T0301616

China's New Industrialization Strategy

China's New Industrialization Strategy

Was Chairman Mao Really Necessary?

Y.Y. Kueh

Chair Professor of Economics and Business Administration,
Chu Hai College of Higher Education, Hong Kong

Edward Elgar
Cheltenham, UK • Northampton, MA, USA

Published by
Edward Elgar Publishing Limited
Glensanda House
Montpellier Parade
Cheltenham
Glos GL50 1UA
UK

Edward Elgar Publishing, Inc.
William Pratt House
9 Dewey Court
Northampton
Massachusetts 01060
USA

A catalogue record for this book
is available from the British Library

Library of Congress Control Number: 2007937726

ISBN 978 1 84720 232 1

Printed and bound in Great Britain by MPG Books Ltd, Bodmin, Cornwall

Contents

Preface   vii

PART I   ECONOMICS OF MAOISM REVISITED

1   Interpreting the economics of the Cultural Revolution   3

PART II   DENG XIAOPING IN MAO'S MANTLE

2   Was Mao really necessary? An economist's perspective   31
3   Dengonomics and the Tiananmen Square incident   47

PART III   AGRICULTURE IN CHINA'S
           INDUSTRIALIZATION

4   The rise of agricultural Dengonomics   63
5   The economics of the 'second land reform'   79
6   Peasant consumption and incomes in critical turn   89
7   Mao and agriculture in China's industrialization:
    three antitheses in a 50-year perspective   116

PART IV   THE NEW INDUSTRIALIZATION STRATEGY

8   The three industrial imbalances   139
9   Growth imperatives, economic efficiency and 'optimum
    decentralization'   162
10 Bureaucratization, property rights and economic reforms   183
11 Inflation and industrial deregulation: the twin travellers   204

PART V   FROM AUTARKY TO THE WTO

12 Foreign economic relations readjusted, 1979–84   227
13 The quest for WTO entry   250

References   262
Index   275

Preface

Deng Xiaoping's economic strategy is widely regarded as a complete anathema to Mao's. This study argues, however, that without the material foundations laid by Mao over his 30-year reign, it would have been very difficult, in the first place, for Deng to launch his reform and open-door policy starting in 1979. Contrary to the popular view, we also argue that Deng basically shared Mao's aspiration and approach in pursuit of China's industrialization and modernization. More importantly, the common aspiration and Mao's material legacy, in particular, had indeed helped to condition Deng to the highly acclaimed 'gradualist' methodology in both domestic economic reform and China's opening to the outside world.

As a matter of fact, Deng's most celebrated, and indeed quite abrupt, open-door strategy may also be traced to Mao's drastic reorientation in foreign economic relations towards the West in the early 1960s (then mainly Western Europe and Japan), following the collapse of Sino-Soviet relations in 1961. More importantly, it was also Mao who personally initiated the 'ping pong' diplomacy in 1971–72 as a prelude to the rapprochement with the United States, which eventually led to the establishment of a formal diplomatic relationship and thus constituted the cornerstone for Deng to 'bring China back to the West'. Thus, as a contrarian view, we also argue that Mao was, *in situ*, not at all 'inward-looking', 'closed-door' or 'autarkic'-oriented, with a predilection for the philosophy of 'self-reliance', entirely ignorant of the technological advances made in the West, as many outside observers believe him to be.

Nevertheless, amidst the generally successful transformation from Soviet-style central planning into a market-based system and integrating with the world economy, Deng, globally branded as the great 'pragmatist', did lose patience at times and resorted to the colossal 'big bang' strategy. The disastrous attempt at an across-the-board price liberalization in 1988 is a good case in point. The political costs of the Tiananmen Square affairs that erupted in 1989 following rampant inflation, and the economic consequences (prolonged western sanction included) seem akin to the Great Leap Forward débâcle of 1958–60. Perhaps Deng, with his maverick flair for totally floating all prices in China overnight, was then also inspired by the favoured dictum of Mao, 'from great disorder to great order' (*you daluan dao da zhi*). That is, both Mao and Deng seemed to subscribe to the dialectic notion that great equilibrium would only come along with great chaos, in seeking a spectacular economic breakthrough for China.

The volume attempts to tell the other story about the economics of China's transition, by focusing on the interplay between the Mao and Deng factors on the road towards a 'socialist market economic system' with Chinese characteristics.

The study consists of 13 essays, of which 12 were written over the past two and half decades or so, the latest one in 2006. They are all grouped into three major subject categories. The first relates to the new agriculture policy programme of Deng, as it may bear on the supremacy of industrialization. The second deals with the new industrialization strategy itself, focusing on the fundamental economic constraints and the search post-Mao for a breakthrough in reforming the economic system. The third discusses the controversial open-door policy and the subsequent quest for WTO, hopefully without compromising the long-established basic premises of pursuing an independent, integrated industrial system for China.

The three main parts are preceded, however, by a lengthy discourse on the economics of Maoism versus Dengism, as it had strongly emerged during the Cultural Revolution. This helps to provide an overall analytical framework for interpreting the nature and scope of the economic policy controversy between Mao and Deng and is, indeed, instrumental in understanding not only the course of economic and institutional changes, but also a series of important practical policy measures adopted in China over the past three decades.

No doubt, as in the former Soviet Union, there has been a crucial link in China between the pursuit of industrialization and political authoritarianism throughout the reign of both Mao and Deng. This may be a matter of the Marxist–Leninist ideology, or sheer Chinese patriotism, but in our discourse 'no moral strings' whatsoever are attached as to whether Mao was *necessary* or not. We follow therefore Alec Nove's (1964) example in his *Was Stalin Really Necessary?* Perhaps ours may be considered as a *phenomenological* approach backed up by the philosophy of Edmund Husserl.

Most of the articles included in the present volume have been published in various journals, and acknowledgements for permission to make use of them are provided in each instance. However, to enhance coherency and 'homogeneity' of subject matter, many of the articles have been refocused, shortened or extended (some very extensively), and updated as appropriate. Many lengthy original notes on material sources are left out to keep the volume manageable as regards space. As a record of the living history at the time of writing, the 'present tense' is generally kept intact for the various articles.

I am indebted to my colleagues at Chu Hai College of Higher Education for various support: Professor C.N. Chang, President, and Professor Y.P. Kong, Vice-President, for great encouragement; and Miss Charmaine S. Chan, Dr Raymond Tse and Dr Zhang Jing for crucial technical assistance at various stages in the preparation of the manuscript.

My gratitude goes, in particular, to Professor Christopher B. Howe and Professor Joseph C.H. Chai for stimulating and inspiring thoughts given over the years.

In memory of my father,
Kueh Chuang Tock,
and
my teachers,
Professor Pikai Tchang
and
Professor K. Paul Hensel

PART I

Economics of Maoism Revisited

1. Interpreting the economics of the Cultural Revolution*

The political upheaval triggered by the Great Proletarian Cultural Revolution in China may be seen as being rooted in the controversy between Chairman Mao and President Liu Shaoqi about the long-term economic development strategy for China. Mao's critique of Liu centres on his 'programme of capitalist restoration', but in essence the Mao–Liu conflict involves two different approaches to implementing the same Stalinist forced-draft industrialization strategy, rather than alternative choices between capitalism and socialism.

Generally speaking, Mao's new venture represents an attempt to revive, with some modifications, the failed Great Leap Forward strategy of 1958–1961. Liu prefers, however, to proceed with conventional Soviet-style central planning and control with enhanced price and income incentives. Liu's approach may tally with the economic reforms in the Soviet Union and her allies in Eastern Europe; hence his being branded as 'revisionist' and the largest 'capitalist roader within the Party'.

In what follows I first highlight the major differences in economic thinking between Mao and Liu. The second and third parts of the chapter examine respectively the crucial implications for the government's policy on agriculture and industry, in terms of institutional accommodating, economic planning and management, and political control. The fourth part evaluates the potential impact of the two divergent economic strategies, Mao versus Liu, on long-term economic development in China. The discussion is concluded with a brief reference to the political and ideological implications of the Mao–Liu economic controversy.

INDUSTRIALIZATION UNDER AUSTERITY

The Mao–Liu controversy on economic development strategy may be evaluated with a highly revealing theoretical model developed by professors Chiang and Fei, called 'maximum-speed development through austerity' (Chiang and Fei, 1966). The basic concept of the model is that an 'optimum', rather than 'minimum' consumption standard will help to maximize the rate of capital growth. This is because a bare subsistence level of consumption imposed by the central planners may impair work incentives, while an 'optimum' wage policy, with a certain degree of austerity, may induce greater labour effort and hence higher output, and thus help to raise, rather than depress, the rate of capital accumulation for investment and economic development.

With his income (and consumption) incentives policy, Liu clearly follows the theoretical postulate of the Chiang–Fei model. Mao, on the contrary, seeks to substitute political control and ideological or moral persuasion for material stimulus, in order to achieve an even higher rate of capital accumulation. In a sense, the entire Cultural Revolution seems to be geared toward this specific end.

Indeed, the 'surplus (over minimum) consumption' outlay, which is bound up with bonus awards, enterprise welfare expenditure, wage differentials and the like, must have appeared to Mao to be quite a sizable growth variable. Notice that bonus awards for workers alone already made up more than 10 per cent of the national total of industrial wage bill in 1956 (Perkins, 1966, p. 151). Likewise, if a bare subsistence income could be consistently enforced in the rural areas, the potential 'acquisition ratio' could be as high as 22 to 24 per cent in 1956–57 (Walker, 1965, pp. 34–5). By implication, Mao's approach to income distribution is therefore inherently egalitarian and austere.

Despite their common adherence to the Stalinist principle of preferential growth of heavy industry, Liu's strategy of 'optimum austerity', as exemplified by the economic readjustments made in the early 1960s following the collapse of the Great Leap Forward,[1] inevitably calls for a modification of Mao's scheme of intersectoral investment allocation in favour of consumer goods production. In agriculture, this would mean lower compulsory delivery quotas, as institutionalized through the 'responsibility farm system' (*zerentian*). By contrast, Mao's harsh consumption policy implies practically an agricultural 'extraction procedure that was tantamount in its effect to a discrete progressive taxation on current production with nearly confiscatory marginal rates on output in excess of the minimum farm subsistence' (Tang, 1968, p. 495).[2]

With his 'maximum austerity' policy, coupled with political and ideological control, Mao clearly aspires to another breakthrough, in both economic and political terms, akin to the Great Leap Forward methodology. Thus, since spring 1968, press reports abound about various industries and enterprises making huge strides in current production from month to month. The observed broad intraindustrial unevenness in output claims is especially highly suggestive that another Great Leap is imminent.

However, the Great Cultural Revolution seems to have been, as yet, essentially confined to the urban centres. The rural sector has remained relatively calm. There is no sign of any mass mobilization being contemplated, as during the Great Leap Forward, for construction of large-scale projects for irrigation and flood control, or for land reclamation. Nor are there signs of a possible resurrection of the notorious 'backyard [iron and steel] furnaces' campaign of 1958. Perhaps Mao is still mindful of the mischief, but for how long will his peculiar strategy tolerate slack utilization of rural resources?

Mao also appears to agree with the agricultural policy reorientation made after the Great Leap débâcle towards enhanced use of modern inputs (chemical fertilizers and pesticides, agricultural machinery, and small and medium-sized farm implements) for productivity growth, rather than relying on such highly labour-intensive farming techniques as 'deep ploughing' and 'close planting'. Perhaps he is also versed in the notion that the 'agriculture-first' policy, as adopted by the Liuist strategists since 1961, may not necessarily compromise the Stalinist primacy of maximizing heavy-industrial growth, to the extent that such added modern inputs of industrial origin may help to raise farm output (wage foods and cash crops) further and thus release industrial expansion from agricultural constraints.

Nonetheless, it seems doubtful that Mao will allow such a neoclassical fashion of intersectoral transformation to continue 'until either capacity production is obtained in the industrial sector or diminishing returns in agriculture render further transformation unprofitable' (Tang, 1968, p. 462). Rather, it seems more likely that, before the equilibrium sets in, Mao will already be attempting another leapfrog.

PHYSICAL PLANNING VERSUS PRICE CONTROL IN AGRICULTURE

Sanzi Yibao as a Policy Programme

Since being officially labelled as the greatest 'capitalist roader' within the Party, Liu has been roundly condemned for his propagating *sanzi yibao* as a fundamental solution to managing Chinese agriculture. Literally, the Chinese abbreviation stands for the extension of the three (*san*) *zi*, plus the single (*yi*) method of *baochan daohu* (contracting farm output quotas down to the individual peasant households, as against the method of collective farming) for farm management. The *sanzi* refer in turn to *ziliudi* (private plots earmarked as an additional source of income, in kind or cash, to supplement earnings from the collectivized farmland), *ziyou shichang* (rural free market) and *zifu yingkui* (the requirements for farmsteads to be made responsible for their own operational profits and losses). Clearly *baochan daohu* should necessarily call for a redemarcation of the collective farmland as individual 'responsibility farms', as alluded to above.

Taken as a whole, the *sanzi yibao* programme complies with Liu's less austere income and consumption policy. First of all, for the entire system to work, the output quotas (given farm procurement prices) must be fixed at such a level that will help to equalize the marginal returns for the peasants from collective farming and private undertakings. Otherwise, prices freely formed on the rural free markets would forcibly help to divert labour resources and farm implements away from the collectives to the private plots and the potentially more lucrative private non-farm undertakings.

Viewed this way, the *sanzi yibao* policy represents, indeed, rather a sophisticated mechanism of price control. While official purchase prices for grain, cotton and the like remain unchanged, there has come into effect, via the manipulation of output quotas, a remarkable shift in relative prices in favour of the peasants in terms of income maximization. Thus, as often complained about in the Maoist-dominated press reports, it has become a widespread practice for peasants to bargain with the collective leadership for lower output quotas. It is not clear to what extent the 'responsibility farm' system has been carried out in the Chinese countryside, but, in a number of provinces, notably Anhui, it seems to have prevailed widely.

For Mao, the upshot of such an 'optimum (or less) austere' policy, by way of reduced farm surplus siphoning, clearly means relative industrial retrenchment. The entire charge against Liu pursuing capitalism seems therefore to be apologetic, belying practical economic considerations on the part of the Maoist planners.

In a way, the practice of *baochan daohu* (or responsibility farm) evolved as an ultimate solution to the initial efforts made by the Party leadership to differentiate, within the three-tier structure of the people commune, performance and income awards among the production brigades (starting in 1959), and then among the production teams (since 1961), when the latter have all been converted into discrete planning and accounting units.[3] Undoubtedly, the differentiations made on the household basis should be much more effective in stimulating current production.

More importantly perhaps, within the broader *sanzi yibao* context, the added price and income benefits for the peasants tend to render redundant any further increases in officially fixed farm procurement prices, as proposed by the prominent economist Ma Yinchu, as an incentive measure, prior to the advent of the Great Leap Forward (Ash, 1998, p. 343). In fact, under collective farming, a decreed price increase may well turn out to be a 'deadweight loss', to the extent that responsible Party cadres, whose primary concern is to fulfil a few key physical output targets imposed from above, may remain unresponsive to price changes, and that individual peasants may as well merely regard the price premium as an income subvention under the egalitarian collectivist–distributive framework.

The *sanzi yibao* programme appears, indeed, to be an even more advanced or 'revisionist' reform approach compared to the Soviet counterpart, where, parallel to the ongoing industrial reform, the emerging agricultural policy seems to focus essentially on profit incentives and price control by taking the conventional agricultural collective as an operational entity, rather than relegating farm decision making to the household level, as under the Chinese 'responsibility farm' system. Clearly, the collective in China still remains intact, with the production team (under the commune system) serving as a collective accounting unit, but, obviously under *sanzi yibao*, collective aggregate decisions made on accumulation and investment have become less coherent and less centralized than in their Soviet counterparts, where peasants still basically work 'for an uncertain share in a future pot of unknown size' (Campbell, 1974, p. 63).

In addition to *sanzi yibao*, which may indeed be regarded as quasi-decollectivization, Liu is also charged, as part of his 'capitalist political plot', with promoting *xida ziyou*: that is, the 'four great freedoms' of employing labourers, lending with 'exorbitant' interest charges, buying and selling land, and running private businesses. It may be difficult to visualize how, prior to the outbreak of the Cultural Revolution, the collectivist rural setting under the Liuist control in China could possibly have disintegrated to such an extent as to allow private transaction of landed properties to take place. However, at least the other three 'freedoms' are clearly either closely intertwined with, or represent a natural extension of, *sanzi yibao* activities. Under *baochan daohu*, for example, it is plausible that individual peasant households occasionally engage outside labour for the contracted farm lot; and some cash-strapped family undertakings in the rural free market may borrow money from neighbours.[4] Taken together, with his policy of *sanzi yibao*, coupled with *xida ziyou*, Liu has virtually realigned himself with Bukharin in the famous industrialization debate of the Soviet Union in the 1920s. Khrushchev himself was in fact on the same runway when he professed himself, in some of his later speeches, as foreseeing a day when the state would not even require deliveries from the collective farms but merely set prices based on the costs of the efficient producers and let collective farms compete for the business (Campbell, 1966, p. 98). However, Liu, dubbed 'China's Khrushchev', appears to be even more 'revisionist' than his Soviet forerunner, as with the 'responsibility farm' system the output quotas are not only relegated to the profit-and-income maximizing peasant households but also subject to bargaining within the increasingly diversified and monetized rural context.

Nonetheless, while Liu's 'less austere' policy may inherently help to move China towards 'market socialism' *à la* Nikolai Bukharin, it still seems quite wide of the mark to brand it as an attempt to restore capitalism.

The Dazhai Model

Mao's Cultural-Revolutionary antithesis to Liuist revisionism in Chinese agriculture is familiar: the highly propagated Dazhai model of maximizing production and farm delivery under conditions of absolute austerity, and discarding price and income incentives in favour of ideological and moral persuasion (Writing Group, 1974, pp. 132–4). The model is named after a large production brigade in Shansi province, which has, presumably 'with boundless loyalty to Chairman Mao and Mao Zedong thoughts', overcome all possible kinds of Nature's harshness to turn food deficit into food surplus, while upholding Mao's teaching of 'self-reliance' (that is, without resorting to any material support from the state).

Carried to the ultimate conclusion, the Dazhai model implies that the pattern of cropping, sown areas and manpower input, compulsory delivery quotas, investment and consumption, and income distribution may all be determined by the central planners, and decisions made relegated through the vertical administrative layers down to the individual collectives to become various operational physical targets, along the lines of the Henselian system.[5] In the circumstances, it is also self-evident that prices, if given (as shadow variables) will merely serve as an accounting medium for facilitating aggregate programming, optimization and choice of plan variants (cf. Gutmann, 1965).

More importantly, granting that, by definition, problems with Leibenstein's X-efficiency should have disappeared, the Leninist principle of *Khozraschyot* (economic accountability) for controlling production efficiency under central planning should also become redundant. The same goes, of course, for the perennial search, common to all Soviet-type economies, for an 'optimum' degree of decentralization in bureaucratic economic management. In other words, the question of optimum managerial unit should have become merely a technical matter involving the relative effectiveness of data collecting, accounting and planning methods.

What is portrayed above is of course an *idealtypus à la* Max Weber. In the Cultural Revolution context, Mao's *realtypus* represents quite a different story, however, being conditioned by both the abortive 1956 attempt with direct physical planning in the wake of the 'socialist high tide' (the collectivization drive) in Chinese agriculture (Perkins, 1966, pp. 65–8, 83–6), and the disastrous 1958–60 Great Leap Forward strategy.

Briefly, the 1956 episode rapidly regressed into indirect control via purchase quotas and price relatives, that was in turn swiftly overrun, however, by the bold, unprecedented, communization drive in 1958, coupled with the great aspiration for a leapfrog on all fronts, economic, ideological and political. The remuneration method of 'part wage and part supply (communal messing)', for example, may be seen as ultimate egalitarianism and austerity. And, since local cadres and the masses were all deemed ideological faithful amidst the spectacular mobilization campaign, financial discipline became superfluous. Budget appropriations and bank loans were then generously extended to support vast uncoordinated and wasteful crash programmes.[6] More fatally, probably the same ideological presumption triggered the unwarranted break-up of the National Bureau of Statistics into discrete local units (Li, 1962). The upshot was, as is well known, immensely exaggerated output claims, and subsequently the great statistical fiasco of 1958–59, which deprived central planners of any reliable statistical foundation for planning. The rest is history.

Viewed against this background, the restoration in 1961 of the production team as a planning and accounting unit for redressing the 'excesses' of the Great Leap is, for Mao, probably a suboptimum choice or, say, an uneasy institutional equilibrium. It not only represents too small an organizational vehicle for potential large-scale labour mobilization, but also helps, in effect, even to sanction income disparity between the teams within the limited confines of a natural village, let alone those of a commune. Worse still, for the radical Maoist ideologue, the disparity may have in fact arisen from differences in natural endowment rather than diligence on the part of the team members; as such, it should therefore be void of any justification.[7]

Thus, no sooner had the famous Tenth Plenum of September 1962 drawn to a close, than Mao called for 'not forgetting class struggle', and forcefully initiated the 'socialist education' campaign to engulf the entire Chinese countryside. With this, the economic policy controversy between Mao and Liu has indeed increasingly turned into political confrontation, to become a prelude to the Cultural Revolution (Baum, 1975).

Interestingly, while private plots, rural trade fairs and the work-point method (for accounting for the relative labour contributions by members of the production team as a basis for income distribution) are all still formally in place,[8] the Dazhai model nevertheless remains defiant, and continues to propagate 'proletarian unselfishness'. Following Mao's call to 'fight selfishness and repudiate revisionism' (*dousi pixiu*) and to 'learn from Dazhai', numerous 'Mao Zedong thoughts propaganda' teams have been dispatched to rurals area to engage individual peasant families in 'self-criticism' and 'self-remoulding', by telling them how '*sanzi yibao*' and a 'capitalist restoration' should bring 'great misery' to all. Once again, Mao's famous slogan, 'the People Commune is great' (launched in August 1958 to trigger the massive communization drive) is overwhelming everywhere.

The practical economic implications of the Dazhai campaign appear enormous. First, should 'unselfishness' prevail and production teams and members therefore be prepared to forfeit any extra income entitlements in favour of Mao's communist course, national savings and investment could truly be maximized to an even greater extent, even without the overriding commune structure. Secondly, being free from the restrictive or prohibitive constraints involved in settling conflicting benefit-and-cost claims among the production teams and brigades, large-scale mobilization by the commune leadership for Nurksian-type accumulation should become merely a technical, and thus much more manageable, organizational problem.[9] Herein, indeed, lies the very quintessence of the economics of Mao, a revolutionary political romanticist aspiring to a great economic breakthrough for his country.

Viewed this way, the rural setting seems to be inherently unstable. Is it 'a calm before the storm'? We really do not know for sure.[10]

CONTROVERSY OVER INDUSTRIAL REFORM

Libermanism in China

On the industrial front, Liu is rigorously condemned for reinstituting bonus awards and promoting wage differentiation among the workers since the early 1960s. In particular, his 'profit-in-command' principle for industrial reform is simply seen as an attempt to 'restore capitalism' in China.

Interestingly, Mao's call for 'not forgetting class struggle', made at the Tenth Plenum in September 1962, precisely coincided with the initial Soviet blueprint put forward by Liberman (1962) for economic reform. In his famous *Pravda* article of 9 September 1962, Liberman proposed, as the title, 'The plan, profits and bonuses' clearly suggests, to substitute 'profit' for the conventional 'output' (in physical or value terms) target as the key success indicator for state-owned enterprises. The proposal immediately hit the headlines in the West, and was certainly picked up in China by such prominent economists as Sun Yefang, who has been constantly vilified as 'China's Liberman' and singled out as the top economic theoretician of the 'Liu Shaoqi clique'.

In a follow-up article, also published in *Pravda*, Liberman (1965) advocated, in conjunction with the September 1965 Kosygin reform, 'direct contractual ties' between user and supplier enterprises to replace centrally planned allocation, although this should initially be limited to consumer goods production and supply. In fact, since July 1964, merchandisers in the clothing, footwear, leather and food-processing industries have successively been allowed to place 'orders' directly with suppliers of their choice in the so-called 'Bolshevichka–Mayak' experiment, as an attempt to introduce competitive market elements. This obviously represents what the Chinese press frequently refers to as 'free markets flooding (all over the place) (*ziyou shichang fanlan*) in Soviet revisionism'.

Perhaps more important, in his 1965 article, Liberman further proposed that centralized control of the 'wage fund' should be gradually relaxed and consumer goods production expanded accordingly, as is also implied by Liu's 'less austerity' policy. Liberman also urged, with equal force, substantially curtailing the nomenclature of centrally planned and allocated materials, extending the 'direct orders' scheme to the higher echelons, and establishing a wholesaler network (to be furnished with appropriate inventory) to replace the conventional 'material-and-technical supply' system. Interestingly, the Liuists have in fact been rigorously condemned in the Chinese press for a similar attempt made presumably in the early 1960s, at creating a 'Second Ministry of Commerce' in place of the familiar State Bureau of Materials Supply (*guojia wuziju*) in China.

It remains as yet unclear to what extent the 'profit target' was applied and the 'free market' prevailed in Chinese industry prior to the outbreak of the Cultural Revolution in 1966. What is clear is that, following the Great Leap débâcle, Soviet-style central planning was returned, vertical ministerial–industrial control and financial discipline were re-enhanced and the policy of material incentives (with bonus awards) readopted as well, as during the 1953–57 First-Five-Year-Plan period.

As a matter of fact, parallel to the industrial reform discussions and experiments in the Soviet Union, articles also began to emerge in *Jingji Yanjiu*, the flagship journal of the Institute of Economics of the Chinese Academy of Science in 1963–64, liberally challenging the Marxian theory of labour value and advocating *produktionpreis* (capital charges to be made cost-price effective). It seems indeed that the 'liberal debate' had already started as early as 1962 (CIA, 1963).

It is nonetheless difficult to ascertain precisely whether the then emerging Chinese 'liberalism' purported to help endorse any official reform ventures given for emulating the Soviet experience, or merely to prepare the intellectual atmosphere needed for launching any new reform initiatives.

The Chinese 'liberals' largely centred around Sun Yefang, Yang Jianbai and their student, He Jiangzhang, all from the Institute of Economics.[11] For both Sun and his Soviet counterpart, profit as an integrated financial variable must have indeed appeared to be the most suitable managerial performance criterion, in light of increased industrial diversification that tends to render centralized control of state enterprises by physical output and input targets all the more cumbersome and ineffective. This applies in particular to the heterogeneous light industries which are being called upon, under the 'less-harsh' consumption policy in the Soviet Union, as well as in China, to expand production capacity to meet improved consumer demands.

In a way, Sun appears to be even more advanced and radical than Liberman in his reform proposals. In his 1962 article, Liberman still proposed to retain, in addition to the overriding profit criterion, the three mandatory planned targets of 'total output', 'output mix' (the so-called 'assortment plan'), and delivery schedule, which are instrumental in upholding central planners' scale of preferences. For Sun, however, these supplementary targets seem to be largely superfluous, judging at least by the widespread charges against him in the Chinese press for 'likening the profit target to the nose of an ox', in that 'by pulling it (with the string attached) the entire cattle may easily be moved around'.[12]

More significantly, perhaps, Sun also seems to be ahead of Liberman (1965) and the 1964 Bolschevichka–Mayak experiment in advocating 'direct contractual ties', as is clearly implied in his groundbreaking proposal for freeing the entire sphere of 'simple reproduction' (replacement investment) from central control.[13] Notice that it is only starting with the Bolschevichka–Mayak experiment that Soviet producer enterprises are allowed to draw up their own output, costs, labour and financial plans on the basis of 'direct orders' (for purchase and delivery) coming from the market buyers (rather than mandatory targets imposed by the planners).

The 'partial marketization' approach clearly implies an important breakup with the conventional *Khozraschyot* principle in Soviet-type planning, under which, as alluded to earlier, 'economic accountability' refers strictly to nothing but financial reckoning for fulfilling centrally imposed output and input production plans, with or without the profit target being attached. This initial breakthrough must have prompted Liberman to swiftly propagate in 1965 the limited 'marketization' process to penetrate the highly centralized 'derived demand' sector, in order consistently to accommodate rising consumerism.

Carried over to China, the emerging Soviet-style approach to economic reform would probably cause the system of central planning to disintegrate even more quickly than in the Soviet Union, especially by virtue of Liberman's proposal for extending the marketization process to the producer goods branches as well. Notice that central planning in China is already less mature and covers fewer industries than in the Soviet Union, and a large portion of producer goods are already 'rationed out' through the manipulation of relatively high wholesale prices, rather than being directly allocated to the various user enterprises (Perkins, 1966, pp. 110–13). The new Soviet approach could therefore easily lead to a more consumption-oriented and increasingly market-based economy, leaving central planners to deal only with a few key sectors in China.

A few words should be said about the highly interesting distinction made by Sun Yefang between 'replacement investment' ('simple reproduction' in Marxist terminology) and 'new investment' ('enlarged reproduction') for economic reform. Sun strongly recommends that, within the context of replacement investment and current production, all decision making should be transferred to the state enterprises. For that purpose the depreciation fund should be retained in full by the enterprises, as against the present practice of being subject to centralized fiscal redistribution. And it should indeed include 'invisible' or 'economic' depreciation as well, not just normal technical wear-and-tear, as is commonly the case among all socialist countries. Sun also considers the existing depreciation rates far too low, being oblivious of the rapidly changing technological context (Sun, 1984, pp. 344–6, 355, 455–6).

Given that the 'simple reproduction' sphere covers both consumer and producer goods sectors, Sun's approach to economic reform is evidently far more systematic and comprehensive, compared to the partial–incremental marketization scheme of Liberman (1965).[14]

As for 'enlarged reproduction', Sun argues, however, that decision authority and control over capital allocation should continue to rest fully with central planners (ibid., pp. 352, 377, 458–9). Evidently this represents the bottom line for the planners to help uphold the long-run scale of preferences of the state. Unlike Liberman, therefore, Sun seems adamant that consumer choice should not by any measure distort the centralized order of allocative priorities.[15]

Sun further strongly advocates a capital charge, on a uniform interest rate, for all fixed assets given to state enterprises by way of budget appropriations, against the practice of levying such charges for working capital only. And, in defiance of the Marxian doctrine, the charges on fixed capital should indeed all be effectively recouped from the output prices. In other words, Sun directly propagates the 'capitalist antithesis' of *produktionpreis*.[16] This flies of course in the face of orthodox Marxism. Indeed, in the early 1960s, Sun's associates, Yang Jianbai and He Jiangzhang, and other similar 'liberal' Chinese economists, all appeared to be rapidly converging on the neoclassical economic paradigm in this respect.[17]

By comparison, Liberman remains ambiguous, whether or not to apply the neoclassical 'one-price' principle in proposing capital charges, although he regards the charges as absolutely necessary for balancing income benefits among state enterprises, relative to differences in scale of allocated capital endowment.[18]

As a matter of fact, in light of ever-increasing capital intensity in production, capital charges are also increasingly considered as imperative in all Soviet bloc countries for stimulating state enterprises to improve efficiency in industrial plant utilization. However, the interest rates as set by the various governments normally vary widely among different industries. This is deemed necessary to compensate for unwarranted intersectoral disparity in cost–price relations (caused by years of official price fixing), and to make interest payment a coherent and sensitive factor in the enterprises' decision making.

Moreover, unlike Sun's proposal, not all the capital charges as levied are meant to be cost- and price-effective, perhaps for fear of sanctioning the *Produktionpreis* theory. In East Germany, for example, the *Produktionsfondsabgabe* (capital levy) (announced in 1963, experimented with in 1964, and formally adopted in March 1966), is charged as a tax on 'gross profit' rather than a cost element, and realized profit net of the charge is set as the key criterion for assessing the performance of state enterprises (Kueh, 1966).

Similarly, the familiar 'differentiated recoupment (payoff) period' method is still widely in use as an investment criterion in the Soviet Union and its Eastern European allies. By contrast, Sun, who like Liberman (1962) defines the profitability criterion as being the western standard of relating realized profits to the combined total of working and fixed capitals, wants to see it being given consistently as the single yardstick for centrally determined capital allocation. This could of course effectively help to divert the bulk of capital resources in China from the priority sectors to the consumer goods sector, given the remarkable disparity in profitability between light and heavy industries. Notice that, as is common to all other socialist countries, consumer goods prices in China, officially fixed, remain relatively high as a means of siphoning off potential income, in place of introducing personal income taxes.

The last point made touches upon the crucial problem of pervasive 'price distortion' as encountered in all Soviet-type economies. From his pre-Cultural Revolution treatises criticizing strongly the policy of 'unequal value of exchange', it may be surmised that Sun should consistently view a rational system of relative prices (given on the basis of *Produktionpreis*) as the very basis for adopting the profit target as the key performance criterion.[19] But he also seems fully aware of the enormous difficulties involved with administrative readjustments of officially-set prices.

Taken together, the reform experiments as conducted in Eastern Europe appear to be a far cry from the consistently structured and far-flung reform blueprint put forward by Sun Yefang (the ambiguity about price reform notwithstanding). If anything, it should perhaps be more appropriate to compare Sun with Ota Sik (1967) of Czechoslovakia, rather than Liberman of the Soviet Union. Nonetheless, Sun is still a long way from Oscar Lange's market socialism, in which, as is well known, both consumer sovereignty and freedom of occupational choice should prevail altogether.

The 'Angang Constitution' as an Alternative Model

In a way, it is tragic that Sun's critique on Soviet-style planning, industrial management and enterprise control as adopted in China should have been launched exactly during the great Sino-Soviet ideological rift in the early 1960s. The upshot is to forcefully trigger an antithesis from the Maoists in the form of the so-called 'Angang Constitution' (*Angang xianfa*) for rigorously enhancing central planning with pervasive physical control in China, blending bureaucratic and mass mobilization approaches.

Named after the Anshan Gangtie (steel-and-iron) Corporation in Liaoning province, the 'Constitution' (presumably formulated by Chairman Mao himself in 1960) spells out five basic principles for managing China's largest metallurgical complex as a model for national emulation (Writing Group, 1974, pp. 70–73). Literally, these are the principles of (1) steadfastly upholding 'proletarian politics in command' (instead of 'profit in command'); (2) strengthening Party leadership (instead of solely relying on the factory management); (3) vigorously deploying mass movement (instead of merely resorting to the experts and technocrats); (4) implementing the 'two participations' (of cadres in collective works, and of workers in plant management), 'one reform' (to get rid of irrational regulations and institutions) and the 'tripartite alliance' (of workers, cadres and technicians), and (5) rigorously promoting technological innovation and revolution.

All five principles should be self-explanatory, manifesting indeed the very spirit of the Cultural Revolution. Many Chinese enterprises are reported to have already adopted the new organizational-cum-mobilization model, the classical example being the Guanghua Saw Mill in Beijing. Several points emerge.

Firstly, the Angan model represents clearly the industrial counterpart of the Dazhai model in Chinese agriculture, propagating egalitarianism and austerity (at least by implication) and substituting ideological and enhanced Party control for profits and material incentives, by restructuring plant management with increased workers' involvement.

Secondly, mass mobilization not only aims at exploiting all possible resources for maximizing production, but, perhaps more importantly, it should also be seen as an attempt to break the monopoly of the managerial staff in manipulating the plan targets for the enterprises. Students familiar with Soviet economics should know that, as common to socialist enterprises, there operates yet another 'tripartite alliance' on the part of the plant director, chief accountant and chief engineer, who consistently collude to distort the 'economic–technical norms' (for labour input, materials consumption and machine-utilization rates, inventory–output ratio, and the like), for setting up a 'soft' or 'easy plan', in order to be able to overfulfil planned assignments, as a means for maximizing bonus awards. Thus the new 'tripartite alliance' *à la* Mao may hopefully substitute for the corrupted one.

Thirdly, the new 'tripartite alliance' for technological revolution does not necessarily imply that workers should be counted on to help develop technical expertise, but it should rather be seen as an initiative to break the impasse encountered in China, as elsewhere in the Soviet bloc, in stimulating technological innovations. Note that, as a rule, Soviet-type enterprises are not motivated in the design of new products and trial manufacturing, or any 'rationalization' of the production processes, as this would normally disturb established routine and therefore interfere with fulfilment of the current production plan, which is the overriding priority for the managerial staff.

Fourthly, while the workers-mobilization approach in the Angang model resembles in a way, say, the East German Massen-Kontrolle (dubbed 'workers–peasants inspection'), it clearly represents a much more structured hedge, built into the individual enterprise management system, against possible managerial abuses and misuses. By contrast, the East German method really amounts to no more than sporadic ad hoc raids or casual auditing.

Fifthly, and most importantly perhaps, the Angang model reflects the fact that, prior to the eruption of the Cultural Revolution, central planning was nonetheless firmly in place, despite the fanfare and rhetoric against Sun and President Liu Shaoqi. 'Capitalism' was in fact nowhere in sight in China, and, if anything, the Chinese system of planning and industrial control had in all likelihood remained as conventional as that prevailing in Eastern Europe in the pre-Liberman years.

Viewed against the broader context of Soviet-style planning, the Mao vs Liu economic controversy therefore appears to be a 'storm in a tea cup'. For Mao the political romanticist, if consumer goods supply could be reduced to bare subsistence requirements in favour of maximizing capital accumulation, the profit target, which is nevertheless increasingly deemed necessary by the Liust planners (especially for steering complex light-industrial production), should indeed become redundant in the first place, notwithstanding its carrying a 'capitalistic' connotation. And if the prole-tariats could all be aroused to become ideological enthusiasts, there should be no place for fear of 'soft plan' manipulation by enterprise–managerial staff in any industrial branches, heavy industry included. In the circum-stances, output would be automatically maximized and technological advances continuously guaranteed.

However, for Liu Shaoqi the pragmatist, and Sun Yefang as a professional economist in search of an optimum solution to the immense and ever increasing complexity involved with the central planning regime, Mao's approach appears definitely to be unrealistic, in that he attempts to throw overboard (with a single 'Cultural Revolution'), all extremely delicate and sensitive problems involved. However, defiant as they may have appeared to be, the few 'revisionist' authors, especially Yang Jianbai and He Jiangzhang, who contributed to *Jingji Yanjiu*, published in the liberal episode of 1963–64, were actually still quite prudent in what they said, being wary of the possible political consequences of compromising the Chairman's over-whelming authority.

All said, Mao seems, nonetheless, to have a point in his concern with 'peaceful transformation' from 'revisionism' to 'capitalism' in China. Soviet experience reveals that any initial Liberman-style decontrol may eventually snowball into an irreversible trend towards a 'capitalist restoration'. This fits into what the prominent German economist, Paul Hensel, calls the 'Systemzwang zum Experiment' (Hensel, 1977). That is, within Soviet-style central planning, any experiment conducted in search of an 'optimum decentralization' will inherently trigger further experiments in a chain of 'trial and error', hopefully without ending up in a 'capitalist solution'.

Viewed this way, the Shangri-La idea of Sun Yefang of freeing the entire 'simple reproduction' (replacement investment) sphere from vertical-line control, while subjecting 'enlarged reproduction' (new investment) to cen-tralized allocation, seems highly problematic. Note that, under Sun's model, both producers of consumer goods and capital goods should, at least by implication, straddle the divide of the two different spheres of 'reproduction'. Should market-oriented 'lateral ties' proliferate, as Sun clearly advocates in his model (similar to the Bolschevichka–Mayak experi-ment and the Kosygin reform), consumer goods suppliers and capital goods producers (for satisfying derived demands) will likely rally to force-fully divert scarce investment resources away from the state's priority sectors. A machine-building enterprise may, for example, attempt to produce more machinery for the lucrative textile industry rather than the high-priority metallurgical industry. Soviet experience also tells that the bureaucratic apparatus cannot always be counted on to rein in such allocative biases. The predicaments may thus end up in either renewed centralization with enhanced but frustrating bureaucratic control, or allowing consumer choice to penetrate further the producer goods sector eventually to erode the centralized scale of preferences.[20]

Barring a full-fledged liberalization of the 'enlarged reproduction' sphere, however, the purported market competition through increased 'lateral ties' in the 'simple reproduction' sector is bound to be limited in both scope and intensity. Thus, as transpires with the Bolschevichka–Mayak experiment, despite high demand for clothing made of *dacron*, the chemical industry is strictly limited in capital stock expansion for producing such artificial fibre to match consumer aspiration (Feiwel, 1967, p. 235).[21]

More importantly, in the absence of a bankruptcy provision for state enterprises, it is unrealistic to expect that 'direct orders' from retailers would all be allowed to converge on a few highly competitive suppliers, leaving idle production capacity to accumulate in the less efficient ones, not to mention that increased output concentration to a few suppliers would in itself only help to defeat the very purpose of promoting market competition. Thus Liberman himself (1965, p. 7) was clearly inconsistent: when being pursued by questions from frustrated industrial branch managers, he simply said that, for those suppliers for which 'direct orders' placed should fall short of the planned targets, efforts must be made (by branch managers in control) to help solicit sufficient orders to fill the gap, so that production capacity may be 'fully utilized'. And, for those enterprises which have received more supply orders than planned for, their output targets should be 'appropriately' readjusted upwards. No doubt, such an eclectic approach would not help much in mitigating the pervasive 'sellers' market' syndrome, as is commonly encountered in the Soviet-type economies.

In this respect, Sun's 'simple reproduction' versus 'enlarged reproduction' dichotomy would undoubtedly encounter even more strongly the same predicament faced by Liberman for his scheme of 'partial marketization' of the producer goods sector. Unlike Liberman, Sun in his model does not really provide for 'new investment' to be partially linked up with or spontaneously 'yield' to market forces, in order to comply with the 'less harsh' consumption or material-incentives policy.[22]

Finally, there still remains the insurmountable 'pricing' problem. Without price competition, how could state enterprises' efficiency really be improved by merely introducing 'direct lateral ties' *à la* Liberman or Sun? And, barring the possibility of effectively redressing the distorted officially fixed prices, how could the profit target serve as a rational performance criterion? Liberman (1962) is strangely vague in this regard, saying only that prices 'should remain (officially) fixed (to adhere, by implication, to the planners' preferences), but be kept flexible as well (to reflect changing demand and supply conditions, including technological advances)'.

Sun, apart from reiterating the *Primat* that prices should be rationalized and 'sales and purchases (between enterprises) strictly (made) according to planned prices' (Sun, 1984, p. 378), seems totally mute throughout, however, regarding ways in which distorted prices may be corrected in practice. Perhaps, being a well-trained economist, he is mindful that any attempt made to liberalize prices across-the-board is simply against the very intrinsic logic of central planning, and is in fact tantamount to bringing the country to the very threshold of 'capitalism'.

It appears therefore that, in the Soviet Union (and in China shortly prior to the Cultural Revolution as well), although the centralized scale of preferences is being increasingly compromised by the improved scope of consumer choice in what the Polish economist Jan Drewnowski (1961) refers to as a 'dual preference system' under socialism, the reform advocates, for political or other reasons, are still wary of the new economic measures eventually degenerating into a 'capitalist' solution entirely in favour of 'consumer sovereignty'.

IMPLICATIONS FOR ECONOMIC DEVELOPMENT

How would the divergent economic development strategy between Mao and Liu, as translated into the two different organizational approaches within the same framework of central planning, possibly bear on quantitative economic performance in China? This is not the place for making any empirical assessment. Outside observers are inclined generally to attribute the economic recovery since the early 1960s to the Liuist 'less harsh' or 'less austere' economic policy. This includes agricultural decentralization, with or without *sanzi yibao*, but certainly with markets and prices playing a greater role in the rural areas. In urban industries, this should include, in addition to reenhanced central planning and control, the reinstitution of the method of bonus awards and increased wage differentiations as well.

However, relative to the particular Soviet paradigm, to which both Mao and Liu subscribe, of maximizing savings and investment for accelerating the pace of industrialization, the critical policy issue involved is not only whether the Liuist institutional alternative is really conducive to increasing output, but, equally important, also whether there are appropriate means available within the given institutional constraints, for converting the largest possible share of marginal output into additional savings for investment. This issue therefore touches upon the two very basic postulates of the Chiang–Fei model which, as alluded to earlier, may help to evaluate the Liuist development strategy.

The first relates to the key behavioural assumption that labour supply (defined in efficiency units) is a positive function of the real wage rate (referred to as 'effort function'), which is supposed to be identical to the consumption standard under near-zero savings capability, as is indeed the case in China. One wonders, however, whether the assumption would hold in the context of an agricultural collective, given that, for the individual peasants, rewards (in terms of basic, guaranteed grain entitlement and cash income) may not always be closely linked to personal work efforts made.

Note especially that cash income distribution (which should count most in terms of peasant incentives as a source of expenditure on industrial consumer goods) is subject to the prerogative of the collective leadership in splitting aggregate income between investment (to be undertaken by the collective) and consumption expenditure (allocated to individual peasant households). Such aggregate decisions made by the production teams (the planning and accounting unit since 1961) may not appear to be as coercive as when previously the larger production brigade was in charge, in favour of collective accumulation. But they are likely still influenced by, if not subject to, the *diktat* of the commune or brigade authority, by way of policy guidelines and regulations. Moreover, even within the production team, it still seems difficult to differentiate strictly among peasant families their relative labour contributions, as a basis for equitable income distribution. That is to say, incentive-impairing egalitarianism should still more or less prevail within the production team.

In the circumstances, one may rather assume that, in response to any decreed increases in income distribution, farm labour supply could nevertheless remain inelastic, if not even becoming backward bending. In other words, peasants may simply regard any added income benefits (in real terms) as a one-off subvention to be forfeited for improving consumption. They may therefore not be prompted at all to render any additional efforts in farming, let alone aspiring to reciprocate the government or collective leadership with any substantial increases in output that should be 'over-proportionate' in size to the added consumption benefits provided, as is hoped for in the Chiang–Fei model.[23] If this is correct, the rate of overall capital accumulation and economic growth would become much lower.

The second key assumption of the Chiang–Fei model relates to the planners' ability to siphon off the bulk of the agricultural surplus (that is, output produced in excess of subsistence requirements) to support industrialization. The surplus should include, of course, grain and cash crops (processed or raw) for exports, in exchange for advanced machinery and equipment to help accelerate technological upgrading, in addition to raw materials needed by urban industries and wage food for the workers. It seems that Chiang and Fei assume implicitly that the bulk of the 'over-proportionate' increases in output, as may be realized, can be extracted one way or the other to enhance accumulation, independent of the institutional setting involved.

Note, however, that agricultural collectives are primarily established to facilitate the siphoning, by imposing compulsory delivery quotas. Granting that *baochan daohu* (the method of collective leadership contracting output down to the individual farm households), with or without the broader context of *sanzi yibao*, may as a 'less austere' policy help to generate a greater amount of output, the de facto decollectivization is nonetheless poised to deprive the state of the most direct and effective means for forced siphoning. Given especially the high consumption-elasticity of income of subsistence peasants, the upshot could be an effective improvement in peasant consumption at the expense of state accumulation.

In theory, there are two possible substitutes for forced farm acquisitions to help maintain the given level or rate of state accumulation. One is to resort even more rigorously to the familiar 'scissors-price' manipulation, that is, to raise further the terms of trade in favour of industry as opposed to agriculture. This was tried out in the Soviet Union in the early 1920s, but ended up in disastrous peasant resentment and the historical 'scissors crisis'. The other is, as Sun strongly recommends, to eliminate the scissors-price differentials altogether, and impose direct agricultural taxes at levels commensurate with the given accumulation rate.[24] Hopefully the confiscatory marginal rates of such a direct taxation would not yet stir up another peasant upheaval, as is familiar in Chinese history.[25]

In this respect, the problem involved with industry seems relatively less significant and less complicated as well. For one thing, as a source of capital accumulation, industry may not really be as important as agriculture, bearing in mind the veiled (indirect) contribution of agriculture via the scissors-price effect. Secondly, unlike agriculture, which is characterized as a 'variable coefficient sector' (Eckaus, 1955), the input–output relations in industry are basically amenable to centralized control. That is to say, the margin of output which may be edged out or curtailed, with government policy imposing a lower or higher degree of 'austerity' in workers' consumption, may be relatively limited. Perhaps it is partly for this reason that Mao rejects even more rigorously profits and bonus incentives for industrial staff and workers, compared to the condemnation of the *sanzi yibao* programme.

Nonetheless, should the 'scissors prices' be entirely done away with, as Sun proposes, prices for urban food supply and industrial cash crops are bound to be raised simultaneously. In the circumstances, the colossal fiscal transfer (agricultural taxes substituting for industrial profit deliveries and taxes as state revenue) may indeed not affect export prices (as is common to

Soviet-type economies, Chinese export quotations are normally given in terms of US dollars according to prevailing world market prices).[26] However, the compensatory wage increases, if they are to be extended, together with the incentive wages, in line with the 'less austere' policy, seem to be inherently inflationary, barring commensurate increases in output.

CONCLUSION: A POLITICAL PERSPECTIVE

Taken as a whole, Liu's economic strategy may eventually end up in a real improvement in consumption standards for both urban workers and the peasants. That is to say, while the extra consumption incentives provided for the peasants under the decentralized rural setting may help to bring about an 'over-proportionate' increase in output, the bulk of the agricultural surplus may in fact remain in the hands of the peasants essentially for consumption, in the absence of forced siphoning through the agricultural collectives, and as well, in light of potentially high consumption elasticity typical of low-income peasants. As a result, capital accumulation may decline, in both absolute and relative terms. This seems critical to the desired pace of economic growth, given that agricultural surplus represents a very significant source of capital accumulation in China.

With respect to the urban–industrial sector, the situation seems even less palatable. Generally speaking, industrial production in China, being not as modernized or capital-intensive as in the West, may not be as strictly governed by 'fixed' input–output coefficients. But there is no doubt that, relative to agriculture, the room left for managerial staff and workers to manoeuvre is still largely circumscribed. In the circumstances, it seems hard to visualize how any incentive-based increases in 'consumption outlay' (to be provided, say, by way of increased wage differentiation and bonus awards) could possibly help to stimulate an 'over-proportionate' increase in output, let alone all the difficult problems associated with the familiar 'ratchet principle' in central planning (Berliner, 1957, pp. 65–7).

It is clearly against this background that the economic reform experiments as currently being conducted in Eastern Europe have increasingly converted to the market-oriented solution, amidst the perennial search for an optimum decentralization within the parameters of central planning. Hopefully, when the day comes for, say, obligatory profit delivery by state enterprises to be converted into western-type profit taxes, the desired capital accumulation rate can still be maintained.

To sum up, for Liu as an economic strategist, economic growth should be more or less a function of the familiar propensity to save, as budgetary savings capacity is limited by private propensity to consume. For Mao, however, consistent with the familiar Fel'dman model, investment, and hence economic growth, are governed by the capacity of the producer goods sector (that is, the Marxian department I), rather than the consumer goods sector (Marxian Department II) (Tang, 1968, p. 461), rightly or wrongly.

Viewed this way, there seems indeed a certain economic rationale behind Mao's political romanticism. It might appear to Mao that, if the 'surplus consumption' could be forfeited by the state, the economic gains from added investment should be able to offset the output decline resulting from adverse incentive effects. Of course, political control should then be tightened up, hand in hand with the multifrontal ideological drive to help transform the superstructure, while at the same time physical planning and bureaucratic control should substitute for the use of market and prices in economic management.

It is with this particular economics of Maoism that many of the apparently non-economic phenomena of the Cultural Revolution should be explained, including the ongoing 'educational revolution' and the *xiafang* (sending down or exile) of the urban cadres and intellectuals to the countryside to 'learn from the peasants'. Similarly, the rigorous criticism of Liu, presumably for his thesis that, after the Communist Revolution, 'the (bourgeois) class has already died out', should mainly serve to enforce the principle of egalitarian distribution. For Liu, however, the 'class distinction' thesis clearly represents an ideology for justifying performance-based wage and income differentiation, as in Marxian reasoning classes are primarily economic shifts in nature. In the circumstances, economic planning and control must be for Mao, as for Stalin, a matter for the Party cadres and technocrats, rather than for such prominent economists as Ma Yinchu and Sun Yefang.

Hopefully, following 1967's enormous distribution in transportation and factory production as a result of fierce political struggle, the situation will soon return to normal, in recognition of the imperatives that life should at least go on as usual.

NOTES

*   This article was written in the heyday of the Cultural Revolution for a China studies conference sponsored by the Leverhulme Foundation and held at the University of Hong Kong in November 1968. As a record of interpreting the living history at the time, I do not find it necessary to make any significant textual alteration. The major tenets of the article, as well as the analytical presentation, are therefore all kept intact. For clarity, however, the original manuscript is extensively re-edited, and many passages substantially expounded on. Some lengthy notes are also furnished to help clarify, substantiate and update a number of material points made with new information flowing from China in the later years. I owe a particular debt to the late Professor William K. Kapp, who, upon a short visit to Hong Kong shortly after the conference, somehow discovered the article from HKU's file, called me for a lengthy discussion, kindly edited the paper and graciously offered to submit it to the journal *Kyklos*, based in Basel, where he taught at the university after his return from the United States. Unfortunately I then declined his offer, citing as reason 'insufficient empirical verification'. Perhaps Professor Kapp realized that I strongly shared his institutional–economic perspective. I am also grateful to Professor Dwight H. Perkins for great encouragement given during my post-doctoral sojourn at Harvard University in 1969–71 under the sponsorship of the Harvard Yenching Institute. The late Professor Alexander Eckstein, who was then at Harvard on sabbatical leave from Michigan, also shared useful comments. Similarly, Professor Benjamin Ward read the article with highly encouraging remarks when he was a Visiting Professor at the Chinese University of Hong Kong in the early 1970s. Last, but not least, my gratitude is due to Professor Alpha C. Chiang, my great teacher and friend, for the irrefutable scrutiny of the comments I made about the two basic postulates of the Chiang–Fei model that indeed underpins the institutional analysis in this and other chapters of the book. See *infra*, note 23.

1. See Kueh (2002a, pp. 207–28) for the origin and collapse of the Great Leap Forward, or note 13 in Chapter 7 for a summary.

2. The quotation is from the pre-publication version of Professor Tang's article which he kindly shared in 1967. I find this original formulation to be more sharply worded than the comparable phraseology given in the published version as cited.

3. The production team (also called a small brigade) is equivalent in size (about 20 to 30 households) to the formal agricultural cooperative which constitutes a hamlet (cun). The (large) production brigade (formerly an agricultural collective with around 250 households) is a natural village (xiang), while the people commune (comprising about 5000 households) represents a rural township (zhen); see Kueh (2002a, pp. 19–20) for details.

4. Nonetheless, there is no doubt that the accusation against Liu of spreading the *xida ziyou* at the time assumed strong Cultural Revolution rhetoric. In Mao (*Maoxuan*, 1977, p. 208), for example, the definitions were much more mildly worded, referring only to the freedom of *jiedai* (lending and borrowing, but not extending *gaolidai*; that is, loans with exorbitant interest charges) and *zudi* (renting, instead of buying and selling (*maimai*) land), in addition to *gugong* (employing labourers) and *maoyi* (trading). In fact, *zudi* might also be bound up with *gugong*, in that, under *baochan daohu*, the responsible peasant household subcontracted wholly or partly the contracted farm lot to the labourers 'employed' from outside the family. It is still not clear how widespread the 'four freedoms' then really were in the Chinese countryside, but the rhetoric of the revolutionary Red Guards was surely absolutely overwhelming. As a matter of fact, the cited remarks of Mao (from an October 1955 speech) were specifically aimed at his opponents in the pre-collectivization debate of the early 1950s (ibid.), rather than the *sanzi yibao* episode of the early 1960s. On balance, it should be clear that the Red Guards deliberately exaggerated Mao's phraseology for condemning the 'revisionist' Liuists, making 'the four great freedoms' their 'original sin'.

5. I refer to Professor K. Paul Hensel's model of *Zentralverwaltungswirtschaft* (centrally administered economy), in which the prominent German economist (Hensel, 1979) systematically attempts to prove that a Walrasian general equilibrium may be established for Soviet-style physical planning with material balances.

6. Notice that this paralleled the 'decentralization' in 1958 of various branch industries from the central industrial ministries to the provincial authorities for purpose of promoting local initiatives for a simultaneous development across the country. Laxity in financial control then inevitably resulted in inflationary pressures, the first round of its kind in the People's Republic; see Perkins (1968, pp. 627–8).

7. Such a notion has developed subsequently, shortly prior to the arrest of the 'Gang of Four' in October 1976, into a radical critique of the 'bourgeois rights'.

8. Under the massive 'class struggle' campaign, the output-contracting method (*Baochan daohu*) seems meanwhile to have been once again replaced by collective farming, coupled

with the conventional work-point method of remuneration (income distribution in cash and/or in kind according to the number of work-points accumulated for farm works done).

9.   Take a large-scale water reservoir and irrigation project, for example. Topographical differences may easily result in unequal distribution of available water among the collectives, relative to costs involved, including travelling time to the construction site, among other things.

10.   What then followed should be familiar: after the dust of the Red Guards upheaval had more or less settled, by 1969, the much publicized 'North China Agricultural Conference' was held to help greatly boost the Dazhai campaign, and launch spectacular labour-intensive infrastructure projects, as epitomized by the globally known Red Flag irrigation canals in Linxian, Henan province. Communes and production brigades were also reactivated as mobilization vehicles for the 'five small industries' set up in support of agriculture, all being reminiscent of the Great Leap strategy. And these all took place while the production teams remained intact and were indeed meanwhile codified, in the New Constitution of 1974 as the standard structure (Kueh, 2002a, p. 21). Note also that by then a peculiar (in fact terrifying) remunerative method also began to emerge in Dazhai. That is, individual peasants were required to 'report their own accumulated work-point total to be subjected to public arbitration' (*zibao gongyi*). (This would spare cadres the cumbersome field-monitoring jobs.) No doubt, for fear of public humiliation, any such self-reports would basically always end up in competitive realignment with the lowest given. Terrifying as the method may be, it clearly intended to comply with Mao's highly demanding egalitarianism regime.

11.   Sun was imprisoned for his 'revisionist' stance in 1968–75. Many of his articles and internal reports written in 1963–65, for which he was purged, were published in 1984 as a collection of essays (Sun, 1984). If read in conjunction with the criticism levelled against him in *Renmin Ribao* of 1967–69, these works provide highly valuable hindsight into the policy disputes between the Maoist and Liuist camps at the time.

12.   The metaphor which was widely cited during the Cultural Revolution was presumably made by Sun in a public speech given in Changchun (provincial capital of Jilin) during an industrial inspection tour around 1963. Sun may appear not to be as outspoken in his internal report on 'The profit target in socialist economic management system' (hereinafter 'The profit target') written in mid-September 1963 (Sun, 1984, pp. 359–67). But, unlike Liberman (1962), Sun nonetheless suggests in the report that central planners should just need to fix the 'broad direction (*dafangxiang*)' of output' for state enterprises. That is to say, as long as the line of production of the enterprises involved is not being shifted to any other industrial branches without permission, it should be left to the supplier and user enterprises to negotiate directly and work out the contractual details about output volume, assortment plan and technical specifications of the product concerned (Sun, 1984, pp. 365, 459). Sun himself regards this method as an integral part of his proposal that state enterprises should enjoy full autonomy with respect to 'simple reproduction' (replacement investment) (ibid., pp. 365–6). Sun later admits that the proposal led to his being accused of 'advocating the revisionist theory of enterprise self-rule' (ibid., p. 459). To do justice to Sun, however, it should also be noted that, unlike Liberman, in his report on 'The profit target', he does not mention whether bonus awards or any other types of material incentives should be provided and tied in with the profit criterion. It is not until 1978 (after the Cultural Revolution) that Sun confesses that he was under enormous pressures, when writing the internal report in 1963, to 'generally negate the bonus and (profit) retention systems' (ibid., p. 538).

13.   The proposal, entitled 'Fixed assets management system and issues on socialist reproduction' (ibid., pp. 339–58), was also written as an internal report in September 1963, just shortly ahead of the one on 'The profit target' cited above (Note 12). Sun himself regards this as 'the most original contribution among both Chinese and foreign economic literatures' which he had ever read (ibid., pp. 492–3).

14.   Notice, however, that Sun also proposes that, when supply falls short of demand within the sphere of 'simple reproduction', central planners should come in to help redress the

balance. He calls this the 'deficit-balancing' method (*cha e pingheng fa*) (ibid., pp. 458–9), but regards such possible supply deficit as likely to be 'insignificant' in magnitude, relative to the bulk of routine production. However, the prerogative reserved for the central planners implies, nonetheless, that any consumer preferences, as may be expressed through the 'direct contractual ties', may still be forestalled from 'spilling over' onto the 'enlarged reproduction' sphere. In this regard, Sun therefore appears less 'liberal' than Liberman.

15. I had the privilege to solicit personally the view of Professor He Jiangzhang in Beijing in the mid-1980s about the emerging 'two-track planning' system in China, under which both current production and investment (for 'simple' as well as 'enlarged reproduction') were bifurcated into a planned and a market-oriented sector (cf. Howe, Kueh and Ash, 2003, p. 116). Interestingly, He, who was then Director of the newly founded Institute of Sociology of the Chinese Academy of Social Science agreed, with some displeasure, however, over the new reform measure, that this had gone well beyond Sun's original idea for strictly keeping investment for 'enlarged reproduction' in the hands of central planners. Former colleagues in the Institute of Economics were amused at He switching positions from a 'rightist' in 1963–64 to a 'leftist' in the 1980s (disapproving of market-oriented reform). Note, however, that shortly after the Tiananmen Square upheaval, in June 1989, He replaced reform-minded Dong Fureng to become Director of the Institute of Economics for a couple of years.

16. Sun rigorously defended his position in a closed-door symposium held in August 1964 to criticize his proposal, when presumably he was already internally branded as the 'greatest revisionist' in China (Sun, 1984, p. 369). As a matter of fact, Sun made the case for *Produktionpreis* as early as 1956 (ibid., p. 407) and then again in 1961 (pp. 257–8, 273), but he became more outspoken with it in 1963 (ibid., pp. 329, 344), and most explicit in his 1964 defence (pp. 369–89; 372–9 in particular).

17. Yang and He and their associates published a number of articles in *Jingji Yanjiu* (see, for examples, 1962, nos 4 and 6; 1963, nos 6 and 12; 1964, no. 5), to help defend and publicize Sun's proposals, especially with respect to *Produktionpreis* as a principle of price formation. There were also contributors to the same monthly journal who strongly opposed their stance, starting in 1964, issue no. 4. The critique against Yang and He became particularly vocal in the last three issues of *JJYJ* for 1964, with one simply titled 'The essence of *Produktionpreis* is to abandon the planned economy' (no. 10, pp. 1–5). Among the critics are such familiar economists as Wu Jinglian, Zhou Shulian and Chen Jiyuan. Wu, now dubbed 'Wu *shichang* (market)' is the most famous advocate of 'the market-economic system' in China since the 1980s.

18. Following his 1965 *Pravda* article, Liberman (1966) makes the point for capital charge much more rigorously a year later. He also advocates differential land rental to help balance locational benefits between state enterprises.

19. As it has surfaced in Sun (1984, p. 378), 'rational price-setting' is indeed set as the single most important precondition in his 1963 internal report advocating the profit target. In other earlier treatises, Sun also rigorously propagates the principle of 'equal value exchange' (ibid., pp. 141, 254–8, 407).

20. A good case in point is the 'two-track system' in China of the 1980s. As is well known, under the system, many state enterprises colluded with officials-in-charge to illicitly divert centrally allocated production materials to the market sector for profiteering. Following massive protests against such corrupted officials (dubbed *guandaoye*) during the Tiananmen Square incident in May/June 1989, the widespread abuse was drastically cracked down on in favour of renewed centralized control, but that was in turn discarded in 1992–93 to pave the way for the accelerated 'marketization' drive initiated by Deng Xiaoping himself (Howe, Kueh and Ash, 2003, p. 117).

21. As Nove (1965, pp. 252–3) also aptly puts it, under central planning it should be very difficult to visualize how the 'direct (merchandise) orders' method could possibly be extended to the producer goods sector.

22. This is clearly implied by Sun's 'deficit-balancing' method as explained in note 14). See also note 12 for Sun's stance on material incentives policy.

23. By making this statement I have in effect just 'replaced one assumption with another', as Professor Chiang rightly points out to me in writing. Surely, more empirical research needs to be done to verify the situation.
24. For Sun this should also represent an integral part of what he regards as the most rational national pricing system (incorporating interest costs) (Sun, 1984, pp. 256–7, 376, 388–9, 465–6, 472). He argues that the method would neither place any extra burden on the peasants, nor jeopardize state revenue. It should amount merely to a fiscal redistribution. Increases in food prices for urban workers could be compensated for by wage readjustments or food subsidies.
25. In fact, in a post-Cultural Revolution article, Sun (1984, p. 529) reveals that he wants to see the direct (agricultural) taxes, once fixed, to remain in force 'for a certain number of years', as an incentive for peasants to increase production. Again this raises the issue of whether the extra output can effectively translate into added capital accumulation.
26. This is because, as a result of years of official price-fixing and insulation, the domestic relative price system in China is simply not comparable to international price relatives.

PART II

Deng Xiaoping in Mao's Mantle

2. Was Mao really necessary?
An economist's perspective*

WHY THE QUESTION AND HOW I ANSWER IT

We are all aware that, twenty years after Chairman Mao's death, his giant portrait still hangs aloft at the Tiananmen Square, and that the Mao mausoleum in Beijing has comfortably survived its builder, Mr Hua Guofeng, the hand-picked heir apparent, who, after serving for the interregnum in 1977–78, had entirely vanished into political oblivion.

There is no doubt that, as the founder of the People's Republic of China, Mao is guaranteed a permanent place in the Chinese pantheon, and that, to historically minded Chinese, Mao will always be revered as the Chinese hero who liberated the country from a century of imperialist plunder and humiliation. However, there is also little doubt that the legendary Chairman, increasingly revered as a distant, historical figure, is becoming an abstraction, remote from the detailed examination of his real role in China's development.

As a matter of fact, for many, if not the majority, of Chinese, Mao's contribution really consisted in the founding of the People's Republic. After that, he is best remembered for the débâcle of the Great Leap Forward and the havoc brought about by the Cultural Revolution of 1966 to 1976. To be specific, in economic terms, the post-1949 Mao is now widely considered to have been more a negative rather than a positive figure. This perception or conclusion of the post-mortem has in fact become so popular, and so deeply ingrained in everybody's mind, that it is now almost impossible to refute.

This is not altogether surprising, because now, just twenty years after Chairman Mao's death, the economic legacy he left behind, in terms of economic institutions and policies, has been virtually reduced to nothing. This is, therefore, a good time to ask whether Mao, the revolutionary romantic, really did more harm than good for the long-term economic welfare of the Chinese population and, indeed, whether the pragmatic policy alternative developed by Mr Deng Xiaoping has done more to realize the grand vision of a modernized and powerful China, the vision formulated by Mao himself and shared by the revolutionary generation.

As history cannot be repeated to verify hypotheses drawn up with hind-sight, it is futile to speculate on whether from the very outset a Deng Xiaoping could have done better than Mao. With this remark, I may allow myself the liberty to shrug off, regrettably, this impossible question which many might want to seek an answer to. Nevertheless, I would argue strongly that, if Deng Xiaoping, instead of Mao, had been given the overriding mandate to bring China into the rank of the advanced industrialized countries as quickly as possible, there was really not much else he could have done, given the particular circumstances which Mao was confronting. I would therefore argue that what Mao did as an economic strategist was absolutely necessary, underpinned as it was by historical imperatives.

I would argue, secondly, that the economic transition from Mao to Deng, (impressive as it may have appeared to be), should be seen as a natural economic evolution that responded to the changing requirements of a maturing industrial structure, rather than as a negation of the established Maoist legacy.

I would argue, thirdly, that the economic heritage of Mao has to be assessed in its entirety to include the massive material foundation in both agriculture and industry, that he helped to create with the particular economic strategy practised. I would argue that Deng owes much to this aspect of the Maoist legacy for being able to undertake fundamental reorientation in economic policy in the past 18 years or so. Specifically, I argue that the Maoist material heritage greatly facilitated Deng's economic reform and opening-up strategy.

All in all, my own answer to the question, 'Was Mao really necessary?', is therefore a definitive yes, from an economic perspective.

MAO'S ECONOMIC STRATEGY AS AN HISTORICAL IMPERATIVE

Let me first elaborate on how the Maoist economic strategy grew out of some historical imperatives which were essentially political in nature. There are two aspects to this which are closely related. The first is that the command economy established from the early 1950s resembles a wartime economic system. Like Stalin in the 1930s, Mao saw the system as a power-ful mechanism for maximizing industrial growth, in order to expand the country's defence capabilities to stand against 'imperialist encirclement and containment', whether perceived or real. The second aspect is the value imperatives for rapid industrialization itself. This was obviously seen as the panacea not only for all economic ills, but also for getting rid of colonialist-type economic control, in the first place.

The major features of the Soviet-style command system as adopted under Mao are familiar. First, all possible capital resources should be diverted to the preferential heavy industry sector, as this represents the material base for future expansion of modern-type light industry or consumer goods industry. More importantly, heavy industry is synonymous with national defence capacity.

Second, the desired scale of investment in heavy industry implies that consumption should be curtailed to the minimum, and savings maximized. Third, agricultural collectivization and nationalization of industrial properties helped to directly control consumption of both peasants and workers to the minimum required for subsistence and thus maximize the national propensity to save.

Finally, to minimize possible foreign interference in the self-contained industrialization and defence development programme, imports were reduced to the bare minimum, allowing for only an inflow of the absolutely necessary technology to bridge the internally insurmountable supply gaps.

This stylized description of the Maoist economic strategy may sound somewhat disparaging, but it transpires, nonetheless, that the aspiration to a forced-draft industrialization drive was shared by virtually all Chinese leaders, Liu Shaoqi and Deng Xiaoping included. As a matter of fact, the grand vision, personally formulated by Zhou Enlai in 1974, of the 'four modernizations' (industry, agriculture, science and technology, and national defence) of China also bears all the hallmarks of the same aspiration and approach.

There seems to be little doubt that the entire economic disposition under Mao was indeed very much conditioned by the protracted Cold-War atmosphere, and probably even more significantly by the abrupt break of Sino-Soviet relations in 1961, and later on by the even more critical Sino-Soviet military confrontation and conflict on Zhenbao Island in 1969, which clearly prompted the Chinese leadership to seek a rapprochement with the United States, and which eventually led to the establishment of Sino-American diplomatic relations in 1978.

It is most interesting to note that it was none other than Deng Xiaoping himself who was personally in charge of formulating the famous 10 'anti-revisionism' treatises (*fanxiu shilun*) during the great Sino-Soviet rift and ideological debate in the first half of the 1960s. And, equally ironical, it was Mao himself, who, during the heyday of the Cultural Revolution in 1971, initiated the 'ping-pong' diplomacy to approach the United States.

Henry Kissinger, shortly after his secret mission to Beijing in 1971, compared Zhou Enlai to Metternich, the nineteenth-century Premier of the Austro-Hungarian Empire. But, obviously, Zhou never lost sight of the fact that China was the weakest side of the US–China–USSR triangle, amidst his grandiose play with power politics, hence his 1974 blueprint for the 'four modernizations' of China.

WHY THE TRANSITION FROM MAO TO DENG?

Now let me turn to my second thesis; that is, why I see the transition from Mao to Deng as a natural economic evolution. Before I give my comments on this point, a brief review of the fundamental economic changes occurring in China is in order.

Figure 2.1 reveals quite clearly that China's industrial base has expanded substantially in the past several decades. By 1978, when the Deng era began, the contribution from industry already made up half of GDP, and stabilized with the same share until 1994, compared with only 23 per cent in 1952 or 33 per cent in 1957, upon the completion of the first Five-Year-Plan.

The backbone to the structural changes represents, of course, exactly the accelerated growth of industry at the relative expense of agriculture we have

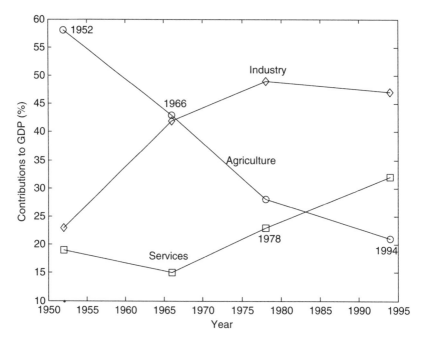

Figure 2.1   *Relative contributions of agriculture, industry and the service sector to Gross Domestic Product in China, benchmark years, 1952–94 (per cent)*

alluded to earlier. This is clearly reflected in Figure 2.2, that shows the markedly divergent growth trends between industry and agriculture.

We may note of particular interest, in Figure 2.3 that, over the three different periods of comparable length, 1952–66, 1966–78 and 1978–95, the industrial growth paths over the long run are indeed quite similar, despite the short disruptions during the Great Leap Forward (1961–62) and at the early stage of the Cultural Revolution (1967–68). More remarkably, for the ten-year Cultural Revolution episode, national income grew at an average rate of about 6 per cent per year, without counting in full the service sector, which has experienced spectacular growth under Deng Xiaoping, and notably without any capital or financial support from outside.

Two major points may be made to explain the imperatives underpinning the economic transition from Mao to Deng. First, after four decades of forced-draft industrialization, increased maturity and diversification within the Chinese industrial structure make it increasingly difficult for the central planners to rely on conventional technical standards and physical norms to control the performance of the state enterprises, or even to formulate and set plan targets effectively. The same phenomenon was observed in the Soviet Union in the mid-1960s. Interestingly, that was also the time when the Soviet economy had gone through roughly four decades of Stalin-inspired industrialization drive.

The second point is closely related to the first one. Under Soviet-style central planning, in the absence of patent right protection, technological diffusion may assure a quicker pace. However, both bureaucratic planners and enterprise managers are accustomed to a standard decision procedure for investment projects. Lack of initiatives to develop or search for new technological alternatives, and lethargy in adapting to changes inevitably led to declining capital efficiency in the long run. This deficiency has also been seen as the fundamental cause of the long-term decline of the Soviet economy (Easterly and Fisher, 1994, pp. 2–5).

Within the Chinese context, declining capital or investment efficiency implies clearly that an increasing share of the national income generated each year has to be set aside for investment, in order to maintain the desired or just the same national income growth rate.

It is against this background that Deng Xiaoping should be seen as more courageous than any other Chinese leaders in seeking a fundamental breakthrough. The approach he has taken is familiar. It is basically a two-pronged strategy. First is the drastic reorientation in income and consumption policy towards what may be called a less harsh strategy, which would (hopefully) help to enhance incentives, and accelerate growth in productivity, and hence further savings for the industrialization drive. The reorientation in

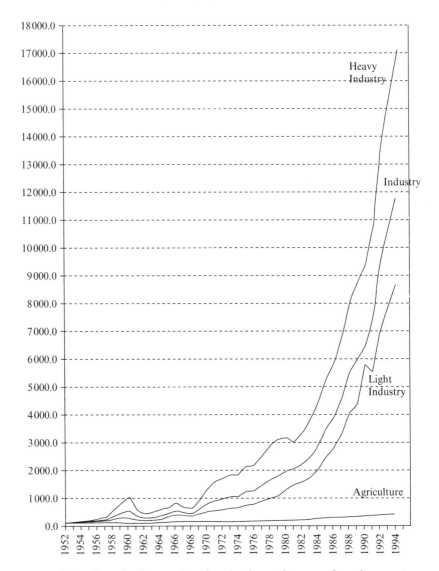

Figure 2.2   Growth of agricultural and industrial gross value of output in
China, 1952–94 (1952 = 100)

consumption policy has already resulted in a marked industrial restructuring. For the first time since the early 1950s, output of light industry, which
is synonymous with the consumer goods industry, has been growing much
more rapidly than heavy industry since 1978, as is shown in Figure 2.3.

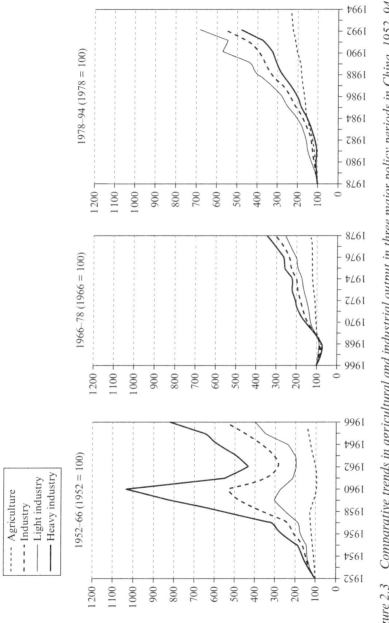

Figure 2.3 Comparative trends in agricultural and industrial output in three major policy periods in China, 1952–94

The second aspect of Deng's daring strategy is consistent decentralization in both agricultural and industrial management, commensurate with the overriding goal of stimulating the necessary productivity growth. I argued in a different context in 1984 that it was the drastic increases in farm procurement prices, as decreed in 1979, that forcefully triggered the de-collectivization process in the early 1980s (Kueh, 1984d).

I argued at that time that, under the collective framework, as was the case in 1979–80, an across-the-board increase in farm procurement prices for the peasants was tantamount to a once-and-for-all income subvention for everybody. That is to say, as long as the egalitarian collective–distributive structure remained unchanged, the marginal income benefits offered through increases in farm procurement prices could really not be counted on as a productivity stimulant. I still hold to the view that it is against this background of pragmatic consideration, rather than any predilection on the part of Deng Xiaoping for 'capitalism', that there had eventually developed a full-fledged agricultural decollectivization and effective reparcel-lization of the collective farmland in early 1984, in order to make effective the purported price-and-income incentives in Chinese agriculture.

The same economic pragmatism of Deng Xiaoping applies of course to industrial decentralization and enterprise reforms. From a simple, egalitarian type of bonus scheme adopted in 1979–80, Chinese enterprises have developed probably the most sophisticated wage-and-bonus payment system one can find in the world.

More importantly, when the enterprise fund, together with provision for profit retention, was adopted in 1979–80, it was construed, in the first place, as nothing more than a device for enhancing enterprises' economic accountability within the conventional Soviet-style setting. But with the profit retention provision came forcefully the demand for profit disposal right. This called, in turn, for enhanced autonomy in investment decision making, and concomitant marketization of the producer goods sector; subsequently, as well, the right of self-marketing allowed market forces to rapidly erode the planning core, culminating ultimately in the strategic reorientation of Deng in 1992 towards establishing a 'socialist market economy'.

Following the same material logic of development for promoting technological progress and productivity is the drastic reorientation in foreign trade policy and, of course, the massive effort made to court foreign investment in China. I must say, however, that in this respect Deng was indeed fortunate enough to be able to benefit from the timely relaxation or détente of East–West relations, particularly the Sino-US rapprochement, which has greatly facilitated the necessary technology transfer. As a matter of fact, I must also say that Deng's entire less-harsh economic strategy seems also to have been formulated against the backdrop of an easing global power constellation at large.

At any rate, the entire open-door strategy is obviously adopted in recognition of the pressing need for borrowing technology from the West, which, together with the emerging competitive market pressures for the domestic enterprises, may hopefully help to redress the fundamental economic ills of declining capital efficiency.

I have yet to mention, but only in passing, another visible hallmark of Deng Xiaoping's pragmatism. This concerns the spectacular growth of the service sector in China since 1979. For Mao, the enormous labour surplus should obviously be maximally channelled into the so-called 'material production' branches, namely agriculture and industry, to be consistent with what clearly was an extensive growth strategy, dictated by the overriding goal for a maximum-speed industrialization. To Deng, however, the new orientation towards technology and efficiency, or specifically the emerging aspiration to an intensive growth strategy to be commensurate with the maturing industrial structure, clearly dictates that a new outlet for the surplus labour is needed.

It is this compelling economic imperative, rather than anything else, that prompted the Dengist policy makers to break the so-called Maoist 'ideological straitjacket', in order to exploit, as we have all seen, every possible potential in the service industries.

HOW HAS DENG CARRIED MAO'S MANTLE?

Now let me finally come to my third major thesis, a contentious one, indeed.

I would argue that, without the solid material foundation left behind by Mao, It would have been very difficult, if not impossible, for Deng to carry out his new economic policy. I would also argue, however, that the essence of Deng's success, with his gradualist strategy to economic reforms, should be seen in his being able to recognize that Mao's mantle, in terms of economic policies and institutions, should not be dismantled overnight in favour of any 'shock therapy', as we have all seen with Mikhail Gorbachev and, especially, the maverick Boris Yeltsin for the former Soviet Union.

In my inaugural lecture delivered in Sydney in August 1989, that is, just two months after the Tiananmen Square incident (see Chapter 3), I argued that, in view of the enormous concentration of economic resources resulting from years of centralized control in China, as well as in the Soviet Union, any abrupt change of direction in favour of a political pluralisation would be highly destabilizing and costly. I argued, specifically, that in a rapidly pluralizing political setting the immense scramble for resources and material benefits by rival interest groups, could lead to an abrupt, large-scale economic disintegration, chaos and destitution.

By virtue of the implied economic imperatives for maintaining stability, I therefore also argued at that time that the political confusion in China would be sorted out very soon and that political unity and stability would soon return to command, as usual, the established economic system. I further argued that, after the dust of the Tiananmen upheaval had settled, economic reforms in China would continue to swing the familiar pendulum of recentralization and decentralization, in the search by the Chinese leadership for an optimum decentralization, and that 'China's door will, in all likelihood, open more rather than less to the West'.

As it turned out, recentralization did take place, and in fact as early as January 1990. I must admit, though, that I am still rather amazed by the pace and intensity with which both renewed decentralization and the open-door policy have been pursued since early 1992 in conjunction with Deng Xiaoping's South China tour.

At any rate, you will have already noted that all the points I strongly argued for in the immediate aftermath of the Tiananmen upheaval were, at that time, all antithetic to the prevalent mood. I remember very well that Gorbachev's approach to economic reform was then acclaimed worldwide for his being able to initiate political reform, presumably as a prerequisite for economic reform. I must say, however, that while I had and still have full sympathy for the students who converged on the Tiananmen Square in June 1989, I do not share, nonetheless, any aspiration for an accelerated process of political liberalization in China, as I believe that it could easily erupt into an economic chaos across the country.

In my inaugural Sydney lecture about the Tiananmen incident, I also quite extensively reflected on the ongoing events in the Soviet Union in comparative perspective with China. Unfortunately, the point I made had eventually proved to be fatal to the adventurist Gorbachev, who could not survive the political storm that he himself had created, and of course even more forcefully to Yeltsin as well, who is at present still struggling to recover from the national economic disorder he has singularly brought about, following the political collapse of the Soviet Union in 1991.

I have still to say a few more words, and in more specific terms, as to how Deng Xiaoping has paid tribute to the Maoist heritage with his gradualist approach to economic reforms in China. But before I do so, let me briefly reveal how, as I see it, Mao's contribution has facilitated the fundamental policy reorientation under Deng Xiaoping. Several points may be made.

First and foremost is that Mao's approach to bold labour mobilization had significantly elevated Chinese agriculture onto a new plateau. Grain output in China stands today at 388 kilograms per head, compared to only

285 kilograms in 1952, the latter being normally considered as the self-sufficiency benchmark. The impressive gain was indeed wrought under enormous population pressures and constant encroachments on farmland by the massive industrialization drive. This is clearly shown in Figure 2.4 and Figure 2.5.

The single most important factor underlying the success is obvious. That is, after years of continuous forced farm investment by way of what development economists normally refer to as a Nurksian type of labour accumulation, the remarkable expansion in the country's irrigation capacity.

Increased irrigation has helped to raise the multiple-cropping area to compensate for the decline in cultivated area. It also facilitates application of chemical fertilizers to boost output per hectare. Equally important, irrigation also helps to stabilize output as well. High and relatively stable grain output is characteristic of present-day Chinese agriculture, compared with the 1950s and 1960s (Kueh, 1984a, 1985b, 2002a). I seriously doubt that, without this well built-up material foundation, Deng would have been able to proceed with his decollectivization programme in the early 1980s.

Second, the greatly expanded heavy industry base, built up over the past four decades through massive forced savings, has facilitated the structural readjustment in the early 1980s in relative favour of light industry and consumer goods production, to support Deng's productivity-oriented less harsh consumption policy (see Chapter 7).

Third, the reorientation towards light industry has also significantly helped promote Chinese exports, which are made up these days overwhelmingly of industrial consumer goods. This helps most crucially to generate the necessary hard foreign currencies for financing imports of most-needed advanced technologies.

Fourth, the millions of township-and-village industrial enterprises, which represent a popular base for export-oriented Sino-foreign joint ventures and which contribute an increasingly significant share in China's exports, are almost all derived from the former five small rural industries established under Mao's reign. The geographically dispersed rural industries are seen by many scholars as the origin of Chinese entrepreneurship which has come to fruition under Deng's reform programme (Walder, 1995, p. 972; Kueh, 1985a).

Fifth, most strikingly indeed, Mao's familiar approach of bold self-reliance left behind for Deng an absolutely clean heritage, free of any external or internal debt. For one thing, there was almost a complete absence of inflation pressures in the late 1970s, when Deng took over (cf. Imai, 1997, p. 201). This certainly greatly facilitated, in the first instance, the drastic increases in state farm procurement prices in 1979 to kick off Deng's policy reorientation. Furthermore, without external debt, the Chinese currency,

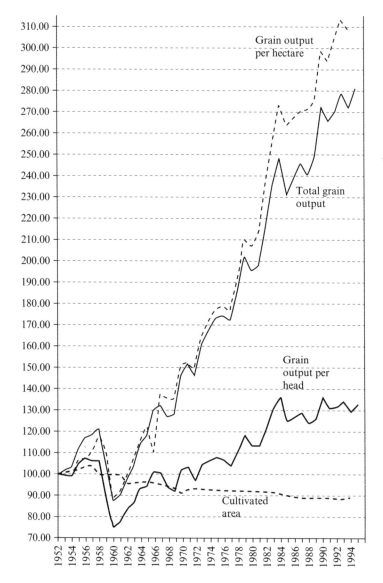

*Figure 2.4   Trends in grain output (total, per hectare and per
head) amidst declining cultivated area in China,
1952–95 (1952 = 100)*

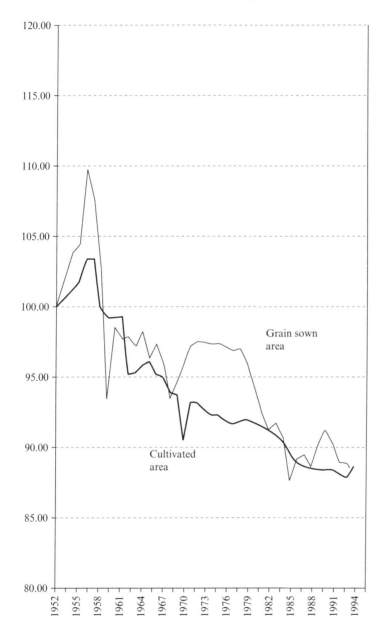

*Figure 2.5   The changing size of grain sown area in relation to cultivated
area in China, 1952–94 (1952 = 100)*

Renminbi, was not at all subject to any major pressures for devaluation. This enabled China to re-enter the world economy with relative ease, and especially to borrow massively from the West, in support of the continuous modernization drive. In this respect, China compares favourably with the former Soviet Union (cf. Lardy, 1995, pp. 1078–80).

I have attempted, briefly, to show how the material legacy of Mao helped ease the economic transition in China, but, more important, Deng's success should really be seen in his awareness that any attempt to cast aside the Maoist institutional legacy could be inherently destabilizing. Deng has been, therefore, very cautious with his approach from the very beginning. This is best manifested in his famous epigram, 'crossing the river cautiously by groping the stone'.

Let me just make one or two major points to conclude my earlier remarks about the implications of the Chinese leadership's position on the Tiananmen Square incident, and indeed, to conclude this chapter.

First, any abrupt political leadership disintegration could result in insurmountable economic chaos, by virtue of the immense rival claims and the scramble from various interest groups, including feuding regional overlords, for resources and power. In practical terms, the entire heavy industry system, for example, could rapidly disintegrate. The large-scale industrial maladjustment that would follow would conceivably manifest itself in serious disruption of the national supply network, and in widespread industrial stoppage, unemployment and wastage. The maladjustment could indeed drag on for years, as has been the case with Russia, before any tenable new industrial structure and consumer benefits could emerge. Obviously, a tenacious political grip was deemed necessary to forestall a potential economic catastrophe of such a nature, and this grip had indeed turned out to be a very tenacious one.

Second, barring any abrupt political disruption, there is also a fundamental economic logic that underlines Deng's gradualist approach to economic transition. Ownership reform is a good case in point. Everybody knows that, in terms of ownership structure, the China of today which comprises a large non-state sector, is already significantly different from that of a decade ago. There is also no doubt that the state sector these days has been largely reduced to the large and medium-scale industrial enterprises and, important as they still are in overall industrial production, state ownership in this respect has indeed been redefined time and again, notably with the operational distinction made between ownership right (by the state) and managerial rights (by the enterprise leadership), to suit the decentralization move. The proliferation of the stockholding systems in China, and indeed the approach made by major state enterprises for public listing in stock markets in Hong Kong and overseas, should be seen in the

same light. I firmly believe that further readjustments in ownership structure will be made from time to time, subject to the dictates of the emerging
market system in China.

For students familiar with elementary Soviet-style economics, whereby
centralized planning and allocation are virtually synonymous with public
ownership, it goes without saying that an outright privatization is tantamount to an abrupt dismantling of the very core of the entire Chinese
economic system. This is, by any measure, not a tenable or realistic proposition. The economic and political consequences would be nothing short of
catastrophic, which I have alluded to briefly, in relation to an outright political liberalization.

Similarly, any policy proposition, such as was often put forward to the
Chinese government in the mid-1980s, for an outright liberalization of the
entire Chinese price system, betrays a gross ignorance of the very basic
element of economics of central planning that officially fixed prices and
mandatory output targets are simply twin travellers, like the body and its
shadow, so to speak. That is to say, any abrupt large-scale freeing of prices
would simply blow up the entire centralized allocation system.

Nonetheless, Deng Xiaoping, the pragmatist, was somehow made to
believe, in early summer 1988, that a full-fledged price liberalization would
help to remove all obstacles to economic reforms, and that 'it would be
better to suffer a sharp, sharp bout of pain, rather than enduring a lingering, long pain'. What followed is familiar: bank runs, panic buying, mounting inflationary pressures and, ultimately, the Tiananmen upheaval, which
had all later proved to be the initial symptoms consequent upon the 'shock
therapy' adopted in the Soviet Union.

Ironically, Gorbachev was himself in Beijing overlooking with Zhao
Ziyang, from the Great People's Hall, the Square that was already heavily
crowded with students. But somehow the flamboyant Gorbachev failed to
look beyond Tiananmen to grasp the fundamentals.

At any rate, the pragmatic Deng was not discouraged by the mishap, and
was indeed resilient enough to re-embark on his gradualist approach,
although it has taken him nearly eight years to gradually free prices to the
extent he attempted to achieve with one shot in 1988.

Let me now turn to a final aspect of the Chinese economic reform to
illustrate how the gradualist approach has worked. Again, ten years ago, it
was a popular proposition that the Chinese system of foreign exchange
control should be abolished altogether, preferably overnight, in favour of a
full convertibility of *Renminbi*. The implications of such a proposal are
rather straightforward: an abrupt liberalization of foreign exchange control
in China would in all likelihood result in a large-scale reallocation of the
most precious hard foreign currencies, in favour of popular and rising

consumer demand for anything foreign, ranging from wristwatches, perfume or soap, to such consumer durables as refrigerators and TV sets. This clearly would be most detrimental to the key priority industries which depended heavily on preferential state allocations of foreign exchange for imports of advanced technology to sustain the modernization drive.

Nonetheless, Deng seemed to have been able to adhere to his pragmatism in this respect, by allowing China's foreign trade and foreign exchange system, gradually but steadily, to move towards a full integration with the world economy. I am certain that, just ten years ago, nobody would have been able to visualize that, through successive readjustments, by way of controlled *Renminbi* devaluations, gradual realignments of domestic prices with international price relatives, abolition of export subsidies and import regulatory taxes, and consecutive import tariff reductions, the Chinese currency is now surely moving towards convertibility; and the country is now verging on the requirement to be a member of the GATT or the World Trade Organization.

CONCLUSION

To sum up, I am convinced that the economic strategy of Deng Xiaoping has worked relatively well. It has given due recognition to the Maoist heritage in terms both of its contribution and of the constraints it imposes on reform policies. It has successfully struck a balance in this respect and charted a viable path to convert the Chinese system into a market economy to be assimilated into the world economy, without incurring excessive costs, be they social, economic or political in nature, the Tiananmen Square incident notwithstanding.

A final word on the question I have posed for this lecture: Mao was by any measures absolutely necessary from a Hong Kong perspective. Without his connivance and tolerance, this tiny colonial and capitalist enclave would have long been part of the socialist system, any time prior to his death. Deng is clearly equally necessary, because I am confident that the 'one country–two systems' model will work. Mao, and Deng especially, indeed bear all the hallmarks of the oriental wisdom of moderation and eclecticism.

NOTE

*   Professorial inaugural lecture delivered at Lingnan University, Hong Kong, 19 March 1996.

3. Dengonomics and the Tiananmen Square incident*

INTRODUCTION

Since the Tiananmen Square incident in Beijing it appears that the situation in China has stabilized as quickly as the eruption of the chaos itself in early June 1989. The Chinese leadership is now very keen to restore normal relations, while the West is still upset by what happened in Beijing. Both central and provincial authorities in China recognize the losses in trade and tourism arising from the incident and are increasingly poised to open the door even more widely, in their effort to court foreign capital, technology and tourists, especially to compensate for the losses incurred.

Of late this continued pursuit of the open-door policy was re-endorsed by none other than Mr Deng Xiaoping, the paramount leader of China, as an integral part of what he calls 'building socialism with Chinese characteristics'. He has given strong commitment to the open-door policy in his choices for the new six-member Politburo, including Mr Jiang Zemin, the former mayor of Shanghai as the new Party Secretary-General, and Mr Li Ruihuang, who was Jiang's counterpart in the equally important port city of Tianjin. Mr Jiang and Mr Li, both Soviet-trained, have been credited for their daring open-door experiments during their earlier tenure.

Mr Jiang was even reported to have once challenged, during his Shanghai years, the central authority, by saying that, if he were given a free hand, he could turn this largest Chinese city into another Hong Kong in a few years.

A number of critical questions, especially as to future directions for China, readily come to mind among Western observers. The questions often asked include the following. What will happen after Deng, who has turned 85, leaves the scene? Will China's door be closed once again? Or, worse still, will there be a fierce succession struggle and unmendable political instability and economic disintegration? If Deng's successors can keep his 'hardline' rule intact, will it be possible to continue borrowing capital and technology from the West without involving the risk of 'bourgeois liberalization'? Or will there be another confrontation with the students in the Square, in say, ten years? Where is China actually heading? Will she

47

continue with her domestic reform programmes, so that the country may eventually be assimilated into the Western world system of free trade and democracy? I hope my brief discussions in this lecture will help to shed some light on the questions raised.

Turning first to the question of the open-door policy, it seems to be a foregone conclusion that China's door will remain open. Nevertheless, to put the question into the proper historical context, let me briefly explain why it should be so.

WHY WILL CHINA'S DOOR REMAIN OPEN?

The most important lesson which the rank and file of the Communist Party learned from the Cultural Revolution was the fact that the Maoist approach of 'self-reliance' leads nowhere in the pursuit of the 'four modernizations'. Deng is certainly clever enough to know, perhaps from his Parisian sojourn in the early 1920s or from his last visit to Japan a few years ago, that sheer enthusiasm on the part of the masses may perhaps help to produce a pair of stainless swords in a backyard furnace (as was already possible in China more than two thousand years ago), but it represents no substitute for steel production using modern technology.

Technology can be learned most effectively from those who are well versed in its application. Even Stalin had to turn to Western Europe in the 1930s for turnkey projects to support his initial five-year economic plans. Most interestingly, after six decades of the forced-draft industrialization drive, Gorbachev has found it increasingly necessary to resort to advanced Western industrial technologies. There seems therefore to be no reason to expect the Chinese to close their doors soon after experiencing the benefits of technology transfer from the West. If anything, the lessons learnt in the late 1950s from their bitter experience with Khrushchev's unilateral and sudden withdrawal of assistance will probably keep the Chinese leadership aware for generations that it would be more beneficial for them to shop in the highly competitive Western markets, rather than resort to the uncertain supplies from the Soviet state monopolies.

A FIERCE SUCCESSION STRUGGLE AND WARLORDISM AFTER DENG?

On the question of succession, one may view the recent showdown between Mr Zhao Ziyang (the deposed Party Secretary-General), and Mr Li Peng, the Premier, as a prelude to a large-scale power struggle in the event of

Deng's death. The showdown has indeed turned out to be quite a violent one, but it is difficult to derive any long-term implications for political instability out of the Tiananmen Square incident. If a scenario of China being divided by a number of warlords fighting against each other emerges, then the situation will clearly scare away investors and traders and thus thwart any increased economic integration of China into the trading system of the West.

I am not a political scientist, and if anyone can produce a crystal ball to predict the outcome of any succession struggle and the effect of any consequent large-scale military clashes and widespread unrest, I would be prepared to vacate this podium for that person. Historical precedents may give some clues to the question of succession posed. The transition from Stalin to Khrushchev in the early 1950s lasted only around three years. The execution of Beria, Stalin's security boss, was no less sensational than the arrest of the 'Gang of Four' in China in October 1976, following the death of Chairman Mao. Likewise, the downfall of the unlikely Hua Guofeng, Mao's chosen successor to pave the way for Deng Xiaoping to return to power in 1978, caught many Western analysts by surprise. Similarly, Gorbachev was by no means the heir-apparent to Breschnev.

Will Mr Jiang Zemin, the new Party Secretary-General, prove to be the Gorbachev of China? Or will another dark horse come to take over the helm in China, in two or three years' time? No-one can really tell. It is nonetheless important to drive home the point that, in both the Soviet Union and China, succession power struggles which have appeared quite violent at times have normally been solved with relative ease, resulting in protracted periods of political stability. Viewed this way the current situation in China is therefore not necessarily 'inherently unstable', as many Western observers may perceive, with their predictions of long-term economic disruption in the country.

Perhaps more important is the fact that the established system of central industrial planning and state ownership control remains basically intact in both the Soviet Union and China amidst the political metamorphoses in their contemporary history. It is to be stressed that this includes the most recent periods, despite all the fanfare about economic reforms, and the adoption of 'capitalist' measures to cure the two countries' economic ills.

HOW IS ECONOMIC CENTRALISM A STABILIZING FACTOR?

The point I would like to make here is that the enormous concentration of economic resources by way of centralized control in all socialist countries, especially China and the Soviet Union, considering their vast size, seems to represent in itself a powerful fiat to preempt any move toward political pluralism. Specifically, any process of political democratization will potentially lead to disintegration of the existing system. The status quo invariably serves what economists call the centralized allocative preferences of the political leadership in terms of economic modernization or defence needs; or, simply, the mere preservation of vested interests and political power. This, together with the built-in Leninist principle of 'democratic centralism', helps to forge consensus among the core leaders as unified leadership keeping the entire system intact.

Perhaps we should turn briefly to the Western analogy in this respect to make the point more clearly. In most advanced Western countries, government changes hands quite frequently, and seldom do Western leaders in office outlive their counterparts in any Eastern bloc countries, including China. Yet, despite frequent leadership changes, the market-type economies have exhibited a remarkable degree of institutional stability. Clearly the markets are the best independent arbitrator of any conflict of interests, and once the system is well established and major conflicts resolved, normally only marginal adjustments are necessary. A similar process applies to the relationship between the government and the people who help to put them into power, here the political process and the voting system act as arbitrators of political conflicts.

By contrast, any significant attempt to decentralize the Soviet-style system of centralized allocation may potentially result in political uncertainty arising from the unmanageable scramble for the previously highly controlled scarce resources. This probably explains why economic reforms in the past two decades in the Soviet bloc have constantly gyrated between the 'remunerative' approach and normative coercion in the perennial search for an optimum decentralization. It has almost proved to be a 'mission impossible' for any Soviet-type economies to enhance workers' material incentives to improve economic efficiency, without compromising the overall policy objective of maximizing industrial growth under the condition of austerity.

Gorbachev was generous enough to the striking Siberian miners, when he promptly conceded in early 1989 to their demands by dispatching consumer goods to the coalfields. However, no sooner had the trains loaded with plain soap and clothes left Moscow for Siberia than the Ukranian coalminers took their turn, making similar demands. And there is no guarantee that workers in the other economic sectors will not follow suit. Where will this lead to? Will everybody flee to the three small Baltic Republics where extended economic autonomy is likely to be granted?

In a way the present-day situation in the Soviet Union resembles the Khrushchevian reorientation towards a less harsh consumption policy in the post-Stalinist era. The important point to be noted then is that, in the past three decades, the core of the Stalinist-style central economic control has remained basically untouched, despite the intermittent and much celebrated Kosygin reform of 1965, inspired by the renowned Soviet economist Liberman, which at that time also prompted the world media to speculate on the imminent surrender of socialism to capitalism.

If what I have just briefly described holds true as the economic *raison d'être* for the political dictatorship and pervasive inertia to changes in the communist countries, then it will indeed be most exciting to see whether the courageous Gorbachev or, for that matter, his followers in Poland and Hungary, will be able to effectively break through the impasse with their daring political experiments.

Let me now turn back to the Chinese scene which I am more familiar with. Here Mr Deng Xiaoping seems to have opted for the more 'pragmatic', albeit the less popular, approach. In a widely circulated internal party document, he recently urged the establishment of a powerful third-generation leadership, after Mao and himself, to preserve the established Party policy line of 'socialist economic construction' without 'bourgeois liberalization'.

Against the Soviet background that I have mentioned earlier, it is not difficult to understand what Mr Deng Xiaoping perceives as economic necessity to enhance centralized political control. China's resource base in relation to a population of one billion is extremely meagre compared with that of the Soviet Union. After years of highly centralized management, any drastic political and economic decentralization in China is, therefore, inherently explosive. This is particularly the case if one takes into account the enormous pent-up demand from years of price and consumption control, notably in the major urban centres.

WHY THE TIANANMEN SQUARE INCIDENT?

In a way it is precisely the over-ambitious attempt at price decontrol made by Deng himself, in summer 1988, that has led to rampant inflation, widespread urban resentment and, finally, the recent unrest. The social groups hardest hit by inflation represent precisely the essential school and university teachers, government office workers and the whole range of intellectuals responsible for the various state research institutes. These are the people who promptly took to the streets in Beijing and other cities to join the student protestors. In this context I should first briefly deal with the economic fundamentals and what Deng Xiaoping regards as the 'little domestic climate' which helped to give birth to the Tiananmen Square incident.

For simplicity, we may first distinguish between three major social groups in China: first, the intelligentsia; second, the economic bureaucrats and technocrats; and third, the mass of industrial workers and peasants. It is obvious that the latter two groups have been able to ride the waves of economic and price reforms better in recent years.

The peasants who make up 80 per cent of the Chinese population have in the first place enjoyed successive price increases for their products as decreed by the state in recent years. These measures were taken to redeem the debts owed to them for being constantly coerced in the past three decades to support the massive industrialization drive by surrendering anything produced in excess of subsistence needs. The offered price incentives, coupled with decollectivization, have also greatly helped to boost farm output and productivity. This has in turn led to the replacement in 1985 of the Stalinist method of forced siphoning by contractual purchases and increased overall marketization of the Chinese rural context.

The success story of Deng's rural reform is well told and that should not detain us here. In relation to the more recent inflationary pressures, the peasants also tend to gain more rather than less compared to the urban masses. For many from the rural areas the initial price and income benefits offered by the state may have been increasingly diluted by rises in prices for both farm input and consumer goods of industrial origin. Generally speaking, however, prices for farm products have risen much faster than those for industrial consumables, at least in the free markets to which the farmers now have access for disposing of their farm surplus. This is easily understandable, for the basket of consumer goods of average urban Chinese is still very much dominated by living necessities, especially farm and farm-related products.

China's major agricultural problems are certainly far from being solved, but the vast numbers of peasant folk are relatively content these days compared to a decade ago. It must indeed be gratifying for Deng to see the payoff from his bold rural experiments. Barring the successive financial concessions made in the past ten years, the peasants, traditionally prone to being organized for large-scale uprisings, could have been a potentially destabilizing factor. Peasant disruption cannot be as easily dealt with by dispatching a hundred tanks and armoured vehicles to the vast rural areas.

Turning to the urban scene, industrial workers have also been major beneficiaries of Deng's economic reforms. Apart from several wholesale wage increases decreed since the late 1970s, the wage bills for many industrial enterprises have also become pegged to the amount of profits realized as part of the incentive measures. This more or less helps to shield them from inflation threats. Economic reforms would also have benefited the tens of thousands of hawkers and peddlers who operate in a virtually non-controlled market environment.

Despite these reforms, official Chinese survey statistics for the last one or two years reveal that around one-third of the urban households in many large cities actually saw their real income reduced as a result of inflation. Undoubtedly, the majority of these households belong to what I have summarily classified as the 'intelligentsia' category who are deprived of any surfboard to ride the inflation waves. Many university students certainly also see their future in this grim picture.

It is by no means my intention to reduce the Chinese intellectuals to *homo economicus*, but for many of them living on government-fixed salary or pension income, it is nonetheless a gross injustice vis-à-vis the workers and peasants. The situation is figuratively underscored by a widespread saying in China ridiculing the scientists: 'making (*gao*) atom bomb (*yuanzidan*) is less rewarding than (*bibushang*) (street hawkers) selling (*mai*) tea-teaf flavoured egg (*chayedan*)'. Their resentment was exacerbated by outrageous corruption on the part of large numbers of economic bureaucrats and technocrats who, by virtue of their official positions and high political connections, took advantage of the so-called 'two-track' economic system to divert scarce commodities from planned allocations for sale in the more lucrative free markets. Many of these, whom I call the 'socialist yuppies' made a great fortune from this malpractice which is officially termed *guandao* (official profiteering). The corruption was one of the three or four main targets of students' protest in Tiananmen Square.

The other major political demands of the students were in fact closely related to the slogan of 'Down with *Guandao*'. The demand for press freedom and democracy, for example, was clearly meant to enhance political transparency (or 'glasnost', in Gorbachev's term) and provide checks-and-balances to prevent any abuse of political power. Carried to the ultimate conclusion, however, these demands for political reform were tantamount to contending for power. This inevitably would lead to political pluralization and was, at least in the mind of the established leadership, inherently destabilizing. Herein should be seen the origin of the Tiananmen tragedy.

CAN THE BASIC CAUSES BE REMOVED?

Now that the bloodstains in Tiananmen Square and the nearby Eternal Peace Boulevard have been removed, can the new leadership dispel the 'little climate', brought about by resentful students and intellectuals simply by cracking down on official corruption? A number of high-profile state corporations which had been engaged in *guandao* have indeed been dissolved recently with renewed resolution by the Chinese government. But will this help?

I am respectfully reminded, in this situation, of a statement made by the prominent Australian–Chinese historian, Professor Wang Gang-wu at a public lecture in November 1977, little more than a year after Mao's death and prior to Deng's return to power. Professor Wang said almost literally that Mao was a unique historical phenomenon which has now gone forever. China from now on will join the ranks of other developing countries in pursuing material wellbeing.

He has indeed been proved correct by Deng's orientation away from ideology and towards economic reform. It is difficult to see why the intelligentsia has been excluded from this pervasive trend of secularization. Atypical as it may appear to be for the pragmatic Deng, he seems to have resorted to renewed indoctrination; hence the recent public appeal for 'hardworking and plain living' to serve the course of socialism.

Is there any economic alternative for Deng? Clearly, any extensive financial concessions made to cope with rising consumerism would inevitably call for a wide-ranging state budgetary reallocation within the Chinese context. This could take the form of price or income subsidies for the beneficiaries, but whatever the form of outlet, barring any real productivity and output breakthrough, it is elementary economics that, within the socialist context of central planning, priority investment projects of the state have to be adjusted to make ends meet.

Tragically, it is precisely the reluctance or inability to adjust the priorities in the last few years in the wake of surging consumerism that forced the Chinese government to resort to banknote printing, which finally ended in near hyperinflation and popular discontent in 1989.

To be fair, substantial concessions have already been made on the part of the leadership to appease the farmers and the workers in the past decade or so. I see a strong link between the wide-ranging concessions and the overtures made to western capital, technology and tourism to bridge the domestic gaps in investment financing and thus help to accelerate the desired productivity growth.

Fatefully, the open-door policy tended to reinforce the secularization trend by virtue of what development economists in the 1950s had already called the 'demonstration effect'. In the socialist context this is understood to include the 'bourgeois influence'. Surprisingly, it was not until the erection by the student protestors in Tiananmen Square of the huge replica of the Statue of Liberty, overshadowing the familiar Mao portrait, that the Chinese leadership suddenly became acutely aware that the 'Trojan Horse' was already on the doorstep of *Zhongnanhai*, the huge and beautiful office and residential enclave for senior Party and Government officials located behind the Square. The 'Trojan Horse' was smuggled in, to borrow Deng's words, by the 'large international climate' which converged with the 'little domestic climate', to bring about the Tiananmen storm.

With these remarks, I shall turn now to the two critical issues raised earlier. The first issue is whether the continuous pursuit of the open-door policy will sooner or later lead to another confrontation with the students in the Square. The second, more fundamental, issue is whether the new Chinese leaders will be coerced by current difficulties to enhance, once again, centralized and bureaucratic controls, thus thwarting any prospect of further economic and political reforms in China.

HOW IMPORTANT IS THE 'INTERNATIONAL CLIMATE'?

Perhaps I should first make the point that economic reforms (*gaige* in Chinese) and opening up (*kaifang*), the two terms frequently treated as synonymous, are actually not necessarily logically tied in together.

The radical Chinese policy reorientation in foreign trade relations from the Soviet bloc to the West in the early 1960s, following Khrushchev's abrupt withdrawal from China, remains the greatest step ever taken in terms of opening up to the West. Even during the Cultural Revolution period when 'self-reliance' was the catchword, China's trade volume with the West hardly declined, in both absolute terms or in relation to GNP, apart from the tumultuous Red Guard years of 1967–69.

In this context I will briefly spell out how Deng's differences from Mao contributed to the external factors leading to Tiananmen Square.

One readily thinks of the massive growth in the past decade of foreign capital and technology, direct foreign investment in China, and tourism in the Chinese economy. Participatory foreign investments provide direct contacts with the outside world in Chinese factories, but the non-economic influence is limited in view of the comparatively small number of joint ventures which in fact are mainly located in the southern province of Guangdong, across the border from Hong Kong.

Tourism has a greater influence than direct investment. The amount of hard foreign currency generated by tourist business in the past few years is virtually the same as capital brought into the country through joint ventures. Dollar for dollar, however, tourism carries a much larger number of foreign messengers of 'bourgeois ideas' (a total of more than 130 million tourists in the past eight years). They are highly concentrated in the urban areas, Beijing in particular.

For many, if not most, Chinese, intellectuals or others, it is clearly humiliating to chase after tourists to exchange money, especially from the 'compatriots' from Hong Kong who are tough negotiators and know the money exchange market better than tourists from the West.

In this regard, it is unfair to blame the deposed Party Secretary-General Mr Zhao for having neglected ideological niceties. Zhao might be blamed for his laxity in monetary control during his term as the Chinese Premier up to 1987, which subsequently led to runaway inflation and the rampant proliferation of black markets for foreign exchange. Nevertheless, it seems difficult, if not impossible, for any serious Chinese leadership to combine the very Dengist brand of pragmatism with altruist socialist ideology within the context of global secularization.

Apart from tourism, there has been yet another unexpected disastrous loophole in Deng's master plan of modernizing China. Unlike Stalin, Deng, in his vigorous search for Western technology, wants not only hardware but also software, hence the tens of thousands of students sent abroad. Typically pragmatic, Deng was once quoted as saying that, if only 20 per cent of students return, it would be sufficiently worthwhile to serve 'the historical mission of motherland construction'. Unfortunately, however, the voice of the students who have returned (or not) seems to have proved even louder than the powerful Voice of America, BBC and Radio Australia.

WHERE IS THE CHINESE GOVERNMENT REALLY HEADING?

What will this lead to, if it is business as usual for the new Chinese leadership? Will there be another confrontation with the students in a few years' time? There were unconfirmed press reports after the Tiananmen incident that the Chinese Government was to step up imports of rubber bullets and tear-gas canisters to replenish the stocks which were rapidly exhausted in early June. Perhaps the waterworks around Tiananmen Square will be re-engineered to enhance water pressure as well. Premier Li Peng reportedly told an American visitor that the pressure was too low for water-cannons to dispel the surging crowds, hence the use of real bullets.

If this is true, Premier Li seems to be poised to walk a tightrope, perhaps along the South Korean way. In Seoul, great confrontation between the students and the police has become a familiar television scene, after the brutal crackdown of the Kwangju uprising in 1980. The Korean economy and exports have nevertheless been faring remarkably well in the 1980s, making it one of the four prospering little 'dragons' in the Pacific Rim, along with Taiwan, Hong Kong and Singapore.

In fact some Chinese leaders are supposed to have begun toying with the idea of 'neo-authoritarianism' since early 1988, in light of the successful experience of the four little dragons. By Western standards the political environment in these small countries or regions is by no means congenial, except perhaps in Hong Kong, where, up to the very recent past, people normally did not care about politics anyway. Yet free enterprise initiatives have greatly helped them to penetrate world markets.

Can the great dragon really learn from the little brothers? The question is essentially whether the present Chinese 'two-track' economic system, which I would say is roughly a combination of some 60 per cent centralized control and 40 per cent market allocation, can be effectively moved toward a full-fledged marketization which, as I argued earlier, is the economic prerequisite for any process of political pluralization to begin.

This is not the occasion for me to get into details about problems of economic reforms in China, but, put briefly, I simply do not see any short-term prospect, Tiananmen Square notwithstanding, for any accelerated economic decontrol to take place. There are enormous fundamental constraints, foremost being the established imperative to maximize industrial growth in the conventional Stalinist sense of priority growth of heavy industry. In the Chinese context, there is also the persistent imperative for the central authority to balance the regional disparities by siphoning any surplus generated in the richer coastal areas for reinvestment in the vast undeveloped interior.

Take Shanghai, for example, which is by far the richest area in China in terms of per capita income. At one time it contributed nearly 20 per cent of the country's total industrial output, but was forced to see around 90 per cent of its revenue handed over to the State treasury for regional reallocation. Shanghai's relative industrial position might have changed, but the system of centralized budgetary redistribution remains largely intact, notwithstanding reform experiments conducted in recent years for converting compulsory profit remittance into profit taxes as in the West. This is the simple economic background against which this once lovely and prosperous pearl of the Orient has been converted into one of the largest urban ghettos in the world. Even though Mr Jiang Zemin from Shanghai has become the Party Secretary-General, he will not be able to entertain appeals from his successor in Shanghai for a free hand.

Another more fundamental point to be made here is that forced industrialization implies strict wage, income and consumption controls which result in persistent worker disincentives. The romanticist Mao obviously failed to revolutionize the world outlook of the workers, but Deng also has failed, with his pragmatism of giving controlled doses of wage incentives, in not bringing about any real breakthrough, especially where workers of the centralized industrial core are concerned. That is what really counts in the overall Chinese context.

More seriously, the difficulties are compounded by the fact that the forced industrialization strategy in China, as elsewhere in the Soviet bloc, inevitably results in chronic supply shortages. This calls for a complex bureaucratic system of physical and price controls. It is inherently inefficient. The Dengist attempt to partially marketize the system has in a way tended to create more problems rather than solve them, *guandao* aside.

Viewed this way, economic reform in China will probably continue to follow the familiar Soviet experience of swinging on a pendulum from decentralization to recentralization for many years to come. If Gorbachev's policies are any indication, hopefully at some future stage, when the necessary material base is established, China may be able to afford real decentralization and political pluralization to accommodate contending popular interests. When that time will come is anyone's guess. Many in the West are sceptical that it will ever come. Zinoviev, the renowned exiled Soviet author of the book *Homo Sovieticus*, for example, predicted recently that Gorbachev would have to return to the Stalinist model in ten years' time. Whatever the outcome, Mr Regan, the former US President, made a good point when he said, just a few days after the Tiananmen incident, that the students were a bit too hasty with their political demands.

WHAT IMPLICATIONS FOR THE WEST?

You may be trying to relate all I have said to the Western business interest. What I have attempted to do here was mainly to place the Tiananmen incident in a historical context. Many of you, with business interests, are perhaps more concerned with the short-term implications.

The situation is indeed not at all rosy: double digit inflation, increased trade deficits, dwindling foreign exchange reserves, suspension of loans by major Western countries and withdrawal of Western investors. To complete the apocalypse, while the initial benefits from agricultural reforms are becoming increasingly depleted, the prospect seems remote for any real breakthrough in industrial productivity. The CIA recently predicted, in its report on China to the US Congress, that pressures may build up, forcing the Chinese government to increase expenditure and money supply to accommodate increased demand from the military, to cover losses of state enterprises and to keep urban wages in step with soaring inflation. All these will presumably result in increased social and political instability in the run-up to the twenty-first century.

If the forecast is correct, then probably only adventurists with a hit-and-run business tactic would be interested in China. The CIA forecast reminds me of a remark made by Professor Peter Wiles of the London School of

Economics, one of the world's authorities on Soviet economics. In a small workshop held a few years ago in London to compare the Soviet and Chinese economic reforms, he said that the Soviet economy had been time and again predicted by Western analysts to be on the brink of the grave. But it had never actually collapsed.

My own explanation for this is simple. Unlike Western economies, the Soviet-style central planning and its monetary–financial process are two quite disparate entities. In case of any significant monetary disturbances, centralized allocation, coupled with powerful, albeit inherently inefficient, bureaucratic–physical control can always help to hold the entire economic fabric together by neutralizing the role of the financial variables. The plain and commonsense (perhaps a bit radical) example of this somewhat eso-teric statement is wartime-like rationing and queuing for consumer goods, which makes money income meaningless.

This is not the occasion to elaborate on the possible business implications of the recent political events in China. Briefly, anyone interested in dealing with the Chinese has to realize, in the first place, that it is a fact of life that the Chinese system of centralized economic and political controls has built up to such a point that it cannot be dismantled overnight. It has remained intact despite the Tiananmen incident and, for the Chinese Government, business will be as usual, with all the possible frustrations one may expect in dealing with the overwhelming Chinese bureaucracy in striking deals, be they business or just cultural exchange.

CONCLUSION

I have made four main points. First, it seems unlikely that any major polit-ical instability will occur in China in the years to come, except perhaps for some sporadic urban unrest.

Second, China's door will, in all likelihood, open more rather than less to the West, but the prospect of a *full* integration of trade and investment with the free trading system of the West still remains quite remote.

Third, domestically, the search for a solution to improving efficiency of state industries and the national economy as a whole will continue, but it seems hard to visualize any real breakthrough, given the built-up impulse to maximize saving and investment in heavy industries, which works strongly against the secular aspiration for consumerism and impairs incentives.

Fourth, continuous, albeit reduced, adherence to Soviet-style planning and control via bureaucratic–physical means to ensure state investment and production priorities makes it difficult for the Chinese leadership to relax political control of the economic process and other spheres of life in general.

Nevertheless, any controlled relaxation in this respect, as has happened in the past decade, coupled with the Chinese search for foreign capital and technology, tends to open up enormous business opportunities for the West, given the vast size of the Chinese market. In this context, by virtue of geographic proximity, Australia, together with Japan and other Pacific Rim economies, could potentially gain more than other countries in their economic relations with China.

NOTE

*   Professorial inaugural lecture delivered at Macquarie University, Sydney, 28 August 1989; reprinted with minor adaptations from Y.Y. Kueh, 'Where will China go from here?', *Australian Quarterly*, **61**(3) (1989), 358–69. By kind permission of the *Australian Quarterly*.

PART III

Agriculture in China's Industrialization

4. The rise of agricultural Dengonomics*

THE ISSUE

There are two major aspects to Deng Xiaoping's economic reform in Chinese agriculture. The first is the drastic increases in state farm procurement prices as promulgated immediately upon his return to power at the famous Third Plenum of the Eleventh National Party Congress (NPC) held in November 1978. The second is accelerated dismantling of the agricultural collectives, more precisely the entire people's commune system, as triggered by the price and income incentives offered in 1979 (what may be considered as a 'less harsh consumption policy'). By early 1984, the process had already culminated in a de facto 'redistribution' of collective farmlands to the individual peasant households throughout the Chinese countryside.

There is no doubt that the changes threaten to tear apart the very raison d'être of Mao's economics of collectivism. That is, to maximize farm surplus extraction to support the massive industrialization drive through the familiar 'scissors-price' instrument and to facilitate Nurksian-type accumulation by way of *non-quid pro quo* labour mobilization, as a means of hedging against natural calamities and exploiting scale economies.

Thus, what could be the economic consequences of Deng's approach? This chapter discusses the impact on national and farm savings, rural investment priorities, overall production stability, and implications for farm procurements and supplies to the urban–industrial sector, and attempts to shed some light on possible future trends. Chapters 5 and 6 look at the decollectivization process and the effect on peasant incomes and consumption. To begin with, the major features of the new agricultural policy programme are briefly sketched.

ASPECTS OF DENGONOMICS

First, beginning with summer harvests in 1979, state procurement prices for 18 different categories of farm products have been raised by a startling average of 25 per cent. The increase amounts to 20 per cent for grain procurements within the scheme of compulsory delivery quotas, which are fixed by the state on a longer-term basis. A new price premium of 50 per cent (up from 30 per cent) is offered for the so-called 'above quota' sales, the amount of which is also predetermined, but may vary from time to time for such quasi-compulsory transactions. In the case of cotton, which is also subject to compulsory purchases, the respective increases were 15 and 30 per cent, while compulsory purchase prices for edible oil and pork were adjusted upward by nearly 25 per cent. On top of these increases, new schemes of 'negotiated prices' (*yijia*) and free-market prices (*shijia*) for voluntary sales add to peasants' incentives.

Moreover, prices for industrial sales to the rural areas, especially producer goods needed by agriculture, are generally to be kept constant or may even be gradually reduced. Agricultural taxes, mostly in kind, have been lowered or abolished altogether for many poorer localities. The same applies to income taxes imposed on rural industries and other non-farm enterprises.

Taken together, the new policy initiatives amount to a genuine effort to eliminate or substantially mitigate the long-established 'scissors-price' differentials. *Postscript*: It was not until 1985, however, that, together with the abolition of compulsory quotas (in force since 1953) in favour of 'contractual procurements', the multi-tier price system converged to the one-price policy (Kueh, 2002a, pp. 236, 242).

The second major aspect is the adoption of the 'agricultural production responsibility system'. This represents initially a method of assigning various farm tasks to the individual peasant households (or groups of households) to replace collective farming and the egalitarian Maoist method of remuneration on a quasi-time-rate basis. However, the experiments have rapidly culminated in the *baogan daohu* system, under which collective farmland is 'reparcellized' down to the household level (*daohu*), and each peasant family contracts with the collective (specifically the production team) to deliver a predetermined amount of output (*baogan*) for state procurement (plus the planned collective retentions for productive investments and welfare expenditure, and the necessary grain reserves). The peasants are allowed to retain anything produced in excess of the contracted 'net delivery'. *Postscript*: By 1985, the new system had rapidly changed to a 'state–tenant' relationship in that, under 'contractual procurement', peasant families started to deal directly with a state procurement agency.

Undoubtedly the *baogan daohu* method amounts to a very favourable lump-sum tax or fixed land rental for the peasants, compared to the past when any surplus production realized over subsistence requirements was forcefully siphoned off by the state. More importantly, beginning in 1982, the same state procurement prices are to be applied to voluntary sales by individual peasant families, while previously they were paid by the collective the lower 'internal prices'. This helps to reinforce peasant incentives, in that, through the 'decollectivization' any increases in state farm procurement prices can directly filter through to individual farm households as income benefits.

A third component of the reform package reflects the need to promote rural economic diversification, in order to absorb farm labour made redundant by the more efficient *baogan daohu* system, and produce more nonfarm consumables to ease increased local demand pressures arising from the 'less harsh' consumption policy on urban light industries. This includes family or organized sideline production, as well as rural trade fairs, which serve as the natural outlets for subsidiary outputs. The most important development, however, is the rapid proliferation of the new 'five small industries' (cotton spinning, knitting, sugar refining, cigarettes and wine making), all consumption oriented. They have largely replaced the old 'five small industries' (cement, chemical fertilizers, farm machinery, metal making and energy, including small coal mines), which were often founded by local government and commune leadership by extorting the savings of production brigades and teams for supplying collective agriculture with the necessary producer goods.

A fourth aim of the reform is the decentralization of agricultural production planning and control. The number of planned product categories and obligatory targets was reduced from 21 and 31, respectively, in 1978 to 16 and 20 in 1981, and further, to only 13 categories, in 1982. In many localities the state crop-acreage targets were ignored or abolished altogether by local authorities. This trend seems to be consistent with the proliferation of the *baogan daohu* system, which tends to make many physical control targets, especially the labour input and planted acreage targets, nugatory.

The final, but not the least important, aim of the reform is to decentralize agricultural investment decision making. Table 4.1 shows that state budget appropriations for agricultural investment have declined drastically, starting in 1980. The decline is evidently meant to be fully or partly offset by the corresponding increases in farm procurement prices, which should help to boost both peasant incomes and local investment capabilities. Note that the reduction in state appropriations apparently contradicts the policy of national economic readjustment (first introduced in early 1979 and then reinforced in early 1981) for correcting 'national economic imbalances' (*guomin jingji bili shetiao*) in favour of the agricultural sector and light industry. But this represents in fact a fiscal redistribution, in that increased state budget expenditure on farm purchases (which have indeed translated

Agriculture in China's industrialization

Table 4.1 State budget appropriations for investment in the agricultural
sector and state bank loans for rural communes and brigades in
China, 1952–82

	Investment appropriations			Bank loans		
		Net increase over previous year			Net increase	
	Total (billions of *yuan*)	(billions of *yuan*)	%	Total (billions of *yuan*)	(billions of *yuan*)	%
	(1)	(2)	(3)	(4)	(5)	(6)
1952	0.38	—	—	—	—	—
1957	1.09	−0.27	−19.80	—	0.27	—
1962	0.87	−0.37	−29.84	—	0.60	—
1965	2.35	−0.27	−10.31	—	0.39	—
1970	2.25	0.46	25.70	—	0.15	—
1975	3.56	−0.14	−3.78	6.22	0.90	—
1976	3.99	0.43	12.08	7.75	1.53	24.60
1977	3.60	−0.39	−9.77	8.55	0.80	10.32
1978	5.11	1.51	41.94	10.20	1.65	19.30
1979	6.24	1.13	22.11	12.29	2.09	20.49
1980	4.86	−1.38	−22.16	15.86	3.14	29.05
1981	2.46	−2.40	−49.38	16.84	0.98	6.19
1982	—	—	—	18.52	1.68	9.98

Notes: Columns 1–3 cover only investment appropriations made for agriculture, forestry,
water conservancy and meteorological services. Column 4 refers to year-end balances of
bank loans for communes and brigades at large, including bank loans for non-farm
enterprises.

Sources: *TJNJ 1983*, pp. 450–53.

into budget deficits since 1979, for the first time ever in China) must be compensated by a reduced investment outlay.

It must also be noted, however, that, with the restoration of the
Agricultural Bank in 1979, state bank loans extended to the collectives
(commune, brigade and team) and their subordinate non-farm enterprises
also increased very substantially in 1980 (Table 4.1). This seems to imply
that part of the direct budget appropriations were also converted into
bank loans consistent with the decentralization drive, or, even more, the
extent of farm-price increases was perhaps considered not sufficient to
help boost local production and investment initiatives under the new rural
setting, hence added liquidity from the banking system.

Table 4.2   Deposits and loans of rural credit cooperatives: year-end balances, 1979–82 (billion yuan*)*

	1979	1980	1981	1982	1979/1982 Trend rate % per year
Total deposits, of which:	21.588	27.234	31.961	38.988	10.32
Commune and brigade agricultural	9.833	10.548	11.324	12.106	7.18
Commune and brigade non-farm enterprises	2.193	2.947	2.973	3.366	15.35
Individual commune members	7.843	11.703	16.955	22.811	42.74
Others	1.719	2.036	0.709	0.705	−0.26
Total loans, of which:	4.754	8.164	9.638	12.115	36.59
Commune and brigade agricultural	2.254	3.454	3.571	3.476	15.53
Commune and brigade non-farm enterprises	1.415	3.111	3.546	4.230	44.05
Individual commune members	1.085	1.599	2.521	4.409	59.58

Source: TJNJ 1983, p. 451.

Notice, however, that with the phasing out of the commune system the bank loan balances were reduced remarkably in 1981 and 1982 in favour of accelerated increases in loans provided to the individual peasant households by the rural credit cooperatives, which are specifically charged to deal directly with them (see Table 4.2 and *JJNJ 1983*, p. IV-144). In fact, private deposits with the credit cooperatives have also increased enormously to capture fully the most favourable impact of farm-price increases for the peasants.

Taken together, the various new policy measures therefore constitute a rather consistent programme of rural decontrol in favour of economic diversification and enhanced marketization and monetization.

IMPACT ON AGGREGATE SAVING

Farm-price increases and various tax concessions for the entire four-year period 1979–82 have added not less than 76 billion *yuan* to the gross income of the rural sector,[1] or 66 per cent of total state budget expenditures for 1982. These concessions to the farm sector have served to change rather

Table 4.3   *Trends in sectoral distribution of Gross Domestic Product and peasants' disposable income and consumption expenditure in China, 1952–82 (at current prices)*

| | Gross domestic product | | | | | | Peasant income (Y) and consumption expenditure (C) in *yuan*/person | | |
| | Billion *yuan* | | | Percentage share | | | | | |
	A	I	S	A	I	S	Y	C	C/Y
1952	34.0	13.6	11.3	57.7	23.1	19.2	1978	133.57	116.06	0.87
1957	42.5	30.2	18.1	46.8	33.3	20.2	1979	160.17	134.51	0.84
1962	44.4	33.5	14.5	48.0	36.3	15.7	1980	191.33	162.21	0.85
1965	64.1	55.8	18.8	46.2	40.2	13.6	1981	223.44	190.81	0.85
1978	106.5	153.3	41.2	35.4	50.9	13.7	1982	270.11	220.23	0.81
1979	131.8	166.6	36.6	39.3	49.7	10.9	1979–1978	26.60	18.45	0.69
1980	146.7	185.7	36.4	40.0	50.4	9.8	1980–1979	31.16	27.70	0.89
1981	165.8	184.4	39.8	42.1	47.8	10.1	1981–1980	32.11	28.60	0.89
1982	189.3	198.6	36.8	44.6	46.8	8.6	1982–1981	46.67	29.42	0.63

Notes: A, I, S stand respectively for agriculture, industry (and construction) and the service sector (transportation and trade only). C does not cover expenditure on such current inputs as chemical fertilizers and pesticides.

Sources: *TJNJ 1983*, pp. 22, 24, 499, 501.

markedly the intersectoral distribution of national income, reflected in the consistent increases in agriculture's share of Gross Domestic Product since 1979, shown in Table 4.3.

The increases in agriculture's share of GDP were more than sufficient to offset the reduction in state budgetary investment appropriations and state bank loans shown in Table 4.1, and have indeed translated into very substantial increases in peasants' income, savings and investment, and consumption expenditure. The distribution of agricultural income between consumption and investment is of course a problem of a different order. If the survey estimates shown in Table 4.3 represent a reliable indicator, then the average marginal propensity to save of peasant families amounted to around 23 per cent from 1978 to 1982. The overall farm sector's saving ratio should be substantially higher if 'corporate savings' at the production team level and by nonfarm rural enterprises are included. Indeed, the Sixth Five-Year Plan 1980–85 calls for a marginal propensity to save of 39 per cent for the rural sector as a whole. Such an achievement would be extremely impressive considering the high income elasticity of demand for consumer goods on the part of Chinese farmers whose level of consumption is still quite close to subsistence.

Now how can such a high level of saving, which was hitherto generated by agricultural collectives, be sustained under the current decollectivization drive? Three possible reasons may be adduced. First, under the *baogan daohu* system, contracted output quotas are controlled by the production team leadership.[2] Specifically, they are set by the team in accord with both the compulsory state procurement requirements and the desired team retentions for financing collective acquisitions of farm machinery and irrigation projects (apart from other collective welfare expenditure). It is conceivable that the possibility of alternative earnings made available to peasants by the rural diversification campaign may force the teams to hold down the contracted output quotas (and hence collective accumulation), so as to make peasants' marginal benefits from above-quota deliveries appear to be at least equally attractive. It is very unlikely, however, that such marginal adjustments will adversely affect the power of the collectives to generate savings.

Second, commune and brigade non-farm enterprises are likely to remain an important source of overall rural accumulation and development finance. Note that, although their development did not gain any momentum until the mid-1970s, their net profits realized in 1979–82 still amounted, nevertheless, to a total of 45.2 billion *yuan*, as seen in Table 4.4. This is equivalent to 55 per cent of the total increase in income (that is, 82.8 billion *yuan*) of the agricultural sector as a whole from 1978 to 1982 (cf. Table 4.3). More noteworthy is the fact that 31.6 billion *yuan* (that is, 59 per cent) of the net profits realized in 1978–82 were reinvested in rural non-farm and farm-capital projects sponsored either directly by the related communes and brigades or by other poor brigades who were beneficiaries of transfers (see Table 4.4). The balance, net of the 6 per cent set aside for collective welfare expenditure, represents mostly profit remittances that were to be redistributed at the discretion of subordinate production teams. A substantial share of the balance was also allotted to team-wide investment activities.

Table 4.4 also implies a consistent trend toward increased transfers of net profits to production teams in recent years. These transfers result from decentralization under the *baochan daohu* and *baogan daohu* systems, which enhanced the economic links of the peasant households to the teams and loosened their links to the commune and brigade leadership at large. Such changes tended to affect investment priorities within the commune system but not the overall saving potential of commune and brigade enterprises.

It should also be noted that, after the promulgation of the new National Constitution in December 1982, a nationwide campaign was launched to free commune and brigade enterprises from the political tutelage of commune leadership. Communes ceased to function as rural governmental

Table 4.4   Realized net profits of the commune and brigade enterprises and their allocations, 1978–82 (billion yuan)

	1978	1979	1980	1981	1982
Total net profits realized in current year	8.80	10.45	11.8	11.3	11.6
Cumulative balance of unused profits from previous year	—	—	4.5	4.4	4.1
Total allocation in current year, of which:	6.82	8.05	9.5	10.0	10.4
(1) Reinvestment in C/B enterprises	3.09	4.06	4.7	4.3	4.8
(2) Acquisition of farm machinery	1.15	1.13	0.9	0.7	0.5
(3) Farm basic capital construction	1.17	1.17	0.9	0.8	0.7
(4) Transfers to poor brigades for productive investments	0.31	0.39	0.4	0.2	0.2
(5) Total in support of agricultural production, (2) + (3) + (4)	2.63	2.69	2.2	1.7	1.4
(6) Collective welfare expenditure	0.40	0.49	0.7	0.7	0.9
(7) Other uses including remittances to subjugated production teams	1.10	1.30	2.6	4.0	4.2
Year-end balance of unused profits	—	—	6.9	5.6	5.3

Sources: NYNJ 1980, p. 366; *1981*, p. 192; *TJNJ 1983*, p. 207.

organs. Their administrative powers were transferred to the traditional *xiang* (township) government. Commune and brigade enterprises were turned into nominally autonomous economic entities (renamed *xiangzhen* (township and village) enterprises subsequently). These changes were primarily designed to enhance enterprise incentives and efficiency but did not reduce the importance of the non-farm enterprises as sources of rural capital accumulation.

   Third, peasant households are also motivated to save to buy more of such essential current inputs as chemical fertilizers, in order to reap the new price and income benefits. This saving motivation seems to be particularly strong under *baogan daohu*, as reflected in the drastic increase in the marginal saving propensity in 1982, the year when the new farming system was in full blossom. The initial fears that *baogan daohu* would render agricultural machinery 'roadless' (*nongii wulu*) have now also proved to be unfounded, for the year 1983 was marked by the peasants' frenzied eagerness to purchase or rent farm machines from the collectives. As a result, the production of farm machines experienced a spectacular increase of 23 per cent in gross value of output in 1983. Of course, this elastic response on the part of supplier industries was only possible because the farm machines involved were mostly small in scale. Thus the output of hand tractors increased by 67 per cent in 1983, while tractors (a separate category comprising larger machines) declined by 7.5 per cent (*TJGB 1984*).

It remains to be seen whether the initial rush to cash in on the attractive earning opportunities offered by higher farm-procurement prices and the *baogan daohu* system will be sustained in the long run. But, in the foreseeable future, increased peasants' saving incentives, coupled with the centralized system of compulsory deliveries and the saving potentials of collectively controlled rural non-farm enterprises, will tend to ensure a high overall saving ratio for the rural sector as a whole.

CHANGING INVESTMENT PRIORITIES

Equally as important as the size of aggregate savings is the question of how they are invested. In the first place, the new policy tends to disfavour larger rural overhead capital construction. Centralized state investment allocations normally designed for large water-conservation projects embracing several communes, *xian* (county), *diqu* (prefecture) or provinces, have been curtailed. In addition the *baogan daohu* system tends to inhibit large-scale labour mobilizations adopted in the past for irrigation projects. This probably explains the declining allocations of funds by commune and brigade enterprises for basic farm-capital construction (Table 4.4). The same goes for the observed reductions in the acquisition by the communes and brigades of farm machinery consisting of larger-sized irrigation and drainage equipment.

It is indeed remarkable that, in favour of satisfying increased demand for such current inputs as chemical fertilizers and farm-product processing, as well as commercial transactions, bank loans from both the state bank and the credit cooperatives for the acquisition of rural equipment have declined drastically, from a cumulative total of 3.7 billion *yuan* in 1980 to 1.3 billion *yuan* in 1981.[3] Likewise, state agricultural bank loans extended to rural farm machinery companies declined from a year-end balance of 2.8 billion *yuan* in 1980 to 2 billion *yuan* in 1981 (*JJNJ 1982*, p. V-334).

It is well known that the Chinese system of 'labour accumulation' (direct investment of labour) was often carried out without any quid pro quo for the collectives or the individual peasants concerned. Now, in order not to further impair peasant incentives, the new policy approach adopted since 1980 stresses voluntary participation with strict cost–benefit calculations made for the collectives and the peasants involved. Adherence to this principle will undoubtedly make the financial costs of 'labour accumulation' prohibitive, especially when set against the alternative potential earnings available under the *baogan daohu* system and the current policy drive for rural economic diversification.

A related phenomenon has been the rapid proliferation of the new 'five small industries' (Yan, 1981) to replace the old 'five small industries', which amounted effectively to an integrated local system of small-scale heavy industries to supply agriculture with the necessary producer goods. Their drastically reduced importance (excepting perhaps chemical-fertilizer plants) was simultaneously caused by (1) the declining demand for such heavy construction materials as cement and iron and steel bars needed by irrigation projects and (2) the enormous effort made at the local level in recent years to shift investment resources to the new five small industries, in response to the mounting income-induced demand for light consumables. Note also that the wide spread between raw material prices and processed output prices for these industries makes them very lucrative.

Declining large-scale infrastructure construction, however, has been compensated by increased investment in small- and medium-sized farm implements, which are more suitable for small-scale operation (Luo, 1983; Da, 1983). This explains the increased transfers of funds from commune and brigade enterprises to production teams (Table 4.4). The teams, which operate in a restricted geographic area, can lend small farm implements to peasant families more easily than communes or brigades. The *baogan daohu* system has also generated a great demand on the part of the peasants, initially for such small farm implements as hoes, sickles, night-soil buckets, animal-driven ploughs, carts and then for such semi-mechanized farm implements as threshing machines and diesel-powered hand tractors. As a Chinese analyst puts it, it is unlikely that the number of large tractors, harvesting machines, heavy transport vehicles and irrigation and drainage equipment will experience 'any substantial increases within a certain period to come' (Da, 1983).

Like the accelerated increase in the use of chemical fertilizers, the new investment emphasis is aimed at quick returns. Coupled with greatly improved incentives, the initial effect of the *baogan daohu* system seems to have been positive. Grain production recorded an impressive 8.7 per cent increase from 1981 to 1982, partly with the blessing of exceptionally good weather.[4] It is, however, difficult to assess to what extent the potential longer-term productivity losses resulting from shifting intrarural investment priorities may be compensated by short-run gains in output.

INSTABILITY IN FARM PRODUCTION

Two questions may be raised about the possible impact of the new agricultural policy on current output. The first is whether decentralization in agricultural planning and control, coupled with the diversification drive, will make the composition of rural output more sensitive to relative prices and profitability. The answer so far has been clearly positive, seeing that the sown acreage for cotton, tobacco leaves and other lucrative cash crops has been greatly expanded in many localities in recent years,[5] in part to feed the flourishing new five small industries (Kueh, 1983a, p. 679). This shift toward cash crops provides the chief explanation for the consistent decline of grain acreage from the 1978 level of 121 million hectare (by no means a record) to the lowest recorded level of 113 million hectare in 1982 (*TJNJ 1983*, p. 154).[6]

In mid-1981, the situation had become serious enough to prompt the central leadership to issue a blanket administrative order to close down or suspend the operation of small factories, notably for cotton spinning and cigarette making (*GWYGB*, **6**, 30 May 1981, pp. 177–80; **10**, 10 July 1982, pp. 474–6). The planned acreage targets, especially for grain crops, which in many areas were abolished earlier have also been reimposed or strengthened to check the price-induced production instability (*JJNJ 1982*, p. V-14). Since centrally fixed procurement prices may not exactly reflect relative scarcities, it is of course difficult to ascertain *a priori* whether the government is justified in blocking the shift from grain to cash crops by administrative means.

The second, more fundamental, question concerns (a) rural infrastructure and (b) peasants' incentives to withstand serious natural disasters. Note first that the grain yields in China have been increasingly stabilized over the past 30 years, although weather conditions remain as variable as in earlier periods (see Figure 4.1). Can this stabilization of the trend in yield be sustained and enhanced in the future in light of the new agricultural policy changes? How will reduced large infrastructure investments in water-conservation works affect the long-term capacity of the country to resist droughts and floods? Although nearly half of China's arable land is now under irrigation, only around a quarter can be classified as 'high-and-stable-yield fields', that is, free from the impact of serious droughts and floods (*NYNJ 1981*, p. 67). To the extent that the less fertile and less stable areas are required to help satisfy the enormous demand for grain, the overall output is likely to remain vulnerable to weather adversities. Regression results from previous analysis show that, for the period 1970–81 as a whole, 35 per cent of annual grain-yield variations can still be accounted for by weather variability. Admittedly this represents a considerable improvement over the period 1952–66, for which a similar regression yielded a R^2 value of 0.59 (Kueh, 1984a, p. 76).

As regards peasants' incentives, it should be noted that the strong 'subsistence urge' of the Chinese peasants has hitherto acted as a powerful

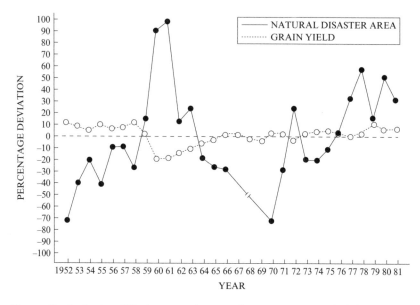

Notes: Production instability is measured as annual average percentage deviations of grain yield per hectare from the log-linear trend value. Weather variability is measured as annual average deviations of the size of natural disaster-affected farm areas from the long-term mean. See Kueh (1984a) for details.

Source: Kueh (1984d), p. 368.

Figure 4.1   *Changes in weather conditions and grain production instability in China, 1952–81*

'harvest stabilizer'. This is understandable under the pre-decentralizatron framework where rural occupational and locational mobility was strictly controlled by the collectives, and the failure to cope with the vagaries of weather could be catastrophic, if not suicidal.[7]

Consider the familiar phenomenon of mass mobilization of labour at times of serious droughts, to carry water from afar and to carry out the most painstaking 'gardening' techniques used to rescue wilting plants (Shanxi, 1975, pp. 182–8). *Baogan daohu* now makes such collective mobilizations less feasible. More importantly perhaps, alternative earning opportunities offered under the diversification drive may render the adoption of such massive labour-intensive approaches economically less attractive from the standpoint of the peasants. Hence there has been widespread fear among the Party cadres that the new system leaves Chinese agriculture more exposed to the mercy of the weather (Zhang, 1983, p. 51).

STATE PROCUREMENTS AND FOOD SUBSIDIES

The *baogan daohu* system may tend to depress the level of state compulsory-procurement quotas but this does not necessarily imply reduced state procurements. In fact, in the past few years, the Chinese peasants have most eagerly responded to the attractive price premium for semi-compulsory sales above predetermined quotas, the so-called 'above-quota sales'. In addition, sales at both negotiated and free-market prices have also increased very substantially (*TJNJ 1981*, p. 343; *1983*, p. 388; *GWYGB*, **18**, 20 October 1981, pp. 562–5). As a result, total state procurement of grain expressed as a percentage of total grain output ('the procurement ratio') has in recent years markedly reversed the declining trend discernible over the past three decades (see Table 4.5).

Generally speaking, such an increase in the total state-procurement ratio implies not only a more elastic grain production but also a more secure local supply. Even more remarkably, this has occurred despite the exceptionally poor weather of 1980 and 1981. It cannot yet be established, however, whether under similar large-scale weather disturbances the

Table 4.5 State grain procurements as a percentage of total grain
production in China, 1952–82

First decade		Second decade		Third decade	
Year	%	Year	%	Year	%
1952	20.3	1962	23.8	1972	20.1
1953	28.4	1963	25.9	1973	21.2
1954	30.6	1964	25.3	1974	21.4
1955	27.6	1965	25.0	1975	21.9
1956	23.6	1966	24.1	1976	20.3
1957	24.6	1967	22.7	1977	20.0
1958	29.4	1968	23.3	1978	20.3
1959	39.7	1969	22.1	1979	21.7
1960	35.6	1970	22.7	1980	22.8
1961	27.4	1971	21.2	1981	24.2
				1982	24.9
Average	28.5	Average	23.5	Average	21.4

Notes: Grain output and procurements are both given in terms of '*yuanliang*' (unhusked grain) and based on the production year (from April to March of the following year), rather than calendar year. The year 1982 is not counted in the average for the third decade.

Source: *TJNJ 1983*, p. 393.

baogan daohu system will respond in the same manner. Apart from this question, one may perhaps assume that interregional grain transfers in China can now proceed in a relatively more secure manner in favour of grain-deficit areas. Likewise, industrial expansion tends to be less constrained by agricultural performance in terms of the supplies of raw materials and food consumed by wage earners.

The peasants' favourable responses to price incentives imply, however, increased state expenditures on farm procurements. This is especially so in view of pervasive attempts made by peasants, and by local authorities as well, to have the compulsory delivery quotas set at lower levels in order to reap the additional cash benefits offered by the four-tier price system noted at the beginning of this chapter. These 'distortions' must have grown to crisis proportions lately. Appeals are constantly being made by the central government, which is also resorting to administrative fiat, to raise or restore quotas (*GWYGB*, **17**, 10 October 1981, pp. 529–34; **20**, 10 November 1981, pp. 632–4). This is another good example of conflicts of interest recurrent in the planners' search for an optimum level of decentralization.

The state has had to incur an additional financial burden from the reform, since resale prices for farm products procured by the state were only marginally adjusted upward, while the bulk of the increases in procurement prices have had to be absorbed by the state budget in the form of reduced collection of profits from the grain-trade department. Moreover, in order to maintain the existing wage-cost and industrial-price structure pending a comprehensive price reform, a systematic scheme of living-cost subsidies from the state budget to urban workers was introduced following the decreed increases in resale prices. As a result, the amount of various forms of price subsidies has increased drastically in recent years. This further complicates the entire structure of the Chinese price system, which for familiar reasons was already highly distorted.

CONCLUSION

Several important points may be made. First, the Chiang–Fei 'labour effort' function (see Chapter 1, pp. 4 and 20) seems to be at work, judging by the frenzy with which the Chinese peasants have attempted to cash in the price and income benefits offered for farm production by the new agricultural policy programme, weather implications notwithstanding. Peasants are more motivated, for example, to shift from the superficial application of fertilizers to the painstaking practice of 'stratified insertion' into the soil for quickening nutrient absorption by plant roots.

Second, despite accelerated rural decontrol under the *baogan daohu* system, peasants seem not to be poised to forfeit the transferred income from the state (via the drastic increases in farm-procurement prices) merely for short-run improvement in consumption, as is reflected in enhanced marginal propensity to save for productive investment. This suggests that the Chiang–Fei 'capital accumulation' function should hold as well, generally speaking, notwithstanding the fact that farm production and peasant consumption have become relatively secure these days.

Third, there has, nonetheless, been a remarkable shift in investment priority, from large or larger-scale rural overhead capital projects (such as irrigation/drainage facilities to withstand droughts and floods) to small or smaller-sized short-run maximizing investments (chemical fertilizers, small farm implements and the like). Hopefully the established foundation will help to hedge against possible long-run production instability and the displacement of economies of scale which may result from the reparcellization of collective farmland.

Fourth, with bureaucratic–physical control under the collectives being abolished, farm production and output mix have also become increasingly vulnerable to short-run fluctuations in market and prices as well. The rural economic diversification drive which helps to provide alternative earning opportunities adds to the instability. Hopefully the ongoing experiments with marketization will eventually help to redress the disequilibria and converge to a more stable rural economic context.

Fifth, increased farm procurement costs associated with higher price incentives (for above-quota and non-quota sales) inevitably call for the improved supply of consumer goods to the peasants; hence the proliferation of the 'new five small industries'. Similarly, rising urban consumerism may help to intercept increased farm supplies (processed or otherwise) originally destined for exports in exchange for needed foreign machinery and equipment. As a matter of fact, not only have grain exports declined steadily since 1978, but grain imports increased most dramatically at the same time (Kueh, 1984b). Hopefully this will not compromise too seriously the established industrialization strategy, for Mao and Deng alike, of focusing on heavy industry growth.

In short, the present rural setting seems very unsettled. It is to be hoped that the added consumption incentives provided will trigger a continuous upsurge in farm production, eventually to help lift the country over the critical threshold of capital constraints in pursuit of maximizing industrialization.

Postscript: Starting in 1985, with the abolition of the compulsory quotas, a new unified farm purchase price formula was given for state procurement agencies, but this all pointed to renewed resort to the price scissors. The upshot was widespread peasant resentment, which was in turn aggravated by adverse weather and other conditions, resulting in a marked decline in grain output (Kueh, 2002a, pp. 242–4). Thereafter, the Chinese government was constantly confronted with the Achilles' heel of balancing peasants' incentives against the perceived broader context of national interests.

NOTES

*   Reprinted with adaptations from *Journal of Comparative Economics*, **8** (4) (December 1984), Yak-Yeow Kueh, 'China's new agricultural-policy program: major economic consequences, 1979–84', 353–75, copyright 1984, with permission from Elsevier.
1.   These include reductions in state budget revenue caused by increases in state farm-procurement (quotas and above-quotas) prices, and reductions/exemptions of agricultural taxes and commune and brigade enterprises' income taxes, and prices for producers' goods of industrial origin sold as inputs for the agricultural sector.
2.   At the beginning of the *baogan daohu* drive in mid-1981, state procurement agencies might also contract directly with a group of farmers or individual peasant households in some localities, but this involved mostly the above-quota and non-quota sales. The provision was prompted by the fact that, at that early stage, many production teams failed to specify explicitly the state procurement quota for the contracting peasant families; and the 'above-quota sales' of some individual households were used to compensate for shortfalls of others, so that the team as a whole could fulfil the state quota deliveries. This has impaired incentives, of course, for the peasants involved were not awarded the stipulated price premium. As a hedge against such abuses it has also become a widespread practice for the state procurement agencies to directly collect the farm deliveries from and settle the payments with the households.
3.   *JJNJ 1982*, pp. V-332–3 and *1983*, pp. IV-142–3; Agricultural Bank of China (1984), p. 26. For a more detailed discussion about the situation in 1982–83, see Liu (1983), pp. 37–8; *ZGJR*, **10** (1983), 5–6.
4.   The 8.7 per cent increase in 1982 is indeed extraordinary, compared with the average rate of increase of 3.8 per cent for 1978–82, or 2.6 per cent for 1952–82. Even if set against the bumper harvest of 1979, the 1982 grain output still represents a record gain of 6.4 per cent (*TJNJ 1983*, p. 162).
5.   Total cash-crop acreage has expanded by 30 per cent, from 14.44 million hectares in 1978 to 18.79 million hectares in 1982. This helped to raise their share in total sown acreage from 9.6 per cent to 13 per cent (*TJNJ 1983*, p. 154)
6.   See Liu (1982) for this background of the reduction in grain acreage. The observed cropping changes are also partly caused by the government's deliberate policy, adopted in the earlier years of decollectivization, to encourage greater regional specialization according to comparative advantage.
7.   See Kueh (1983b) for a more detailed discussion of the 'subsistence urge' and other socio-economic types of 'harvest stabilizers'.

5. The economics of the 'second land reform'*

THE BACKGROUND

For peasants who have been collectivized for nearly three decades, the national campaign initiated by the Party Central Committee's Document No. 1, 1984, to promote the reparcellization of collective farmland, by extending the peasants' leasehold right to over 15 years (para. 3-1),[1] is certainly not less spectacular than the land reform of 1949–52, when land was confiscated from the rich for redistribution among poor peasant families. This 'second land reform' has now firmly consolidated the long-fought policy of Deng Xiaoping for a decentralized approach towards rural management. All the cats – 'black or white' – seem to have now been totally unleashed to run after their best catch. This stands in sharp contrast to the uneasy equilibrium of the 'two-line struggle', which existed throughout the entire 20-year period following the abortive communization drive of 1958–59. Nevertheless, while probably no Chinese leader today can afford to play the role of Mao's Liu cum Deng, one wonders whether, for economic reasons, the present rural institutional solution as envisaged in Document No. 1 will mark the end of the perennial Chinese search for an 'optimum' level of decentralization.

In a way, the agricultural reform of recent years has begun with the drastic increases, decreed in 1979, in state farm procurement prices. For a regime very much obsessed with the value imperative of modernization, the farm price increases should clearly be construed as income incentives for promoting agricultural production to ease the economic constraints on industrialization. This is nothing new, but is precisely the policy developed by the prominent Chinese economist, Ma Yinchu, some 25 years ago in his then much condemned 'balanced growth model' for China (Walker, 1963). Thus the strategy fits well the Chiang–Fei model, which advocates an 'optimum austerity' consumption standard as a 'roundabout' approach to achieving an even higher rate of capital accumulation and economic growth.

Yet, for the purported price and income incentives to work in the first place, the established egalitarian collective–distributive structure must obviously be altered, otherwise the decreed price increases may amount to nothing but a once-for-all windfall for the peasants. That is to say, barring substantial rural reform, the additional outlay incurred by the government might represent a formidable loss from the standpoint of the state planners.

However, up to late 1981 – that is exactly two years after the initial price increases – the reorganization in the form of the *nongye shenchan zeren zhi* (agricultural production responsibility system) was largely limited to the restoration, or refinement, of the work-point system, the convention of the mid-1950s and, in a more constrained fashion, of the early 1960s.

Table 5.1 explains the various operational variants of the responsibility system. It is clear that, from the incentive point of view, the *baogan zhi* (net-output delivery system) is much more attractive than the *baochan zhi* (output-contract system), which in turn should be more preferable than the *baogong zhi* (labour-contract system). More importantly, the *hu* (household) contract should be much more effective than the *zu* (group) contract, and both are, for the peasants, undoubtedly more beneficial than working for and sharing in some future common plot of the collective of an unknown size – unknown not only because it depends on the unpredictable work effort of fellow collective members, but also because it may vary greatly according to possible changes in government policy or the collective attitude towards farm accumulation and distribution.

Thus, it is no wonder that there has been a forceful trend, as revealed in Table 5.2, for the responsibility system to converge from the *baogong zhi* to *baochan zhi* and then rapidly to *baogan zhi*, on the one hand, and from the *zu* to *hu* as the contracting tenant on the other hand, to complete the rush to *baogan daohu*. Specifically, *baogan daohu*, which Document No. 1 now attempts to perpetuate, and which prescribes a rather favourable lump-sum tax (or rental) obligation on the part of the peasant tenants, may be regarded as the officially tested solution for making the price incentives work effectively. The entire decollectivization process seems to have grown mainly out of spontaneous local economic pressures rather than from a master plan.[2] In any case, it has certainly enjoyed the blessing of Dengism, which essentially advocates 'the indiscriminate testing of truth through empirical performance' *(shijian shi jianyan zhenlide weiyi biaozhun)*.

THE RATIONALE

Why then issue Document No. 1, 1984, at all? Apart from the crucial need for granting the peasants a long-term leasehold right, which I shall discuss later, it has been necessary to formulate a new policy and to create a new organizational framework to cope with the many fundamental issues

Table 5.1   The agricultural production responsibility system in China: types and variants, 1980–83

---

1. *baogong zhi* (labour-contract system)

    contractor: *zu* (group of farmers), *hu* (peasant household) or *lao* (individual labourer)
    obligations: to fulfil certain specified farm work (sowing, transplanting, harvesting, etc.) fixed in terms of quantity/quality/time limit and material costs involved, under the unified management of the team
    rewards and penalties: agreed work-point entitlements (or reduction in case of contract failure) as a basis for participating in the team-wide distribution of final output, in kind or in cash

2. *lianchan zhi* (output-linked system)

2.1 The *baochan zhi* variant (output-contract system)

    contractor: same as above, hence the familiar term *baochan daohu* (contracting output down to the household, in the case of *hu* contract)
    obligations: to fulfil a specified amount of *final* farm output for a fixed land area, either under the unified team management (as in the case of *zu* or *lao* contract) or separately by the individual peasant household (*hu*), with current inputs being fixed and provided by the team
    rewards and penalties: agreed work-point entitlements (reductions) as in the case of *baogong zhi*, plus full or partial retention (compensation for) the overfulfilled (underfulfilled) proportion of the contracted output targets in the case of a *hu* contract

2.2 *baogan zhi* (net-output delivery system)

    contractor: *hu*, hence *baogan daohu*
    obligations: to fulfil the contracted output quotas for both state procurements and collective retentions with land area being fixed for the absolute disposal of the peasant households, and draught animals and farm implements (normally small and medium-sized) reconverted into their possession through either direct title transfer or conditional assignment
    rewards and penalties: entitlements to any amount of output realized in excess of the fixed delivery quotas, or compensation for any proportion underfulfilled

---

Sources: See Kueh (1984d), p. 356.

associated with, or arising from, the system of *baogan daohu*. For one thing, the greatly increased rural labour reserves released by the much more efficient private farming system has seriously aggravated the problems of rural unemployment and underemployment. Much more needs to be done than just to reiterate the appeal for increased rural economic diversification

Table 5.2   *The agricultural production responsibility system in China:*
            spread and changes, 1980–83 (per cent)

		Lianchan zhi (Output-linked system)				
		Baochan zhi (Output-contract system)		Baogan zhi (Net-output-delivery system)	Baochan plus Baogan zhi	
	Baogong zhi (Labour-contract system)	Total *hu* and *zu* contract	*Zu* only	*Hu* only	Total *hu* and *zu*	*Hu* only
	(1)	(2)	(3)	(4)	(5)	(6)
1980 (January)	55.7	29.0	24.9	0.02	29.1	4.2
1980 (December)	39.0	42.1	23.6	5.0	47.1	23.5
1981 (June)	27.2	45.1	13.8	11.3	56.4	42.6
1981 (October)	16.5	37.4	10.8	38.0	75.8	64.6
1982 (December)		22.0	13.3	*c.* 70.0	92.0	78.7
1983 (November)			3.0		98.0	95.0
1983 (November)					99.0	
1983 (December)				94.5		

Notes: The figures refer to percentage share of production teams or equivalent basic accounting units of the people's communes employing the system. The December 1983 figure of 94.5 refers to percentage of total number of peasant households.

Source: Kueh (1984d), p. 357; (1985d), p. 125.

as a means of accommodating the mounting labour surplus, and the stylized commune system, with all its 'puritan' facades, was certainly incompatible with the scale of labour mobilization needed for tapping the greatly diversified non-farm resources in rural areas. The emerging new task appeared to be far too difficult to be handled by Maoist-style ideological persuasion or collective coercion within the communes, in order to organize mass labour mobilization for large-scale water conservation works and other rural overhead projects.[3]

It is against this background that specific operational arrangements are provided for in the Document. These include: (1) the provision of flexibility for peasants to establish rural cooperatives of any scale and type, including those which break through local administrative barriers and specialize in particular branches of business (para. 3-5); (2) the stipulation that capital owned by the peasants and collectives may move freely around the country for investment in existing or in new rural enterprises (para. 3-2); (3) a clearer (albeit still rather restrictive) formulation about the extended freedom for both private and collective enterprises to employ rural wage labourers (para. 3-3); and (4) an instruction to the local authorities to bring about, where necessary, income reallocation within the cooperatives concerned, in favour of grain *zhuangye hu* (specialized households), with a view to balancing their incentives against the very prosperous non-grain households and the rural, non-farm economic sectors (para. 3-4).

The second, and closely related, fundamental issue is that increased diversification and specialization, and increased peasant income, inevitably result in increased commercial flows, not only within rural areas, but also between rural and urban–industrial sectors, however limited the counterflows from the latter sector may be, in view of the established strategy giving preference to the growth of modern industries. Therefore an appeal is now being made for accelerating the removal from the state's hands of the entire rural supplies and sales cooperative network (para. 4-2), which curiously was converted into state ownership as late as 1978. Likewise, rural credit cooperatives which have seen both their deposits and loans volumes increased tremendously in recent years, as a result of the creeping decollectivization process and increased peasant incomes, are now to be given greater powers in financing rural industrial/commercial activities, and the freedom to change interest rates charged (para. 4-3).

The third, and probably most crucial, issue remains how directly to provide the peasants with sufficient income benefits, especially those specializing in the production of grain, cotton and other major cash crops which are subject to state control. The substantial increases in procurement prices were certainly not meant to eliminate totally the scissors-price differentials. Agricultural prices remain depressed, not only relative to industrial products of urban origin, but perhaps more crucially to those produced by the rural non-farm enterprises. The changing and sharpening intrarural differences are certainly more immediate in the attitude of the Chinese peasants than the established rural–urban differentials. It is against this background that the provision mentioned earlier for possible intracooperative income reallocation should be understood, and considered against the recent drain of rural manpower from the agricultural sector proper, with rural–urban migration still being controlled (Kueh, 1985a).

What can be done in this respect? A total liberalization of farm prices would be inconsistent with the policy of forced-draft industrialization. Thus, Document No. 1, 1984, cannot but be limited to reiterating the established policy guidelines for gradually reducing the nomenclature and quantity of compulsory purchases on the one hand (para. 5-1), and to keeping their amounts fixed for a number of years on the other hand (para. 5-2). It is extremely difficult to determine the comparative price and income benefits which may arise from complete relaxation of physical target controls, especially in view of the fact that prices for the 'third category' farm products which are not subject to unified controls, and are in many cases important input materials for rural non-farm enterprises, 'are to be genuinely freed' (para. 5-1). It is indeed interesting to note that Document No. 1, 1984, ends up on this issue with a rather awkward clause proposing that 'the State Council authorizes the related ministries to establish special committees for systematically studying the entire circulation and price systems and producing fundamental reform methods therefore' (para. 5-4). How this would eventually be done is anybody's guess, pending perhaps the reform of the national price system as envisaged in the latest Decision of the Party's Third Plenum of 20 October 1984, which is being regarded as another watershed in Chinese economic policy.

There are of course other crucial issues related to the system of *baogan daohu* which the Document, surprisingly, tends to ignore. Two important examples are water conservation works and agricultural extension services. These are two areas which have, comparatively speaking, benefited from collectivization, but can a decollectivized agriculture still draw on the Maoist approach towards irrigation projects for example, using Nurksian-type labour accumulation? With respect to the second issue, *baogan daohu* is not necessarily incompatible with the requirements of a Green Revolution, as some western experience based on private farming shows. But the recent Chinese performance in this area seems not to be particularly encouraging (Kueh, 1985b).

All the issues raised here are certainly not unique to Document No. 1, 1984. As a matter of fact, exactly a year ago the emerging institutional arrangements already prompted the Party leadership to review, in a similar document, its overall rural economic policy, and to spell out its long-term perceptions about agricultural development, rural specialization, commercialization, employment and technological innovations.

Nevertheless, while Document No. 1 for 1983 also laid down essential groundwork (notably the depoliticization of the commune system) for the subsequent organizational changes, as illustrated above, its preoccupation with 'grand visions' somehow concealed the most serious problem of land use inefficiency associated with *baogan daohu*.

Specifically, by autumn 1983 at the latest, it became clear that the meticulously short tenancy duration of one to three years would give rise to widespread *Raubwirtschaft* of the most radical and disastrous forms China had ever encountered (*NCGZTX*, **3** (1984), pp. 13 and 15; and **8** (1984), p. 5). In a major speech delivered at the National Rural Work Conference in November 1983 for summing up the experience of implementing the policies of Document No. 1, 1983, Wan Li, the vice-premier responsible for agriculture, states that the foremost task for 1984 was how to encourage the peasants to invest in such a way as to preserve soil fertility (*NCGZTX*, **2** (1984), p. 7). He asked for proposals from the floor, but obviously the answer was already around the corner.

I shall discuss shortly what the extension of the leasehold to 15 years may imply, but mention should first be made of another crucial land use problem which also greatly bothered Wan Li. In his view the prevalent egalitarian practice of allocating farmland to individual families on a per capita basis, regardless of inter-family differences in the size of the labour force, inhibits efficient land use across the country and within localities. As a remedy, Document No. 1, 1983, allowed for 'labour swapping between farm families' and for 'families which have lost their labourers or which are short of labour force, to employ occasional farm workers, for the purpose of maintaining their living' (para. 6). No matter how modest these initial stipulations may sound, their subsequent implementation has forcefully yielded the 'truth' for a full-fledged endorsement in Document No. 1, 1984, of virtually unlimited transfers of leasehold rights, with all the compensatory provisos (para. 3-1) which elementary western economics would simply regard as differential land rent.

This surely flies in the face of orthodox communist ideology and the real impact is profound. Scores of peasants, driven by poverty into the various non-farm sectors, rush back to participate in the 'second land redistribution' which they regard as a 'social insurance', in the hope that the 15-year leasehold will automatically transfer into private ownership upon its expiration, to sustain the extra rental bonanza (*NCGZTX*, **7** (1984), pp. 30, 33). Leasehold markets, akin to property transactions in the distant past, have begun to mushroom (*NCGZTX*, **8** (1984), p. 14), despite constant appeals from the authorities for the surrendering of redundant or unused land parcels for non-compensatory reallocation by the collectives, as is also stipulated in the Document (para. 3-1).

For the collectives, which are responsible for the reallocation within the hamlet or village, the scramble for land inevitably results in widespread quarrels among the peasants, and hence produces tremendous tasks relating to arbitration. In the localities where 'uxorilocal' marriage is widespread, for example, attempts have now been made by male chauvinist peasants to block such a custom, for fear that prospective bridegrooms from outside may encroach upon their land share.[4] Many collectives are forced to draw up a 15-year plan of land balances which incorporates the mandatory birth control scheme and provides for inter-family clearing on the basis of projected changes (death, birth, marriage) in family size (*NYJJWT*, **8** (1984), p. 42 and *NCGZTX*, **6** (1984), pp. 34–5).

Fears of large-scale social disturbance clearly make 'Dengonomics' appear to involve danger, for the 'black cat' premise would, *ceteris paribus*, lead to an outright public auction of collective farmland rather than to land being allocated on a basis of population. Hence the economically more sensible allocative device of tender biddings is limited to such farm subsidiaries as fishponds, pig sties, fruit orchards, and so forth (*NCGZTX*, **8** (1984), p. 12).

THE IMPLICATIONS

Where will all these dramatic changes converge? The year 1984 was greeted with yet another 'high-tide of rural socialism' – this time with 'Chinese characteristics'. Jubilant Chinese peasants very often capture the scene these days in Chinese television broadcasts at both the national and provincial levels. Peasants are shown with various measures to enhance and preserve soil fertility. Long-term land use efficiency is of paramount importance to China for, despite increased industrialization, the good earth is still the single most important source of economic surplus, which ultimately determines the pace of industrialization at large, and the possible scale of rural investment, non-farm employment, diversification and commercialization. But will the tide eventually subside? It seems premature to attempt a full evaluation of this new social experiment, but it is nonetheless worthwhile to give some brief thoughts about how it may relate to the established system of central planning and the broad policy goal of modernization.

Recall first of all that it was the enormous need to siphon off an agricultural surplus to finance the First Five-Year Plan that created the entire system of compulsory farm purchases and monopolized sales by the state. This in turn prompted the subsequent collectivization and communization process (as an expedient for implementing and expanding the compulsory delivery scheme). One wonders whether the current 'decollectivization' will bring the Chinese peasants back to the pre-1953 land reform situation, which was essentially dominated by free market relations rather than by planning and coercion (Perkins, 1966, pp. 28–42).

Note, however, that compulsory purchase quotas for the major farm products are to remain intact (para. 5-1 and Document No. 1, 1983, para. 7-1). They are now directly relegated to the peasant households in the form of *baogan* targets (Table 5.1) which represent nothing but land rental. The state is not necessarily a bad landlord, as Gale Johnson, the prominent American agricultural economist, aptly puts it, provided that the tenure relationship is well defined (Johnson, 1982, p. 845). However there are two important sources of uncertainty within the present Chinese context.

First, the collective cadres are very often compelled to adjust upwards any agreed *baogan* targets which are overfulfilled to an unpredictably large extent, perhaps on account of sheer hard work (*NCGZTX*, **8** (1984), p. 12). The pressures often originate from jealous peasants who have done less well. Perhaps they are less skilful or less industrious or less lucky in obtaining lower rental commitments. Whatever the cause, there has evidently been a fierce backlash of the deeply ingrained egalitarian ideology. The situation is certainly more difficult for the demoralized rural cadres to handle than for the powerful landlords of the past, vis-à-vis the free tenants.

The second, and certainly more fundamental, source of uncertainty arises from the fact that, while Document No. 1, 1984, specifically calls for the compulsory purchase quotas 'to be fixed for a number of years' (para. 5-2), the official commentators constantly refer to the necessity for any 'irrational' (that is, 'unrealistically low'), *baogan* target, to be readjusted from time to time (*NCGZTX*, **8** (1984), p. 4, and **3** (1984), p. 12). This is not a matter of difference in semantics. Rather, it is difficult to visualize how the quotas can be kept constant for any extended period of time at all: it is difficult by virtue of the rationale of the adopted development strategy which, analogous to the Chiang–Fei model, will call for the extra output induced by the marginally increased consumption outlay over the maximum austerity, to be effectively siphoned off to support modernization.

In a way, all the major farm quotas are biased downwards these days, in light of the massive diversification and commercialization drive. Specifically, rural non-farm activities enjoy higher output prices and profitability, because of the irrational price structure. And, for the entire *baogan daohu* system to work, peasants' earning potential net of the imposed state deliveries (or rental) must obviously be made comparable, by manipulating (that is, lowering) the *baogan* targets. Otherwise, simple marginal allocative rules would dictate that manpower and other farm resources should be further diverted away from the good earth.

All this is precisely the institutional arrangement for the 'optimum austerity' consumption strategy, which has indeed prompted the observed upsurge in incentives and agricultural productivity. However, the constant upward revision of targets would be tantamount to imposing confiscatory marginal income tax rates. Nor, I think, could the peasants be bullied with any policy reversal of the declining scissors-price differentials for taxing away their gains. Thus, in terms of the Chiang–Fei model, there seems to be no practical organizational solution within the socialist context, to help guarantee that the 'additional output' generated can be effectively converted into state capital accumulation. If correct, the outcome may be a slower rather than higher overall economic growth rate.

There are other major areas of concern which tend to enhance the government's policy dilemma. Water conservation works represent a crucial one. After years of massive investments in irrigation/drainage works, China seems basically to have power over the traditional 'grand agony', but the 'lifeline of agriculture' is by no means firmly secured, judging by the degree of yield instability relative to weather changes (Kueh, 1984a). At the same national conference at which Wan Li delivered the key speech as a prelude to Document No. 1, 1984, Li Bening, vice-minister of Irrigation and Power Generation, was concerned about the possibility of irrigation works being consistent with the much-publicized grain output target of 480 million tons for the year 2000 (*XHYB*, **1** (1984), 117–18). Not only has it been difficult to increase the irrigated area in recent years, as he clearly noted, but 'after the implementation of the responsibility system, maintenance works (of existing irrigation facilities) lag behind in some areas, and some were destroyed, and (the misdeed) has not yet been completely halted. This also accounts for the decline in irrigated area' (ibid., p. 117).

In short, the present rural solution represents by no means an 'institutional equilibrium'.

NOTES

*   Reprinted with adaptations from Y.Y. Kueh, 'The economics of the "second land reform"
     in China', *The China Quarterly*, **101** (March 1985), 122–31; copyright School of Oriental
     and African Studies, published by Cambridge University Press.
1.   The Document is dated 1 January 1984, and published in *Renmin Ribao* on 12 June 1984.
     The two digits, 3 and 1 in parentheses, refer respectively to the relevant section and para-
     graph of the Document. This chapter provides an interpretative study of the Document,
     hence similar citations hereinafter.
2.   Note that, in similar decrees in 1979, *baochan daohu* was explicitly prohibited (*NYNJ
     1980*, p. 58), and in the so-called Document No. 75 of September 1980, only a negligible
     number of production teams regarded as poor were allowed to practice *baochan daohu*
     (*NYNJ 1981*, pp. 409–11).
3.   See Eckstein (1975, pp. 268–72) for a good discussion about the relationship between
     mass mobilization and communization, and the role played by the Maoist ideology.
4.   See *NCGZTX*, **2** (1984), p. 45, **8** (1984), p. 5. The custom is for the men to be 'married
     into' and live with the wife's family.

6. Peasant consumption and incomes in critical turn*

AGGREGATE TRENDS AND STRUCTURAL CHANGE

The pace with which the new Dengonomics has helped to boost peasant incomes and consumption since 1978 is truly amazing. By a large measure, the increases in farm procurement prices since 1979 have immediately translated into disposable income for the peasant households and improvement in consumption standards. As shown in Figure 6.1, per capita peasant consumption has accelerated most markedly relative to that of the urban residents since 1978, narrowing the gap from 1:3.2 in 1978 to 1:2.6 in 1986. Note also that the growth in urban consumption has slowed down equally remarkably in the early 1980s, as a result of drastic curtailment in urban investment, in heavy industry in particular. Undoubtedly, by the advent of the Deng era, the decades-long industrialization drive was considered basically mature enough to afford a relaxation in rural control.

However, Figure 6.1 also reveals that, once the 'Economic Readjustment' was completed, from 1983 onwards, there has been a marked equalizing trend in growth rates between urban and rural consumption; and the trends are indeed underscored by the parallel decline in 1985–86. As a matter of fact, the absolute figures given in Figure 6.1 show that the relative difference in per capita consumption in 1986 between the peasants (191.02 *yuan*) and non-peasants (496.50 *yuan*), is exactly at par with that prevailing in 1957 (respectively 72.6 and 186.9 *yuan*), with both years bearing the same 1:2.6 ratio. This seems to imply that any prospective growth in peasant incomes and improvement in their consumption standard should be carefully judged against the constraints inherent in the established Stalinist economic strategy of maximizing heavy industrial expansion, by controlling consumption at the relative expense of the peasants.

Nonetheless, the rapidly rising peasant consumption and income have also been accompanied by accelerated rural economic specialization and diversification, making a break from the Maoist pro-grain strategy, which had dominated the Cultural Revolution period. Thus, as shown in Table 6.1, non-farm income has become an increasingly important source of peasant incomes, while household consumption of domestic produce

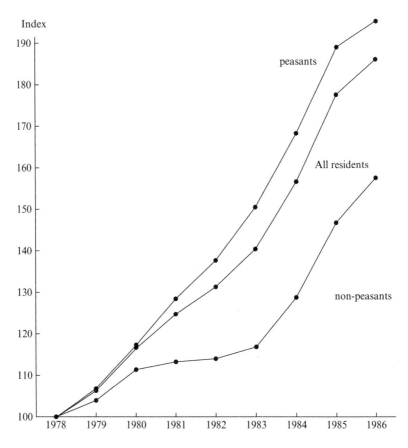

	yuan/*head* (*in 1952* yuan)			*Annual growth* (%)	
	1957	*1978*	*1986*	*1957–78*	*1978–86*
All residents	93.4	134.8	251.03	1.8	8.1
Peasants	72.6	97.7	191.02	1.4	8.7
Non-peasants	186.9	315.5	496.50	2.5	5.8

Notes: The figures are from the national income accounting of consumption versus savings net of 'social' or 'collective' consumption. Urban residents are normally provided with a greater share in social consumption than the peasantry, especially in terms of education and medical care benefits.

Sources: TJNJ 1987, pp. 670–71.

Figure 6.1   *Growth in personal consumption per capita of the peasants*
relative to that of the non-peasant residents in China, 1978–86
(in 1952 yuan)

Table 6.1   *Per capita net income of the Chinese peasant households by*
origin of sources, and their expenditure on consumer goods by
direction of outlay, 1978–85

	Total income yuan/head			FSM income %		Outlay on consumer goods %	
	UCM	FSM	Others	Farm	Non-farm	Market purchases	Self-supply in-kind
1978	66.3	26.8	6.9	75.9	24.1	39.7	60.3
1979	63.7	27.5	8.9	77.9	22.1	—	—
1980	56.6	32.7	10.7	76.2	23.8	50.4	49.6
1981	52.0	37.8	10.2	73.2	26.8	56.1	43.9
1982	21.5	69.4	9.1	—	—	56.5	43.5
1983	11.6	79.0	9.4	84.4	15.5	58.8	41.2
1984	10.0	80.3	9.7	79.8	20.2	58.6	41.4
1985	8.4	81.1	10.5	76.1	23.9	60.2	39.8

Notes: (1) UCM and FSM stand for unified collective management and family self-management, respectively. (2) 'Others' include incomes from cooperative undertakings (*jingji lianheti*). (3) For absolute *yuan* figures, see Table 6.3. (4) The data are all from household surveys conducted by the National Bureau of Statistics.

Sources: Kueh (1988), pp. 636–7.

has been steadily replaced by purchases from the market, in peasants' consumption outlay. These all signal improvements in rural consumption and living standards after the death of Mao.

Note that, in Table 6.1, family 'self-managed' net income in both absolute and percentage terms increased drastically from the watershed year of 1982, as a result of the 'transfer' of regular large-scale collective farming activities to the private households under the *baogan daohu* system. The shares between farm and non-farm income may appear to have not changed as much (except for 1982), because income from the flourishing non-farm activities (handicrafts, rural industries, construction, transport, trade, catering services and the like) has increased equally remarkably. No doubt the new rural institutional setting is now firmly in place, although, despite the abolishment of the forced siphoning system (compulsory deliveries) in 1985, farm sales continue to be subject to monopsonist manipulation by state procurement agencies – a more moderate 'scissors-price' control.

The main parts of this chapter examine the peasants' savings and consumption behaviour, changes in consumption pattern and the problem of food consumption adequacy, with a particular reference to interprovincial inequality and stability. The discussions should, however, be preceded by an analysis of the sources of short-run fluctuations in overall peasant income and consumption.

SHORT-RUN FLUCTUATIONS

Peasants' income and consumption fluctuate from year to year, subject to a number of factors associated with farm production. The most important ones include prices for inputs and outputs which are largely subject to the government's 'scissors-prices' policy in the new setting. No doubt the weather also plays a crucial role, but this is, unfortunately, often ignored in most analytical exercises. Using the data given in Table 6.2 for 1978–86, a regression equation may be estimated to ascertain the relative influence of these major factors, as follows:

Table 6.2   *Yearly fluctuations in peasants' net income, farm output and input prices, and the weather conditions in China, 1978–86 (per cent)*

				State farm				
	Nominal net income			Procurement prices		Input prices		The weather
	Index	Yearly changes	Detrended fluctuations	Index	Changes	Index	Changes	Index
1978	100		−5.18	100		100		+18.95
1979	119.9	19.91	−1.98	122.1	22.1	100.4	0.4	−13.25
1980	143.2	19.45	0.93	130.8	7.1	101.4	1.0	+14.13
1981	167.3	16.78	1.60	138.5	5.9	103.1	1.7	−1.70
1982	202.2	20.89	5.87	141.6	2.2	105.1	2.0	−16.58
1983	231.9	14.68	4.66	147.8	4.4	108.3	3.0	−14.68
1984	266.0	14.71	3.48	153.7	4.1	117.9	8.9	−20.47
1985	297.7	11.90	−0.19	166.9	8.6	123.6	4.8	+15.10
1986	317.3	6.58	−8.30	177.6	6.4	125.0	1.1	+18.50

Notes: (1) Detrended income fluctuations are percentage deviations from the log-linear trend value. The 'detrending' helps to isolate the magnitude of income fluctuations net of the yearly secular increases in nominal prices. The calculated percentages (with plus or minus signs) may, therefore, be roughly regarded as income fluctuations caused by changes in weather/output conditions or peasant incentives in response to variations in state farm output/input prices. (2) The weather index is similarly defined as in Figure 4.1.

Source: Kueh (1988), p. 643.

$$Y = 15.5567 + 0.1307\,P_1 - 0.3118\,P_2 - 0.1774\,W$$
$$(0.691) \quad (0.420) \quad (-0.563) \quad (-1.632)$$
$$R^2 = 0.52 \quad \text{T-value in parentheses,}$$

where Y, P_1 and P_2 stand for the yearly changes in net income, and output and input prices respectively, and W the weather index, all as defined in Table 6.2.

The estimated results reveal that the year-to-year changes in per capita net income are, as expected, positively correlated with state farm procurement prices, but negatively correlated with farm input prices and the weather index. In fact, the weather appears to be a much more powerful explanatory variable compared to both farm output and input prices.

Thus, as shown in Table 6.2, the three years, 1982, 1983 and 1984, which are known for having exceedingly good weather, all saw large increases in per capita peasant income. This occurred despite the fact that the increases in state farm procurement prices in these three years were the smallest in extent, compared with those of other years in 1978–86. The year 1979 is also noteworthy. It saw the largest increase in state farm procurement prices (by an average of 22 per cent over 1978), and an equally substantial increase in peasant net income (by 20 per cent). Farm input prices remained virtually unchanged in 1979. However, the increase in peasant income was also associated with an abrupt improvement in weather. Thus, from the point made above concerning the three years 1982, 1983 and 1984, it is clear that, without the good weather, the peasants would probably not have been able to reap the price benefits offered in 1979, and thus to increase their income to the extent that they were able in that year.

State farm procurement prices continued to increase considerably, from 4.1 per cent for 1983–84, to 8.6 per cent for 1984–85. For 1985–86 the increase still amounted to 6.4 per cent. Nevertheless, the possible output and income effects of these price increases were greatly offset by the drastic deterioration in weather conditions in 1985 and 1986, both of which were the worst years since 1978 (Table 6.2). The result was a substantial slowdown in peasant income growth from 1984 to 1985 (down from 14.7 to 11.9 per cent), and again from 1985 to 1986 (down further to 6.6 per cent). The deceleration occurred amid substantial downward adjustments in the rate of increase in state farm input sales prices (Table 6.2). More strikingly, the years since 1983 were all marked by accelerated agricultural decollectivization and economic diversification. Thus the improvements in peasant incentives could not offset the negative impact of poor weather and, had it not been for the remarkable increases in non-farm employment and income to compensate for the losses occurring in the farming sectors, the slowdown in peasant income growth in those few years could have been even more drastic.

In short, the year-to-year fluctuations in per capita net peasant income during 1978–86 can be consistently explained by the weather, although the extent of the weather's influence may have been reduced, compared with the 1950s or 1960s. Apart perhaps from 1979, when the sharp increases in state farm procurement prices were reinforced by exceptionally good weather, to bring about a record increase in peasant income, the price incentives arising from the marginal yearly adjustments in state farm output and input prices seem to have been greatly overwhelmed by the impact of the weather in the period from 1979 to 1986 taken as a whole.

SAVINGS AND CONSUMPTION EXPENDITURE

The statistics in Table 6.3 show the yearly fluctuations in peasant consumption expenditure and savings in relation to income realized in 1978–86. For the entire period, the savings ratio and marginal propensity to save (mps) averaged 18 and 17 per cent, respectively. Between these years, the mps varied quite substantially. Several interesting points should be made.

First is the remarkable high mps of 31 per cent in 1979. No doubt this reflects the immediate effect of the increases in state farm procurement prices made that year. Note that the price increases did not take effect until the summer harvests. Peasant consumption in the first half of the year was basically unaffected. The price increases amounted, therefore, to an extra bonanza for the peasants. It is also possible that the supply of consumer goods lagged behind the sudden increases in peasants' purchasing power in the second half of the year. The high mps may, thus, partly represent an element of 'forced savings'.

Secondly, the mps was substantially scaled down to around 11 per cent in both 1980 and 1981. This occurred despite the fact that peasant income continued to grow substantially, by 19.5 per cent in 1980 (which saw further price increases to offset the negative output effect of deteriorating weather conditions) and, to a lesser extent, by 16.8 per cent in 1981 (a mediocre year in terms of weather). The implied acceleration in consumption expenditure in 1980 and 1981 (an increase by 20.6 and 17.6 per cent, respectively), suggests that the peasants might by then have become confident that the price increases were real and sustaining, and they, therefore, might have finally opted to express their consumption elasticities of income, after the prolonged suppression of the previous 30 years.

Third is the spectacular growth of mps in 1982, 1983 and 1984, amounting to 37, 29 and 44 per cent, respectively. More strikingly, this occurred against the background, in these three years, of the lowest rates of

Table 6.3   Trends in per capita net income and consumption expenditure of the peasant households in China, 1978–86

	Net income			Consumption expenditure			Savings ratio	Marginal propensity to save
	In current prices	Yearly changes		In 1978 prices	In current prices	Yearly changes			
	yuan	yuan	%	yuan	yuan	yuan	%	%	%
1978	133.6			133.6	116.1			13.1	
1979	160.2	26.6	19.9	n.a.	134.5	18.5	15.9	16.0	30.6
1980	191.3	31.2	19.5	184.5	162.1	27.7	20.6	15.2	11.1
1981	223.4	32.1	16.8	n.a.	190.8	28.6	17.6	14.9	10.9
1982	270.1	46.7	20.9	n.a.	220.2	29.4	15.4	18.5	37.0
1983	309.8	39.7	14.7	265.0	248.3	28.1	12.7	19.9	29.3
1984	355.3	45.6	14.7	309.0	273.8	25.5	10.3	22.9	44.0
1985	397.6	42.3	11.9	350.1	317.4	43.4	15.9	20.2	–3.2
1986	423.8	26.2	6.6	357.6	357.0	39.5	12.5	15.8	–51.1
Total	2465.1	290.2			2020.3	240.7		18.0	17.1

Notes: The total income and consumption expenditure series in current prices imply an annual growth rate of 15.5 and 15.1 per cent, respectively. This is only marginally higher than the deflated rate of 13.1 per cent for the income series. In fact, the major inflation occurred in 1985, at 8.5 per cent. (n.a. = not available).

Source: Kueh (1988), p. 641.

increases in state farm procurement prices, compared with any of the other years in 1978–86, while state farm input prices continued to be adjusted upward, reaching the record high of 8.9 per cent in 1984 (Table 6.2). Clearly, the improvement in peasants' mps was, in the first place, brought about by increased income (exceptionally good weather), but, more importantly, it was also made possible by the rather moderate increases in peasant consumption expenditure in 1982–84, compared with those of 1978–81 (Table 6.3).

Fourthly, the above point, about peasants' consumption behaviour in relation to income gains, has a very significant implication. That is, the creeping decollectivization process had, by 1982–83, probably given the Chinese peasants the impression that rural decontrol was both real and lasting. The traditional virtue of thrift and the household income-maximizing motivation unfolded forcefully, by way of maximizing savings and investments, in order further to cash in the offered price benefits. An important conclusion, which can be drawn from this reasoning, is that farm savings may not necessarily suffer, when forced savings institutionalized by agricultural collectivization disappear. Note that the de facto redistribution of collective farmland in China did not take effect until 1983, when the commune system began to disintegrate.

Fifthly, the mps of the Chinese peasants plummeted from the record high of 44 per cent in 1984 to a negative rate of 3.2 and 51 per cent in 1985 and 1986, respectively (Table 6.3). This can also be explained in rather straight-forward terms. Of the utmost importance is the substantial slowdown in peasant income growth during 1985 and 1986. The rates of income increases in these two years were the smallest since 1978, due to very bad weather conditions (compare Tables 6.2 and 6.3). The decline could not even be arrested by the considerable increases in state farm procurement prices, and the reduction in farm input prices. However, the negative mps also tends to reflect the fact that the Chinese peasants did not want to reduce their consumption expenditure in response to reductions in income. They preferred instead to dig into their savings from the previous good harvests to make ends meet in the lean years, so as to maintain their newly established consumption levels. A certain trend of consumerism has thus been emerging in rural China.

CHANGES IN CONSUMPTION PATTERNS

This section examines the magnitude of improvements in peasant consumption between 1978 and 1986, in terms of its overall level and composition. For the Chinese peasants, who had been living at a subsistence level in the previous 40 years or so, the most important question to ask is whether Engel's law has begun to work in post-Mao China. This law states that consumption expenditure on food declines as a proportion of total income or expenditure, as income rises. The decline implies that an increasing proportion of the income can be set aside for consumption of less essential, but nonetheless desirable, goods or services, such as housing, clothing and daily articles, or cultural entertainment.

Figure 6.2 shows the Engel's ratios for China taken as a whole, based on national time series and cross-provincial data. Taken together, the Engel's ratio declined from around 67 per cent in 1978 to 57 per cent in 1986. This is rather a remarkable decline. It could have been even more· impressive, had it not been for the sampling bias for 1978, which covers only 19 out of 29 provinces, and excludes such poor provinces as Gansu, Ningxia, Qinghai, Shaanxi, Xinjiang, Xizang and Guangxi. Judging by international standards as given in Table 6.4, the improvement in peasant consumption in China is, however, marginal. The average Engel's ratio for the country as a whole advanced only from the 'absolute poverty' category (in 1978) to the very upper end of the 'marginal' category (1986). In 1986, it still stood well above the 1970 standards of such developing countries as Kenya, Iran and Malaysia.

However, increased income and consumption expenditure (Table 6.3), coupled with the declining food budget share, imply gradual improvement in the living standard and in the consumption patterns of the peasants, no matter how marginal the improvement may have been. The perceived changes are reflected in the elasticities of peasant consumption of goods and other living necessities, with respect to income or total consumption expenditure (that is, income net of savings). The elasticities relate the percentage changes in realized consumption to that of realized total expenditure (or income gross of savings). As such, they measure the different responses of consumer demand to increases in income, and show the direction and intensity of changes in consumption patterns.

Table 6.5 presents the various expenditure elasticities of consumption of the Chinese peasants in 1978–86, again based on national time series and cross-provincial data. Some brief comments should be made about the content of the major consumption categories. The two food sub-categories, that is, staple and non-staple food, include respectively, (1) foodgrains and beans, and (2) vegetables, pork, beef, mutton, fish, poultry, eggs, edible oils, sugar, salt and spices. A third sub-category covers fruit, milk, wine and meals consumed in restaurants, but it is not treated separately in our elasticity estimates. The housing category is also noteworthy. It includes mainly expenditure on building materials for new houses or house improvements. Rents and payments for utilities are negligible in rural China.

The first interesting point to be made is that, for both the national time series and the cross-provincial estimates, the expenditure elasticities for non-staple food, housing and the 'others' category, which includes fuels, household utensils, small appliances, wristwatches, radio, television sets and, not least, furniture (to go with new houses), are consistently greater than unity. This implies accelerated consumption of these goods and services.

By contrast, the elasticities of staple food consumption are, as expected, smaller than unity (0.36 in 1980). The latter tended to decline markedly over the years, reaching the exceedingly low level of 0.07 in 1986. However, as is discussed shortly, this should not be taken to imply saturation of foodgrain consumption, and consequent diversification of the consumption structure. The demand for clothing (another basic need) shows similar, though less pronounced, trends, the elasticity declining consistently from 0.87 in 1978 to 0.72 in 1986.

per cent

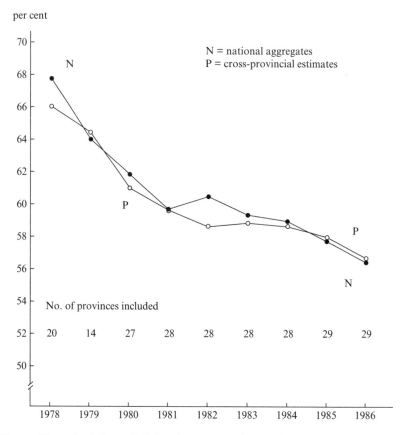

Notes: The national time series is based on current prices. To the extent that food prices may have changed from year to year relative to those of other consumer goods, the estimated food outlay proportion may be biased either upward or downward for any particular year. Nevertheless, both the national time series and the cross-sectional estimates using provincial data show a consistently declining Engel's ratio, except for the chance marginal reversal in 1982 for the national time series.

Source: Kueh (1988), p. 648.

Figure 6.2 Engel's curves of the Chinese peasants: percentage share of food in total consumption expenditure, 1978–86

Most startling, however, is the demand for housing. Housing expenditure elasticities are consistently much higher than those for the much-sought-after non-staple food, for all the years between 1978 and 1986. Whenever possible, the Chinese peasants are prepared to squeeze the consumption of high protein food items, so that cash can be made available

*Table 6.4   International standards of food budget share in total
consumption expenditure*

Engel's ratio (%)	Quality standard	Sample countries, 1970 (in descending order)
>59	absolute poverty	China (67.7 in 1978), India (66.7)
50–59	marginal	Philippines (56.5), China (56.4 in 1986) and South Korea (55.9)
40–50	fair/moderate	Kenya (48.9), Iran (46.7) Malaysia (41.0) and Colombia (39.6)
30–40	rich	Italy (37.5), Hungary (35.6), Japan (32.3), and United Kingdom (29.5)
<30	very rich	France (26.5), Belgium (25.8), Netherlands (25.7), West Germany (22.6) and United States (17.4)

Source: Kueh (1988), p. 649.

for building new houses. This fits in very well with the traditional Chinese value imperative of having a house to boost the family image. The estimates show that the expenditure elasticities of housing increased most dramatically from 1.46 in 1978 to 1.94 in 1980, and were sustained thereafter at levels ranging between 2.23 and 2.55. These are exceedingly high elasticities, and are clear manifestations of the building boom in rural China in those years.

It is also interesting to note that the expenditure elasticities for the 'others' category of peasant consumption, which captures all the 'luxurious' items, are consistently lower than those for housing demand, but they rank, nevertheless, exactly between the elasticities for non-staple food (greater than unity) and clothing (smaller than unity, but still quite high compared with those for staple food). This implies that the urge to improve the diet is still more intense than the demand for relative luxury goods. But, beyond the satisfaction of basic clothing needs, the Chinese peasants have now become increasingly interested in *zhongdangci* (medium-class) or even *gaodangci* (high-class) commodities. How this emerging consumerism will evolve in the future depends to a great extent on peasants' satisfaction with food consumption, especially with respect to non-staple food.

Table 6.5   Elasticities of food and other major consumption outlays with respect to total consumption expenditure (TCE) by the peasant households in China, 1978–86

	TCE vis-à-vis net income	Food expenditure			Other expenditure		
		Total	Staple	Non-staple	Clothing	Housing	Others
National series							
1978–86	0.9351	0.8622	0.4949	1.0705	0.7089	2.1397	1.1557
Cross-provincial							
1978	0.8437	0.9266	n.a.	n.a.	0.8728	1.4557	1.2374
1979	0.9010	0.9643	n.a.	n.a.	0.8563	1.5200	1.2121
1980	0.9269	0.8289	0.3576	1.2390	0.8719	1.9350	1.1836
1981	1.0566	0.7897	0.2169	1.3063	0.8025	2.2609	1.1014
1982	1.0347	0.7636	0.1407	1.3747	0.6848	2.4716	1.0788
1983	0.8773	0.7501	0.1260	1.2629	0.7028	2.5511	0.9070
1984	0.8506	0.7591	0.1591	1.2156	0.5950	2.4134	0.9293
1985	0.9784	0.7007	0.0731	1.0713	0.7192	2.3140	1.0937
1986	0.9698	0.7214	n.a.	n.a.	0.7205	2.2271	1.0503

Notes: (1) The elasticities are estimated on the equation, $\log E_i = a_i + b_i \log Y + U_i$, where E_i and Y denote respectively expenditure on the *i*th item and total per capita consumption expenditure. U_i is a disturbance term, and a_i (a constant) and b_i (the elasticity) are parameters to be estimated. (2) n.a. stands for 'not available'. (3) The number of provinces included are 27 (for 1980), 28 (1981–84) and 29 (1985–86). The sample is not as complete for 1978–79.

Source: Kueh (1988), pp. 650–51.

ADEQUACY OF PEASANT FOOD CONSUMPTION

Figure 6.3 shows the increases in per capita peasant consumption of the major items of non-staple food, compared with foodgrain consumption, in 1978–86. The contrast in the rates of increases between the two categories of food consumption is striking. A minor exception which should, however, be briefly noted concerns vegetable consumption which, like grain consumption, in 1986 remained basically at the same level per capita as in 1978. The discrepancy between the growth in the supply of staple and non-staple food may become somewhat less drastic, if the increased proportion of fine grain consumed (from 50 per cent in 1978 to 82 per cent in 1986) is taken into account (*TJNJ 1987*, p. 700). Nevertheless, the discrepancy still looms large, and points to the fact that, in 1978, the diet of the Chinese peasants was highly vegetarian, comprising not much more than a simple combination of foodgrain and vegetables, and that, from 1979, however, any increases in grain production and supply have been largely converted into meat and, notably, wine.

The increase in poultry consumption, by an average of 21 per cent per year from 1978 to 1986, is especially noteworthy. Meat consumption which includes pork, beef and mutton, also increased substantially, by nearly 10 per cent per year. This is comparable to the 11 per cent increase recorded for aquatic products, comprising mainly fish and shrimps. These improvements become all the more remarkable if set against the stark background of 1957–78. In this earlier period, there were hardly any increases in such categories, with the consumption of high protein foods, such as eggs and aquatic products, even exhibiting negative consumption growth.

The accelerated increase in poultry consumption during 1978–86 may partly be explained by the fact that the base amount consumed in 1978 was exceedingly small; that is, only a quarter of a kilogram per head/year, compared with 5.8 kilograms for meat. However, three points must be made relating to the peasants' preference for poultry consumption. In the first place, poultry consumption is the most economical in that the grain to poultry conversion rate amounts, as a rule, to only 2:1, compared with 4:1 for pork and 6:4 for beef. Secondly, compared with pork and beef, poultry production requires a smaller amount of overhead investment. Thirdly, peasants could easily take advantage of the decollectivized rural framework to raise chickens and ducks. At any rate, the haste with which the Chinese peasants made use of the new rural environment to make up their dietary deficiency is truly remarkable.

Now the question is, after the massive drive towards dietary improvement, has the food consumption of the Chinese peasants become adequate? As a rough yardstick, we may consider the quantity of meat consumed. This amounted to 11.8 kilograms per head in 1986, or less than one kilogram per month. If poultry and seafood are included, the monthly per capita consumption still stood at hardly more than one kilogram. This is around the weight of one and a half medium-sized chickens, and is scarcely enough even for a child.

Table 6.6 gives the standardized measurement of food sufficiency in terms of nutrient intake per head/day for peasants in selected provinces. The first interesting point to emerge is that, for the peasants (surveyed), the overall calorie intake of 2,515 per day for 1983 seems to be basically sufficient. It represents an increase of 11 per cent over 1978, and is only 3.3 per cent short of the 'normal' requirement of 2,600 calories. Note also that,

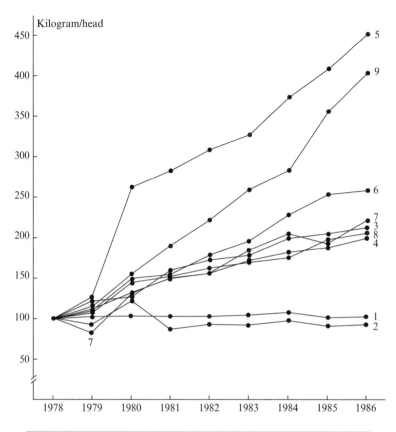

	Kilogram/head		Annual growth (%)	
	1978	1986	1957–78	1978–86
1. Grain (unhusked)	248	259	0.41	0.54
2. Vegetables	142	134	1.56	−0.72
3. Edible oils	1.96	4.19	1.00	9.96
4. Meat	5.76	11.79	3.10	9.37
5. Poultry	0.25	1.14	—	20.88
6. Eggs	0.80	2.08	−0.06	12.69
7. Aquatic products	0.84	1.87	−1.28	10.52
8. Sugar	0.73	1.59	2.12	10.22
9. Wine	1.22	4.96	4.14	19.16

Source: Kueh (1988), p. 654.

*Figure 6.3   Increases in per capita consumption by the peasant households
of the major items of staple and non-staple foods in 1978–86,
in comparison with 1957–78*

for rural China as a whole, a figure of 2,806 calories is given. This may have included the non-farm residents in the countryside.

Secondly, for virtually all the sample provinces, the nutrient intake of the Chinese peasants is, however, still overwhelmingly dominated by plant, rather than animal, sources. This is true not only for calorie intake taken as a whole, but also for protein and, to a lesser extent, fat. Note that soybean and vegetable oil are still very important sources of protein and fat intake in China.

Thirdly, judging by the required combination of calorie sources, that is, 1 (protein):2 (fat):5 (carbohydrates), there is a serious bias towards carbohydrates in all the provinces shown in Table 6.6. Heilongjiang represents perhaps the only exception, where fat supply seems to be comparatively sufficient. Protein deficiency is visible in most of the provinces. Note also that even the more favourable all 'rural China' figures show the dietary structure to be seriously biased towards carbohydrates, with a nearly 40 per cent deficiency in fat supply.

In short, despite significant increases in the consumption of non-staple food in 1978–86, the absolute consumption levels of high protein foods such as meat, fish, poultry and eggs are still rather meagre for Chinese peasants. The peasants' diet remains largely vegetarian. Viewed against this background, the declining food budget share, discussed earlier, should be interpreted with care. It should by no means be taken to imply saturation of food consumption, so that any increases in peasants' income could be set aside for non-food consumption. Rather, peasant incomes in China seem to have just increased to a point at which they may consider it worthwhile to shift consumption to other, non-food expenditures, especially housing.

This point has in fact prompted a Chinese analyst to question the usefulness of the Engel's law, by referring to the interesting case of Shandong province (Ji Changzhong, 1986). Shandong ranks consistently as the most 'advanced' province in China in terms of the Engel's curve for 1978–86. Shandong peasants are, in this respect, comparable to, or even better than, their counterparts in such rich areas as Beijing, Tianjin and Shanghai for any of the years in the post-Mao era. By 1982–83, the Engel's ratio of Shandong had already dropped to the record low of 50 per cent, the lowest for the whole of China (see Figure 6.5 in next section). Nevertheless, our nutrient analysis shows that the diet of the Shandong peasants remained remarkably poor. Not only is their calorie intake insufficient, but their protein and fat components are dominated by plant rather than animal sources (Table 6.6).

Shandong peasants may be especially well known for their hardworking nature and their thriftiness regarding food consumption, but there is no reason to suggest that peasants elsewhere in China are markedly different. If this observation is a general indication, then, after the rural

Table 6.6   Nutrient intake per day of the Chinese peasants in selected provinces, 1983

	Calories	Protein (P) (grams)	(grams)	Fat (F) (grams)	Carbohydrates (C) P:F:C
Normal requirement	2600	75	73	394	1:2.21:5.25
All China	2877 (92)	83 (93)	47 (53)	512	1:1.29:6.18
Urban China	3183	88	75	519	1:1.94:5.93
Rural China	2806	82	41	510	1:1.13:6.25
Peasants surveyed	2515 (92)	68 (95)	35 (44)	466	1:1.18:6.88
North China					
Shanxi	2111	57	28	394	1:1.13:6.03
Liaoning	2683	84	57	441	1:1.56:5.27
Heilongjiang	2316	63	66	352	1:2.41:5.64
Anhui	2530 (93)	69 (95)	39 (53)	459	1:1.29:6.69
Shandong	2428 (85)	74 (76)	29 (69)	452	1:0.88:6.08
Henan	2076	56	22	400	1:0.88:7.11
South China					
Zhejiang	2503	62	39	460	1:1.42:7.41
Fujian	2599 (95)	57 (88)	22 (40)	523	1:0.86:9.20
Hubei	2627 (90)	76 (93)	43 (51)	469	1:1.27:6.18
Hunan	2809 (90)	77 (90)	49 (41)	497	1:1.44:6.45
Guangxi	2224	54	38	403	1:1.57:7.45

Notes: (1) Figures in parentheses refer to the percentage shares of plant versus animal sources. Most of the carbohydrates figures are derived from the standard formula of 1 gm fat = 9.3 Kcal., 1 gm protein = 4.1 Kcal., and 1 gm carbohydrate = 4.1 Kcal.

Source: Kueh (1988), pp. 656–7.

house building boom is over, the Chinese peasants may well be expected to improve their food consumption to a considerable extent. The possible result would of course be a reversal of the declining Engel's curves for the individual provinces, and for the country as a whole.

INTERPROVINCIAL INEQUALITY AND INSTABILITY

The handful of provincial samples shown in Table 6.6 already point to a considerable degree of inequality in nutrient intake between peasants of different provinces. The calorie intake of Henan peasants, for example, was 18 per cent less than the average of 2,515 calories for all the peasants surveyed in 1983, while that of Hunan peasants stood at 12 per cent above the average. Thus, if the conclusion drawn about food consumption adequacy at the national level is projected down to the provincial level, the Chinese picture of nutrient deficiency certainly becomes all the more stark.

In addition, there is the problem of annual fluctuations in peasant food consumption. It is understandable that, the poorer the province, the greater the degree of farm output, income and consumption instability. In view of our earlier analysis about the magnitude of year-to-year changes in peasant net income in 1978–86, at a time of bad harvests, peasants in the poor provinces can be expected to be drawn into a hopeless situation of hardship. It is therefore necessary to examine further the degree of interprovincial inequality in peasant incomes and consumption, and to show to what extent it has changed over the years 1978 to 1986, as a result of the interplay between the weather and policy factors. Several points emerge from Figure 6.4.

First, the interprovincial inequality index for peasant income declined in the years 1978–79 to around 1982–83, and then started to rise sharply thereafter. By 1986, the index was already well above that of 1978–79. This 'U'-shape change can, first of all, be explained by the sharp increases in state farm procurement prices and by the massive tax concessions granted to the poor provinces in 1978–80. More importantly, up to 1982–83, income distribution was still basically chanelled through the collectives. With the farm accumulation ratio being controlled by the collective leadership, the increased price benefits in the richer provinces were largely converted into investment funds, rather than redistributed to the peasant members. By contrast, the tax and other concessions made to the poor provinces were mostly intended to improve peasants' living conditions, hence the equalizing trends.

Secondly, the weather certainly accounts for something in explaining the income equalizing trends, in that the main weather hazards in 1980 and 1981 mainly affected the relatively rich provinces in the middle and upper reaches of the Yangzi River (Kueh 1984a, pp. 78–80). Likewise, under the collectivized framework that still existed, the bumper harvests of 1982 tended to benefit the peasants in the poor provinces comparatively more than those in the rich provinces, in terms of redistributed and disposable net income.

The third point concerns the abrupt upturn in interprovincial peasant income inequality in 1984. This coincided with two noteworthy events. The first was the decreed perpetuation of the reparcellization of the collective

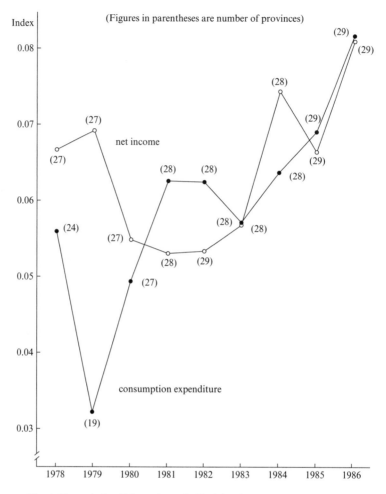

Notes: The Atkinson index (I) is mathematically defined as

$$I = 1 - \left(\sum_{i=1}^{n} (Y_i - \bar{Y})^{1-\varepsilon} \right) 1/(1-\varepsilon)$$

where Y_i stands for the per capita net income of the peasants' households of the ith province, $\bar{Y}$ the corresponding mean for all the provinces, and ε the 'explicit distribution parameter', which is assumed here to be 2.0. See Atkinson (1983, pp. 56–8) for a detailed explanation.

Source: Kueh (1988), pp. 661–2.

Figure 6.4   Trends in interprovincial inequality of per capita income and consumption expenditure of the Chinese peasants, as measured by the Atkinson index, 1978–86

farmlands. Peasants' leasehold rights were extended from three to over 15 years, commencing in January 1984. The second factor was the all-time record harvest in 1984. It is only natural that, starting from the new basis of 1982–83, a good harvest across the country in the decollectivized rural environment would lead to much increased interprovincial income inequality.

The fourth point refers to the temporary reversal of the rising trend in interprovincial income inequality in 1985. The reversal seems to be rather marginal in relation to the dramatic upsurge in the inequality index in 1984 and, as a matter of fact, it only helped the index to reach the all-time high in 1986. Nevertheless, the zigzag occurred precisely in 1985 when the compulsory farm deliveries were being replaced by the new system of purchase contracts, to be signed between the peasant households and state procurement agencies. Increased decollectivization and rural marketization should have resulted in an increase in income inequality, yet the reverse occurred. It is difficult to explain this but, again, the weather was probably a major factor. The weather conditions worsened namely considerably from 1984 to 1985 in quite a number of comparatively rich provinces, notably Jilin, Heilongjiang, Hubei, Guangdong and Sichuan. From 1985 to 1986, however, some poor provinces, for example, Hebei, Gansu, Ningxia and Xinjiang, were adversely affected, while there were considerable weather improvements in the rich or average provinces (*TJNJ 1985*, p. 303; *1986*, p. 209; *1987*, p. 199).

With regard to the problem of interprovincial inequality in peasant consumption expenditure in 1978–86, it should, first of all, be noted that the provincial samples for 1978 and 1979 are too incomplete to draw a conclusive statement from the estimates, although the sharp decline in the interprovincial inequality index for consumption expenditure from 1978 (sample of 24 provinces) to 1979 (19 provinces), is probably more than a matter of possible sampling bias (see Figure 6.4). The increases in state farm procurement prices and the rural tax concessions granted in 1979 should have partly helped to correct the regional disparities in peasant consumption which existed in the early post-Mao era.

Even if we omit the year 1979, and link directly the two years 1978 and 1980 (for which the provincial samples are more comparable), the interprovincial consumption inequality still declined markedly. After 1980, however, the declining trend was reversed and followed, generally, the upward path of interprovincial inequality in peasant net income. It deserves, therefore, no further elaboration, except perhaps for one relatively minor point. That is, the inequality in consumption expenditure started to increase in 1981, a year or so earlier than the reversal in the declining income inequality trend. One possible explanation for this is that, by 1980–81, peasants in the richer provinces might have already been convinced that the new price benefits offered by the state were genuine and lasting. They therefore opted to improve their consumption. This point is underscored by the fact that the average marginal propensity to save for the country as a whole declined very sharply from 1979 (31 per cent) to 1980–81 (both years 11 per cent) (see Table 6.3). This led to increased consumption inequality among the provinces, for peasants in the poor provinces still had to find ways to make ends meet.

The absolute magnitude of the regional disparities in per capita peasant income and consumption expenditure must have thus become quite significant by 1986. Looking across the provinces, the inequalities are even more pronounced. The mean value of per capita peasant net income for all the provinces was 445 *yuan* in 1986, with a substantial standard deviation of 153 *yuan*. The comparable figures for consumption expenditure are 378 and 137 *yuan*, respectively. Using either measure, in 1986 Gansu peasants stood at the lower end of the spectrum, with their per capita income (269 *yuan*) and consumption expenditure (233 *yuan*) only 47 per cent of the Jiangsu level (*TJNJ 1987*, pp. 701–2). The inequality in percentage terms may not appear to be too grave, but the absolute *yuan* income for the peasants in Gansu, and many other provinces, can only support a subsistence living. Moreover, there are wide ranging intraprovincial inequalities. In Gansu, for example, peasants within the lowest net income bracket of 200 *yuan* and below still made up 51 per cent of the provincial total in 1985 (*Gansu TJNJ 1985*, p. 378).

We turn now to examine how the changing inequality of peasant income may translate into interprovincial inequality in per capita food consumption. In Figure 6.5, the Engel's ratio for the peasants in different provinces are plotted for each of the years 1978 to 1986. The graph is self-explanatory, and needs little interpretation.

We first note the deteriorating interprovincial inequality in the food budget share of the peasants, reflected in the increasing coefficients of variation from 1978 to 1986. Secondly, for all these years the standard deviations remain exceedingly large, implying very variable food budget shares from province to province.

The average (unweighted) food budget share in all the provinces declined consistently, from around 66 per cent in 1978 to 57 per cent in 1986. Such improvement is also shown by the fact that the number of provinces falling within the category of 'absolute poverty' in terms of Engel's law, has declined from 19 provinces (note incomplete samples) in 1978, or 17 provinces in 1980, to only eight provinces in 1986. Nevertheless, 16 out of the 29 provinces still remain in the 'marginal' category in 1986. As a matter of fact, only peasants in a handful of provinces (or their administrative equivalents), notably

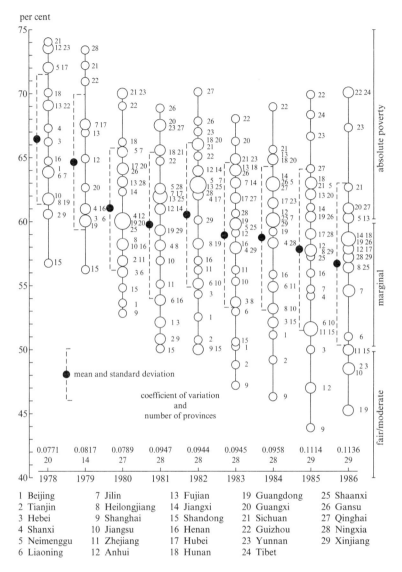

Note: See Table 6.4 for definition of the three categories of 'fair/moderate', 'marginal' and 'absolute poverty'.

Source: Kueh (1988), p. 664.

Figure 6.5   *Interprovincial inequality in food budget share in total consumption expenditure of Chinese peasants, 1978–86 (per cent)*

Beijing, Tianjin, Shanghai, Jiangsu and perhaps Hebei and Shandong, may now be considered as having attained the *xiaokan* (fairly sufficient) standard of livelihood (Yang, 1986, p. 63).

Reading across the years from 1978 to 1986, Figure 6.5 reveals some interesting comparative provincial trends. First, most of the provinces showing a consistent decline in the Engel's ratio are to be found in the east, notably Jiangsu, Zhejiang and Liaoning. Secondly, in quite a number of provinces, that is, Guizhou, Yunnan, Guangxi and even Guangdong, there has been hardly any improvement in this respect. Thirdly, in many provinces in which there has been either some or no long-term improvement, the Engel's ratio has fluctuated considerably from year to year. Shaanxi and Shanxi, for example, belong to this category. This implies that their food consumption is still vulnerable to weather conditions.

The most important point to be noted in this context, however, is that the Engel's ratio for most, if not all, of the provinces, represents highly self-restrained food consumption. This applies not only to the peasants in Shandong, as discussed earlier, but also to their counterparts in Hebei, or, for that matter, the residents in urban Tianjin, all of whom had an Engel's ratio comparable to that of the Shandong peasants.

The persistent contraints on peasants' food consumption can best be highlighted by the per capita foodgrain consumption levels, as revealed in Figure 6.6, which make up 80 to 90 per cent of their calorie requirements. It should, first of all, be noted that, in terms of the coefficient of variation, no particular trend of widening interprovincial inequality in grain consumption is discernible from 1978 to 1986. This is not surprising, for grain is the most basic necessity for the poor peasants, but at the same time it is an inferior good for the higher-income groups.

Nevertheless, as with the Engel's ratio, there was a considerable degree of interprovincial inequality in per capita grain consumption in 1986, as in, say, 1980 (ignoring the different sizes of provincial samples available for 1978, 1979 and 1981). To the extent that the national average per capita grain consumption for the peasants (taken together with the much-restrained consumption of non-staple food), can at best be considered as adequate, in terms of calorie requirements and dietary structure a great number of the Chinese peasants in the poor provinces must still be seriously undernourished. This generalized picture becomes starker if the following qualifications are made, which classify the provinces largely into three contrasting categories.

The first category covers provinces in which the per capita grain consumption is consistently below the national average. These are provinces which have a food budget share which is well above the national average. In this category are, for example, Yunnan, Guizhou, Shanxi, Gansu and,

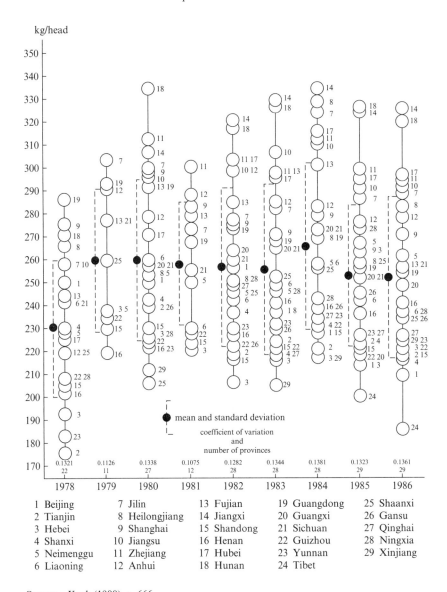

Source: Kueh (1988), p. 666.

Figure 6.6 Interprovincial inequality in per capita grain consumption by the Chinese peasants, 1978–86 (unhusked kilogram)

to a lesser extent, Shaanxi and Ningxia. These are the least favoured provinces.

The second category is characterized by provinces in which the per capita grain consumption is also below the national average, but which, however, have a food budget share which is below the national average. This category includes Beijing, Tianjin, Hebei, Shandong, Henan and Liaoning. These provinces stand in the middle of the spectrum of food consumption welfare.

The third category is represented by provinces in which the per capita grain consumption is above the national average, but their food budget shares are below the national average. This group includes Jilin, Heilongjiang, Zhejiang, Jiangsu and Shanghai. They constitute the upper end of the welfare spectrum.

Other provinces are distributed between the three categories, with different possible combinations. Hubei and Hunan, for example, combine very high per capita grain consumption with near-average food budget shares.

The most fundamental overall point which should be made, however, is that, except for a few provinces, peasant foodgrain consumption is still a self-restrained one throughout the country. This seems to have been reflected in the abrupt increase in the national mean of per capita grain consumption in 1984 (Figure 6.6). In fact, almost all the provinces show parallel increases in this respect in that particular year. This can only be understood in the light of the unprecedented good harvest of 1984. This means that for most, if not all, Chinese peasants, grain may indeed not be an inferior commodity at all.

The situation resembles the decline in the Engel's ratio for the country as a whole, from 65.8 in 1957 to 60.9 in 1962, and its renewed increase to 63.3 in 1963 and 68.4 in 1965 (Ji, 1986, p. 36). The decline was, in the first instance, caused by the dramatic downturn in food supply in the immediate aftermath of the Great Leap débâcle. It should in no sense be seen as denoting any improvement in food consumption. The reversal in the Engel's ratio in 1963, and especially in 1965, indicates, in turn, the recovery in food supply. This analogy helps to explain the increase in per capita grain consumption in 1984. It may also explain the minor reversal, as noted earlier, in the food budget share in 1982 (see Figure 6.5). Note that the year 1982 was second only to 1984 in terms of weather and harvest conditions (see Table 6.2).

Finally, a few words should be said about food consumption instability. As revealed in Figure 6.6, the per capita grain consumption figure for Jilin peasants, for example, jumped by 14 per cent, from 283 kilograms in 1983 to 323 kilograms in 1984, only to be scaled down again in 1985–86 almost to its original 1983 level. Similar drastic fluctuations occurred in Fujian (down by 13 per cent, from 302 kilograms in 1984 to 262 kilograms in 1985), Shaanxi (down by 8 per cent, from 257 kilograms in 1985 to 237 kilograms in 1986), and other provinces. For provinces such as Shaanxi, with a per capita grain consumption below the national average, fluctuations of such magnitude could, of course, be associated with considerable hardship.

CONCLUSION

The personal income and consumption expenditure of the Chinese peasants increased, in real terms, by about two and a half times from 1978 to 1986. These exceedingly large gains abruptly ended the prolonged failure, under the Maoist regime, to raise peasants' living standards. Probably for the first time in Chinese history, their Engel's curve has shown some sustained trends of decline, although, by international standards, the ratio is still extremely high, only marginally below the category of 'absolute poverty'.

The increases in income have allowed the Chinese peasants to improve their consumption of non-staple food, notably poultry and meat. However, their calorie intake, which can at best be deemed adequate, is still overwhelmingly dominated by plant sources, foodgrain in particular. It is seriously deficient in protein and fat. Against this background, the emerging consumerism, as reflected in the relatively large expenditure elasticities of income for the peasants' non-food purchases (notably clothing, housing and semi-luxurious consumer durables), should be viewed as the familiar 'demonstration effect', rather than any sign of saturation in food consumption.

There has been a considerable degree of interprovincial inequality in peasants' income and consumption expenditure, as well as in the supply of foodgrain. The inequalities were reinforced by increased marketization and monetization of the rural context. This is a significant departure from the Maoist era, when any farm surplus was forcefully siphoned off by the state to minimize regional inequalities. Judged against the average national standards as briefly summarized here, the existing inequalities still imply the existence of absolute poverty for peasants in many provinces.

Moreover, peasant income as a function of farm output is still subject to weather influence. It has thus fluctuated substantially from year to year. For peasants in poor provinces with less capacity to withstand bad weather, such instability brings extraordinary hardships in basic consumption and, for peasants in better-off provinces, savings can easily be drained to make ends meet in the lean years. This is clearly reflected in the drastic changes in the national average of peasants' marginal propensities to save in 1978–86.

Several points may be made concerning the long-term implications. First, China's rural and agricultural policies will continue to be preoccupied with concern about the pressing peasants' demand for better food and shelter. The pressures will tend to be intensified as a result of continuous rural liberalizations and the ensuing rising peasants' expectations of improving income and consumption.

Second, overall improvements in peasants' consumption and living standards since 1978 made it possible for the Chinese government to tolerate some increases in provincial inequalities in this respect. However, the disequalizing trend is bound to be constrained by the political–economic imperatives to extract farm surpluses from the rich peasants, to balance the basic needs of the poor.

Third, the established economic strategy of forced industrialization will also continue to dictate that farm surpluses are extracted for the urban–industrial sectors, as in the Maoist past. Thus it will be difficult for the existing gap between rural and urban income and consumption standards to be closed or even to be narrowed to any substantial extent in the years to come. As a result, any further liberalization in rural areas would inherently help to enhance the existing tension between the state and the peasants, in view of their mounting pressures for resources to be redirected to meet their rising consumption demands.

Fourth, in conclusion, the Chinese peasants can, in the foreseeable future, at best expect some carefully guarded relaxation in the government's income and consumption policies. The relaxation is likely to take place by way of continuous state manipulations of farm input and output prices within the present system of 'farm purchase contracts'. Given the enormous need to siphon off farm surplus to support the industrialization programmes, farm prices – and hence peasants' income – will continue to be controlled by the state in varying degrees.

Thus it seems unlikely that the quasi-compulsory system of state farm purchases can give way to a full-fledged marketization of the entire rural economy in the near future. In the meantime, however, a vigorous policy effort will probably continue to be made to promote rural non-farm employment and income, as a means of improving peasants' living standards. For the Chinese peasants, this of course represents a more acceptable variant of local self-sufficiency, compared with the Maoist one, which tended to confiscate any amount of farm or non-farm output produced in excess of what was required for bare subsistence.

NOTE

*   Reprinted with adaptations from Y.Y. Kueh, 'Food consumption and peasant incomes in the post-Mao era', *The China Quarterly*, **116** (December 1988), 634–70; Copyright School of Oriental and African Studies, published by Cambridge University Press.

7. Mao and agriculture in China's industrialization: three antitheses in a 50-year perspective*

INTRODUCTION

Fifty years ago, in July 1955, Chairman Mao delivered his speech 'On the question of agricultural co-operativization' (*Maoxuan*, 1977, pp. 168–91). The speech, which was addressed to Party secretaries from all the provinces, municipalities and autonomous regions, immediately triggered a 'Socialist High Tide that during 1955–56 engulfed the entire Chinese countryside in a radical upheaval and a shift of agricultural organization towards collectivization' (Walker, 1966). The High Tide did not completely recede until the full cycle of Chinese agricultural collectivization was completed following Mao's death in 1976. From the vantage point of post-Mao reforms, the basic questions that arise are clearly, first, why the 'Socialist High Tide' in the first place? And secondly, was the three-decade-long collectivization really worthwhile? To many Western scholars and analysts, and indeed to many of their Chinese counterparts, the conclusions are as follows: collectivization impaired peasant incentives; rural bureaucratic control and non-market methods distorted the allocation of resources and inhibited productivity growth; the drive for grain self-sufficiency, especially during the Cultural Revolution, retarded rural specialization and intraregional exchange; and, above all, agriculture was consistently undervalued in the national scale of investment priorities.

Taken together, agricultural collectivization/communization is thus seen to have been responsible for the slow growth or stagnation of Chinese agriculture, and hence of depressed peasant income, widespread poverty and even prolonged malnutrition for many. Above all, the Great Leap Forward phase was deemed to have cost China 'almost a decade of economic growth', and to have made Mao and China objects of global ridicule. In short, Mao is seen more as a 'revolutionary romanticist' than as an economic realist: a man who cared more for ideology, politics and class struggle than for practical economic issues.

Some scholars have, of course, noted the significance of advances in agricultural technology under Mao, notably in the forms of irrigation and drainage systems and the increased application of chemical fertilizer. But these advances are rarely emphasized in major Western studies. Rather, the potential productivity gains are seen as having been offset by the waste and inefficiencies of rural bureaucratization. On this view, the only positive phases in the story of agricultural development are seen to be 1952–55 (prior to the High Tide) and the first half of the 1960s, both seen as periods when markets and prices still played a significant role in the rural economy (Lardy, 1983).

No wonder, therefore, that the post-Mao agricultural reforms that dismantled the Peoples Communes and the compulsory farm delivery system and replaced bureaucratic power with market mechanisms are regarded as the negation of Mao's approach to agriculture. But is this really the whole story of Chinese agricultural development in the modern period? I believe not. And the fiftieth anniversary of *On Co-operativization* seems an appropriate moment to review this topic of fundamental historical importance, because we have now reached the point where the Mao and post-Mao eras are of almost equal length.

In what follows I attempt to provide an alternative framework of interpretation for understanding the performance of agriculture under Mao and relate this to the course of development since his death. The three major propositions put forward may be regarded as the antitheses to widely held views on the economics of the Mao period. The discussion may raise more questions than are answered, but they are offered mainly in qualitative form to develop the longer-term debate. Further quantitative analysis can be left to students interested in the econometric analysis of Chinese affairs.

COLLECTIVIZED AGRICULTURE AND THE INDUSTRIALIZATION IMPERATIVES

My first proposition examines the problem of how to evaluate the long-term performance of Chinese agriculture. I argue that one should not just look at the agricultural sector and evaluate performance in terms of comparative rates of output, productivity and income growth. Evaluation must take into account the wider context of industrialization performance, since this was the sector that agriculture was mainly to serve. For Mao (as for Stalin), steel was the 'final good' and agricultural output the 'intermediate input'.[1] Viewed this way, judgments about performance based on the impact on peasant incomes or poverty alleviation belong rather to the realm of ethics and welfare choices.

The major criterion has to be whether the agricultural sector did deliver sufficient agricultural surplus to promote industrialization. The 'surplus' needed for this includes not only foodgrain consumed by industrial workers, but also cash crops (such as cotton and tobacco), as well as the livestock, poultry and aquatic products used as inputs for textile/garment manufacturing and the tobacco and food processing industries. The final products among these goods may be consumed domestically, but, by virtue of the strategy of maximizing industrial growth, they are bound to be primarily destined for the export markets where they are exchanged for advanced steel products, machinery, equipment and high-technology goods required for the industrialization drive.

This seems to state the obvious, but if we think now in terms of Simon Kuznets' analysis of the tripartite contribution of agriculture (to product, market and factor supplies) the matter becomes quite complex (Kuznets, 1964). Setting aside the 'product contribution' illustrated above, the potential of agriculture as a market for China's own industrial goods (let alone imported ones) was obviously deliberately limited by Mao's strategy of forcing agriculture to rely on internal resources to build up the necessary production capability to raise agricultural surplus further and to meet its own consumption and producer goods demands.

In this respect, we must elaborate on Mao's thinking on the consequences of the High Tide. In *On Co-operativization*, Mao considered in some detail his 'grand vision' of 'socialist industrialization' for China and the role to be played by agricultural collectivization in achieving this. He made three major mutually reinforcing points.

The first was that cooperativization would facilitate agriculture's leap, from small-scale management with farm implements powered by draught animals, to large-scale operation with machinery. Barring this, he argued, 'it is not possible to resolve the contradiction between the ever increasing demand for commercial grains and industrial raw materials, and the presently very low output level common to major agricultural crops' (*Maoxuan*, p. 181).

Secondly, 'only on the basis of co-operativized large-scale management will agriculture be able to make use of the supply from heavy industry (the single most important branch of socialist industrialization) of tractors and other farm machines, chemical fertilizers, modern transportation equipment, kerosene, electricity, etc. (in order to expand production)'.[2]

Thirdly, cooperativization, he argued, would help facilitate the overall process of accumulation since, in addition to the immediate contribution of direct agricultural taxes, 'a substantial proportion of the large amount of capital needed for the completion of socialist industrialization and farm-technological renovation' will in future come from a 'large-scale agriculture'. This new sector will greatly raise peasants' purchasing power, thus facilitating 'large-scale development of light industry' to supply peasants 'with large amounts of living materials [consumer goods] in exchange for commercial grains and light-industrial raw materials'. It is through this exchange, Mao is arguing, that the rate of accumulation will be raised (*Maoxuan*, pp. 182–3).

Hence, while the pursuit of a modernized agriculture has merit for Mao in terms of peasant well-being, the ultimate point of reference in the July 1955 speech is the maximization of capital accumulation as required by the Stalinist principle of preferential growth of heavy industry.

A few months after his *On Co-operativization* speech, Mao translated this grand vision into a more practical policy approach in his famous treatise *On the Ten Great Relations* (*Maoxuan*, pp. 267–88), which he himself regarded as the first ever blueprint for a uniquely Chinese route to national construction which 'is similar in principle to that of the Soviet Union but has our own substance' (*Wansui*, 1969, pp. 151, 163). Mao cautiously argued that 'our problem at present is still how to appropriately readjust the investment [allocation] ratio between heavy industry and agriculture and light industry, in favour of a greater development of agriculture and light industry. . . . [Heavy industry] should still remain the main focal point, but investment proportions for agriculture and light industry should be raised a little bit. . . . This will help to better supply living necessities to the people on the one hand, and increase capital accumulation on the other hand; and hence to develop [even] more and better heavy industry' (*Maoxuan*, p. 269).

It is against this background that Mao has at times been regarded as being in favour of a 'balanced development strategy' or a more 'developmental' versus a purely 'extractive' strategy (cf. Lardy, 1983, p. 16). The former type of strategy should perhaps be understood in the ethical sense of balancing peasants' welfare against excessive investment in heavy industry. The latter, however, is strictly a strategy in the literal sense that to 'develop' and enhance agricultural productivity with appropriate doses of state investment may eventually help to extract an even greater amount of agricultural surplus in the relatively short run.

Whatever the case may have been with Mao, it is evidently very difficult, if not impossible, in practical policy deliberations to determine in either case what the 'optimum trade-off' may be. What is clear, however, is that under the Stalinist pro-heavy industry bias, both strategies imply 'austerity' for the peasantry. Thus, the only yardstick available to gauge the performance is whether they effectively release industrialization from agricultural constraints.

In this respect, the most remarkable departure from the Stalinist model should really be seen in the rigorous attempt made during the Great Leap

Forward to substitute the principle of rural 'self-reliance' for supplies from the modern urban industries, in order to save even more resources for promoting the heavy industry. This strategy was indeed carried out with full force through the entire Cultural Revolution period (Riskin, 1987, ch. 9; Eckstein, 1966, pp. 31–6). The upshot was of course added hardship for the peasantry in terms both of consumption losses and of increased work loads.

In a way, the legacy of the agriculture–industry dichotomy remains relevant today, judging by the emergence in recent years of the so-called *sannong* (three-agriculture) problem; that is, the general problems of agriculture (*nongye*), of peasants (*nongmin*) and of the rural areas (*nongcun*).[3] In the eyes of the new Chinese leadership under President Hu Jintao and Premier Wen Jiabao, it appears that only now is Chinese industry finally mature enough to 'return-feed' (*fanbu*) agriculture or the rural sector at large, and thus at last begin to achieve a more 'harmonious' development sought in *On the Ten Great Relations*.[4]

Now to return to the question: should Mao's agricultural policy really be considered as successful, bearing in mind the enormous burden placed on the Chinese peasantry? Obviously this must be assessed within Mao's own frame of reference, as outlined above.

In a pioneering study completed in 1968, Anthony M. Tang conducted a standard correlation analysis between the growth rates of Chinese agriculture and industry in 1949–57 (Tang, 1968, pp. 466–80). His conclusion was quite straightforward: the agricultural policy of the Chinese government was correctly 'development-oriented' (as a means to 'extract' more agricultural surplus to support industrialization), but industrial development in the period was, nevertheless, still effectively constrained by the vagaries of agricultural production. Tang noted the sharp contrast on this point between China and the former Soviet Union. Per capita grain availability stood at 480 kilograms per year for the Soviet population in 1928 when Stalin started to collectivize Soviet agriculture. The comparable figure for China was only 220 kilograms in 1952 or 256 kilograms for the 1957 baseline. Thus, while fluctuations in agricultural output had virtually no effect on Soviet industrial growth, in China the spillover effects of poor agricultural years affected both light and heavy industries. This is explained by the harsh reality that subsistence-level Chinese peasants had to be accorded a priority share of agricultural output, leaving industry as the 'residual claimant' of output.

A similar analysis is needed for subsequent periods, but some basic aggregate indicators seem adequate to reflect the changing situation since the inception of the Chinese First Five-Year Plan in 1953. The figures in Table 7.1 show that the continuous industrialization drive based on highly collectivized agriculture had, by the time of Mao's death, already brought

Table 7.1   China's Gross Domestic Product (GDP) and total employment (TEM) by sectoral origin, 1952, 1978, 2004 (per cent)

	1952		1978		2004	
	GDP	TEM	GDP	TEM	GDP	TEM
Agriculture	51	84	28	71	15	47
Industry	21	7	48	17	53	23
Services	29	9	24	12	32	31

Sources: *TJZY 2005*, pp. 20, 45 for 1978 and 2004; *2001*, pp. 50, 108 for 1952.

the share of industry in the country's GDP up from 21 per cent in 1952 to the startling high of 48 per cent in 1978. Since then the share seems to have basically stabilized at between 49 per cent (1998) and 53 per cent (2003). Meanwhile, the corresponding GDP share of agriculture declined by 23 percentage points between 1952 and 1978, and since 1978 by 13 more percentage points to a mere 15 per cent in 2003.

Note also that agriculture's contribution to GDP growth in 2004 is estimated to be only 9 per cent of the total, in sharp contrast to shares of 62 per cent and 29 per cent, respectively, for industry and the services sector (*TJZY 2005*, p. 24). This suggests that industrial growth in China has now been basically released from agricultural constraints to become a self-augmenting sector. Three important points may be made, but only briefly, about the background to these impressive economic changes.

First, of course, is the role of the compulsory farm procurement scheme (in force during 1953–85). Mao himself made it very clear that the agricultural collectives were created to ease implementation of this device.[5] The forced siphoning was in practice 'a progressive tax on current production with nearly confiscatory marginal rates' (Tang, 1968, p. 495). The Kuznets' product contribution of agriculture was achieved both by direct tax and by manipulation of prices (the 'scissors effect'). For Mao's reign taken as a whole, there was, therefore, an enormous 'imbalance' in investment allocation between agriculture and industry relative to the respective output generated.[6] This is precisely what is considered by many Western scholars to be the source of many of the economic ills in Chinese agriculture. I remain to be convinced that a substantial reallocation of investment in favour of agriculture would have promoted the planned industrialization drive more effectively.

The second point involves the Kuznetsian 'factor' contribution, which is obscured by the relative figures given in Table 7.1. Being a classical model of 'unlimited labour supply', Chinese agriculture can always release redundant labour to support industry. Much more important, however, is the factor of 'land' as a contribution from agriculture. I refer to the continuous encroachment on farmlands during the process of urbanization and industrialization. The Chinese peasants were (and still are) constantly compelled to relinquish precious farmland at the discretion of the bureaucratic apparatus without due (if any) monetary compensation. Strangely enough, no effort has ever been made to compute the 'implicit price' for such 'factor' contribution. Of course, any computation would only help to aggravate further the estimated 'intersectoral imbalance' between agriculture and industry. At any rate, the hard fact is that, to meet production targets, the agricultural sector had increasingly to resort to multiple-cropping practice to compensate for reductions in cultivated areas.

The third point relates to Mao's strategy for regional autarky and national self-sufficiency. This involves international politics. It is clear that Mao was obsessed by fears of regional and international conflicts, conditioned as he was by the 1962 war with India, the 1969 Zhenbao Island clash with the former Soviet Union and, of course, the prolonged Dulles/Truman legacy of 'containment' (cf. Sinha, 2003). Denied any direct support from outside, agriculture, as the foundation of the national economy, clearly bore the full brunt of the massive drive towards building an independent, comprehensive industrial system. Interestingly, Hong Kong was a key instrument for acquiring indirect assistance through the mechanism of multilateral trade. On the eve of the open-door strategy, net foreign exchange earnings from the former British colony alone were more than sufficient to balance the combined trade deficits incurred with Japan and Western Europe – deficits that reflected imports of the much-needed advanced machinery and equipment and steel products (Kueh and Howe, 1984, p. 823). These were paid for by China's exports to Hong Kong that were almost exclusively agricultural, subsidiary agricultural and processed agricultural products (including textiles), which made up the bulk of total Chinese export value (Lardy, 1983, pp. 127, 137).

Viewed this way, Lardy's 'paradox' of 'the persistence between the mid-1950s and mid-to-late 1970s of chronic malnutrition and low income in a significant share of the rural population, despite a doubling of per capita national income between these two periods' (ibid. pp. ix, 159) may not really appear to be that problematic, given that a very substantial proportion of per capita national income takes the form of output of machinery and equipment, including weaponry. Even so it is a remarkable fact that Guizhou province, which had by far 'the greatest concentration of chronic rural poverty in the late 1970s [and] the lowest reported life expectancy of any province – 59 years' (ibid. pp. 171, 173), still compared quite favourably with the national average life expectancy of 40 years in 1950 and only

47 years in 1960, although it was lower by six and nine years, respectively, compared to the national averages of 65 and 68 years for 1975 and 1981, respectively (Chai, 1997b, p. 253).

COLLECTIVIZATION AS AN AGRICULTURAL-GROWTH STRATEGY

My second proposition examines the popular perception that agricultural collectivization in China was a major source of inefficiency and resource waste. I argue rather that, from the outset, collectivization was conceived by Mao as a resource-mobilizing vehicle for expanding physical output as required by the industrialization imperative. Agricultural performance in China should therefore be assessed as such, rather than in terms of norms of static efficiency and income maximization. In the circumstances, any given agricultural output mix should clearly also be understood against the industrial planners' preferences rather than those of peasants or consumers in general.

I would therefore argue that, from the planners' perspective, as long as the aggregate output growth brought about by the mobilization strategy outweighed the sum total of potential losses associated with peasant disincentives and inefficiency, the strategy is serving its purpose. For Mao, however, this was clearly a second-best approach. He actually aspired to having 'the best of both worlds' and, although he could always resort to 'Politics in Command' as a substitute, the problems of peasant incentives and material well-being seem to have been constantly in the forefront of his mind.[7]

At any rate, the collectivization was clearly a case of an extensive growth strategy. Such a strategy initially involves movement from inside the full employment points, on to the production possibility frontier. Achievement of this may be called 'growth efficiency' and it should be distinguished from an intensive growth strategy that attempts rather to shift the production possibility frontier upwards by more intensive use of given resources and technological innovation. This represents dynamic efficiency in the neo-classical sense.[8]

Whether or not, prior to collectivization, Chinese peasants actually operated at the transformation frontier (that is they achieved static efficiency by virtue of centuries of intensive cultivation under the private landholding regime) is a separate issue.[9] What seems clear is that, under such a system, siphoning off the farm surplus would entail an enormous financial burden for the planners and thus seriously compromise the industrialization imperatives, even if we ignore the problem of the inability of planners to interfere with peasants' choices between work and leisure. (In the traditional system, idleness was a common phenomenon during the slack season.)

In the eyes of the planners, therefore, there was a clear case for collectivization to enforce the extensive growth strategy. The entire mechanism required bureaucratic control and direct agricultural planning with targets for the physical sown area and individual crop outputs. The first experiments with these were in 1956 and 1958–59 and they were rigorously enforced during the Cultural Revolution of 1966–76 (Perkins, 1966, pp. 65–8, 83–6; Lardy, 1983, pp. 19–21, 37–8, 41–3, 46–8). This system rendered the neoclassical paradigm of economics inoperative, since under it it does not really matter whether the cotton/grain price relatives were correctly set or not, as these prices were simply an accounting device. As long as the officially fixed 'scissors' differential allowed peasants a minimum net revenue (the rural counterpart of urban wage) to purchase such basic necessities as cloth and edible oil and vegetables, plus perhaps occasional meat products (if not self-supplied from the private plot) and some minimal consumer goods, the mechanism, draconian and robust as it might appear, was working. Note that the peasants were not only guaranteed the basic grain ration (*kouliang*) but cotton cloth was subject to prolonged rationing as well.

Viewed this way, it appears redundant to argue that rural cadres in charge of farm decisions were deprived of the price signals needed to guide intercrop sown area allocation, or that, worse still, they were constantly subject to political pressures to maximize key physical output targets in disregard of proven rational cropping patterns, as was widely believed to be the case under the 'grain first' strategy during the Cultural Revolution.[10] Nonetheless, two major points must be made to clarify such perceived 'allocative biases' and their potential impact.

First, the issue here parallels the familiar argument that former Soviet bloc countries were all 'trading in the dark', because highly distorted domestic prices (as a result of years of government price fixing), compounded by distorted official exchange rates, could not be compared with overseas prices to determine the optimum export mix. However, in practice, central exports planners were basically aware, perhaps via trial and error, where comparative advantages lay, and the analogous problem faced by the agricultural planners and local rural bureaucrats was evidently much more manageable. The case was similar in industrial or enterprise planning, although this was clearly much more complex in terms of product differentiations.[11]

A closely related argument is that, unlike industry, agriculture is a 'variable coefficient sector' (Richard Eckaus) and peasant behaviour is therefore less conducive to centralized management and control. Under the diktat or 'extortion' by rural cadres, Chinese peasants could thus become resentful and act irrationally, resulting in gross inefficiency in farming. However, I would rather argue that, once the farming routine was established, they would simply or subtly yield to the practice to earn, say, their own grain and cotton cloth rations, unless they wanted to strive for something else. These considerations help us to understand why, under the prolonged period of Mao's hegemony, the rural fabric of production and exchange remained intact and worked reasonably well.

The second point relates to the apparently extremely 'grain first' strategy of the Cultural Revolution. There are three aspects to a possible appraisal of the widespread charges about the excesses committed in terms of unbalanced cropping pattern. One is how the perceived excesses can possibly square with the fact that the entire Chinese exports programme – which comprised overwhelmingly non-grain but essentially farm-related products and which was indeed so precious to the industrialization imperatives (as alluded to earlier) – managed to remain intact. It had in fact been consistently expanding.

The second aspect is slightly more technical. It is that the 'grain first' strategy resembles the 'output-maximizing model' of the former Soviet economy (Ames, 1965, p. 54). Unlike the perfectly competitive market economy model, output in any state-owned enterprise was to be maximized subject to the constraint of 'average-cost equal to [the given] price [average revenue]' (that is, the enterprise just breaks even). This principle replaces the familiar 'marginal cost equal to the price' formula for profit maximization. Any output extension beyond the break-even point would clearly entail financial losses. Was the Chinese government really prepared to foot the bill (fiscal subsidies) at any cost that might arise under the 'grain first' strategy? It seems doubtful, given that, under the given scissors differentials (highly depressed farm procurement prices versus expensive modern inputs), the peasants could easily incur financial losses for which they could not be held responsible.

The third aspect involves what may appear to be some exceptional cases. Sichuan was cited as one such case, where multiple (third) grain-cropping was rigorously expanded 'at all costs': in other words, despite continuously increasing financial losses. Similarly, North China rigorously substituted grain for cotton, entirely ignoring, presumably, the law of comparative advantage in sown area allocation. The 'grain first' practice was indeed said to have been carried to such an extent that cotton had to be imported on a large scale to feed the country's textile industry, totally defying the simple arithmetic that the hard currency outlay on cotton imports could have otherwise been saved for importing a much higher quantity of grain than that produced domestically (Lardy, 1983, pp. 63–4, 82–6, 201). More research has to be done to unravel these puzzling 'paradoxes'. Perhaps the principles of regional autarky and grain self-sufficiency were simply given as strategic imperatives.[12] We really do not know for sure.

The most conspicuous characteristic of Mao's agricultural growth strategy is mass labour mobilization. This phenomenon is familiar but an important aspect of Mao's approach to this has remained relatively unappreciated. This is that, from the outset, Mao regarded agricultural collectivization as a good means for 'fighting natural calamities' (*Maoxuan*, 1977, p. 179). I refer to this elsewhere as the 'institutional hedge' (Kueh, 2002a, pp. 18, 48). This is closely linked to restrictions on migration and occupational flexibility to prevent what was commonly referred to in pre-war China as '*taohuang*' – large-scale rural exodus to seek shelter and food in the wake of overwhelming floods and droughts. The new 'institutional hedge' left peasants with no alternative but to stay on their farm and, hence, for what I would term the 'subsistence urge', to redress the havoc caused by floods by, for example, reclaiming the inundated farmland. In this way they can still help fulfil the compulsory sown area and output targets. As shown below, this indeed proved to be a most powerful incentive.

It seems that, once this 'institutional hedge' was established, Mao turned to the other two equally important aspects of mass mobilization: that is, labour mobilization for water conservancy projects or expanding the irrigation and drainage capacity, and for rural support industry (iron bars and cement, such as for building water reservoirs), as well as farm technological innovations in general. Such mobilization clearly converged in the 1958 policy slogan of 'the Great Leap Forward' and forcefully triggered the amalgamation of the agricultural collectives into the people's communes.

What caused the GLF strategy to collapse and result in the food crisis of 1959–61 should perhaps not detain our discussion.[13] What seems clear, however, is that the Cultural Revolution strategy was in many ways built upon the Great Leap blueprint and experiments conducted during 1958. These included labour mobilization for large-scale irrigation and drainage projects that enabled China to build up and enhance what I would call the 'technological hedge'.[14] Equally noteworthy was of course the campaign for the 'five small industries' (metal making, machine building, cement, chemical fertilizers and energy, such as coal mining or small hydropower plants), all to be run by the communes and production brigades. Being rural-based and farm-oriented, these were widely hailed by many Western observers as the 'Chinese road to [rural] industrialization', but they in fact all evolved from the experiences of the abortive 'backyard furnaces' campaign of 1958.[15] Taken together, these two campaigns were what produced the 'high and stable yield fields' areas where harvests were substantially protected against floods and drought (Kueh, 1985a, p. 51).

The 'institutional hedge' certainly worked. Chinese agriculture in the 1950s was basically in a similar technological environment to that of the 1930s, in that it lacked modernization and the 'technological hedge'. However, while the weather in the 1950s remained as volatile as in the prewar era – disastrous floods in the Yangzi and Huai River basins in 1931 and 1954 and similar scale droughts in 1934 and 1959 – for virtually all grain crops (rice, wheat, maize and others), the fluctuations in sown area, yield per hectare and hence total output were all consistently less in the 1950s than in the 1930s (Kueh, 2002a, pp. 47–50).

Figures 7.1a and 7.1b show the sharp contrast between the two periods.[16] It may be noted further that the output stabilization trends were clearly in evidence across *all* major regions in the 1950s. The 'institutional hedge' worked consistently across the nation. More important, output in the various regions all showed a rising trend in the 1950s, whereas in the 1930s the trends were at best stationary. Increases in output were in fact brought about by a combination of sown area stabilization/expansion and gains in yield per hectare sown. This clearly suggests that the 'institutional hedge' was at work, given that, as Lardy (1983) has pointed out, 'there were few industrial inputs used in farming and little evidence of technological change' (p. ix). Thus what made the 1950s different was that, apart from the collectivized effort to stabilize and expand sown area, the peasants were 'coerced' to exhaust systematically all possible sources of organic fertilizers, both human and animal, for field application (Kueh, 1984c), and to tend the fields with greater care, especially upon or in the immediate aftermath of serious floods and droughts, for subsistence and plan fulfilment.

There is no doubt that, during the Cultural Revolution, the 'institutional hedge' was greatly reinforced by the draconian collectivist approach of the time, coupled with the rapidly emerging 'technological hedge' after the mid-1960s, to help further strengthen agricultural production. National grain output increased by an average of 2.6 per cent per year in 1966–77, or 3.0 per cent if 1978 is included. These are quite impressive growth rates, particularly when viewed against the background of a highly pro-urban–industry policy bias, which left little state investment for agriculture, except perhaps that for harnessing the major untamed rivers (Kuo, 1972).

Lardy has argued that agricultural growth during the Cultural Revolution was 'no more rapid than or even somewhat below the pace of development in 1953–57' (grain output increased indeed by an annual average of 3.5 per cent); he sees this as surprising given especially what he perceives as a great disparity in farm inputs between the two periods and the internationally significant breakthrough in the breeding and field dissemination of new rice hybrids in the 1970s (Lardy, 1983, p. ix). Lardy attributes the 'paradox' to the two different Chinese approaches to

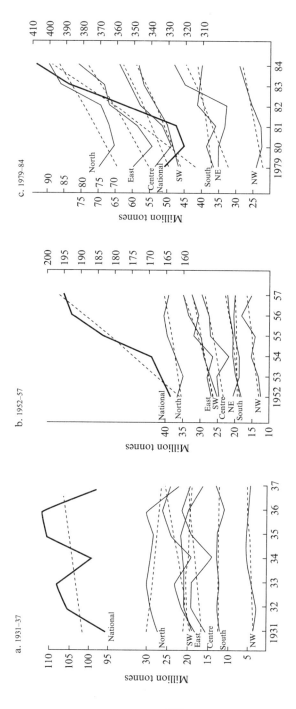

Source: Kueh (2002a), pp. 92–4.

Figure 7.1 Yearly fluctuations in regional and national grain output in China, 1931–84, sub-periods

managing agricultural development. That is, in the earlier period, despite collectivization, markets and prices still played a significant role. By contrast, in 1966–77, direct, quantitative planning and bureaucratic control impaired peasant incentives, distorted the cropping pattern and hence depressed agricultural productivity.[17]

This argument is not supported by the data if we start with a comparison of 1952–57 with 1931–37 (see Figures 7.1a and 7.1b). In the 1930s, the rural institutional framework was close to the market paradigm and I would argue that the superior performance in the 1950s was already a reflection of the initial impact of collective-mobilization economies, rather than of any lingering price and income incentives for the peasants. As for 1966–77, I would prefer to argue that the 'less impressive' performance referred to by Lardy – especially as shown by 'declining total factor productivity' – can, in the first place, be easily explained by the fact that the growth impact of the 'institutional hedge' had, by the 1970s, become more or less saturated. We need also to bear in mind the widely known point that we still lack independent, reliable aggregate output and input indices for gauging the 'total factor productivity' changes in Chinese agriculture. Depending on the data used and assumptions made (appropriate 'weights' for land, labour and capital inputs) the estimated 'total factor productivity' index can easily swing to the positive or negative sides.[18] The Chinese data used by Lardy (1983, pp. 86–7) (farm survey or national data for production and labour costs and official aggregate agricultural output value in gross or net terms) are clearly not entirely satisfactory.

Also any serious estimation of changes in 'total factor productivity' must take into account the accelerated expansion in capital stock that occurred during the Cultural Revolution, when there were big investments in enhanced irrigation and drainage facilities (Lardy, 1983, p. 88). Statistically, in the short run, this will tend to inflate 'input costs' (no matter what procedure is used to account for the depreciation costs) and thus to depress 'total factor productivity'. The output effects of big doses of investment take some time to come through as the 'technological hedge' becomes fully effective. In this case, the effects were probably not fully noticeable until the 1980s.

A few words should be said about the weather, which I have dealt with in detail elsewhere (Kueh, 2002a). The 'institutional hedge' profoundly helped 'dilute' the weather impact in the 1950s (compared to the 1930s) and, coupled especially with the 'technological hedge' built up in the 1970s, further minimized the weather disturbance in agricultural production. It is against this background that I believe that the post-Mao agricultural decollectivization needs to be understood.

POST-MAO DECOLLECTIVIZATION AS A TRANSITION TO INTENSIVE GROWTH

My final proposition examines the view that the decollectivization since 1978–79 represents a complete negation of Mao's approach to agricultural development in China. I would argue, on the contrary, that the new agricultural policy programme was built upon Mao's legacy to reap the benefits made available by the material and technological foundation he had left behind.

As I have explained elsewhere, decollectivization was necessary for making the purported income incentives – coupled with the massive increases in farm procurement prices in 1979 – work, in the first place (see Chapter 5). By 1984, collective farmland was effectively redistributed for private farming, which brought Chinese rural institutions back to the situation of the 1949–52 'land reform'. This was followed, in 1985, by the dismantling of the compulsory procurement scheme (in force since 1953) and the 'reserve' or 'support price' system, in favour of procurements based on negotiated contracts. The rural Chinese economy was thus returned quite close to that of the pre-war era, save that there were no large-scale private land holdings. Since then, agricultural production in China has been increasingly subject to a new breed of instability: the instability of the market (Kueh, 2002a, ch. 12).

The radical 1985 rural reforms might have been prompted by the successive bumper harvests in 1982–84, which then made it difficult for the government to stockpile grains procured from the peasants and indeed rendered redundant the long-established urban foodgrain-rationing system. However, the new policies, which have since been firmly in place, should obviously not be regarded as simple expedients, but rather evolving from highly improved physical conditions in Chinese agriculture.

Figure 7.1c reveals that, as in the 1950s and 1970s, grain output trends in China continued to exhibit the pattern of a rising trend in 1979–84. This growth was surely associated with drastic increases in the application of chemical fertilizers, as peasants rushed to cash in on the new price benefits (Kueh, 1984d). However, this obscures the vital point that fertilizer and other modern current inputs can only be effectively used if irrigation water is adequately available, and if, during the growing season, crops will not be seriously damaged or wiped out by floods or droughts. This is why the period 1979–84 is so profoundly different from the 1930s, although, as discussed, rural institutions in the 1980s were rapidly converging on those of the 1930s.

In the 1980s, the weather was as volatile as in earlier periods, as suggested by the fluctuations in grain output as it moves upward in Figure 7.1c. Note especially the sharp downturns in total grain output in 1980 (down 3.6 per cent after the great Yangzi River floods) and in 1981 when there was a slight recovery of only 1.4 per cent. This reflected the equally serious but more confined floods in Sichuan province and offset the impact of the reform incentives. The equally powerful recoveries in 1982 (by 9.1 per cent), 1983 (9.3 per cent) and 1984 (5.2 per cent) were all prompted by exceptionally good weather in three good years, although accelerated decollectivization also helped to stimulate the Chinese peasants to cash in as fast as possible.

In order to measure weather impact under reform the effect of policy-induced sown area fluctuations on grain output have to be removed. I do this by making use of the yearly deviations in grain yield per sown hectare from the (log-linear) trend values to regress against the computed weather index. The results reveal that weather influence, while clearly discernible between the prewar and postwar years, were consistently and indeed markedly reduced in the 1930s to 1950s (the 'institutional hedge' at work). Improvement continued in the 1970s (the 'institutional' and 'technological hedge') and these gains have continued on into the 1980s ('technological hedge' firmly established to enable dismantling of the 'institutional hedge') (Kueh, 2002a, pp. 125, 239). Interestingly, starting in the 1980s, residual variations in grain yields which cannot be explained by the weather variable have tended to increase. This is the new instability in Chinese agricultural production.

Nonetheless, the new instability reflects precisely that agricultural performance in China has now become much more secure compared to the past, in that Chinese peasants, coupled with the massive rural economic diversification drive, are now poised to readily express their price elasticity of production and supply. The year 1985 is a good case in point which saw total grain output curtailed by a hefty 6.93 per cent (from the 1984 level), as a result of both massive sown area contraction and reduced current inputs for sustaining per hectare yield. The weather was also implicated, but there is no doubt that the single most important culprit should be the new monopsonistic pricing formula adopted (to replace the 'reserve' or farm 'support price') by the state procurement agency, which was then already overwhelmed by mounting grain stock-piling (Kueh, 2002a, pp. 242, 249–51). It was against such a backdrop that, in 1994, in the wake of rising farm input prices, the government found it necessary to raise procurement prices as well (even amidst good harvests), in order to forestall a similar sudden downturn in grain production (see Chapter 11).

At any rate, grain production continued to surge and peaked in 1998 (see Table 7.2). The relative abundance in the ensuing decade clearly suggests that food insecurity in China has now become a matter of the past.

Twenty years ago, I rather feared that the decollectivized rural setting would continue to prompt Chinese peasants to engage in short-run income-maximizing investments at the expense of the maintenance/expansion of

Table 7.2   *China's population (P) in millions, grain sown area (SA) in*
            million hectares, grain yield per hectare (GY) in kilograms, and
            grain output, total (Q) in million tonnes and per capita (PQ) in
            kilograms, 1952–2004, and growth rates in % per year for sub-
            periods

	1952	1978	1998	2004	1952–78	1978–98	1978–2004
P	574.82	962.59	1248.1	1299.9	2.00	1.31	1.16
SA	123.99	120.59	113.79	101.61	−0.11	−0.29	−0.66
GY	1322	2527	4502	4620	2.52	2.92	2.35
Q	163.92	304.77	512.30	469.47	2.41	2.63	1.68
PQ	285	317	411	361	0.41	1.31	0.50

Sources: *TJZY 2005*, pp. 39–40, 119–20 for 1978, 1998, 2004; *TJNJ 1983*, pp. 154, 158; *1984*, p. 81.

essential capital stock such as irrigation and water control facilities (see Chapter 5). However, between 1978 and 2004, built upon the Maoist legacy, the 'effectively irrigated area' increased by 0.7 per cent per year, from 44 965 thousand hectares to 54 478 thousand hectares and diesel-driven agricultural drainage and irrigation machines by 3.2 per cent, from 25 216 to 57 729 thousand kilowatts. In the same period farming machinery (comprising large, median and small-sized tractors and complementary farm implements) grew by 6.7 per cent, from 117 499 to 637 560 thousand kilowatts; rural hydropower stations' generating capacity grew by 5.8 per cent, from 2284 to 9938 thousand kilowatts, and total electricity consumed in rural areas by 11.1 per cent per annum, from 25 310 to 393 300 million kWh (*TJZY 2005*, pp. 115–19; *TJNJ 2004*, pp. 477–78). These impressive statistics suggest, ironically, that the Chinese peasants behave as if they are treating the Cultural Revolution as a 'role model' to emulate.

Note also the enthusiasm with which Chinese peasants have continued to plough back farm earnings in expenditure on chemical fertilizers in order to take advantage of the improved infrastructural capital: consumption has risen from 8840 to 46 370 thousand tonnes in 1978–2003, an annual growth rate of 6.6 per cent.

Another important point is that the basic farm mechanization statistics as cited reflect not only improved agricultural-technology capacity. The implied pace of machine-for-labour substitution also helps point to the massive post-Mao rural economic diversification and industrialization drives. This activity is indeed partly reflected in the new rural power-generating capacity and total electricity consumed, because these are by no means only directly related to farming operations.

CONCLUSION: A 50-YEAR PERSPECTIVE

Table 7.2 shows the basic statistics for grain production (China's most important agricultural product) for the benchmark years 1952, 1978, 1998 and 2004. The year 1978, which marks the end of the Mao period, divides the past five decades into the two periods of equal (26-year) length: 1952–78 and 1978–2004. The year 1998 is used as a point of reference, as it marks the highest ever grain output in China in both total and per capita terms.

Several important points emerge from these data. First, total grain output increased at an annual average rate of 2.41 per cent in 1952–78, a rate remarkably close to the 2.63 per cent for 1978–98 and, in fact, that surpassed by a wide margin the 1.68 per cent achieved for the more comparable period of 1978–2004. Second, in terms of per capita grain output (or 'availability'), the 1952–78 performance would have been even more impressive, had it not been for the much higher population growth rate recorded for the period of 2 per cent per year, compared to 1.31 per cent for 1978–98 and 1.16 per cent for 1978–2004. Third, the rate of increases in grain yield per hectare in 1952–78, by 2.52 per cent per year, was also comparable to that of the two later periods.

To assess further the agricultural performance in 1952–78, we also have to bear in mind the interim 'Great Débâcle' of 1959–61. Grain output was in fact not restored to the 1958 peak until 1965–66, with the advent of the Cultural Revolution. In other words, had it not been for the disastrous GLF experiments, Chinese agriculture would have perhaps been able to complete the transition to the intensive-growth strategy at an even earlier stage. Nevertheless, the relatively slow agricultural growth during the post-Mao era, taken as a whole, also clearly suggests that, against the backdrop of the Maoist legacy, Chinese agricultural production was by the early or mid-1980s already entering a phase of relative saturation, as alluded to earlier, in terms of enhanced grain stockpiling, for example.

In other words, by the close of Mao's period, China's historic food security problem was basically solved. Further, there was a continuous upgrading in the composition of grain consumption (Table 7.3). With fine grain consumption saturated, the share of maize has increased remarkably since 1978 (18 per cent of the total) or 1985 (17 per cent) through to the peak of 2003 (27 per cent). This reflects grain now grown to feed livestock or used for edible oil or confectionery. This factor also explains the relative slowdown in per capita grain output in the past two decades, as can be seen in Table 7.2.

The improved safety margin now available to the peasants is reflected in the chaotic aftermath and 'havoc' brought about by the abolition of the 'reserved' prices in the 1985 reform. In this episode grain prices fell, and I estimate that probably three-quarters of the subsequent loss of output in

*Table 7.3   Trends in grain output and output composition in China,
             selected years, 1952–2004*

	Grain output (million tonnes)	Fine grains (%)			Coarse grains (%)		
		Rice	Wheat	Total	Maize	Others	Total
1952	163.92	41.8	11.1	52.9	10.3	36.9	47.2
1957	195.05	44.5	12.1	56.6	11.0	32.4	43.4
1970	239.96	45.8	12.2	58.0	13.8	28.2	42.0
1978	304.77	44.9	17.7	62.6	18.4	19.0	37.4
1985	379.11	44.5	22.6	67.1	16.8	16.1	32.9
1990	446.24	42.4	22.0	64.4	21.7	13.9	35.6
1995	466.62	39.7	21.9	61.6	24.0	14.4	38.4
2000	462.18	40.7	21.6	63.3	22.9	13.8	36.7
2001	452.64	39.2	20.7	59.9	25.2	14.9	40.1
2002	457.06	38.2	19.8	58.0	26.5	15.5	42.0
2003	430.70	37.3	20.1	57.4	26.9	15.7	42.6
2004	469.47	38.2	19.6	57.8	27.8	14.4	42.2

Source: *TJNJ*, various issues.

1985 (down by 7 per cent on 1984) was the result of deliberate limitations
on the sown area and current inputs by the disillusioned peasants. Clearly,
the peasants had by then sufficient income alternatives that could be earned
as a result of rural diversification, but these alternatives, available even in
the early-to-mid 1980s, did not emerge from a vacuum. Their origins lay in
the 'new five small industries' (cotton spinning, knitting, cigarette-making,
wine-making and sugar-refining) which themselves were often conversions
from the five heavy small-scale rural industries of the Cultural Revolution
(Kueh, 1985a, pp. 6, 34). During the 1980s, moreover, these industries were
increasingly being consolidated into rural collectives that became the backbone of China's export expansion.

   In conclusion, perhaps the most important point is that agriculture and
rural development in the broader sense remain subject to a pro-urban and
pro-industry strategic bias. It may be hoped that the new initiatives taken
by the Hu-Wen leadership to address the *sannong* problem will finally begin
to correct this imbalance. Already, however, the average peasant household
has an Engel coefficient (outlay on food as a percentage of total consumption) that has declined from 68 in 1978 to a relatively comfortable 47 in 2004
(*TJZY 2005*, pp. 110–12). Fine grain as a proportion of total staple foods
consumed increased from 50 per cent in 1978 to 87 per cent in 2004, and,
beyond these food indicators, in 2004 three-quarters of all rural households

possessed colour television sets (113 per cent of them if black and white sets are included); 37 per cent had washing machines, 55 per cent telephone lines, 142 per cent electrical fans and 36 per cent motorcycles. Clearly, the *sannong* problem today is very different from that facing China at the time of the 1955 High Tide. Even so, I remain unconvinced that, had Mao failed 50 years ago, China today would have been better off in terms of industrial and agricultural progress.

NOTES

*   Reprinted with adaptations from Y.Y. Kueh, 'Mao and agriculture in China's industrialization: three antitheses in a 50-year perspective', *The China Quarterly*, **187** (September 2006), 700–723; copyright School of Oriental and African Studies, published by Cambridge University Press.
1. I borrow an epigram by the Harvard Professor, Abraham Bergson, that 'steel was a final good to Stalin, and bread an intermediate one', as quoted by Wiles (1962); see Tang (1968, p. 460).
2. *Maoxuan*, p. 182. This suggests that, by summer 1955, Mao was fully confident that agricultural cooperativization should precede mechanization, not vice versa. See Howe and Walker (1977, p. 181) about this significant controversy between Mao and Liu Shaoqi on the issue, and Perkins (1966, p. 60) for a brief discussion about the relevance of the Soviet experience of mechanization to China.
3. See Wu and Liu (2004) for a comprehensive definition of the *sannong* problem, and Tang (2002) for the critical problems involved.
4. Hu made the point at the Fourth Plenum of the Sixteenth National Party Congress (NPC) held in September 2004, and again more specifically at the National Economic Work Conference in November 2004. In the words of Wen Jiabao, 'the first phase of the (post-Mao) rural reform, i.e. the implementation of the basic economic system of household management is completed, and the country is now entering into the second phase of reform with industry "return-feeding" agriculture and urban centres supporting the countryside' (press interview given in conjunction with the National People's Congress held in March 2005; see *XBCJ Ribao*, 15 April 2005. Wen also proclaimed that all agricultural taxes would be eliminated in 2005.
5. See Mao's 'Two talks on agricultural mutual-aid cooperation', *Maoxuan*, 1977, p. 122. He made the point even more explicit in 'Reading notes on the Soviet textbook of political economy' (1961–62), *Wansui*, 1969, p. 330. Note that the scheme was adopted as soon as the First Five-Year Plan (1953–57) was launched.
6. Lardy (1983, pp. 126–8) conducted a sophisticated estimate of the size of the 'imbalance'. He shows that, for 1950–77, light industry contributed (profits and taxes) 29 per cent of state budget revenue, which was equivalent to 70 per cent of all state investment, of which only 8 per cent was reinvested in light industry, with the bulk used to finance investment in heavy industry. He also cited a respectful Chinese source to the effect that 'as late as 1978 more than two-thirds of light industrial goods still were manufactured from inputs procured from agriculture'.
7. See also Mao's 'Summing Up Speech at the Sixth Expanded Plenum' (September 1955), *Wansui*, 1969, pp. 12–25, with which he campaigned for the official endorsement of his cooperativization drive.
8. Bergson (1968), pp. 15–18. In his Harvard class, 1969–70, Professor Bergson made use of the transformation curve to illustrate the differences between growth efficiency and dynamic efficiency, to be distinguished from static efficiency (producing on the frontier) (my lecture notes).

9. Cf. Elvin (1982, pp. 13–35) and of course the monumental contribution by Buck (1937) about the situation in the 1930s.
10. See Lardy (1983), pp. 47–8, 52–3 for the very explicit views expressed in this respect.
11. As a matter of fact, industrial planning in China was then already considered as much less difficult than in the Soviet Union. As Perkins (1968, p. 601) puts it, '(China) produces a far fewer number of commodities' and 'There are fewer interdependencies between industries and sector.' Moreover, as Howe (1978, p. 54) sees it, planning and decisions did not evolve from 'scratch', but normally involved 'marginal adjustments and appropriate expansion' from existing plans.
12. As was then epitomized by Mao's familiar call for '*shen wa dong* (digging deep into the ground to build air-raid shelters), (and) *guang ji liang* (storing abundant grains)' to be '*bei zhan* (prepared for wars), (and) *bei huang* (against natural calamities)'. See also Wheelwright and McFarlane (1970) for an interpretative study of Mao's approach to 'regional autarky'.
13. Delve into the origins of the disaster at great length in Kueh (2002a), ch. 11. The widespread views are familiar: extreme egalitarianism, peasants' disincentives and labour exhaustion, coupled with failure in technically untenable large irrigation projects and the 'deep ploughing and close planting' farming practice, plus the notorious 'backyard iron and steel furnaces' campaign. I argue, however, that the upheavals were all phenomena of 1958, for which grain output actually hit the all-time high. Put simply, my view is that the culprit should be the central planning fiasco brought about by the grossly faulty information feedback from the provinces. This resulted in the disastrous delusion that only one-third of arable land would be needed for grain cultivation, and hence in the adoption of the 'three-three system' (one-third for horticulture, and the rest to lie fallow). Note that total grain sown area was deliberately curtailed in 1959 by 9 per cent from 1958 or 13 per cent against the 1957 level. On top of this, state grain procurements based on highly exaggerated output claims were absolutely excessive. For survival, peasants were forced to dip into seed and feed grains (for livestock and draught animals). The upshot was inadequate sowing in 1960 and, coupled with the extraordinary droughts, a reduction in grain output by nearly 28 per cent or 26 per cent from the records of 1958 and 1957, respectively. The droughts were prolonged into 1961, preventing any quick recovery. Famine followed nationally. From the present-day mass media perspective, it still remains an intellectual myth how the catastrophic statistical fiasco took place.
14. For advances made in this respect see Stone (1993), pp. 311–60; Howe (1978), ch. 3.
15. Cf. Kueh (1985a). Many of these small plants are by their very raison d'être 'inefficient' (lack of scale economies, excessive vertical integration etc). But here, again, the 'costs' involved should not be considered as outweighing the 'benefits' obtained from such a mobilization approach. Cf. also Donnithorne (1972).
16. The year 1959 is not included in Figure 7.1b, because the sharp output decline in that year was substantially caused by the deliberate sown area curtailment, as alluded to. If 1958 is included, the picture will not change much.
17. Lardy (1983), pp. 40, 47. Chow (1985) has a similar neoclassical economic point of view. He sees the Chinese farmer not being 'paid according to the marginal product of his labour' (p. 47) as a core problem in Chinese agriculture. The other problem is 'misuse (by the central planning authority and its staff) of farmland and (hence) low productivity' (p. 48). Such arguments are of course completely at odds with the very character of Mao's strategy of forced farm siphoning and double taxation via scissors differentials; that is, of forced savings to promote 'growth efficiency' (see Bergson, 1968, pp. 15–18).
18. See Chao (1970, p. 238); Tang (1968, p. 482); (1984, pp. 87–94) and Wiens (1980) for possible sources of biases, reservation and disagreement between different estimates.

PART IV

The New Industrialization Strategy

8.   The three industrial imbalances*

There are three major aspects to the Maoist legacy that are important for understanding the new industrialization strategy adopted in China since Deng Xiaoping's return to power in 1978. First is the massive orientation towards heavy industry in pursuit of a maximum-speed 'socialist industrialization' at the expense of agricultural growth. This is the familiar Soviet-style 'industry–agriculture dichotomy'. Second is the attempt made, abortive at times, to correct the regional imbalances in industrial distribution. That is, to narrow the enormous gap between the underdeveloped interior and the more advanced coastal areas. Third is parallel to the large-scale modern-type industries, the rigorous promotion of small-scale indigenous industries, in part for the purpose of labour absorption. This is what Professor Eckstein regards as 'local adaptations' of the Soviet model of forced-draft industrialization (Eckstein, 1966, pp. 31–3).

The chapter falls into two main parts. The first looks at China's industrial development under Mao with respect to the three basic strategic policy goals alluded to, and analyses the quantitative changes that have taken place under Deng and his followers during the process of economic transition. The second part attempts to define the nature and scope of the modifications made to the Maoist strategy of industrialization since the late 1970s and examines, in particular, the long-term impact of the new strategy on sectoral, regional and technological imbalances.

I begin the discussion, however, by highlighting, from a global perspective, China's achievements in industrialization and technological advances by the early or mid-1980s, in order to provide a benchmark for assessing the emerging records of the new industrial strategy.

CHINA'S STATUS AS AN INDUSTRIAL POWER

Hardly had Deng completed the initial 'Economic Readjustment', by 1984, than the three-decade long Maoist style industrialization drive had already brought China to the front rank of world economic powers. The country was then the seventh-largest country in the world in terms of the absolute level of GNP, and ranks sixth in size of industrial output, after the United

States, the Soviet Union, Japan, West Germany and the United Kingdom. China is also a major international producer of certain key industrial commodities: she ranks sixth in power generation and the production of crude oil, fifth in chemical fibres, fourth in steel output, third in chemical fertilizers, second in the production of coal and cement; and she is the largest producer of clothing in the world (*GYJJTJZL 1949–84*, p. 206). Per capita production indicators compare favourably not only with China's own pre-war peaks, but also with the postwar records of other developing countries, including India.

Technological advances have powered rapid industrial growth and brought about significant changes in the sectoral composition of gross domestic product. From 1952 to 1978, the contribution of the industrial sector to GDP increased most remarkably by 27 percentage points, from 21 to 48 per cent. The corresponding share of agriculture declined by 23 percentage points, from 51 to 28 per cent, during the same period (Table 8.1). This sharp rise in industry's share of China's national income is a rare historical phenomenon. For example, during the first four or five decades of their drive to modern industrialization, the industrial share rose by only 11 per cent in Britain (1801–41) and 22 per cent in Japan (1878–82 to 1923–27) (Yeh, 1984, pp. 701–2). In the postwar experience of newly industrializing economies, probably only Taiwan has demonstrated as impressive a record as China in this respect (Kuznets, 1979, pp. 56–7, 124). Of course, the small island economy, which benefits greatly from the huge US export market, should not be compared directly with the vast Chinese Mainland's, which has, until the advent of the open-door policy, remained basically a closed system.

Perhaps even more remarkable is the fact that technological transformation in China has embraced a capacity for imitating Western high technology. An obvious example is that of the development of interballistic missile and satellite technology, although there are other areas too in which China by no means lags behind the industrial technology of her Western mentors.

Moreover, there is an irony in the fact that, while China's per capita income remains a mere fraction of those of West Germany, France, Sweden and Australia, such countries – China's industrial precursors – now consider it beneficial to use Chinese rockets to place their commercial satellites in orbit. This is no doubt an extreme case of technological dualism, but it is not the only one that exists in China: technological contrasts between industry and agriculture, as well as between different industrial branches and different regions, are hardly less striking.

THE DICHOTOMY BETWEEN INDUSTRY AND AGRICULTURE

Several important points emerge from Table 8.1. Firstly, when the Mao era ended, by 1978, the industrial sector taken as a whole already contributed to nearly half of the country's GDP, but it took up only 17 per cent of the national labour force. By contrast, for the agricultural sector, the corresponding figures were 28 and 71 per cent. In other words, every 1 per cent of workforce taken up by industry from the national pool contributed 2.8 per cent of national income, compared with a mere 0.4 per cent in the case of agriculture. Industry's labour productivity, in terms of 'relative product per worker' (RPW), was therefore seven times the level of agriculture. In 1970, the heyday of the Cultural Revolution, when anything for the services sector, apart from, say, 'productive' freight transportation was repudiated as capitalist remnants, the productivity discrepancy between industry and

Table 8.1   Industrialization and intersectoral imbalances in China, 1952–2005 (per cent)

	1952	1957	1970	1978	1987	2005
Industry's share in						
GDP	20.9	29.7	40.5	48.2	43.9	47.3
employment	7.4	9.0	10.1	17.3	21.9	23.9
relative product per worker	2.8	3.3	4.0	2.8	2.0	2.0
Agriculture's share in						
GDP	50.5	40.3	35.2	28.1	26.8	12.4
employment	83.5	81.2	80.7	70.5	60.0	44.7
relative product per worker	0.6	0.5	0.4	0.4	0.5	0.3
Services' share in						
GDP	28.6	30.1	24.3	23.7	29.3	40.3
employment	9.1	9.8	9.2	12.2	17.8	31.4
relative product per worker	3.1	3.1	2.6	1.9	1.7	1.3
Total inequality (amongst sectors)	65.8	81.9	93.4	84.4	64.4	69.4

Notes: Relative product per worker (RPW) = % share in GDP (Y) / % share in employment (W). Total inequality amongst sector (TIAS) = $\Sigma[1-Y_{(i)}] \cdot W_{(i)}$ (ignoring the minus sign); where $Y_{(i)}$ = RPW at sector i, and $W_{(i)}$ = % share in employment of sector i. The TIAS formula was formulated by Simon Kuznets (see Liu, 1968, p. 124). He estimated the index for India to be 41.4 in the early 1960s – the highest among developing countries (ibid., p. 128).

Sources: *TJZY 2006* and *2005*, and earlier issues.

agriculture amounted to a startling high of ten to one. The upshot is the incredibly high 'total inequality amongst sectors' (TIAS) index of 93, which has remained unsurpassed by the economic history of any other country in the world. There is no doubt that, with his zeal to help industrialize China to catch up with the West, Mao had pushed the Stalinist rationale for a maximum-speed industrialization to its ultimate conclusion.

Secondly, ten years into the Deng era, the GDP share of industry declined from 48 per cent in 1978 to 43.9 per cent in 1987, but that was essentially to pave the way for a remarkable increase in the share of the services sector, from 23.7 to 29.3 per cent. As a result, the TIAS index declined consistently, from 84.4 to 64.4 in the same period. Note, however, that agriculture's relative product per worker remained depressed. Had it not been for the massive effort made in the early post-Mao years to boost agricultural production, the sector's share in GDP would have in all likelihood been reduced to an even greater extent than the marginal decline from 28.1 to 26.8 per cent, respectively. This would further lower the relative product per worker, given that the sector still needed to absorb 60 per cent of the national labour force, despite relaxed restriction on rural–urban migration.

A few more words must be said about the characteristics of the Dengist economic transition against the backdrop of the Maoist heritage. First and foremost should be the rapid rise of the services sector in terms of both GDP and employment shares. This not only reflected the fact that the Maoist ideological straitjacket was discarded, but also increased rural exodus, including the return of tens of millions of urban youths from their Cultural Revolution exile in the countryside. Venues must obviously be opened up for highly labour-intensive service undertakings to help absorb such masses, in addition to the existing huge pool of urban unemployed. More importantly, the large number of peasants rendered redundant under the new agricultural programme must also be given work as well. This included peasants who no longer needed to be engaged in the more efficient *Baogan Daohu* farming system, as well as those who used to work on large-scale Nurksian-type infrastructure projects which have now been abandoned in favour of small-scale short-run income-maximizing investments made by the peasant households (see Chapter 4).

The influx tended of course to help lower the average labour productivity of the services sector, and of the urban industries as well (Table 8.1), to the extent that many of the new peasant arrivals were also taken up by small-scale labour-intensive urban collective industrial undertakings (Kueh, 1985a). These all clearly explain the 'equalizing' productivity trends between the three broad economic branches towards the end of the first decade of Dengist economic reforms.

There is yet another important factor, though mainly statistical in nature, that helps to explain the 'equalizing' productivity trends. This involves the reclassification of small rural industries run by villages from agricultural to industrial production effective as of 1984 (*TJNJ 2006*, p. 504). The effect is to pull down relative product per industrial worker, since most of what were previously regarded as rural industries (with output being incorporated into the agricultural (rather than industrial) gross value of output) are labour-intensive, farm-processing undertakings with comparatively small value-added components. Bear in mind too that the 'rural-industrial' workers, who used to constitute only a small proportion of the 'agricultural' work-force, now represent a substantial part of the urban-industrial labour force, even though the latter remains small in relation to the total rural workforce.

Looking back, one may conclude that, while Mao, with decades of spectacular mass mobilization, was able basically to build up a workable rural overhead foundation (especially with respect to irrigation and drainage facilities) to help sustain agricultural growth, the Dengist strategists have been left with the liability of how to put up with the ever-increasing surplus labour in China by expanding the services industries, as well as highly labour-intensive small industrial undertakings. Table 8.1 shows that, three decades on, by 2005, they have actually been quite successful as well, judging by the remarkable increases in the sector's share in both GDP (40 per cent) and employment (31 per cent). Nevertheless, agriculture and the peasants, or the rural society at large, still lag far behind their urban counterparts these days in the pursuit of material well-being; hence the current rigorous campaign launched by the third-generation Hu-Wen leadership for tackling the so-called *sannong* problems, as discussed in Chapter 7.

REGIONAL INDUSTRIAL DISPARITIES

The disparity between coastal and interior regions was already a preoccupation in the 1950s. In his *On Ten Great Relations* in 1956, Mao stressed the need to correct industry's coastal bias in favour of the interior (Croll and Yeh, 1975). This preoccupation became an obsession in the Cultural Revolution, when the perceived need for war preparation led to the adoption of a strategy of regional industrial autarky. In the consequent scramble to create a comprehensive network of self-sufficient local industries which would meet China's defence requirements, economic rationality, based on interregional or intraregional specialization and cooperation, was largely ignored, as was widely reported.[1]

The most remarkable evidence of the move towards industrial autarky was the so-called 'third-line construction', adopted during the Cultural

Table 8.2   Distribution of gross value of industrial output between the coastal and interior regions in China, 1952–2004 (%)

	1952	1957	1978	1987	1997	2004
Coastal	69.4	66.8	60.9	61.1	59.8	73.2
Interior	30.6	33.2	39.1	38.9	40.2	26.8

Notes: The coastal regions comprise officially Beijing, Tianjin, Hebei, Liaoning, Shanghai, Jiangsu, Zhejiang, Fujian, Shandong, Guangdong and Guangxi provinces) (*GYJJTJZL 1949–84*, p. 362).

Sources: *GYJJTJZL 1949–84*, pp. 139, 143; *TJNJ 1988*, p. 326; *1998*, p. 434, 2006, p. 508.

Revolution. An estimated 53 per cent of national investment funds during the Third Five-Year Plan (1966–70) were diverted to industrial and related construction projects located in areas west of the second north-west railway line (Hsueh and Woo, 1986, p. 72). The bias persisted until the death of Mao.

As shown in Table 8.2, in terms of gross value of industrial output (GVIO), the contribution of the 11 provinces officially defined as 'coastal' did consistently decline from 69 per cent in 1952 (67 per cent in 1957) to 61 per cent in 1978. Strangely enough, two decades into the Dengist reform (by 1997), the 'coastal' share still remained basically constant, despite the shift in policy emphasis 'from the development of the interior – where investment costs are relatively high – to development of areas in which the infrastructure is more fully developed' (Field, 1986, p. 528), coupled with the accelerated influx of foreign direct investment (FDI) into the coastal areas. It seems that the policy reorientation has merely served to halt the rise in the industrial share of the interior until the late 1990s, and the trend was then forcefully reversed for the coastal share to reach the startling high of 73 per cent, in 2004.

Nonetheless, as Figure 8.1 reveals, the picture of regional industrial distribution in 1978–97 will look quite different if the narrowly defined coastal region is extended to embrace the adjacent Central provinces of Henan, Anhui, Hubei and Hunan, to the exclusion of Beijing and Tianjin (reclassified into the North), as well as Liaoning (Northeast).[2] The broadly defined coastal belt (comprising the East and Central-South regions) did indeed see their GVIO shares increase most remarkably since 1981, at the expense of virtually all the other four regions, the Northeast (China's traditional heavy-industry bulwark) included.

Note also, from Figure 8.1, that the East and Central-South regions both now not only command the overwhelming absolute GVIO shares in China but also enjoy the highest degree of industrialization in terms of relative

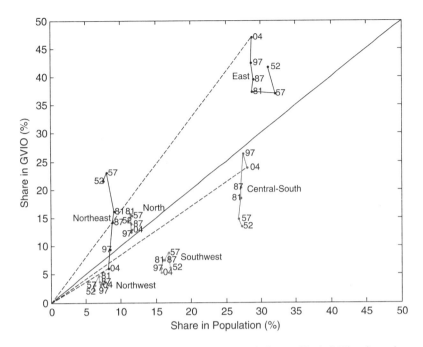

Note: The provinces included are: Northwest (Shannxi, Gansu, Qinghai, Ningxia, and Xinjiang); North (Shanxi, Neimonggu, Beijing, Tianjin, and Hebei); Northeast (Jilin, Liaoning, and Heilongjiang); Southwest (Sichuan, Chongqing, Guizhou, Yunnan, and Xizang); Central-South (Henan, Hubei, Hunan, Guangdong, Hainan, and Guangxi), and East (Jiangsu, Zhejiang, Anhui, Fujian, Jiangxi, and Shandong).

Sources: Kueh (1989a, p. 427) and *TJNJ 1998* and *2006*, various pages.

Figure 8.1 *Comparative regional shares in national gross value of industrial output (GVIO) and population in China, 1952, 1957, 1981, 1987, 1997, 2004 (per cent)*

GVIO per capita of total population, as may be measured by the slope of the broken line linking the origin to the respective coordinates for the years concerned. The minor exception is that the North at present still shows a slightly higher per capita GVIO than the Central-South region, but there seems no doubt that the gap is poised to be closed very soon.

It is clearly against this background that the celebrated 'Go West' campaign was launched in 2000 for promoting investments in the Northwest and Southwest for correcting what Mao regarded as intolerable regional bias, and the appeal frequently made in recent years for reinvigorating the 'old industrial base of the Northeast'. Note, however, that the post-Mao regional industrial bias has basically evolved from market-driven forces, with massive export-oriented FDI being concentrated on the coastal provinces. It is nowadays virtually impossible to resort to the Maoist past practice of forced siphoning of revenue from, say, Shanghai and Liaoning province for investment in the interior (cf. Lardy, 1975).

Another important remark is still in order to the credit of the Dengist strategists. This relates to the significant intraindustrial spillover to help augment the pace and degree of regional industrialization. In 1981–87, for example, the share of Shanghai in national GVIO declined from 12 to 8 per cent, in favour of gains by neighbouring Jiangsu, Zhejiang and Anhui provinces, totalling five percentage points. Similar intraregional shifts occurred from Beijing and Tianjin to Hebei, and, for that matter, Shandong province as well. Clearly, the expanding market-based regional conglomeration economies, with or without the impact of FDI, have helped to absorb an enormous amount of surplus labour from the rural areas. The accomplishment is truly remarkable, by virtue of the fact that, by the late 1980s, restrictions on rural–urban migration (in force since the early 1950s) could largely be lifted as a result, without causing any major disorder in the urban centres.

TECHNOLOGICAL DUALISM

The concept of 'technological dualism' was developed by R.S. Eckaus in the 1950s to characterize the contrast in most developing countries between their relatively developed coastal area (as a result of colonial rule) and the vast underdeveloped rural hinterland. At about the same time, Mao in his *On the Ten Great Relations* (1956), promoted the simultaneous application of indigenous and modern Western technologies, parallel to simultaneous development of coastal and interior industries. This had subsequently led to the familiar Maoist economic strategy of 'walking on two legs' as adopted during the Great Leap Forward of the late 1950s (Eckstein, 1966, p. 32). Obviously Mao regarded the phenomenon of 'technological dualism', not as a liability, but as an asset. What followed is familiar: the abortive 'backyard iron and steel furnaces' campaign of the GLF, the renewed attempt at rural industrialization through the 'five small industries' run by the communes and brigades during the Cultural Revolution, and subsequently under Deng Xiaoping, the 'new five small industries' undertaken by rural townships and villages (see Chapter 7).

However, neither Mao nor Deng ever really lost sight of the grand vision of a 'socialist industrialization', based on modern, large-scale, capital-intensive investment projects focusing on the preferential development of heavy industry, as a means of catching up with the West. As a matter of fact, judging by the zeal with which Deng attempted to court foreign capital and technology, he certainly appeared no less ambitious than Mao in this respect. Of course, the major difference is that, unlike Mao, Deng was fortunate enough to enjoy the advantage of political détente with the West, the United States in particular, for facilitating the desired technology transfer, no matter how limited that may have later proved to be after the embargo imposed by the West following the Tiananmen Square incident.

Nevertheless, while Mao and Deng shared Soviet-style industrial 'gigantomania' (cf. Campbell, 1966, p. 108) based on advanced Western technology, they were confronted with the overwhelming task of coping with the mounting masses of rural and urban unemployed. In this respect, the situation in China was undoubtedly very different from the former Soviet Union in, say, 1928, when Stalin regarded it as essential to 'tractorize' Soviet agriculture in the wake of collectivization and the first wave of industrialization, in order to release farm labour to support industrial expansion (Perkins, 1966, p. 60). At any rate, the upshot of the Maoist, and especially the much more pragmatic Dengist approach, in pursuit of maximizing industrial modernization and labour absorption is a phenomenon of technological dualism rarely seen elsewhere in the world. To point to the obvious: satellite technology or manned spacecrafts existing alongside the 2000-year-old method of manufacturing fire-crackers or hand-driven cargo carts, or the Lenovo computer juxtaposed to the traditional Chinese abacus.

Thus, within the first decade of the Dengist transition, the share of industrial output churned out by highly labour-intensive cottage-type undertakings (which are not classified as 'industry proper' in official statistics), increased from less than 5 per cent in 1981 to around 15 per cent in 1987, and a startlingly high of 38 per cent in 1997 of the national GVIO (gross value of industrial output), as shown in Table 8.3. Between 1987 and 1997, they amounted to some seven, to more than seven-and-a-half, millions of 'industrial enterprises' dispersed across the country. This represents 93 per cent of the national total, leaving the remaining 7 per cent to be accounted for by the proper industrial establishments. The larger ones of the cottage-type industries are run by the village/hamlet collectives or cooperatives, but the overwhelming majority are the rapidly emerging private individual businesses located throughout the Chinese countryside.

Comparable statistics for 2005 or 2004 are unfortunately not available, but there is no doubt that the stark technological disparities between the industry-proper sector and the millions of mini-industrial undertakings as implied in Table 8.3 should still remain in place in China today as it was a decade ago, owing to ever-increasing new entrants to the labour force, especially in the rural sector.

Within the industry proper the distinctions among L, M and S-scale enterprises are also generally speaking quite striking, as shown in Table 8.4,

Table 8.3 *Distribution of gross value of industrial output (Q) and number of enterprises (N) between scale (large, medium and small) and non-scale enterprises in China, 1981–2005 (million* yuan, *units and per cent)*

| | | Total (1) | Scale enterprises | | Non-scale enterprises | Percentage shares | | |
			L + M (2)	S (3)	NS (4)	L + M	L + M + S	NS
1981	Q	545 547	220 869	299 014	27 780	40.1	95.3	4.7
	N	(381 500)	5 000	376 500	—			
1987	Q	1 381 300	577 512	605 366	198 422	41.8	85.6	14.4
	N	7 474 100	9 865	483 708	6 980 527	0.1	6.6	93.4
1997	Q	11 373 271	3 686 874	3 387 893	4 298 504	32.4	62.2	37.8
	N	7 922 900	23 950	510 417	7 388 533	0.3	6.7	93.3
1998	Q	11 904 815	3 755 234	3 018 480	5 131 101	31.5	56.9	43.1
	N	7 974 565	23 408	141 672	7 809 485	0.3	2.1	97.9
2004	Q	(22 231 593)	13 337 468	8 894 124	—			
	N	(1 375 263)	27 692	1 347 571	—			
2005	Q	(25 161 950)	16 770 072	8 391 878	—			
	N		29 774					

Notes: (1) Q for 1981 is at 1980 prices, others at current prices. (2) Bracketed N and Q are sum total of L + M + S only. (3) Q total for 2005 refers to above-scale enterprises, and SQ is obtained by subtracting LQ. (4) Since 1998, enterprises are reclassified into above- and below-scale (annual revenue of five million *yuan* as the cut-off point), in place of the multi-tier distinction by administrative jurisdiction. The L + M + S figures for 1998 all refer to above-scale enterprises; hence the drastic reduction in number of SN from 1997. (5) L + M + S are redefined in 2003, but N total for 2004 is still markedly small compared to 1998, owing to exclusion of NS (millions of village-run and private-individual undertakings). (6) The L + M figures represent, however, a rather consistent statistical series for 1981–2005. (7) It is nevertheless not possible to ascertain how changes in output composition and prices between the years may have affected the series.

Sources: *TJNJ 1981*, pp. 208, 212; *1987*, p. 157 (for 1981); *1988*, pp. 44, 301, 310–13 (1987); *1998*, pp. 431, 437 (1997); *TJNJ 1999*, Tables 13.5 and 13.6 (1998); and *2006*, pp. 505, 550 (2004, 2005).

although, owing to redefinition and reclassification it is not possible to compare exactly the differences between the years under study. Note that, in 1987, for example, L and M enterprises, taken together, constituted only 2 per cent of all industrial enterprises, but absorbed one-third of the labour force and two-thirds of fixed capital stock, and contributed around 50 per cent of national GVIO; their turnover taxes and remitted profits accounting for 65 per cent of state revenues, based on the absolute statistics

Table 8.4 Comparative scale of output (Q), capital (K) and labour (A) inputs by large (L), medium (M) and small (S) industrial enterprises in China's industry proper, 1987–2005

	Q mill. *yuan*	A persons	K mill. *yuan*	K/A yuan	Q/A yuan	Q/K ratio
	Average per enterprise					
1987						
L+M	53.00	2616	40.59	15 518	20 263	1.3057
L	108.11	5058	99.28	19 627	21 372	1.0889
M	29.45	1572	15.51	9 868	18 738	1.8988
S	1.12	111	0.45	4 082	10 163	2.4888
1997						
L+M	153.99	—	114.31			1.3471
L	375.63	—	292.78			1.2830
M	58.68	—	37.56			1.5623
S	6.67	—	2.79			2.3907
1998						
L+M	160.48	—	135.52			1.1842
L	370.17	—	333.30			1.1106
M	60.41	—	41.15			1.4680
S	21.31	—	8.77			2.4299
2004						
L+M(a)	517.68	1389	234.30	168 671	378 435	2.2095
L+M(b)	481.64	1267	—		380 153	
L	3254.99	6456	—		504 113	
M	250.00	833	—		299 942	
S	6.60	43	—		153 466	
2005						
L+M	563.25	1276	222.12	174 085	441 444	2.5358

Definitions: 'Industry proper' is defined as total minus non-scale industry as shown in Table 8.3; A total number of staff and workers; K capital stock at original purchase prices net of depreciation; and Q GVIO at current prices.

Notes: (1) For 1987 Q (originally given at 1980 prices) are converted into current prices, and K (given as gross of depreciation) into net terms by applying the relevant aggregate index/ratio as may be estimated from statistics given in various *TJNJ* pages listed above. (2) The absolute Q and enterprise number underlying the average figures for 1987 do not exactly tally with those in Table 8.3 (which are not used here for lack of accompanying A and K). (3) For 2004, no explanation is given for the difference between L+M(a) and (b). The absolute Q for L+M(a) is not provided, but obtained by assuming that the difference in total number of enterprises (as given) between (a) and (b) is accounted for solely by M and that each has an average Q of 250 million *yuan* as given for (b). (4) K series may be affected by differences between the years in depreciation rates adopted for capital stock. See other comments made in notes to Table 8.3.

Sources: Kueh (1989a), p. 432 and *TJNJ 1988*, p. 318; *1989*, p. 266; *1998*, p. 461 (for 1987); *TJNJ 1998*, pp. 444–5 (1997); *1999*, Tables 13.6 and 13.7 (1998); *2005*, Table 14.15 (2004 L+M(a)); *2006*, p. 505 (other 2004 figures); and *2006*, pp. 550–51, 558 (2005).

underlying the average figures given in Table 8.4 (see also Kueh, 1989a, p. 431). Nonetheless, when compared to such familiar mammoth steel complexes as Anshan, Wuhan, Shoudu and Baoshan, or for that matter the Daqing Oilfield, even the average L enterprises as shown in Table 8.4 appear to be minuscule, in terms of scale of output, employment and capital stock (Kueh, 1989a, p. 434).

One or two points should be made for qualifications, however. First is that, to some extent, the predominating absolute scale of L and M enterprises vis-à-vis the S ones may indeed be a matter of horizontal agglomeration or vertical industrial integration, although there is no doubt that the comparative capital-intensity (K/A) figures, as in the case of 1987 (for which statistics are available), also point to substantial intraindustrial technological disparities. Second is that the difference in labour productivity (Q/A) between M and L (ratio of 1.14), however, is disproportionately small relative to that in capital intensity (K/A) (ratio of 1.99). The same goes for S versus M (respectively 1.84, 2.42).

The discrepancies clearly contradict the empirical rule about capital productivity. Apart from possible implications of X-efficiency (Leibenstein), this may be explained by the fact that many modern, large-scale industrial complexes in China each represent an excessive vertical integration of industries. That is to say, within one and the same such large industrial establishment, highly mechanized, capital-intensive core industries may be supported by a wide range of highly labour-intensive, peripheral factories comprising preponderantly manual processes or operation (Eckstein, 1977, p. 288), which all help to pull down the average labour productivity. There is no reason to suggest that such intraindustrial technological disparities have been mitigated to any substantial extent since 1987.

MAO IN DENG'S INDUSTRIAL STRATEGY

The morphological changes in the agriculture–industry dichotomy, regional industrial imbalances, and intra-industrial technological disparities as highlighted above, are all closely related. An integrated view of the relationships should be provided, however, as a background for understanding how the Maoist past may have impinged upon the new industrialization strategy under Deng and his successors.

Note again that, after nearly three decades of economic reforms, Chinese agriculture has still remained basically depressed in terms of labour productivity and income, relative to industry and the rapidly emerging services sector (Table 8.1). This is bound up with enhanced coastal bias in the distribution of modern, large-scale industries, as exacerbated by the influx of foreign direct investment in the East and South China regions. Meanwhile, the accelerated expansion of small-scale industries and the veritable ocean of 'mini' industrial undertakings have also taken place overwhelmingly in the densely populated, and more broadly defined coastal regions, especially in the provinces of Shandong, Jiangsu and Guangdong (Figure 8.1). At the same time the economic imperatives for focusing on modern industrial technology on the basis of a heavily labour-biased factor endowment have brought into even sharper focus the stark technological disparities between highly capital-intensive, large-scale industries and those millions of nascent small, rural-based undertakings lying outside the conventional orbit of the industrial sector (Tables 8.3 and 8.4).

In short, in the post-Mao era, the 'three imbalances' (industry versus agriculture, coastal versus interior regions, and lopsided technological development) inherited from the Maoist past have actually tended to deteriorate, in absolute or relative terms. There are three aspects to the specific Dengist strategy that contributed to the aggravation, namely the role of heavy industry in intraindustrial allocation, the specifically Dengist approach to labour mobilization, and the open-door policy.

The Role of Heavy Industry

As alluded to in Chapter 2, in the early Dengist transition in the 1980s, it appeared that the well-established Maoist or Soviet-style economic strategy for the preferential development of heavy industry was being abandoned amidst the drastic 'Economic Readjustments' made in favour of consumption-oriented light industry and agriculture. Table 8.5 reveals that the share of heavy industry in GVIO was drastically reduced from the high of 56 per cent for the 1970s (dominated by the highly austere Cultural Revolution strategy) to the low of 52 per cent in the 1980s.

A comparison of 1978–87 with 1971–77, for example, reveals that there had been an accelerated growth of light industry, relative to that of heavy industry. Against a base of 100 for 1978, by 1985 the index of heavy industrial output was 175 (incidentally, implying the same rate of growth as that experienced by both light and heavy industry during the previous seven-year period, 1971–78), while that of light industry had reached 227. The implied annual rates of growth were 11 per cent for light industry, 7 per cent for heavy (Kueh, 1989a, p. 439).

The divergent trends between capital-intensive heavy industry and labour-intensive light industry persisted through the late 1980s, reversing the pattern of changes which occurred in the early years of forced-draft industrialization in the 1950s, when heavy industry expanded rapidly at the expense of both light industry and agriculture. Meanwhile, the rate of agricultural

Table 8.5 Shares of heavy (H) versus light (L) industries in gross value of industrial output (GVIO) at current (C) and 'comparable' (K) prices in China, 1953–2004 (per cent)

	Share at C prices			Share at C prices			Share at C prices		Share at K prices	
	H	L		H	L		H	L	H	L
1953	37	63	1978	57	43	1992	53	47	—	—
1955	41	59	1980	53	47	1994	57	43	53	47
1957	45	55	1982	50	50	1996	56	44	54	46
1959	58	42	1984	53	47	1998	57	43	54	46
1970	54	46	1986	52	48	2000	60	40	56	44
1972	57	43	1988	49	51	2002	61	39	58	42
1974	56	44	1990	49	51	2004	67	33	—	—
1976	56	44	1991	51	49		(68)	(32)	—	—
1980s	48	52	1980s	52	48	2000s	63	37		
1990s	56	44	1990s	56	44					

Notes: (1) Figures for the 1950s (1953–59), 1970s (1970–78), 1980s (1979–89), 1990s (1990–99) and 2000s (2000–04) are weighted averages. (2) Prior to 1988–89 the figures refer to 'all industries' including sub-township enterprises. (3) For 1994–97 only industries at and above the township level are included, whereas the 1998–2004 figures cover solely 'above-scale' enterprises (see notes to Table 8.3 for redefinition). (4) The H and L shares are therefore not exactly comparable between the relevant periods. To the extent that the narrower measures exclude smaller-scale, labour-intensive light industries, the H shares may err on the high side. Nevertheless, the 2004 broader measure (bracketed figures) suggest that the reverse may also be true. (5) Figures for the 'abnormal years' (the Great Leap Forward and débâcle, the subsequent recovery, and the tumultuous Cultural Revolution of 1966–69) are omitted.

Sources: TJNJ 1988, p. 44 (for 1953–86); 1989, p. 269 (1988); 1994, p. 377 (1989–93); 1995, p. 381 (1994); 1996, Table 12.7 (1995); 1997, p. 417 (1996); 1998, p. 437 (1997); 2004, p. 516 (1998–2003); 2005, p. 488 (2004); 2006, p. 505 (2004 figures in parentheses).

growth in 1978–87 was also higher than that of both 1952–57 and 1971–78, but not 1961–66, when sharp rises in farm production largely represented recovery from the great depression of the early 1960s. Rapid agricultural growth in the 1980s, reflecting the combined effects of good weather and productivity-enhancing policy measures associated with post-Mao decollectivization, had of course helped support the expansion of light industry (Kueh, 1989a, p. 440).

Nevertheless, the comparative trends in Table 8.5 also show that, overall, heavy industrial growth has been able to keep up with that of light industry. More importantly, from the early 1990s onwards, synchronized especially with the landmark decision of the 14th National Party Congress held in October 1992, to formally establish a 'socialist market-economic system' in China, the share of heavy industry started to gain momentum again, increasing to the pre-Readjustment high of 57 per cent by 1998, and perhaps propelled by the country's admission to the World Trade Organization, to the startling all-time high of 67 per cent by 2004.

It should also be of interest to note that the GVIO share of heavy industry as measured at current prices consistently exceeded that given at 'comparable prices' since the early 1990s. This 'price effect' seems to suggest that the sector, being increasingly represented or dominated by such new industries as automobiles, electronics, petrochemical and the upgraded steel-making technology, has gained even greater importance as the leading vehicle of industrialization in China.[3]

The industrial restructuring, of heavy versus light industries over the past two and a half decades or so, as briefly sketched, implies several important points, however. First, by the time of the economic transition from Mao to Deng in the late 1970s, China's heavy industry, after three decades of self-perpetuating reinvestment in the sector, had already built up and matured to such a stage as to be able to facilitate the new leadership's strategic reorientation towards a 'less harsh consumption' policy, as highlighted in Chapter 2. Second, heightened consumerism and increased market-oriented reforms beginning from the mid-1980s had further helped to promote a closer economic integration of the heavy industry sector with light industry. Third, it is indeed quite remarkable that enhanced market forces not only did not help to derail, but had in fact strongly underpinned, the renewed acceleration of heavy industrial growth, especially since the celebrated NPC decision of October 1992 to dismantle altogether all mandatory SOEs' output and input targets and the long-established system of bureaucratic–physical control to further help pave the way for WTO accession.

Looking back, the process of economic changes in China therefore strongly drives home the point that the massive forced-draft industrialization drive under 'maximum austerity' during the 30-year reign of Mao has paid off quite handsomely, considering the marked improvement in the country's overall economic strength and in income and consumption standards of both urban and rural residents over the entire post-Mao era.

The Non-Maoist Mobilization Approach

Of all the industrial changes discernible since 1978–79, the one which most characterizes the specifically Dengist approach lies in the rigorous promotion of the non-Maoist type of small or mini-scale enterprises for developing small industries (ignoring for the time being the much-celebrated open-door policy). Prior to 1978, private individual undertakings were strictly prohibited, and collective ownership confined exclusively to 'street neighbourhood' enterprises in urban centres and the commune and brigade enterprises in the rural areas (Kueh, 1985a). With Mao's ideological straitjackets removed, however, resource constraints have imposed the only limits to ownership diversification and expansion. More importantly, the changes were strongly underpinned by the significant policy reorientation of the early 1980s from developing farm-support rural industries towards the production of any types of consumer goods (be it handicraft or machine-operated), in line with the 'less harsh' consumption policy.

Thus, not only had the number of collective and privately-owned industrial enterprises multiplied since the early 1980s (Table 8.3), but, taken together, they tended to rapidly 'crowd out' the GVIO share of the state-owned industries as well. As shown in Table 8.6, by the time the path-breaking October 1992 reform was promulgated, the SOEs' share was already reduced from the high of 78 per cent in 1978 to only 52 per cent, in favour of accelerated increases in the combined share of the collective and private enterprises from zero to 41 per cent, respectively. By 2004, the balance was then completely tilted, with the share of SOEs (including state-controlled shareholding corporations) being curtailed to a mere 15 per cent, to the benefit of a myriad of non-state-owned enterprises (combined share of 55 per cent) and foreign-invested ventures (30 per cent).

Given, however, that state-owned industries used to constitute the very core of central planning and the collectives were then only marginally incorporated into the system of centralized allocation (let alone private-individual and foreign invested enterprises), it should be absolutely clear that the accelerated increases in the GVIO shares of the 'informal sectors' since the early 1980s have all been market-driven. This stands therefore in sharp contrast to the Maoist approach of cohesive mass mobilization, although in a way the post-Mao *modus operandi* in this respect undoubtedly also owes its origin to the Cultural Revolution experiences with the rural industries run by the communes and the subordinated brigades, as alluded to earlier.

Table 8.6   *Comparative shares of gross value of industrial output (GVIO)*
by different ownership categories of enterprises in China,
1978–2004 (per cent)

	State-owned	Collective	Individual	Other types	Total
1978	78.0	22.0	0	0	100
1980	76.0	24.0	ngl.	0	100
1985	64.9	32.1	1.9	1.2	100
1990	54.6	35.6	5.4	4.4	100
1991	56.2	33.0	4.8	6.0	100
1992	51.5	35.1	5.8	7.6	100
1993	47.0	34.0	8.0	11.1	100
1994	37.3	37.7	10.1	14.8	100
1995	34.0	36.6	12.9	16.6	100
1996	28.5	39.4	15.5	16.6	100
1997	25.5	38.1	17.9	18.4	100
1998	28.2 (21.6)	38.4	17.1	22.9	107 (100)
1999	28.2 (20.3)	35.4	18.2	26.1	108 (100)
2004	15.1	32.1	22.4	30.2	100

Notes: (1) The 'state-owned enterprises' (SOEs) category includes (for the later years up to 1999) state-controlled share-holding (*kongu*) corporations. (2) 'Other types' cover predominantly (or exclusively for 2004) foreign-funded enterprises including Sino-foreign joint ventures. (3) The figures for 1998 and 1999 do not round up to 100. The likely sources of error should be the overstated absolute GVIO size for SOEs. Similar error occurs with 1997, but it can be reconciled with the figures given (in *TJNJ 1998* as cited), however. The bracketed figures are taken as the residual of the sum total of the other three categories. (4) A comprehensive recategorization of the enterprises by forms of business registration rather than ownership types from 2000 onwards makes it impossible to extend the statistical series consistently through 2005. (5) Unlike the pre-2000 figures, official statistics for 2000–03 also refer to 'above-scale' enterprises only (see explanation in Table 8.3) and hence are not used here. (6) For 2004, the figures (from the 2004 National Economic Census) cover both above and below-scale enterprises, however. To make them comparable to the pre-1999 series, SOEs (*kongu* included) are lumped together with solely state-funded corporations with limited liability, and collective enterprises with all other (domestic) joint ventures (including cooperatives, joint ownership enterprises and shareholding and other corporations with limited liability). Note also that 'individual enterprises' now include not only solely *geti* (individually)-funded businesses, but also partnership enterprises, private corporations with limited liability (now by far the largest grouping) and private shareholding corporations.

Sources: *TJNJ 2000*, Table 13.3 (1978–99); *1998*, Table 13.3 (1997); and *2006*, p. 505 (2004).

More interestingly perhaps, throughout the Dengist transition, up to the mid-or-late 1990s, the non-state-owned enterprises were basically organized by and subordinated to the different vertical layers of administrative jurisdiction (*cun* or sub-village unit, village, township, *xian* or county, and the province), essentially for the purpose of meeting local or regional demands. This is indeed quite similar to the organizational pattern under Mao. Although from the mid-1980s onwards rural–urban or regional cooperative joint ventures had also begun to emerge between private-individual and collective undertakings, it was, however, not until as late as the year 2000 that all enterprises, state-owned or otherwise, were recategorized according to forms of business registration, distinguishing therefore only between sole proprietorship, business partnership, private/collective/state-owned business entities with limited liability, shareholding corporations and the like (see Note 6 to Table 8.6), similar to the Western pattern of business organization.

Thus, with the overall economic context being increasingly marketized in China, private and collective entrepreneurship has strongly unfolded to break both horizontal (regional) barriers and vertical-line control under the Maoist rule to finally turn the country into a unified market. Needless to say, the process of market integration has also been strongly enhanced by accelerated decontrol of the SOEs from the central industrial ministries and the respective regional authorities, amidst the market-oriented reforms (Chai, 1997a, ch 3 and 4).

The Open-door Policy

The most drastic policy change made under Deng of course is the open-door strategy launched in 1979. This embraces the readiness both to drastically expand external trade volume and to rigorously court foreign direct investment (FDI) in China. The new venture is indeed very often considered complete anathema to the Maoist approach of autarky ('self-reliance' and self-sufficiency). However, here again, the pragmatic traces of the Maoist past are still very much in evidence.

First of all, the 'opening up' resembles in a way the dramatic reorientation made in 1962 to China's external trade from the former Soviet Union to Japan and Western Europe, following the abrupt withdrawal by Khrushchev of economic and technical aid to the country. In the same vein, no sooner was the bloody Zhenbao Island (in the Amur River bordering China and Russia) conflict (1969) ended than Mao himself initiated the rapprochement with the United States (the 'ping-pong' diplomacy of 1972). The overtures not only immediately brought China into the United Nations but also triggered the first batch ever of American technology transfer to the country (1974) as embodied in the 14 Kellogg chemical fertilizer plants. What followed is familiar: the formal normalization of Sino-American relations in 1978, which may indeed be seen as the most critical cornerstone for the launching of the open-door policy in the following year.

Secondly, there is no doubt that, for both Mao and Deng, foreign trade carries the single most important mission of importing Western technology to support the massive industrialization drive. As a matter of fact, throughout the Maoist years, the country's imports were overwhelmingly (to the tune of 70 to 80 per cent) dominated by machinery and equipment, transport vehicles, and iron and steel products which could not be produced domestically. The practice had consistently penetrated the late Deng era and, indeed, with political restrictions on Western exports being increasingly lifted since the late 1970s, foreign exchange earnings have virtually become the only major constraints on technology transfer from the West. This also explains the fact that foreign exchange control was strictly imposed under Mao, and it was not until shortly before Deng's death in 1997 that, with accelerated accumulation of foreign exchange reserves, the current account began to be gradually relaxed, while there has not as yet been any sign of an imminent abolishment of the capital account control.

Thirdly, while the most remarkable effort made under Deng for courting FDI might appear truly to be a breakaway from the Maoist doctrine, it is nonetheless conspicuous that, since 1979, 'import-substitution' FDI (especially in major capital-intensive heavy industries) has been strictly restricted in favour of 'export-oriented' FDI (labour-intensive light industries in particular), which helps to generate foreign exchange earnings for technology imports to support the independent forced-draft industrialization campaign along the Maoist lines (cf. Kueh, 2002b). It is in fact not until China's entry into the World Trade Organization in 2001 that, in compliance with the global rules for liberalizing trade and investment, the highly protected import-substitution industrial system began to be earnestly opened up as well for foreign investment. It is of course a separate matter whether an earlier direct foreign technological involvement in this closed industrial sector would have proved to be even more beneficial to the long-term interests of the country. But, obviously, Deng shared Mao's philosophy and long-run aspiration for building an 'independent and comprehensive (integrated) modern industrial system' for the country, comprising both heavy and light industries.

A word or two should perhaps be said about the boldest Cultural Revolution rhetoric on 'self-reliance' as a strategy for promoting technological innovations and breakthrough. Again, this is often seen in the West to be a specific Maoist ideological predilection completely detached from the harsh reality that China lagged far behind the highly industrialized countries in technological advances, and that, barring accelerated technological borrowing from the West, the prospect would remain absolutely remote for the country to close or narrow the enormous technological gap with the advanced Western counterparts. Nevertheless, behind the Maoist revolutionary rhetoric and facade was concealed the hard fact of the prolonged Cold War that pre-empted any significant technology transfer under the US-led embargo that simply left Mao with no tenable alternatives but to resort to his draconian and at times abortive approach of 'self-reliance'. By contrast, Deng was indeed blessed with a much less hostile global political milieu in this respect.

LONG-TERM BEARINGS ON THE 'THREE IMBALANCES'

The market-based system is now firmly in place in China, and the country closely integrated with the global economy. Any policy readjustments made for correcting the national pro-industry bias and regional industrial imbalances are bound to be marginal in magnitude, and are certainly not as effective as under the Mao era.

The familiar Maoist or Stalinist-style industry–agriculture dichotomy (that is, forced-draft industrialization financed by forced savings institutionalized by agricultural collectivization at the expense of rural investment and peasant income and consumption), has now completely yielded to the market-oriented reforms. Despite earnest efforts made by the government to mitigate the established scissors-price differentials through renewed increases in farm procurement prices over the past two decades or so, the terms of trade have indeed continued to prevail against the agricultural sector and the peasants. Accelerated industrial expansion and technological progress, as exacerbated by the continuous influx of FDI into various manufacturing branches, have now effectively turned the industry–agriculture relations in China into a pattern similar to the global North–South disparity against many developing agriculture-based and raw materials producer countries.

To be sure, the non-Maoist mobilization approach under Deng has greatly helped to divert tens of millions of surplus rural labour into a wide range of labour-intensive non-farm employment. However, with new entrants being constantly added to the good earth, agricultural productivity and peasant income are bound to fall behind that of the flourishing industries and urban residents; hence the extended *sannong* policy initiatives launched since 2004 (see Chapter 7).

Briefly, the celebrated government effort (all promulgated, as a rule, in 'Document No. 1' of the Party Central Committee in January each year to underscore the national priority accorded to), comprises a series of policy measures for redressing the ever widening industry–agriculture divide. For 2004, it aims essentially at raising the income of *nongmin* (the peasants). In

2005, relative emphasis shifts to boosting the 'all round-capability' of *nongye* (agriculture). This is followed, in 2006, by the vision of establishing a 'new socialist *nungcun*' (countryside), and, in 2007, of moving Chinese agriculture towards a 'modernized system'.[4]

Thus, from 2004 onwards, cumbersome local levies began to be eliminated, and by 2006 the agriculture tax (intact for more than two thousand years) was abolished altogether. Direct farm subsidies of various types are provided for current inputs and purchases of farm machinery and equipment. Public services (medical and health care, and education and cultural) are to be enhanced, and public utilities (electricity, roads and drinking water supply) expanded in the countryside for aligning, hopefully before too long, with the prevailing urban standards.

The policy measures all fall under the rubric of 'give more, take less, and enliven (the rural setting)' (*duoyu, shaoshou, fanghuo*), culminated in the 2007 master plan for creating a 'modern agriculture' complete with advanced irrigation system, mechanized operation and information technology. The plan also envisages the emergence of big farm businesses, diversified industrial processing, new types of logistics and market conglomeration, and eventually a new outlook of the peasantry as well.

Clearly, the new *sannong* policy implies substantial fiscal transfer under the pronounced strategic reorientation for 'industry and the urban centres to reciprocate the past contributions of agriculture and the rural areas'. As spelled out in Document No. 1 of 2007, total yearly support–*sannong* allocation from the state budget should henceforth grow faster than total recurrent budget revenue. This is not the place for making a quantitative assessment of the possible scale of industry-to-agriculture fiscal transfer and its potential impact.[5] However, the bulk of funds seems to be earmarked for 'public investments', resembling in a way the past Maoist approach, save that the sources were then all accumulated from the rural base.

The present Chinese strategy for rural development and poverty alleviation has drawn global acclaim. Jeffrey Sachs, for example, sees it as much more practical and effective, compared to the World Bank's approach in Africa. The latter, being dominated by 'extreme free-market ideology', has failed to see 'public investments – in agriculture, health, education and infrastructure as necessary complements to private investments', 'wrongly seen such vital public investments as an enemy of private-sector development', and thus 'pushed for privatization of national health systems, water utilities and roads and power networks', and blamed government corruption, mismanagement and lack of initiatives for the failure (www.project-syndicate.org, 26 May 2007).

Nonetheless, the prospect still remains remote for the Chinese countryside to get rid completely of the mounting population pressures. And, given the imperatives to engage the masses continuously in primitive labour-intensive undertakings in industry and the tertiary sector, the phenomenon of 'technological dualism' will persist long into the future.

In the Maoist past, the state strongly relied on forced fiscal transfer for investment in the interior provinces to correct the stark regional industrial disparities. This was facilitated by compulsory profits delivery from the coastal SOEs, which used to make up around 90 per cent of total state revenue. Since the mid-1980s, however, such forced siphoning was gradually converted into a Western-type tax-linked system under the 'tax-for-profit' revenue reform. Initially, for many SOEs, the 'after-tax' profits were still subject to 'regulatory income taxes' imposed for balancing major inter-branch inequality in profitability caused by pervasive price distortions (Kueh, 1990a, p. 263), but now, being effectively deprived of such highly confiscatory levies, the government's redistributive fiscal manoeuvrability is clearly strictly circumscribed.

Thus the highly publicized 'Go West' campaign has essentially become a matter of state investment in crucial overhead structure, the transportation network in particular. Plant investments are, however, left to individual market-based corporate entities, including foreign joint ventures. In the circumstances, capital flows from the coastal to the interior regions are bound to be constrained, with or without the provisions of tax incentives and other types of investment stimulants. Both domestic and foreign-funded enterprises will likely still favour the conglomeration economies offered in the coastal belt.

The more recent government initiatives taken by the new Chinese leadership for boosting investment and economic development in the middle parts (*zhongbu*) of the country will also face similar, though perhaps less stringent, constraints (by virtue of geographical proximity to the advanced industrial cosmopolitans to the east). Besides, with Vietnam now rapidly opening up as well, its extended coastal belt, coupled with an enormous cheap labour supply, certainly looks no less attractive to foreign investors than the remote Chinese interior regions.

No Chinese government would also find it easy to weigh the relative urgency of promoting the industrial development of the north-west and south-west against the potential benefits of concentrating investment in the already-advanced coastal region, where there are potential scale economies to exploit. Thus the gradual infiltration or migration, as envisaged in the Seventh Five-Year Plan, for example, of coastal industries to the interior seems more a conceptual scheme than a truly operational programme. One way or another, China's vast hinterland will continue to play a part in the Chinese leadership's long-term economic strategy for national development.

CONCLUSION

Chinese industry has been consistently projected to grow considerably faster than agriculture. The widening disparity will continue to call for the necessary state budget reallocations to the countryside for public or collective investments. This should help to promote agricultural productivity and modernization and mitigate (hopefully) the scale of industry–agriculture dichotomy.

Likewise, continual concentration of industrial investments and inflows of foreign capital and technology in the coastal areas will help to perpetuate interregional imbalance. Barring any accelerated and sustainable industrial growth on the basis of its own factor endowment, the interior will almost certainly continue to fall well behind the coastal region for many years to come – this notwithstanding any possible corrective fiscal transfer to be effectuated by the central government.

The Chinese search for advanced technology is insatiable, yet the government continues to be confronted with overwhelming imperatives for accommodating the mounting surplus labour. The glaring bifurcation of the country into 'two industrial systems' (a modern, highly capital-intensive core surrounded by primitive, extremely labour-intensive undertakings) is bound to persist into the distant future.

In short, the three fundamental imbalances as observed will continue to exercise the minds of China's policy makers for many years to come.

NOTES

*   An extensively revised, extended and updated version (with complete new statistics) from Y.Y. Kueh, 'The Maoist legacy and China's new industrialization strategy', *The China Quarterly*, **119** (September 1989), 420–47; copyright School of Oriental and African Studies, published by Cambridge University Press.
1.   There is a host of Western literature available on this subject, with differing viewpoints and judgments. The earlier ones include Wheelwright and McFarlane (1970). Lardy (1975), for example, differs substantially from Donnithorne (1972) concerning the degrees of centralized control and regional self-sufficiency and autarky. Cf. also Lyons (1987).
2.   Compare notes to Table 8.2 and Figure 8.1 for definitions of the regions. According to Ma (1983, p. 131), Anhui should be added to the coastal region as defined in Table 8.2.
3.   Cf. Howe, Kueh and Ash (2003), pp. 150–54. It also appears that the accelerated increases in heavy industry's GVIO share towards the mid-2000s are partly contributed by the booming housing construction industry.
4.   See http://news.aweb.com.cn/2007/1/30/9031289.htm for Document No. 1 of 2007. For 2004–06, the documents are also easily accessible on a Google search.
5.   See http://www.China.com.cn, 1 March 2006 for some illustrative statistics given by Chen Xiwen, a senior officer from the Ministry of Agriculture to the Standing Committee of the National People's Congress.

9. Growth imperatives, economic efficiency and 'optimum decentralization'*

THE SEARCH FOR AN 'OPTIMUM' SOLUTION'

All the policy signs emanating from China following the crushing of the Tiananmen Square protests of mid-June 1989 point clearly to a 'backlash' to the ten-year-old programme of economic reforms. There is little doubt that the new policy measures are more than a matter of how to enhance the 'fight inflation' campaign launched in September 1988. The perceived need for re-strengthening economic controls is most clearly spelled out by none other than Yao Yilin, the veteran central planner, who until December 1989 was chairman of the powerful State Planning Commission. Shortly prior to his departure, Yao granted a prominent Chinese-American journalist a rare interview in which he stressed the need for renewed centralized financial and allocative controls over the economy (*DGB*, 23 December 1989).

At the same time, the Chinese leadership has, however, also repeatedly stated that enterprise reforms will continue to be 'intensified' (*shenhua*) by way of the continuing campaign of economic retrenchment (Zhang Yanning, 1990; Li, 1990). This 'intensification' can literally only be taken to imply continued decentralization or some mild modification of the existing reform measures as the means to solve the persistent problems of ailing enterprise performance. While the term may appear to be semantically confusing, the message should be clear enough for students conversant with the perennial search by all the Soviet-type economies since the early 1960s for an 'optimum' decentralization.

Specifically, this decentralization should help to improve enterprise efficiency by way of increased profit and consumption incentives, to be coupled with extended enterprise decision-making powers. But any measures adopted should not, in the mind of the Soviet planners, be pushed to such a point as to compromise the overriding Stalinist rationale of maximizing savings and investment – aimed ultimately at accelerating economic growth according to the centralized allocative priorities. These preferences are conventionally accorded to heavy industries, which are seen as the backbone of the forced-draft industrialization drive. And with the predominant share of accumulated investment funds constantly ploughed back into the producer-goods sector, any potential improvements in consumption benefits for the populace tend to be indefinitely deferred to the distant future.

Within the Chinese context, there is yet another complicating dimension in relation to the same dilemma as encountered in the Soviet and Eastern European reforms. That is, with per capita income (and hence saving capabilities) remaining low in China, the Chinese planners seem, in the first place, to be more concerned with how to impose a greater degree of austerity in order to produce the necessary amount of capital accumulation to promote economic growth. By contrast, the relatively well-off Soviet Union and its former Eastern European satellites seemed more preoccupied with the problem of how to cope with declining industrial efficiency.

This is not to say that problems of comparative economic efficiency are not high on the Chinese agenda. In fact, around half of the country's GNP has been generated since the close of the Mao era from the industrial sector, which has seen its capital stock expanded enormously in the past four decades. Any productivity increases that can be achieved through industrial reforms will therefore represent an important source of further economic growth in China and, given the ever-rising capital intensity of the Chinese economy, the opportunity costs of inefficient industrial investments incurred for lack of a breakthrough in reforms and productivity may increasingly become untenable in both economic and political terms.

Thus the new generations of Chinese planners are not only confronted with the basic policy dilemma of how to reconcile, on the one side, the conventional Maoist imperative to maximize economic growth under austerity, with, on the other, the increasingly visible popular aspirations for consumerism. As a result of increased diversification of the industrial structure, they are also confronted with the same problems as the Soviet Union in the 1960s, of how to tackle the much more complicated issues of industrial efficiency through some 'managed' delegations of decision-making powers, hopefully without losing their grip on the desired direction and structure of the national economy.

Any attempt to examine the pattern and relative magnitude of economic decentralization and marketization in China should therefore be set against this particular policy background.[1] Viewed this way, the Chinese economy has remained further from the threshold of a self-regulating market-based system than has been quite commonly believed. Thus it is not appropriate to regard the current 'recentralization' measures as any fundamental reversal of the much celebrated 'market-oriented' reforms of the past decade.

The first half of this chapter highlights the major changes that have occurred since 1979 and examines the relative magnitude of the reform experiments.[2] The second half of the chapter explains how the decentralization drives and the subsequent reversals following the Tiananmen Square crackdown are related to the common policy imperative shared by both Mao and Deng for maximizing economic growth. This is followed by a detailed discussion of the possible implications for long-term productivity and capital accumulation. It is hoped that the interpretations in the concluding section will help to shed some light on the possible impact of the current policy reversal and the future course of China's economic policy.

PACE AND PATTERN OF MARKETIZATION

The process of marketization in China by the mid-1980s did indeed tend toward dismantling the conventional Soviet-style system of centralized planning and control. This markedly distinguished the Chinese approach to economic reforms from the various experiments that had been conducted in the Soviet Union and other East European countries since the 1960s.

In the Soviet Union, for example, in the hey-day of the Kosygin Reform adopted in 1965, 'market regulation', notably the familiar Bolshevichka–Mayak experiment in the clothing industry, was largely confined to the consumer goods sectors. The method of so-called 'direct-contractual ties', as advocated by Liberman, the intellectual architect of the Soviet reform, was to enable user industries, or buyer agencies in the case of consumer goods supply, to seek their own suppliers and thus exert competitive pressures to improve supply efficiency (Chapter 1). However, producer goods supply was still subject to centralized allocation according to the planners' preferences. This effectively prohibited any penetration of consumer preferences into the entire allocative system.

More importantly perhaps, with consumer goods supply continuing to be constrained by input supplies in the early economic reforms in the Soviet Union, the possible improvement in supply efficiency in terms of quality, specifications and delivery was bound to be marginal. In fact, economic reforms in the entire producer goods sector in the Soviet Union and its European satellites were largely confined to measures for refining the Leninist principle of *Khozraschyot* (economic accountability of state industries), without touching upon the integrity of the Stalinist approach of centralized control.

Against this Soviet background, the post-Mao economic reforms in China may really be regarded as a breakthrough. In the first place, the adoption of the so-called 'two-track' planning system has resulted in the state industrial sector being bifurcated into planned and market sectors, allowing the marketization process to penetrate the producer goods sphere. Consequently, shortly prior to the eruption of the Tiananmen Square incident, there were mounting calls from both academics and policy makers for a redefinition of property rights commensurate with the expanded decision making autonomy in state enterprises. In fact, in addition to the officially sanctioned experiment with stock-share systems for state industry, there were also explicit calls for the state to relinquish its ownership control over state property.

Economic reform in the rural areas is of course much more advanced in this respect. 'Reparcellization' of the collective farmland in the early 1980s, coupled with the extension of the leasehold rights to 15 years starting in 1984, brings Chinese agriculture very close to the private land-tenure system of the West. The replacement in 1985 of the Stalinist scheme of compulsory farm delivery with a system of purchase contracts to be signed between the peasants and the state procurement agencies is also meant to further enhance the privatization and marketization process in rural China (Ash, 1988). No less important is the rapid proliferation of rural non-farm industries, which operate largely on a cooperative or de facto private basis, being detached from any hierarchic–vertical controls following the abolition of the People's Communes in 1982–83.

Similar decentralization took place in foreign trade, especially in the export sector, which for the most part is not conducive to centralized control, and in which provision is now given for exporting industries and local authorities to retain part of foreign exchange earned as an incentive. Decontrol in the import sector is understandably much less drastic, because foreign exchange earnings still remain generally subject to centralized allocations to ensure compliance with import priorities.[3] Nevertheless, the foreign exchange retention scheme, though highly limited in scale, also implies some marginal relaxation in import control. Also, under the 'trade agency system' adopted in late 1984, users of imports are allowed direct contact with the world markets through competitive sourcing services rendered by specialist trading agents.[4]

More significant in this respect is, clearly that, in addition to the Special Economic Zones, all coastal provinces are now made available to foreign capital and technology. Guangdong and Fujian (and now Hainan as well) have become largely free in shaping their own external economic relations. Thus, despite Tiananmen Square and subsequent Western sanctions, the Chinese leadership, with Jiang Zemin as the new Party Secretary-General, has repeatedly made clear that the 'open-door' policy would remain intact. It remains to be examined how this open-door policy stance may stand in relation to the observed 'recentralization' trends.

Reference is first made to the much celebrated Resolution of October 1984 which was charted by none other than Zhao Ziyang (who was then the Chinese Premier) in order to put the various reform measures into a proper context. The Resolution not only endorsed the 'creeping' decentralization process in agriculture, trade and some minor industries, but also contemplated the abolition of 'mandatory planning', that is, the very core of Soviet-style central planning, comprising major industries, and heavy industries in particular. Mandatory planning was to be gradually discarded in favour of 'guidance planning' which, in turn, was to be replaced ultimately by a system of 'market regulation'. Practical measures were in fact taken to reduce the numbers and types of essential consumer and producer goods which are subject to mandatory planning and centralized allocation. This tended, of course, to widen the relative manoeuvrability of state enterprises under the two-track system of planning and pricing.

However, while the official notion of the October 1984 Resolution was to establish a '*planned* socialist commodity economy', by 1987–88 the Chinese policy slogan was rephrased as 'the state regulates the market, and the market guides the enterprises'. The aim was obviously to bring more clearly to light the government's *long-term* policy goal of creating some kind of full-fledged market economy, although the radical policy slogan concealed at the same time the fundamental issue of whether state ownership of the large and medium-scale industrial enterprises (the lynchpin of central planning) would eventually be replaced by private ownership, the single most important legal institutional prerequisite for the operation of any market economy.

At any rate, the process of marketization gained momentum after 1985 and has, by the advent of the Tiananmen upheaval, indeed appeared to have increasingly touched upon the integrity of Soviet-style central planning in China. Rampant inflation, coupled with the spread of *guandao* (that is, SOE managers and government officers colluding to divert scarce, centrally allocated materials from planned use to the market sector for profiteering), seemed to have brought the Chinese system of centralized planning and control to the brink of collapse by 1988–89. This had even led some Western observers to believe that China's economy had virtually become a market economy.

SOME MEASURES OF RELATIVE INTENSITY

While there was a strong trend toward dismantling Soviet-style industrial planning, it is difficult to determine exactly the depth and scope of the marketization process in quantitative terms. For students familiar with the Soviet practice of central planning, the most important indicator would be a reduction in the number of the centrally compiled 'material balances' and their commodity coverage. Unfortunately, information on this is scanty.

The material balances are compiled by the State Planning Commission and its provincial counterparts as a basis for the respective State Materials Supply Bureaus to allocate centralized supplies to user industries. The procedure implies clearly that output of state industrial enterprises is in turn subject to centralized distribution. In other words, for all SOEs, both the physical input and output plan targets are determined by the superior authority, together with the necessary finance.

Prior to the reform launched in 1979, around 80 per cent of the national gross value of industrial output (GVIO), which originated overwhelmingly from the large and medium-scale enterprises, was integrated into the central planning system. This included, of course, both producer and consumer goods, as well as output earmarked for export. Non-industrial consumption necessities, notably grain, cotton, pork and edible oils, were also subject to balancing (hence compulsory deliveries from the peasantry) and urban rationing one way or the other. Consistently, prices had to be officially fixed to ensure financial compliance with the planned physical transactions. However, it is by no means easy to measure to what extent this system of centralized control has disintegrated amidst the marketization process, especially given increased adoption of the double-track system in planning, investment and pricing.

Take, for example, one or two of the familiar statistics as shown in Table 9.1. It is not at all clear whether the nomenclature of producer goods (subject to unified distribution by the State Materials Supply Bureau), which showed a decline by broad category from 256 commodities in 1983 to 26 in 1986–87, includes materials which fall under double-track planning. The same question probably also applies to product categories subject to mandatory planning, which were reduced from 123 in 1983–84 to around 20 in 1988, although it is not at all clear how the two categories of 'unified distribution' and 'mandatory planning' in Table 9.1 are related to each other.

Judging, however, by the fact that for such product categories as steel, coal, cement, and timber only parts of the output are subject to unified distribution (see Table 9.1), it seems obvious that the double-track system also applies to the broad categories of output referred to above. If correct, the decontrols in favour of market regulation must be more extensive than is suggested by the reduction in the number of the aggregate output categories.[5]

At the same time, though, the 'deregulated' output proportions (to be taken as the balance of the percentage shares subject to mandatory planning or 'unified distribution'), as shown in Table 9.1, declined comparatively less than the reduction in the number of broad categories of commodities. In fact, the output shares of steel, coal and timber industries under unified distribution declined from 1983–84 to 1987 to a much more limited extent, compared with the reduction in terms of aggregate product

*Table 9.1   Major indicators of economic decentralization and
marketization in China, 1978–88*

	Prior to 1980	1983/84	1985	1986	1987	1988
Output subject to mandatory planning by State Planning Commission						
No. of categories		123	60		20	
Shares in gross output value (%)		40	20		17	12
Producer goods subject to 'unified distribution'						
No. of categories	259	256	23	26	26	
Shares by major products (%)						
steel	74.3	62.3	56.9		47.1	
timber	80.9	44.3	30.7		27.6	
cement	35.0	24.1	9.4		15.6	
coal	57.9	49.0	50.0		47.2	

Source: Kueh (1990b), p. 101; Howe, Kueh and Ash (2003), p. 112.

categories. This implies that key inputs are still quite substantially subject to centralized control.

Moreover, products outside of 'mandatory planning', or for that matter 'unified distribution', include those which fall under the category of so-called 'guidance planning'. According to the October 1984 Resolution, this is meant to be a transitional arrangement in the long-term shift from 'mandatory planning' to full-fledged 'market regulation'. It is difficult to visualize how such a mixed system may work, but it is interesting to note that, at one time, television sets were placed in the category of 'guidance planning' so as to encourage output in order to satisfy popular demand, while TV tubes, the single most important component, fell under 'mandatory planning', like other similar electronic products of national defence importance (Kueh, 1989b, p. 390).

It is also unclear how the category of products subject to centralized 'branch-ministerial balancing and distribution' (*buguan wuzi*) stands in relation to the entire deregulation process of outputs subject to 'unified distribution' (*tongpei wuzi*). This concerns such products as copper, nickel and aluminium, which presumably are 'branch-specific' in terms of output and input demand. It seems doubtful, however, that all such products are really of such 'limited use' that they can be totally deregulated without causing any problems in balancing supply against demand. In other words,

Table 9.2   Major indicators of price deregulation in China, 1979–88

	Year	At		
		'State price'	'Guidance price'	'Free market price'
Shares in total transactions by value (%)				
Farm and subsidiary products,	1988	35		65
Industrial consumables,	1988	45		55
Industrial production materials,	1988	55		45
Peasants' sales of farm products,	1979	92	2	6
	1986	37	23	40
Total 'social commodity' sales,	1979	97	0.5	2.5
	1985	47	19	34
	1988	29	22	49

Note: The last item is defined in official Chinese statistics as retail sales of all consumer goods plus producer goods to the rural sector.

Source: Kueh (1990b), p. 104; Chai (1997a), p. 113.

a considerable part of this category of output is probably still under ministerial control.[6]

Perhaps more importantly, the process of deregulation as depicted in the figures given in Table 9.1 is very much a matter of decree by the central planning authority. The provincial authorities normally have their own mandatory planning system. Besides, it is not unusual for the provincial authorities to acquire needed materials *en bloc* from other provinces for centralized reallocation at highly subsidized prices to user industries under their jurisdiction (Zhao, 1986, pp. 12–13; Zhao, 1989). This of course resembles the Khrushchevian approach of 'administrative decentralization' (1957), rather than a genuine relegation of decision-making powers to the state enterprises per se.

Even more revealing is the extent of concomitant price liberalization (see Table 9.2). It is much more limited in relation to the volume of deregulated material supplies (Table 9.1). Moreover, apart from the ambiguous category of 'guidance prices', free market prices also include 'negotiated prices' and 'floating prices', which are subject to officially fixed ceilings. However, deregulation in the centralized physical allocation system has certainly facilitated the efforts of state industries to escape from state price controls. Under the pressures of chronic supply shortages, the immediate upshot was rampant inflation, as seen in 1985 and since 1987–88, in particular.[7]

Turning to the rural sector, where the degree of marketization is higher than anywhere else, state farm procurements at officially fixed prices still accounted for 35 per cent of total transactions of farm and subsidiary products in 1988 (Table 9.2). If turnover at 'guidance prices' is excluded, truly free market prices probably cover no more than 40 per cent of the transactions by value. In fact, the state procurement agencies' purchase contracts with peasants are normally tied to 'preferential' supplies of key inputs such as chemical fertilizers, pesticides, diesel oil and so on, to ensure compliance on the part of the peasants (Kueh, 1990a; Sicular, 1993). Thus the situation somewhat resembles the system of input and output target controls in state industries. It is often difficult to distinguish clearly the practical differences between the new contractual purchase system and the former system of forced Soviet-style quota deliveries.

The foreign trade sector is similarly constrained. Pervasive foreign exchange controls aside, attempts have been made time and again by central authorities to stave off or mitigate price and market competition among exporters (for fear of impairing foreign exchange earnings), despite the adoption of the 'trade agency system' since 1985. Likewise, despite the strong urge for Western capital and technology, Sino-foreign ventures have been largely kept out of the centralized materials balance and supply system for fear of their causing planning instability. This is also clearly reflected in the grand 'international circular flow' strategy advocated by Zhao Ziyang himself in 1988, whereby foreign investors should turn to the world markets for *both* their outputs *and* supplies of raw materials, in pursuit of hard currency earnings to support the country's carefully guarded programme for industrialization and economic independence.

CONSTRAINTS ON FULL LIBERALIZATION

At any rate, despite all the economic metamorphoses, the scope and intensity of the marketization drive (or for that matter the move towards capitalism) in China in the past decade were certainly much less dramatic than some uncritical Western observers tended to suggest. There is no doubt that a lot had altered, especially against the background of the Cultural Revolution period. But the fact remains that the core of the Soviet-style central planning and bureaucratic control of state industries was still far from dismantled. With substantial shares of key industrial inputs still subject to centralized allocation at both the national and the provincial levels, controls permeate the interindustrial linkages into other sectors. Agriculture, for example, is brought directly into this network of control because there remains an enormous need to extract sufficient farm surplus to support the massive industrialization drive.

Western observers may like to see, in the mounting inflationary pressures and the outrageous practice of *guandao*, the system of centralized control being blown apart by enormous market forces. What is nearer the truth, rather, is the fact that, precisely because the quantity of goods available for sales and purchases at the market is still severely limited by the centralized system of bureaucratic–physical allocation to the priority sectors, open inflation and *guandao* only helped to bring into sharper focus the persistent phenomenon of supply shortages, which is built into all Soviet-style economies. What is new, compared with the Maoist past, is that the two-track system made such explicit expression via market signals possible. But Tiananmen notwithstanding, it is doubtful that in the foreseeable future the predominating planned sector would completely yield to pressures from the market sector, so that more goods could be made available to match the enormous pent-up demand left over from years of overinvestment, depressed consumption and price controls.

Western traders and investors in China are certainly aware that the situation there is still very different from that in Hong Kong and Taiwan, both dominated by the same Chinese culture and tradition. But it can be difficult for anyone trading with China, but not familiar with the economics of Soviet planning, to trace the sources of their frustrations with bureaucratism, favouritism, corruption or, more specifically, highly discriminatory tax and quasi-tax treatments, and supply and cost uncertainties. For the most part, these difficulties are again rooted in the highly cumbersome and inefficient system of centralized material supplies, rather than in, say, Chinese feudalism or some cultural mysticism, which, interestingly enough, many Chinese themselves (Marxist or otherwise), frequently refer to as apologetics.

Students conversant with Soviet economics know, nevertheless, that the cumbersome bureaucratic supply system has been, for both the Chinese and the Soviet planners, the necessary evil, indispensable for centralized allocation. The situation is more seriously complicated by the arbitrary character of official price setting. Fixed prices are necessary for making the planned physical transactions financially accountable. But, once fixed, they cannot be frequently adjusted to account for constantly changing supply and demand conditions. The outcome is pervasive cost–price irrationalities, and economically indefensible interindustrial discrepancies in profitability, which in turn makes it difficult to construct an equitable taxation programme.

For foreign investors concerned, any standard tax rates should therefore imply sufficient room for negotiating with the Chinese authorities for discretionary reductions and exemptions for any proposed joint investment projects. Foreigners trading with China have of course long encountered similar predicaments. Viewed against this background it is doubtful that, under the current Chinese leadership, the situation will really ever become worse for potential Western investors. Rather, under the established FDI policy, readjustments and concessions will probably continue to be made from time to time, as has been the case in the past decade, for improving investors' incentives. And, especially if the open-door policy is to be understood in terms of Zhao's 1988 grand strategy of converting the entire coastal belt into an export processing zone, then there is no reason why China's door will ever be closed again for strictly economic reasons. It seems nonetheless unrealistic to suggest at the same time that in the foreseeable future the well-established planning core would eventually yield to the dictates of world market rules, so as to fully integrate the Chinese economy with the free trade system of the West.

It is difficult exactly to characterize the present Chinese economic system as a whole. Some Western scholars, notably Professor Robert Dernberger, see it as a 'mixed economy' (Dernberger, 1989, p. 21), but it is probably one which is skewed more towards the planned rather than market sectors. And as the prominent Princeton economist Professor Gregory Chow aptly put it in October 1988, 'short of very drastic and unexpected political changes, this system is unlikely to be greatly changed in the next decade' (Chow, 1989).

REFORMS AS AN ECONOMIC GROWTH POLICY

Our foregoing discussions clearly point to the case of a *controlled* decentralization in China within the conventional Soviet-style system of central planning and control. The policy approach fits in well with our conceptual framework (given in the introductory section), for interpreting the various reform measures as a series of searches for some kind of an 'optimum' decentralization. Specifically, the decentralization, or for that matter partial marketization, should help to improve producers' efficiency as a source of further economic growth, but the process should not be allowed to distort the economic priorities of the planning authorities. Most of the reform measures adopted in China since 1979 can be understood in this light, including the ambitious long-term reform programmes as envisaged in the October 1984 Resolution.

Thus, in the perceived replacement of 'mandatory planning' with the system of 'market regulation' at some future stage, the role of the state in controlling the direction and pattern of economic growth is still very much in evidence, according to the 1984 Resolution. The state would presumably still make use of such economic policy levers as taxes, bank loans, interest rates, prices and the allocation of foreign exchange, to forcefully make the behaviour of state enterprises comply with the centralized scheme of allocative preferences. How this could possibly be achieved is anybody's guess.[8] What seems certain is that the Chinese leaders, including probably Zhao Ziyang himself, were not envisioning, say, the dictum of consumers' sovereignty eventually to substitute for the well-established policy goal of maximizing industrial growth under austerity.

The points made here about the tactical policy considerations underlying the observed decentralization and marketization drive should be spelled out in more definitive terms, before we turn to examine their possible implications for long-term economic growth in China.

Take the entire process of agricultural decollectivization, for example. The fact that basic farm procurements continue to be monopsonized by state agencies (albeit in a lesser way compared to the Maoist past) only helps to highlight the important practical consideration that, with the added incentives provided to the peasants in the form of higher farm prices and greater disposal over incomes on the basis of household farming, a greater amount of agricultural surplus may be generated to support centralized investment in the preferential industrial sectors.

Similar policy objectives have commanded economic reforms in the urban industrial sectors as well. This started with the restoration of the enterprise funds in 1979 for bonus awards and innovative investments. The related partial profit retention scheme and the 'profit contracting' methods adopted after the October 1984 Resolution are all efficiency-oriented incentive measures, yet, amidst all the concessions made, the output and input targets of major state enterprises have continued to be centrally imposed upon them.

Likewise, the bifurcation of state industries into the planned and market sectors can be seen as a tactical arrangement aimed at encouraging state enterprises to exert extra efforts to increase output by tapping disguised resources that otherwise would have remained untapped under centralized planning and control. An even more radical measure along these lines was the experiment for selected small-scale state enterprises to be totally detached from the planning system and 'leased' out to private individuals or collective teams for management on a 'tax-linked' basis.

This also applies to the hundreds of thousands of urban and rural collective industrial enterprises which have been largely unleashed from any vertical lines of administrative control and encouraged to make use of any local resources for increasing output that they can market on their own account on a profit-and-loss basis. It should be noted, nevertheless, that all these small enterprises are very much overshadowed by the large and medium-scale state industrial enterprises which form the core of central planning in China.

The entire open-door policy fits neatly into the same overall economic strategy. Zhao's 1988 strategy of making available the whole of China's seaboard for tapping foreign resources and technology is a clear case in point. So is the fact that, amidst the export decentralization drive, the bulk of foreign exchange earnings has continued to be subject to centralized allocation all along, to ensure compliance with strategic import plans of the central, or for that matter, provincial authorities.

The most fundamental question involved here is clearly whether, given the value imperatives for maximizing industrial growth in the Stalinist mode of preferential growth for heavy industries, it would be possible for the concerted package of income and consumption incentives truly to result in higher output efficiency *and* thus greater savings capabilities to help accelerate the pace of economic growth. To reinforce this point, a few words should first be said about why the Chinese economic strategy is still seen as highly growth-oriented.

Generally speaking, heavy industrial output in the past decade or so has actually never been scaled down significantly in favour of agriculture and light industry for purposes of increasing consumers' goods supply. Specifically, after the initial retrenchment made in the late 1970s, its output rapidly gained momentum in the early 1980s, surpassing the growth rate of agricultural output by 1984, and widening the gap between the two sectors in very much the same way as the intersectoral patterns of growth observed for the 1950s. Against light industry, its output share rapidly stabilized at around 52 per cent of the national industrial output totals from the early 1980s through to the late 1980s. This adjusted share is only marginally lower than the share of 57 per cent in 1978 (Kueh, 1989a, pp. 439–41).

Likewise, expenditure on capital construction for heavy industry as against light industry and agriculture dropped by less than 10 percentage points from 49 per cent of the national total in 1978 to 40 per cent in 1980, but it quickly recovered ground to reach a share of 45 per cent in 1988 (*TJNJ 1989*, p. 487). In other words, the established priorities accorded to heavy industry remain very much intact, leaving only marginal room for incentive-oriented improvement in the supply of consumer goods.

Reference may be made again to the analytical scheme developed by Professors Chiang and Fei in the mid-1960s, to explain the possible rationale for the observed policy reorientation of the decentralization drive (Chapter 1). Note, in the first place, that the Chinese capital accumulation ratio has been consistently scaled down from the high of 37 per cent in 1978 to around 30 per cent, at least until 1983–84 (*TJNJ 1989*, p. 36), to allow for the consumption share to increase accordingly. Nevertheless, this is still an exceedingly high accumulation ratio by the standards of any developing market-type country with a per capita income comparable to that of China. This implies, of course, continued wage and consumption controls, although the degree of austerity may be less severe than in the Maoist past.

Viewed this way, what distinguishes Deng from Mao is really not so much a matter of any sharp departure from the model of 'maximum-speed development through austerity', but the specific Dengist 'round-about' strategy of maximizing heavy-industrial growth, in line with the particular Chiang–Fei postulate that an 'optimum' (or 'less harsh') rather than minimum (bare-subsistence) consumption standard (that Mao rigorously attempted to impose) may eventually help to raise rather than depress capital accumulation. Specifically, a 'less harsh' consumption policy for correcting the Maoist excesses may be more conducive to enhancing labour input. As a result, total output may grow 'overproportionately' to the required increase in consumption expenditure. And capital accumulation may therefore increase (in absolute terms, and eventually even relative to GDP), to help further enhance long-term economic growth.

THE VALUE IMPERATIVES OF GROWTH VERSUS EFFICIENCY

The main problem with the Chiang–Fei model lies perhaps not so much with the key behavioural assumption that productivity will increase in response to any improved consumption environment, although, as we shall discuss shortly, a distinction between agriculture and industry may have to be made in this respect. Rather, within the present Chinese context, the more important question is whether the anticipated increases in output can be effectively converted into savings (instead of being consumed), so that the desired rate of increase in capital accumulation can be maintained. A few points may be made.

First of all, turning to the assumption about potential productivity gains, it should be noted that the strategic reorientation from 'maximum' to 'optimum' austerity tended to be precisely coupled with the process of marketization. From the planners' perspective, the best way to satisfy increased consumer demand is obviously to generate supplies through exploitation of resources *external* to those already earmarked for the established industrial core. In this respect the rapid proliferation of rural non-farm industries in the post-Mao era can indeed be regarded as a spectacular success.

These small-scale industries helped to accommodate tens of millions of redundant farm labourers released from the more efficient new farming system, and mobilized enormous material resources that otherwise would have remained idle in the rural areas. By doing so, they increased the supply of consumer goods, which helped to absorb the hundreds of millions of *yuan* of excessive rural and urban purchasing power.[9] The liberalization of urban collectives (or for that matter, the small-scale state enterprises), and private industrial and service undertakings also works in the same direction. The margin of disguised resources to be tapped in the urban centres is understandably meagre, compared to the rural areas.

One or two points of qualification need to be made, however, regarding the new-found initiatives for mobilizing idle resources. Rural collective industries had become so lucrative that very often the responsible local authorities were prompted to intercept the necessary raw materials such as cotton and tobacco leaves, which had been originally earmarked to feed the established large-scale urban state industries. This, of course, threatened to disintegrate the centralized planning core (Kueh, 1985a, p. 34).

Moreover, uncontrolled proliferation of rural industries has led to 'blind duplication' of investment projects, totally ignoring problems of diseconomies of scale.[10] It is against this background, together with the overall policy demand for retrenchment (fighting inflation) that tens of thousands of rural factories have lately been wound up, resulting in mounting unemployment pressures.

As regards agriculture proper there is no doubt that the desired productivity effects also materialized at least up to 1985, judging by the vigour with which the Chinese peasants attempted to reap the new price and income benefits offered via the decreed increases in state farm-procurement prices after 1979. This was, however, not just a matter of income incentives per se. Equally important was the new distributive framework provided under the quasi-private farming system, which helped greatly to enhance the personal effort–reward link for Chinese peasants.

Nevertheless, the incentives promoting increased farm output that had resulted from the initial realignments in the terms of trade between agriculture and industry have been rapidly exhausted within the past several years. With farm procurements continuing to be basically monopsonized by state agencies and with the 'price scissors' opening once again, it is difficult to envisage how the much celebrated breakthrough in agricultural productivity of the early 1980s can be sustained. Already burdened by uncertainties pending the solution of the land-tenure problem (limited leasehold rights), peasants have viewed the dwindling price incentives with alarm, giving rise to nothing short of an investment crisis in Chinese agriculture.[11] This is obviously one of the important factors underlying the current campaign to strengthen investments in rural overheads.

Clearly the situation in urban industry is even more complicated, and probably less promising as regards the given objectives of spurring output growth via enhanced material incentives. First, indiscriminate bonus awards have been a widespread practice. Within the complex intra-enterprise structure of large and medium-scale enterprises, it is understandably difficult, as an incentive measure, to define workers' performance criteria for closely linking their awards to work effort. Second, the two-track system enables large and medium-scale enterprises to profiteer by redirecting centrally allocated materials to the high-priced open market. Third, the partial marketization process makes it more difficult to control enterprise performance in the planned sector itself, in terms of product quality, specifications and deliveries to meet the demand of user industries, because there now are increased 'outside-plan' opportunities for raising profitability. Fourth, the highly distorted input and output price relationships tend to render any overall profit criteria inoperative as an enterprise control measure. In an increasingly decentralized context, profitability can be raised with relative ease simply by manipulating the input and output mix.

Thus, unlike the experience with agricultural reforms, it is doubtful that decentralization and a partial marketization process coupled with enhanced income incentives has brought about any real efficiency improvement in Chinese industry, apart from some marginal mobilization of idle capacity and resources. Rather, with supply shortages a chronic phenomenon the predictable outcome clearly has been that state enterprises are resorting to various profiteering 'malpractices' to erode the effectiveness of the centralized planning core, thus defeating the very rationale underlying the search for an 'optimum' decentralization.

Let us turn to the question of whether any extra incentive-induced output can be effectively siphoned off for investment – the other postulate of the Chiang–Fei model. The question appears more relevant to the agricultural sector, not only because the added price and income incentives did result in substantial productivity upsurges (at least up to 1984), but more importantly for the reason that industrial growth and investment in China will continue to depend primarily on the volume of farm surpluses, which can be converted into food for urban workers and especially into exportables to be exchanged for Western machinery and equipment to support the country's industrialization programme.

As we have shown elsewhere, following the agricultural reforms of the early 1980s, grain procurements (*viz.*, extraction of farm surplus) by the state did increase remarkably and in fact more quickly than total grain output (Chapter 4). This was the case also for such essential economic crops as cotton and oil-seed. Nevertheless, not only have grain exports declined steadily since 1978, but at the same time grain imports had to be increased dramatically to match increased demands for higher consumption by the urban populace and by rural residents who are not engaged in grain production (Kueh, 1984b, pp. 1248–52). The high farm procurements resulted in part from pressures exerted by the peasantry for the state to offer higher prices for 'above-quota' and 'non-quota' sales of farm produce. The resultant increases in state budget expenditure inevitably led to further curtailment in investment in the preferential industrial sectors.[12] It also necessitated a diversion of resources to light industries to match increases in rural consumption demands. Obviously the established policy imperative to preserve the integrity of the government's industrialization programme posed a limit to the price and income concessions made to the peasants. This explains why, even under the contractual purchase system, the peasants are bound to yield to the terms imposed by state agencies.

Theoretically speaking, it may be possible for the extra peasant output that was induced by the price incentives to be 'recycled' by, say, an increase in the prices of both consumer and producer goods of industrial origin sold to the peasants. This represents, however, a return to the familiar price scissors. Another alternative is to raise direct agricultural taxes. Both methods would tend to defeat the very aim of the present policy of providing greater material incentives to peasants.

In the absence of any effective policy mechanism for siphoning off the extra incentive-induced farm output, an overall relaxation of controls on peasant consumption seems to be inevitable. This cannot but have adverse consequences for the country's massive policy goal of industrialization, if the Chinese government is to continue to rely mainly on increased capital accumulation as a source of long-term economic growth.

In this respect, the situation *vis-à-vis* urban industries is of course even worse. The added incentive outlays in the form of wage increases, bonuses and subsidies probably largely represent a 'deadweight' loss in terms of anticipated productivity increases, let alone possible marginal gains in capital accumulations *à la* Chiang–Fei model. This is the background for the continued appeals from the central authorities to 'enliven' (*gaohuo*) the large and medium-scale state enterprises, and lately to 'intensify' (*shenhua*) enterprise reforms.

As long as the major state industries are woven into the fabric of centralized planning, it is hard to visualize how 'intensification' of enterprise reform may possibly promote productivity, apart from some refinements of the centrally controlled 'success indicators' (performance criteria), coupled with some bureaucratic measures to stave off 'abuses' of the limited provisions for engaging in market activities. Note that, in contrast to the centralized industrial environment, the initial breakthrough in agricultural productivity was largely a matter of decollectivization. But it was precisely decollectivization which rendered it difficult for the state to siphon off farm surplus effectively, given the exceedingly high income/consumption elasticity of the Chinese peasants.

Thus, barring any productivity breakthrough in urban industries, an escalation of the relative degree of austerity seems inevitable. Already, the overall capital accumulation ratio, after an initial downward adjustment to around 30 per cent of the national income, has swiftly increased and been sustained at a high 35 per cent since 1985. This is only marginally lower than the record of 37 per cent for 1978.[13]

A final word needs to be said, too, about the foreign trade sector. Clearly, apart from agriculture, this has been the most dynamic sector ever since China's door 'opened' in 1979. This is not the place to examine the impressive contribution of foreign capital to the country's capital formation, and the drastic increases in trade volume relative to the size of China's gross national product. The important point here is that the enormous gains were brought about without any significant economic opportunity costs. The major impetus has come from the provision of powerful foreign-exchange retention incentives to export industries and to local authorities for exploiting resources outside of the central planning system. Interestingly, even Gorbachev has recently seen this as a possible panacea – to offer the Soviet peasants hard foreign currencies for enhancing grain deliveries. With some skilful manipulation of the incentive package, there still seems to be plenty of room for the Chinese to promote additional exports.

Nevertheless, the very rationale of the Chiang–Fei model is also clearly at work in this respect, in that the bulk of the foreign-exchange earnings continue, as mentioned before, to be forcibly remitted to the central authorities. And with the current recentralization drive, it can only be expected that such transfers will increasingly be enforced. Already, as a matter of fact, the exporting industries' 'quota entitlements' (as against cash retention) of foreign exchange earnings have become larger than the total foreign-exchange reserves that the central authorities had held in recent years. Hopefully, these remissions to the central government will not eventually impair the decentralized export incentives.

CONCLUSION: RECENTRALIZATION AND WHAT NEXT

There is no doubt that the very pragmatism associated with Dengonomics has brought about a burst of output growth that the romanticist Mao could have never dreamed of, with his desperate revolutionary search for an economic breakthrough. More remarkably, the growth under Deng was accomplished without essentially dispensing with the core of Soviet-style central planning and control. In the words of Professor Gregory Chow, who like many other liberal economists in the West was a great sympathizer of Zhao

Ziyang, 'a balanced, mixed system can achieve respectable economic results, especially when compared with the past' (as cited in Dernberger, 1989, p. 24)

The crux of the problem is, however, to what extent the centralized planning system can really tolerate the centrifugal effects of market forces. In this respect, the current 'recentralization' measures seem to have been prompted more by economic imperatives rather than any political antagonism toward Zhao Ziyang. There might have been factional differences in terms of particular economic policy issues, but it seems unlikely, for example, that Zhao was totally ignorant of the compelling need for a centralized reallocation of fiscal and material resources from the richer coastal provinces to support the planned transformation of the underdeveloped interior region. It was under his reign, after all, that the Seventh Five-Year Plan was drawn up, which envisages an accelerated economic transformation of the vast Northwest and Southwest regions. Judgements among the Chinese leaders might differ as to the relative urgency of such resource transfers, but it seems incredible that Zhao would have preferred to leave the process totally to market forces.

Another closely related issue is how far income and consumption incentives can continue to be offered by the state as a means of spurring productivity growth. Undoubtedly, there was an immense aspiration for consumerism in China, once the appetites of the Chinese peasants and workers were aroused in the past decade. However, in view of the meagre Chinese margin of personal savings, any successive compromises made in this respect will inevitably touch upon the very integrity of the continuing Stalinist policy to maximize savings and investment so as to accelerate industrial growth. This is particularly the case given the difficulties faced in regenerating an upsurge on agricultural output or making any significant breakthrough in productivity-oriented industrial reforms. This explains, in a way, the recent policy appeal for renewed emphasis on austerity and ideology, a return to the virtues of the 1950s, or even to the exacting 'Protestant ethic' of the Cultural Revolution period.

Viewed against this background, the current 'recentralization' measures obviously represent no more than another swing on the familiar Soviet-style pendulum of decentralization and recentralization. The swing back this time may appear to entail particularly painful effects, for, unlike the previous experience in China (and the Soviet Union as well) the pendulum has swung in the past decade well beyond the Khrushchevian type of regional decentralization to allow for partial marketization of the producer goods sector down to the enterprise level. But there is, nevertheless, no reason as yet to suggest that the pendulum will collapse altogether.

Whatever the outcome, probably the single most important lesson Zhao Ziyang, and Jiang Zemin as well, have learnt from their common mentor

Deng Xiaoping, the paramount leader of China, is that the open-door policy represents a vital approach to break the economic impasse, in that it may help to tap world resources and technology, hopefully without injuring the established strategy for a forced-draft industrialization. With the Tiananmen legacy, Jiang of course has the much more arduous task of balancing the possible economic benefits of the open-door policy against the ideologically disastrous 'bourgeois' influence of the West.

NOTES

* Reprinted with adaptations (with new statistics added) from Y.Y. Kueh, 'Growth imperatives, economic recentralization, and China's open-door policy', *The Australian Journal of Chinese Affairs* (now *The China Journal*), **24** (July 1990), 93–119; plus inputs from Y. Y. Kueh and Zhao Renwei, 'Market-oriented transformation of China's economic system as a development strategy', in Dieter Cassel and Günter Heiduk (eds), *China's Contemporary Economic Reforms as a Development Strategy*, Baden-Baden: Nomos Verlagsgesellschaft, 1990, pp. 13–36.

1. The terms 'decentralization' and 'marketization' are used interchangeably, although in general the latter term refers to a more radical approach to decentralization as compared with, say, the Khrushchevian type of 'administrative decentralization', that is, the delegation of economic decision-making power from the central to the regional (*Sovnarchoz* or provincial) authorities.

2. See Kueh (1990a) for a systematic and fuller account of economic reforms in China.

3. By 1988, the amount of foreign exchange earnings at the disposal of the central government was presumably reduced to 40 per cent of the national total (*Renmin ribao*, 17 January 1990). The amount under provincial control was similarly curtailed. If the same degree of central control (40 per cent) applies in the provinces, at most one-third of the national total is available for 'free disposal' (import quotas and licensing apply, however).

4. For details of trade reform as highlighted herein, see Chapters 12 and 13.

5. At any rate, after the October 1984 Resolution, the relative degree of 'marketization' of key producer goods, notably steel products, certainly became more substantial than during the heyday of the 'Economic Readjustment' of the early 1980s. During the 'Readjustment' the highest ever proportion of steel production that enterprises marketed was only 20 per cent, in 1981 (Tang, 1987, p. 232).

6. Note especially that the number of such 'ministerially controlled goods' has been consistently much greater than that of 'nationally allocated goods' (*viz.*, 'unified distribution'). For 1982, for example, the numbers are 581 and 256, respectively (Tang, 1987, p. 229).

7. The background to Chinese inflation in recent years is, of course, more than a matter of increased 'deregulation'. It involved continuous state budget deficits, excessive printing of banknotes, and runaway capital expenditure. For a comprehensive discussion, see Naughton, 1990).

8. In a way, the perceived future Chinese system resembles the postwar French *Planification*, but apart from the major differences in ownership system, the Chinese planners' scale of preferences would probably entail much greater centralization, requiring a greater degree of enterprise coercion compared with the French experience of 'indicative' planning (which foundered eventually under the pressures of market forces).

9. It is obvious that, without the added mobilization of idle resources for producing consumer goods, the enormous pent-up demand resulting from years of overinvestment, and consecutive increases in farm procurement prices and urban wages, would not have been able to find an outlet.

10. The comparative merits of rural industries in terms of scale diseconomies versus transportation economies (as compared with large-scale urban industries) have been a subject of extensive discussions in China and the West (see, for example, Wong, 1982).
11. The 'investment crisis' is characterized as a reluctance on the part of the central authorities to appropriate funds for rural infrastructure investment, and peasants' strong inclination towards short-run maximizing activities, rather than such long-term undertakings as irrigation and flood-control projects. See Watson (1989) for a good discussion of the problems. It is not clear, however, exactly to what extent, for example, the irrigated area in China has declined in the post-Mao era as a result of the 'investment crisis' (Stone, 1993).
12. Strictly speaking, increased state-farm procurement prices resulted in reduced budget revenue, rather than higher budget expenditure on farm purchases. This is because, with the price of grain sold to urban residents remaining largely unchanged, state-farm procurement agencies incurred losses and hence had less or nothing at all to remit to the state budget.
13. *TJNJ 1989*, p. 36. The national aggregate for 1985 includes of course 'voluntary' accumulations by the peasantry for largely short-run maximizing investment, but the relative magnitude is bound to be limited, compared to centralized investments in state industries.

10. Bureaucratization, property rights and economic reforms*

BACKGROUND: THE NECESSARY EVIL

Central planning as transplanted in China from the Soviet Union must in the first place be seen as a vehicle for implementing the Stalinist strategy for accelerating industrialization. In a nutshell, the strategy focuses on the preferential development of heavy industry. It clearly implies exhaustive resources concentration, centralized allocation, persistent income and consumption squeezes, forced savings, and pervasive official price fixing. These all call for the establishment of a huge, coercive bureaucratic apparatus to facilitate control and arbitration.

The entire bureaucratic mechanism also forcefully renders, *ipso facto*, any system of private property rights inoperative. Thus, nationalization of industry and commerce, as well the banking and financial sectors, followed in tandem the inception of central planning in 1953. Agriculture was then also swiftly collectivized, and compulsory farm delivery quotas imposed, in order to bring the sector (together with the entire Chinese peasantry) into the orbit of centralized allocation and bureaucratic control.

If anything, the degree of bureaucratization in China should be much greater than anywhere else in the Soviet bloc, given the sheer size of the country in terms of both population and geographical coverage. Enormous 'transaction costs' are clearly involved to help hold the entire fabric together. These include not only direct outlay as salary for the bureaucrats and on necessary physical administrative overheads, but also wastes associated with bureaucratic inertia and abuse, operational inefficiency, disincentives and misallocation in economic terms. Taken together, however, the entire bureaucratic set-up undoubtedly represents a necessary evil.

Compared to the familiar Western-type government administration, the bureaucratic system in China (or in any other Soviet-type economies) is not only vast and pervasive, but it targets overwhelmingly economic activities, penetrating virtually all spheres and layers of production and distribution. Even more conspicuously, as a substitute for the market-price mechanism, its basic mode of operation is highly characterized by direct physical input and output target control, and a system of highly centralized system of materials allocation based on the supply and demand (material) balances compiled by the planners.

Whether or not central planning via 'material balancing' may in theory bring about a 'general equilibrium' similar to the Walrasian system may remain a contentious issue, but the 'economic bureaucracy' that it has entailed in practice clearly derives its *raison d'être* from the economics of Soviet planning. That is, to help ensure that the planners' allocative priorities be consistently adhered to via bureaucratic coercion. In short, the system should indeed not be seen, as is often the case, as being built upon some cultural value imperatives of Chinese or Russian origin.

This chapter will first highlight the abortive attempts made by Mao to dismantle the entire bureaucratic system, hoping not to prejudice his aspiration for a maximum-speed socialist modernization for China. The second part examines the intensity and extent to which the Stalinist model of centralized industrial planning and control was implanted on Chinese soil. The third and fourth major parts review how the industrial reform experiments conducted since 1979 have encountered fundamental political–bureaucratic and economic constraints inherent in the very rationale of the Stalinist economic strategy of maximizing industrial growth, and how the Henselian 'Systemzwang zum Experiment' (Hensel, 1977) tended eventually to culminate in a full-fledged marketization drive. Special reference is made to the so-called property rights issue. The discussions are concluded with a brief reflection on the long-term contributions and drawbacks of central planning, as it may bear on the post-Mao market-oriented reforms.

THE MAOIST ANATHEMA

By virtue of his ideological predilection, Mao – the revolutionary romanticist – was from the very outset unequivocally against 'bureaucratism' and related work-style manifested in what was often referred to as 'commandism', 'subjectivism' and 'factionalism' (cf. *Maoxuan*, 1977, p. 73). The widely known anathema had clearly dominated parts of his famous 1956 treatise *On the Ten Great Relations* (ibid., p. 275) and the 1957 'rectification campaign' (p. 476). By early 1958, it was swiftly translated into the unlikely decentralization campaign of the Great Leap Forward. While both campaigns appeared to be grossly overwhelmed by the anti-bourgeoisie ideology, the boldest 1958 GLF initiatives triggered profound organizational reshuffles that eventually brought central planning to the brink of collapse.

There are two aspects to the drastic anti-bureaucratic decentralization of 1958. The first is to relegate SOEs hitherto controlled by the central industrial-branch ministries to the jurisdiction of the provincial authorities.

The second is that, by appealing to ideological zeal, local cadres should defy bureaucratic red tape in boosting production to help advance the socialist cause. Thus, while the Chinese provinces then seemingly became a replica of Khrushchev's *Sovnarchoz* created just a year earlier, the SOEs all began to reign freely, oblivious to the overriding context of central planning and bureaucratic control.

Equally crucial is the role played by Mao's dialectic philosophy which strongly underpinned the decentralization drive. As was later also frequently quoted by the Cultural Revolutionary vanguards, Mao saw 'equilibrium (or balance) as a relative, temporary (phenomenon), while disequilibrium (imbalance) an absolute, permanent one'.[1] In a major speech given in May 1958 to help boost the Great Leap Forward, Mao forcefully made the point that 'the breakdown of a balance is a leap forward, which is more superior than the balance itself', and that 'imbalance is a good thing, as it makes life difficult for such (worrying) industrial ministries as machinery, metallurgy, geology and the like, and thus compels them to greatly develop (the supply potentials)' (*Wansui*, 1969, p. 213).

Earlier, in March 1958, in launching the GLF, Mao clearly spelled out, however, that the general (policy) line (*zongluxian*) of 'greater (*duo*), faster (*kuai*), better (*hao*), and more economical (*sheng*)' should be conducted as a 'wave-like' strategy (*Wansui*, 1969, pp. 166–9). That is, 'advance' should alternate with 'retrenchment' as a pattern of economic development, consistent with the 'law of unity of the opposites'.

Another equally peculiar aspect of Mao's strategy is his arguing time and again for 'leaving leeway (*liuyou yudi*)' in planning or balancing demand against supply.[2] The *yudi* is clearly not meant for lessening the economics of shortage *à la* Kornai (1980) per se, but it should rather help to facilitate 'overfulfilment' of given production targets, as a means for boosting morale of the workers. As such it clearly acts against the familiar ratchet principle in Soviet-style planning and management, under which planners normally attempt with all means possible to edge out from the producer enterprises every bit of built-in reserves for maximizing output.

Taken together, the entire GLF strategy as inspired by Mao had turned out to be a colossal mobilization scheme that inherently defied the very logic of Soviet-style planning and bureaucratic control which stressed (at least in theory) plan consistency and proportionality, and involved, once firmly established, usually relatively marginal year-to-year expansion, no matter how tight the output targets might appear to be (cf. Howe, 1978, p. 54). The catastrophe brought about by the drastic anti-bureaucratic reshuffle is familiar: widespread, uncoordinated crash programmes and, most fatefully, the breakdown of the entire hitherto strictly vertically controlled national statistical system, depriving the planners of the single most important instrument for formulating the national economic plans. In the words of Mao, at the famous Lushan Plenum in late July 1959:

> A great many things were not anticipated. Now the planning bodies do not take care of planning, or have not done so for a certain period . . . Not only the State Planning Commission, but also other ministries, as well as local (authorities) have not cared about comprehensive (aggregate) balancing for a certain time. Local bodies may be forgiven, but SPC and the central ministries have carried on for ten years. Suddenly, after the Beidaihe (August 1958) meeting, they gave up. They call it planned directives, but it is equal to no planning. The so-called not taking care of planning means rejecting comprehensive balancing, with absolutely no calculation as to the amount of coal, iron and transportation required. The coal and iron cannot travel by themselves, they must be hauled by carriage. This is what I did not foresee. (*Wansui*, 1969, p. 302; Howe, 1978, p. 54)

After the dust of the GLF upheaval had settled, conventional Soviet-style planning did return, effectively commencing in 1961. But no sooner had the Cultural Revolution erupted than centrally managed SOEs were re-relegated to the provinces, coupled with the Mao-inspired pursuit of regional autarky – in preparation for war or anything else. Once again, the 'remunerative' approach was also rapidly and indeed much more rigorously replaced by ideological persuasion (or political coercion) as a means of controlling economic performance. Nonetheless, 'law of planned development', 'proportionate relations', comprehensive balancing and '*leeway* planning' (to be allowed *in full*) then became the new rules of the game (Writing Group, 1974, pp. 106–9, 119–20, 123).

In the meantime, the restoration of the central branch-ministries in the early 1960s was vehemently repudiated by the CR vanguards as a political plot to create 'industrial empires' in China. Interestingly, the abortive initiative presumably taken at the same time by the reform-minded planners to establish a 'Second Ministry of Commerce' to substitute for the National Bureau of Materials Supply (by far the largest bureaucratic apparatus then in existence in the country) was similarly condemned as a move to restore capitalism.

Postscript: Note that it has so far taken more than two decades for the post-Mao economic reforms to eventually dismantle this highly cumbersome, non-market-conforming bureaucratic system.

THE INDUSTRIAL–ECONOMIC BUREAUCRACY

The entire bureaucratic machinery represents a huge and complex, vertically organized logistical system, needed for implementing the centrally determined allocation scheme, comprising both the physical input–output

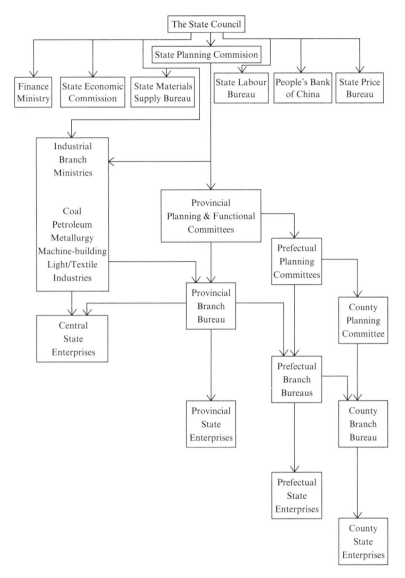

*Figure 10.1   A simplified model of Chinese centralized planning and bureau-
cratic control*

and financial spheres. The chart shown in Figure 10.1 gives a simplified
version of the Chinese organization.

A host of state agencies, all of ministerial rank, are involved. The
Finance Ministry is responsible for planning the financial flows to be

commensurate with the planned physical production and investment process. The state budget represents essentially the consolidated financial accounts for the entire national physical plan system. Unlike its Western counterpart, economic expenditure, notably state investment appropriations, takes up the lion's share of total budget expenditure. The other side of the coin is forced siphoning of realized profits and amortized capitals. Moreover, failure to comply with the remittance schedule on the part of the state enterprises may help to reveal irregularities in plan implementation, and thus call for enhanced state control.

The People's Bank, which is the Chinese replica of the conventional Soviet Gosbank, is essentially the 'cashier' of the Finance Ministry. It provides, on behalf of the Finance Ministry, the necessary fixed capital to the state enterprises, normally free of interest charges. Working capital may in turn be given as state budget appropriations, or bank loans. All enterprise transactions are to be completed by automatic clearing through the Bank. Cash outflows are strictly limited to wage payments and some very minor purchases. This is the familiar Soviet wisdom of 'control through the Ruble'. The purpose is to prevent any non-planned liquidity from building up to become a disintegrating force.

The most peculiar aspect of the entire national economic bureaucracy represents the various branch ministries, together with the State Bureau of Materials Supply and the State Labour Bureau. These agencies help to break down the planned national aggregates into mandatory input and output targets for individual state enterprises. The provinces, as also shown in the chart, are comparable to the branch ministries within the national allocative framework, in that allocations are made *en bloc* from the central authorities for redistribution to the producer enterprises under the provincial jurisdiction. As a matter of fact, the allocating mechanism within the province is, in most cases, identical to the national one. The entire bureaucratic hierarchy thus comprises the so-called departmental and regional (or territorial) principles of management.

We have yet to turn to the most comprehensive state agency of control. That is, the State Economic Commission (SEC). Generally speaking, its function is twofold. First is to help improve enterprise efficiency in current production and investment projects, and motivate state enterprises to engage in technological innovations. Second is to resolve conflicts of interest among the various branch ministries, and the provinces. These could involve, for example, conflicting claims for materials and fund allocations, arising from necessary adjustments in the mandatory output targets. The SEC certainly has some broad set of priority order to base their decisions on, but, in the absence of any market arbitrations, any decisions made in this respect are bound to be bureaucratic in nature, involving consideration of political power relations, personal favouritism, and reckless lobbying, rather than monetary cost and profit calculations.

The very linchpin of the entire Chinese system of bureaucratic control is, however, the Chinese Communist Party. The Party is omnipotent and omnipresent. Every government unit and every state enterprise is planted with a Party cell, and its members appointed to all the critical positions. Put simply, it is the Politburo which formulates the major economic policy guidelines which the State Planning Commission helps to translate into operational allocative schemes. It is the Party units at the various levels which help to make sure that the detailed plans imposed from above be strictly adhered to. In short, it is the Party which holds the entire system together.

Now, what is actually wrong with this Soviet-type system of planning and control? Most of the problems involved have become familiar facts to the West. There are, however, one or two important points which deserve some elaboration in the Chinese context. That is, that the entire planning system is in effect not as coherent as it may appear to be. The State Planning Commission, the Finance Ministry, the People's Bank, and the various branch authorities, are all huge, complex organizations *sui generis*. For sheer technical reasons, the physical planning system established for any particular plan period simply cannot be expected to be consistently synchronized with the financial and monetary planning. Besides, officially fixed prices are, in many cases, meaningless in accounting for costs and economic efficiency.

Worse still, widespread inconsistencies between value variables and physical variables are compounded with chronic inconsistencies in material allocations in relation to output targets. The background for this is simple. Again for technical reasons, the material balances normally have to be compiled separately, for each broad category or goods. It is difficult sufficiently to account for the interindustrial input–output relationships. Any shortfall or output target adjustments made in those industries with strong backward and forward linkages would have called for an insurmountable number of iterations in the balancing procedure, to the extent that an internally consistent and balanced system of material is deemed desirable.

To make things worse, any officials appointed to take charge of planning and balancing tasks naturally tend to impose the maximum in terms of output targets and try to squeeze every bit of input allocations. This is the very background of Kornai's economics of shortages. As a result, it is not uncommon for many factories in major Chinese cities to run for just three or four days a week, for want of electricity supply, for example. It is not uncommon for key investment prospects to be abruptly suspended, for want of such construction materials as cement and iron bar. And it is also not uncommon for goods to be piled up at major ports, and railway stations, for weeks or months, waiting for their turn to be loaded.

Plan inconsistencies and pervasive supply shortages call forcefully for enhanced Party control and endless bureaucratic arbitrations. This is the fundamental cause of confusion, frustration and corruption, or lethargy, on the part of all those involved in the broad sphere of implementing the state plans. All the familiar Soviet phenomenon of *tolkach* (the pusher), and *blat* (back-door activities) (Berliner, 1957, pp. 182, 209) probably find their most radical variants in China.

It is against this background that the constant tussle between 'regionalism' and 'departmentalism', which has been confronting the Chinese, as well as the Soviet authority, for the past several decades should also be understood. The provincial authority naturally tries to get as many goods produced within the province as possible, and prevent any unwanted outflow of resources from the province. This regionalist approach clearly prohibits interregional specialization and cooperation along the lines of regional comparative advantages.

Under the 'departmentalist' approach, however, the same urge for minimizing dependence on outside supplies often leads to excessive vertical integration of industries within each of the branch ministries. It also often results in unnecessary cross-hauling of goods across the country, and thus inhibits integrated use of regional resources. Many practical examples can be cited for illustration, but the point made here should be clear enough.

At least three main areas of inefficiency associated with the Chinese system of management may be identified. The first is the allocative biases within the national and regional context, as just illustrated. The second is the enormous transaction costs involved in maintaining the entire system of bureaucratic control. Finally, the third is pervasive microeconomic inefficiency, in terms of input use and output quality, for lack of managerial and worker incentives, or for that matter, due to the 'softness of budget constraints' *à la* Kornai.

All these efficiency problems associated with bureaucratization represent clearly the very source of Deng's aspirations for economic reform. Unlike Mao's romantic–revolutionary approach, however, Deng sees decentralization and market arbitration as a much more practical and viable long-term solution. How much can really be done to solve all these problems?

MAJOR TRENDS IN ECONOMIC REFORMS

China's economic reform started out in 1979, essentially with the provision for state enterprises to retain part of the realized profits for both bonus awards and reinvestments in minor innovative measures. Expanded financial liquidity requires, nevertheless, a concomitant expansion in enterprise decision autonomy in investments, production and marketing. This in turn called for *partial* decontrol of state allocations of producer goods, and *partial* liberalization of state-controlled prices, on top of increased production of consumer goods for matching rising purchasing power and workers' incentives.

As a result, the entire state industrial system began quickly to be bifurcated into a 'planned' versus a 'non-planned' sector. More importantly, with the producer goods sector being bound for 'deregulation', albeit quite marginally at the initial stage, the Chinese approach tended subtly to break through the familiar Soviet-type constraints of confining reform experiments to the Leninist principle of *Khozraschyot*; that is, to improve 'economic accountability' without compromising the Stalinist framework of centralized planning and control. In other words, 'consumer preference' has begun to emerge as a positive, albeit limited, factor in partially influencing national resources allocation. Note again that, under central planning, the prerogative basically rests with the planners to determine on behalf of the political leadership the level and output mix of consumer goods.

As a matter of fact, the bifurcation does not occur along the product line, in the sense that some industrial branches remain centrally planned, while others are totally deregulated. Rather, the dividing line cuts across all state industries. Even the Anshan Iron and Steel complex, the most prestigious and largest of its kind in China, is allowed to sell, on its own account, any amount of outputs produced in excess of the plan targets. It is also allowed to negotiate with the buyers the prices for such so-called 'supplementary' outputs and sales. The negotiated or free-market prices should of course be substantially higher than the officially fixed prices, which are only applicable to the planned outputs. The corollary of this new reform provision is evidently the fact that the user enterprises are allowed to make their own investment decisions, and that they may finance such investments with liquidity acquired under the profit retention scheme.

This is what has been frequently referred to as the 'double-track system' in production, investment, supply and pricing – a widespread phenomenon in China. Nevertheless, the system has remained essentially skewed towards the 'planned sector'. The truly marketized sector probably amounts to not more than 20 per cent of total output (in gross value terms) within the system of state industries. The share may vary from industry to industry, but in the heyday of 'Economic Readjustment' in 1981–83, it generally appeared to be biased upwards. Many industrial giants, heavy industry included, were then compelled to turn to market demand to keep the factories running.[3]

No matter how limited the 'marketized sector' may be, the double-track system represents an inherently disintegrating force. State enterprises concerned would naturally attempt to undermine the centrally imposed output targets as fully as possible, in order to expand output and sales to the market to reap the price benefits.[4] Viewed this way, by the mid-1980s, economic reforms in China seem to have already arrived at a crossroads. The upshot could be renewed centralization with physical–bureaucratic control or a continuous drift towards market arbitration and free prices.

The Chinese leadership preferred to walk the tightrope, however. Throughout the 1980s, the floating market prices for the 'non-planned' portion of outputs were at times officially capped at a certain limit. In 1984, for example, it was 20 per cent above the fixed prices for mandatory quota delivery. A similar ceiling was applied in 1988 and 1989 in the wake of horrendous *guandao* abuses. In 1985, when the dual-price system was formally put in place, the 'market prices' were all freed, nonetheless (Chai, 1997a, p. 99). As a matter of fact, the 1985 sanction was closely preceded by the path-breaking 'October (1984) Resolution' (made at the Third Plenum of the Central Committee of the 12th National Party Congress) for establishing a 'planned socialist commodity economy'.

The Marxist–Leninist jargon of political economy as applied may sound intriguing, but the October Resolution represents not only a most significant Chinese breakthrough in Soviet-style ideological constraints.[5] It in effect also calls for a concerted conversion of central planning into a market-based system in the long run. Specifically, the transition should begin with the adoption of 'guidance planning' alongside with, and to eventually substitute for, 'mandatory planning'. But the ultimate appears to be for 'market regulation' to replace 'guidance planning'. Meanwhile, the planners should also begin to learn how to apply macroeconomic-type planning and control for regulating aggregate demand and supply, accumulation and consumption and intersectoral reallocation of investment funds, labour and material resources. These should all take place, hopefully, without compromising the *primat* of state ownership, hence the 'socialist' connotation.

The pace with which new policy measures were adopted to support the October 1984 Resolution was quite amazing. To create a level playing field for the SOEs, around the time of, or following, the Resolution, state budget appropriations for both fixed and working capital were converted into interest-bearing bank loans for the SOEs, and compulsory profit delivery into fixed rate income taxes. The monobank system was split into a two-tiered, Western-like structure: the People's Bank of China to serve as the central bank, and four commercial banks created to specialize in lending to industry and commerce, agriculture, foreign trade, and investment for basic construction.

Meanwhile, control of SOEs' decision making on employment and wage determination began to be relaxed and SOEs of lesser economic importance 'leased out' for management by collective enterprises or private individuals. For large and medium-scale SOEs (that is, the linchpin of the entire industrial system), an attempt was also made to extend managerial autonomy by drawing an operational line between state ownership and management rights, in search of an 'optimum decentralization'.

In an effort to break both 'regionalism' and 'departmentalism', SOEs were to be increasingly released from vertical control by both the industrial-branch ministries and respective provincial authorities. The 'liberalized' SOEs should in fact all converge to the jurisdiction of selected municipalities which command the natural endowment to develop urban conglomeration economies. Serving as the critical industrial links, such SOEs should also help to promote *lateral* (horizontal) cooperation between enterprises of different ownership categories, and across regional administrative barriers, by setting up joint stock corporations and similar new types of business entities.

Clearly, one need not be familiar with elementary economics to appreciate that these new reform measures all clearly point in the direction of a market-based system, let alone that they were also being accompanied by enhanced price liberalization, as alluded to earlier.

Perhaps more astonishing, despite accelerated inflation in the interim (which led in part as a factor to the downfall in winter 1986–87 of Hu Yaobang as the Party Secretary-General under Deng Xiaoping, the paramount Chinese leader), the 13th NPC convened in October 1987 (with Zhao Ziyang serving as Hu's successor), and promulgated with real courage a new Resolution for 'the state to regulate the market, and the market to guide the enterprises'. Taken literally, this seems to suggest that, just three years on from 1984, both mandatory planning and guidance planning should now be considered dated to pave the way for a full-fledged system of 'market regulation' with indirect macroeconomic control.

Moreover, the new Resolution of 1987 also advocates that the state administration (essentially of economic affairs) be detached in principle from Party control. All state enterprises should, in turn, be freed from state-administrative tutelage. The entire national system of economic management should be 'depoliticized' as much as possible to facilitate economic decisions to be made on a 'democratic and scientific' basis. Evidently, excessive Party and bureaucratic control associated with 'mandatory planning', or for that matter 'guidance planning', is now seen as a serious obstacle to facilitating economic transition to 'market regulation' as envisaged in the October 1984 reform resolution. In fact, for many senior reform-minded Chinese officials and scholars, the 1984 blueprint has essentially remained a paper work. And as Deng himself sees it, the broader Chinese political context seems indeed to have proved a formidable constraint on pursuing his bold reform initiatives.

It is clearly against this background of heightened aspiration for market liberalization that Deng somehow made the colossal decision in May 1988 consistently to free the entire Chinese price system as well. Perhaps Zhao Ziyang, Deng's new heir-apparent, who was at the time frequented by high-flying American economists, was vulnerable to the philosophy of the Chicago School. But, coupled with the sprouting liberal political ideas, the abortive attempt to sweep across the board all official price fixings was in effect tantamount to a shock therapy. *Postscript*: Fortunately, the catastrophic Tiananmen incident that followed had not prevented the resilient Deng embarking anew on his ambitious venture in 1992 and eventually to make China qualified for the global system of free trade and investment.

ECONOMIC AND POLITICAL–BUREAUCRATIC CONSTRAINTS

Overbureaucratization represents undoubtedly the single most important constraint on economic reform in China. However, it should not be seen, in the first place, as rooted in the country's culture and history. Most of the compatriots in Hong Kong and Taiwan are basically conditioned by the same Chinese value imperatives, yet these are two of the most vibrant market-based economies in the world. It is none other than Soviet-style planning, as adopted in China, and bound up with the forced-draft industrialization strategy, that has called for pervasive bureaucratic control and Party surveillance. Many Chinese reform strategists, in charge or armchair, who are frustrated by renewed market-oriented experiments, therefore see an immediate dismantling of central planning in favour of a full-fledged marketization as the panacea.

Such unlikely ideas are in fact shared by many prominent economists in the West, Nobel laureates included. Thus, shortly prior to the Tiananmen incident, coupled with Chinese modesty – typical of Zhao Ziyang, in granting audience to selected American economists, a couple of radical liberals – from Hong Kong in particular, strongly advocated an *overnight* liberalization not only of officially fixed prices, but also the fixed exchange rates and foreign exchange control altogether and, as well, an across-the-board privatization of all state-owned enterprises in China. This of course helps us to reminisce about the favoured dictum of Mao, that the way to 'a great order' is through 'great chaos' (*cong daluan dao dazhi*).

Obviously, Boris Yeltsin was trapped in such a simplistic projection from the familiar competitive market model, and probably not adequately briefed about the disastrous consequences of the relatively modest version of the Big Bang strategy adopted in China scarcely a year ahead of the Tiananmen upheaval in 1989; hence the 'great chaos' following the collapse of the Soviet Union.

The hard fact remains, however, that the enormous concentration of resources in the hands of the planners and the indispensable gigantic bureaucratic apparatus at their disposal cannot be readily compromised by any drastic measures of deregulation. In other words, the wrangle between 'market regulation' and bureaucratic control is bound to persist in line with the Henselian *Systemzwang zum Experiment*. Hopefully, the balance will tilt towards the market at some stage.

A good way to examine how the built-in bureaucratic constraint may have impinged, for example, upon the new policy measures for mitigating gross allocative distortions caused by the 'departmentalist' and 'regionalist' behaviour, is to look at the possible increases in the relative size of investment and output accountable by the so-called domestic joint ventures, which are set up for promoting 'lateral economic ties'. Unfortunately, relevant statistics are not available for verification, but, conceivably, the scale of such new cooperative industrial undertakings is still highly restricted.

As a People's Daily editorial puts it, most of the branch and provincial authorities involved simply do not heed the central policy call for freeing the hands of enterprises under their jurisdiction. And various 'invisible tariff barriers' are indeed erected to help block the desired flows of resources across different industries and regional boundaries (*Renmin Ribao*, 18 April 1986). If anything, SOEs relegated to the various 'natural-economic' municipalities are normally of lesser importance and poor performance. Besides, apart from operational input and output decisions, the required finances and scarce materials are still subject to centralized allocation by the respective ministerial/provincial bureaus (Chai, 1997a, p. 46).

Evidently, it is not at all easy for any accelerated decontrol of this kind not to comprise the vested interests of the established bureaucracy, and to touch upon the integrity of the broader 'industrial empire' and 'regional fiefdom' concerned. After all, central planners simply need to hold on to vertical branch-line control or the territorial alternative to basically help keep the entire system intact in support of the overriding economic strategy for industrialization. Hopefully continuous accumulation of economic strengths will eventually reach the necessary 'critical threshold' to trigger accelerated industrial deregulations toward greater use of markets and prices, but meanwhile the envisaged economic transition is bound to take place one dose at a time.

A close look at the *modus operandi* of the various functional bureaucracies should help to shed further light on the important sources of resistance to economic reforms. Take the State Bureau of Materials Supply, for example. As a ministerial-rank body it works in parallel to the various industrial branch ministries to make sure that enterprises within its purview will be supplied with the right amount of input materials (raw or intermediate) and the necessary machinery and equipment for carrying out the approved production plans. At the same time it is of course also charged with the responsibility to centralize compulsory output deliveries from the producer enterprises for the planned redistribution. The entire, vertically strictly controlled system of so-called material–technical supplies therefore involves sophisticated planning of acquisition and supply logistics, and is in fact mounted by hundreds of thousands of cadres across the country.

Viewed this way, a full-fledged marketization or commercialization of the huge national bureaucratic apparatus should be tantamount to creating a multi-tiered system of wholesale and retail network, as proposed by Liberman for the Soviet Union as early as 1965 (Liberman, 1965). This would indeed turn all the bureaucrats into businessmen to be responsible for their own profits and losses. Barring a full privatization, however, the emerging commercial operators would still be left without any prospects for substantial private wealth accumulation to hedge against possible risks and uncertainties. Moreover, should the liberalization really help to improve operational or allocative efficiency to any substantial extent, there is no doubt that tens of hundreds of workers and cadres of the state agency would become idle. This would in turn add enormous pressure to the equally cumbersome placement works of the state agencies for labour allocation.

As a matter of fact, the State Bureau of Materials Supply is often singled out by Chinese reformists as one of the two state agencies most resistant to reform measures, the other being the Ministry of Finance. There are two major aspects to the portfolio of the Ministry of Finance that make it vulnerable to any market-oriented measures of decentralization. The first is to maximize state budget revenue for financing investments in the massive industrialization programme. The second is to help bring about a national financial equilibrium, that is, balance between aggregate demand and aggregate supply. These aspects present equally complex problems, closely intertwined.

Briefly, unlike the Western counterpart, the Ministry of Finance in China is not any *passive* tax collector, in the first place. It acts on behalf of central planners to make sure that any amount of profits realized by the enterprises will be remitted to the state coffers. The various experiments with profit retentions for state enterprises, as conducted since 1979, and the subsequent 'tax-for-profit' substitution have, however, proved to be much less comfortable for the responsible cadres in the various finance bureaus, compared to the straightforward practice of compulsory profit deliveries in the past.

Added to the uncertainty are clearly the complex regulations and bureaucratic procedure involved with the 'income-regulatory (adjustment) taxes' and 'profit-contract responsibility' system. Both are adopted to compensate for the inadequacy of the 'tax-for-profit' fiscal reform. The former is intended for balancing interindustrial discrepancy in profitability due to pervasive price distortions; the latter, comprising an array of sophisticated variants for different industries, aims at edging out every possible profit margin of the enterprises (cf. Chai, 1997a, pp. 76–8). Taken together, the entire new fiscal system is therefore basically similar to the past practice of forced siphoning, save the purported incentive effect of the 'profit-contracting' method which, for the finance bureaus in charge, might not be worthwhile at all.

To maintain aggregate balances was also a relatively simple matter in the past. Both the State Bureau of Prices and the People's Bank involved functioned basically as parts of the Finance Ministry. The former helps to fix prices for the supply of consumer goods (aggregate supply, or 'consumption fund' in Marxist jargon), and the latter make sure that cash flows to wage earners would accordingly be limited to the 'wage fund' (aggregate demand) fixed by the Finance Ministry. Since transactions of producer goods (subject to central planning and allocation) all proceeded in a 'cashless' manner (strictly decreed to be directly settled through bank account transfer), virtually all possible sources of aggregate imbalances were held in check.

However, the established bureaucratic routines began to be quickly upset, as soon as various profit retention schemes (implying expanded liquidity) were put in place and commercial banks (extra credit facilities) created, alongside the adoption of the double-track system (increased market-oriented production and investment). Coupled with renewed incentive-linked wage hikes, the reform measures have all added to the unpredictability of aggregate investment and consumption expenditures. On top of this, of course, accelerated price liberalization under the dual price system tends only to help make the country increasingly inflation-prone.

There is no doubt that the old guards of central planning who have continued to man the Finance Ministry have yet to learn the very basic but complex skills of Western-type macroeconomic control, no matter how frustrating this would prove to be.

In this context, a few words should be said about the much publicized 'guidance planning', which is evidently construed as a means to help ease the political–bureaucratic constraints in the transition towards some kind of market socialism. Two problems are involved. First is the continuous predominance of mandatory planning (at least in terms of physical output); nevertheless, major inputs required for production under 'guidance planning' are often subject to centralized allocation. Second, unlike the postwar French experience with *planification*, for example, output targets under 'guidance planning' are normally presented in physical terms as well, rather than in value terms, and are in fact binding rather than truly *indicatif*.

The problems encountered may of course be considered as characteristic of such an economic transition. For example, supplemental physical target control seems indispensable for hedging against abuses by enterprises under the Chinese 'guidance planning'. Specifically, with prices grossly distorted in many cases, output mix may be manipulated with relative ease to fulfil targets given in value terms; what is more, increased freeing of prices against the backdrop of 'monopoly overhang' could add salt to the wounds.

Nevertheless, the prerogatives retained by central planners for physical–bureaucratic injunction inherently threaten to pre-empt any possible application of regulatory fiscal and monetary instruments. Carried to the ultimate conclusion, the basic question really is again whether the established forced-draft industrialization strategy may be substantially compromised or abandoned altogether, in favour of an accelerated relaxation of centralized control or a full-fledged deregulation (including the eradication of the dual-price system) towards the market-allocative regime. Barring this, the 'economics of shortage' *à la* Kornai, coupled with the built-in political–bureaucratic impulse for perpetuating investment in the producer goods sector (*viz.* 'investment hunger') will likely continue to prevail. And, with this, there will be hardly any prospects of a decontrol of prices for both investment and consumer goods.

THE PROPERTY RIGHTS ISSUE

More often than not, state ownership is considered to be the most fundamental constraint on economic reforms in China. In the mid-1980s, in particular, when reforms began to gain momentum, some liberal economists associated with the Chicago School but based in Hong Kong (dubbed by Hayek and Friedman as the bulwark of the laissez-faire model), argued strongly for an *outright* privatization of state-owned enterprises, as alluded to earlier. The familiar Coase theorem (about property rights) was then often cited to support the 'big-push' paradigm. Practical problems emerging from the process of economic transition were, however, hardly subjected to any analytical scrutiny. If anything, Coase's theorem was often resorted to summarily as a critique of the established Chinese system of state ownership, in terms of 'externality' and 'transaction costs' involved.

The crux of the problems is, however, that nationalization (or for that matter collectivization) of the 'means of production' in China was, in the first place, closely associated with or prompted by the adoption in 1953 of the Soviet-style economic strategy, as manifested in the First Five-Year Plan of 1953–57. Specifically, state ownership was then established not necessarily on consideration of any merits of its own or out of some ideological imperatives, but, rather, it purported specifically to serve the industrialization drive. There are two aspects to this. First is to help raise the necessary investment funds through confiscation of private land rentals, interest income and entrepreneur profits (parallel to rural forced savings institutionalized through agricultural collectivization). Second is to put private industrial and commercial properties at the disposal of the planners altogether, de jure or de facto, for centralized allocation.[6]

The situation resembles, indeed, the wartime mobilization acts imposed in many Western countries, notably Germany, under which many major branches of heavy industry such as iron and steel, machinery and equipment, shipbuilding, chemicals and the like all remained privately owned, but just in name. In the circumstances, consumption was bound to be depressed and consumer goods supply very often subject to rationing as well. And such forced physical mobilizations inevitably also rendered markets and prices inoperative, let alone labour conscriptions without due quid pro quo.

Carried over to the postwar Chinese analogue, it would of course verge on the realm of ethics to question the relative desirability of the forced-draft industrialization strategy: very much the same as to challenge the 'value-imperatives' for the Germans to fight the war or defend the country against it. Philosophical issues notwithstanding, central planners in China are, however, clearly also confronted with the practical problem of how to weigh all the 'transaction costs' cum 'social costs' incurred with state ownership and overbureaucratization, against the possible sum total of long-term economic benefits deemed to be arising from that particular economic strategy of pursuing a maximum-speed modernization. Note also that, from the perspective of such a national assessment, it would also fall wide of the mark to specifically argue against SOEs on the grounds of any negative 'spillover' effect, as 'social costs' incurred as such are already 'internalized' in the overall trade-off equation.

Obviously the trade-off cannot be easily settled. It seems inapt, however, to make any unqualified arguments, say, along the lines of the Coase theorem, for an immediate dismantling of central planning in China, in favour of a full-fledged privatization and marketization programme. To do so would be tantamount to a bluffing ideological campaign, propagating a revolution (rather than reform) in the Chinese system, as it stood around the time of the Resolution of October 1984, or for that matter that of October 1987.

A few words should be said about the prevalent Chinese price system which is closely related to the property rights issue, and has thus also become part of the reform critique in and outside China. It is simple logic that free market transactions in the West presuppose private property rights to be the single most important legal foundation, and that under the competitive market system prices generally converge to demand-and-supply clearing equilibrium as scarcity indices. Viewed this way, prices in China, as well as in the Soviet Union, are doomed to be grossly irrational, as bureaucratic price fixing can never really keep abreast of the constantly changing demand and supply conditions, even just attempting to adhere to the centralized scale of preferences. Thus Liberman's reform prerequisites that prices should remain officially fixed but yet kept flexible, remains at best an axiom (Liberman, 1962).

Nevertheless, to argue the case, on the grounds of the familiar (static) efficiency criteria, against central planning and state ownership seems to be wide of the mark, if not tautological. For decades, the potential impact of prices in China has virtually all been sterilized under the system of planning with material balances. Especially during the decade-long Cultural Revolution, when physical targets coupled with bureaucratic control were driven to the verge of the Henselian model of *Zentralverwaltungswirtschaft*, it was largely irrelevant to what extent input and output prices were distorted. Specifically, prices then hardly played any allocative role, serving purely as an accounting variable.

Following the close of the Mao era, the practice of property rights as an 'accommodating agent' as explained is of course bound to be readjusted, in the wake of increased uses of markets and prices. Thus, beginning in the mid-1980s, small-scale SOEs have been increasingly 'leased out' or sold to the public altogether under 'compensatory use' or 'compensatory transfer' schemes. For the medium- and large-scale SOEs, an attempt has been made to separate 'rights of control (management)' from 'ownership rights (entitlement)' in conjunction with the adoption of the contract-responsibility system. Moreover, experiments are also under way for converting larger state enterprises into 'joint-stock corporations' (Zhao Ziyang, 1987). Nonetheless, the prospect for a full privatization seems to remain remote, given the overriding national importance of such SOEs.

Postscript: With the establishment of the stock exchanges in Shanghai and Shenzhen in the early 1990s, an increased number of SOEs have been floated in China and Hong Kong, as well as overseas. But, as a rule, the state remains hitherto the majority stake-holder, although SOEs now all operate in the market environment.

CONCLUSION

One or two points emerge from the arduous Chinese transition towards a market-based economic system. First is that the transition has been characteristically constrained by the legacy inherited from the Maoist past. Second is that, by the close of the Mao era, however, the massive decades-long industrialization drive seemed to have in itself triggered the market-oriented reform. This relates, in the first place, to increased industrial maturity and structural sophistication that made central planning and bureaucratic control increasingly unpalatable and difficult to impose. The complications were indeed similarly encountered in the Soviet Union in the early 1960s. In addition, the Khrushchevian-type 'less harsh' consumption policy adopted also necessarily called for improved market supplies and continuous industrial deregulations.

The market-oriented experiments in China will likely continue to alternate between periods of advances and setbacks, being conditioned by vested political interests, power relations, inherent bureaucratic resistance or sheer inertia, but, given the forceful economic fundamentals, the course of reforms appears to be irreversible. Nevertheless, a full-fledged replacement of state industries by private ownership should probably not be expected in the near future, much to the chagrin of 'socialism-sceptics' who are keen on seeing 'the prophesy of capitalism' fulfilled overnight.

Sceptics frustrated by the enormous 'transaction costs' incurred with socialism and bureaucratism may also like to query whether, after all, it would have been much better for China to engage from the beginning in the capitalist approach to economic development, open-door policy included. Such a thesis can of course neither be refuted nor proved, but an official comment on the colossal Cultural Revolution strategy by none other than Mr Li Chengrui, Director of the National Bureau of Statistics (an economist *cum* statistician who has helped to reconstruct the official Chinese statistics for the blackout period of 1961–78), seems highly revealing of the circumstances. Interestingly enough, in his own words,

> The reason why the Cultural Revolution could still achieve high GDP growth rates is that, although the workers and peasants were highly suppressed by the Gang of Four, they all kept on working hard, with the future good of the motherland constantly staying at the forefront of their minds.[7]

Indeed, GDP scored a rather impressive growth rate of around 5 per cent per year during the Cultural Revolution period of 1966–76 (*TJNJ 1994*, p. 34) and, if both the two most tumultuous initial years of 1967 and 1968 and the terminal year of 1976 (which all saw negative GDP growth as a result of disastrous political in-fighting verging on civil war), are excluded from the calculation, the record would turn out to be quite startling. Perhaps the massive 'transaction costs' involved with the Cultural Revolution type of economic and industrial management and bureaucratic control should be considered as worthwhile. We do not know for sure.

Postscript: After 14 years of deliberations marred with controversy and disputes, China's first ever 'Property Law' (*Wuquanfa*) was finally promulgated in March 2007 to take effect from 1 October. For ideologically blinkered property-rights theorists or liberal economists, this might be hailed as 'prophesy realized'. But here again, the logic for the metamorphosis should be made clear: it is obviously the landmark Resolution of October 1984 for deregulating and increasingly 'marketizing' the central planning system (rather than the Chinese authority aspiring for and contemplating from the very beginning a full-fledged privatization per se), that had forcefully triggered continuous attempts to refine the ownership system and refine 'trial' property-rights legislations to conform with the requirements of the emerging market-oriented economic reforms that had led to the conclusive codification in 2007.[8]

Note also that despite formal codification of the protection of private properties, the Chinese system is presently still officially branded as 'socialism with Chinese characteristics'. A major pillar underpinning the characterization represents of course the continuous economic significance of the SOEs, although they have all been basically 'deregulated' and are now subject to the diktat of the market system.

NOTES

* An extensively revised, extended and updated version from Y.Y. Kueh, 'Bureaucratization and economic reform in Chinese industry', in Wolfgang Klenner (ed.), *Trends of Economic Development in East Asia*, Berlin and Heidelberg: Springer Verlag, 1989, pp. 381–92, with kind permission of Springer Science and Business Media; and with inputs from Y.Y. Kueh, 'China's economic reforms: approach, vision and constraints', in Dieter Cassel (ed.), *Wirtschaftssysteme im Umbruch: Sowjetunion, China und industrialisierte Markwirtschaften zwischen internationalem Anpassungszwang und nationalem Reformbedarf*, Munich: Verlag Franz Vahlen, 1996, pp. 255–75.

1. Similarly worded, Mao made the point in his landmark discourse 'On the Correct Handling of Contradictions among the People', published in 1957, in relation to the formulation of the annual national economic plan (*Maoxuan*, 1977, p. 375). These phrases were later also quoted in a standard textbook on socialist political economy published during the heyday of the Cultural Revolution (Writing Group, 1974, pp. 107–8). See also *Wansui*, 1967, p. 123 for similar *dialectic* exposition.

2. Mao first toyed with the idea in December 1958, when he suspected the notorious '1070 tonnes' target for steel output for that year (*Wansui*, 1969, p. 264). It was repeated in April and again in May 1959, in affirmative and positive tones, well before the catastrophic readjustments were made for the unrealistic GLF targets for 1959 (*Wansui*, 1967, pp. 51, 58). He considered the 'leeway' approach as also consistent with the *dialectic* 'wave-like' theorem.

3. The Readjustment – made in favour of increased consumer goods production – resulted in drastic curtailment of investment and demand for producer goods and hence accumulated idle capacity in heavy industry. This has prompted many high-priority SOEs to resort to the widespread practice dubbed 'seeking rice to fill one's own cooking pot'.

4. See Tidrick (1987) for the possible allocative implications of the price discrimination against the planned output; and Chai (1997a, pp. 98–9) for more details about the evolution of the dual price system.

5. Stalin made a distinction between 'product exchange' and 'commodity exchange'. The former refers to exchange of producer goods ('means of production') among SOEs which for Stalin should not involve any 'change of ownership', hence not a commodity transaction. The latter term was used by Stalin in line with Marxist terminology to denote sales of consumer goods from SOEs to wage earners, and as well those of producer goods to the peasants (transfer of ownership from the state to peasant collectives). Interestingly, in his *Critical Notes* on Stalin's famous pamphlet, *Economic Problems of Socialism in the U.S.S.R.*, Mao rigorously challenges Stalin's dichotomy and wants to see producer goods being treated at par as a commodity as well (*Wansui*, 1967, pp. 156–66). To my knowledge, Mao's criticism of Stalin was indeed made (as early as 1959) well ahead of similar exposition by some prominent Eastern European economists, notably W. Brus and O. Sik in the 1970s. Equally interesting, the Cultural Revolution vanguards preferred, nonetheless, to adhere to Stalin's definition, although Mao's points were also heeded, in that 'exchange among SOEs' was regarded as 'still possessing certain characteristics of commodity exchange' (Writing group, 1974, p. 167). In this regard, the October Resolution of 1984 tended therefore to side with Mao, but it was nevertheless not until October 1992 that, with the decisive Resolution of the 14th National Party Congress for establishing a 'Socialist *Market*-Economic System', the conventional Marxist term of 'commodity' was finally discarded.

6. Note that, in 1958, when communal messing was rigorously promoted, even such minor privately-owned durable goods as cooking utensils, kitchen knives, door locks and anything made of metals were all thrown into the 'backyard furnaces'. Notorious as the 'iron-and-steel making' campaign might appear, it was not necessarily triggered by, say, Mao's ideological predilection for 'destroying the traditional Chinese family', as many sociologists then tended to believe.

7. This is an approximate quotation. I remember the statement was made in a major Chinese periodical in the mid-1980s, but unfortunately I cannot relocate the sources.

8. In this connection I recall with pleasure my several rounds of discussions in the late 1980s with Li Yining, the prominent Professor of Economics at Beijing University. For Professor Li – dubbed Li '*Gufen*' (stock share) in China for his persistently advocating the *Gufen zhi* (system) as a solution to the property-right issue – then argued that 'straightening out the ownership system (*lishun suoyouzhi*) should be the primary task in economic reforms'. I countered, however, by maintaining that 'price reforms (implying market deregulations) should be preceding'.

11. Inflation and industrial deregulation: the twin travellers*

BACKGROUND

Economic transition in China not only represents an arduous process, but has also characteristically been inflicted with bouts of inflation over the past 20 years or so. As a matter of fact, the occasional outbursts of inflation as observed were indeed all triggered by abortive attempts to deregulate the state-industrial sector. This seems therefore quite atypical of the celebrated 'incrementalist' or 'gradualist' approach propagated by Deng Xiaoping himself. At any rate, the disruptive Chinese inflation experience compares unfavourably with the 'graduated' cyclical fluctuations in the West. In mature industrialized countries, the established market system normally does not provide room for any drastic institutional reshuffle and any anti-cyclical fiscal and monetary policy readjustments made are bound to be marginal in scale.

There are two aspects to the background of inflation breaking out in China. The first refers to what may be called the 'monopoly overhang'. That is, the backdrop of pervasive sellers' markets which may be readily exploited by any state-run suppliers operating on grounds of the 'economics of shortage' *à la* Kornai. The second is the familiar 'monetary overhang'. This relates to involuntary accumulation over the years of purchasing powers or financial claims that threaten to burst out, once officially fixed prices begin to be unfrozen in favour of the deregulated SOEs. Both types of 'overhang' are clearly inherited from the Maoist past to constrain the pace of industrial deregulation,[1] much as the material foundation laid down by Mao has in itself helped to facilitate the market-oriented reforms in China.

There are of course other hard variables that fit into the equation of inflation as well. A good or bad harvest, for example, may help to mitigate or aggravate the inflationary pressures. Note that the food basket carries a significant weight in the composite Chinese price index.

This chapter attempts therefore to examine how the various key factors interplay to affect the course of inflation in post-Mao China, by focusing on the pace and pattern of industrial deregulation. A particular attention is given to the extraordinary inflation episode of 1993 to 1995, which closely followed the effective dismantling of mandatory planning and non-market type of control in the country. The discussion concludes with a brief evaluation of the new institutional setting, as it may bear on long-term macroeconomic stability in China. We begin, however, by highlighting the major benchmarks of inflation occurring since 1979, as a background for the discussions.

RIDING THE TIGER OF INFLATION

The periodic bouts of inflation in China are clearly visible in Figure 11.1, although the magnitude of fluctuations tends to vary quite substantially from case to case. Ignoring perhaps the first incident of 1980,[2] the other benchmark inflations – 1985, 1988–89, 1993–95 – are all closely associated with the known cycles of industrial deregulation. In fact, the practical channels through which industrial deregulation translated into inflationary pressures can be identified with relative ease.

Thus, the 1985 inflation (at the record high of 8.5 per cent) followed in tandem the promulgation of the grandiose reform blueprint approved at the Third Plenum of the Party's Central Committee held in October 1984. Many of the policy measures adopted shortly thereafter are clearly more or less inflation-bound, compared to the past practice. In a nutshell this includes, as alluded to earlier, extended credit facility from newly created state-run commercial banks, replacement of budget appropriations by bank loans, tax-for-profit substitution, and pervasive wage reforms that basically ridded SOEs of any mandatory obligations to adhere to the centrally set wage norms and employment restrictions.

These all came on top of the double-track system, formally put in place in 1985 for production, investment, marketing and pricing. Note also that, in the same year, the officially imposed ceilings for both free market prices and bonus awards were lifted as well. Similarly, from 1985, the limit for investments in 'productive' capital projects and major technological innovations requiring screening by the State Planning Commission was raised from 10 to 30 million *yuan*, while incidentally, from 1987, the corresponding figures for projects relating to energy, transportation and basic materials were increased to 50 million *yuan* (Kueh, 1999a, p. 12).

There are two more tactical policy measures that had at the time proved to be fatefully disastrous in causing inflation and indeed made the national top planners a mockery. The first is the provision announced as early as October 1984 (in conjunction with the celebrated Third Plenum Resolution) that, effective January 1985, the 'quotas of bank credits' to be assigned (by the People's Bank) to the four major commercial banks for the year should

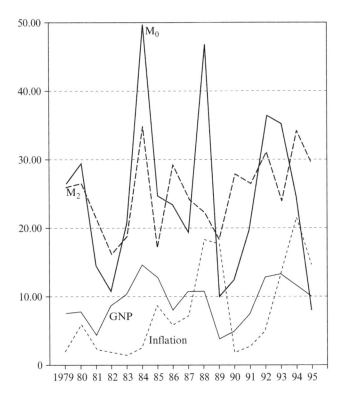

Notes: Inflation rates are based on the overall retail price index. M_0 = currency in circulation by the end of the year. M_2 = M_0 plus M_1 (which comprises transaction demand deposits of firms and institutions, and passbook saving and time deposit of households).

Source: Kueh (1999b), p. 264.

Figure 11.1   Growth rates of GNP, inflation and money supply in China, 1979–95 (per cent)

be determined by the cumulative total of bank loans extended for the whole of 1984. The second, similar measure relates to the 'wage fund'. Specifically, the total wage bills (including bonus payments) that an SOE would be allowed to charge for 1985 would be given as the 1984 record plus an appropriate mark-up.

The upshot should be self-evident. As divulged by Zhao Ziyang himself (then the Premier) in his *Government Work Report* delivered at the National People's Congress in March 1985, the banks all scrambled to lend money, in order to secure the maximum quota by soliciting as many borrowers as possible before the end of 1984. And with the 'budget constraint' still hardly 'hardened', the SOEs were of course absolutely thrilled at the windfall for the greatly expanded built-in buffer for expansion in both investment and employment. As a result, bank loans extended in December alone amounted to a spectacular 50 per cent of the total for the whole of 1984, which represented an increase of nearly 30 per cent over 1983 (Kueh, 1999a, pp. 18–19).

By similar reasoning, wage expenditure recorded an equally staggering increase of 38 per cent in the fourth quarter of 1984, generating an overall increase of 19 per cent in 1984 over 1983 (ibid., p. 19). As a matter of fact, in 1985, the Chinese government was compelled, as a result, to spend hundreds of millions of US dollars from its precious foreign exchange reserves on imports of such consumer durables as television sets and refrigerators, to help absorb the enormous excess purchasing power and match the emerging tide of consumerism. Perhaps it is against this particular background that Hu Yaobang, then Secretary-General of the Party, was later charged for advocating the 'two highs' (high consumption and high investment).

While the 1985 inflation spell may be considered as some teething problem in deregulating the complex structure of state industries, the background to the most fateful rise in inflation, in 1988 (a new record high of 18.5 per cent) appears, nonetheless, to be even more puzzling.

In May 1988, Deng Xiaoping, when meeting an African leader, somehow declared that, in coping with price reforms, it should be 'better to endure a short bout of sharp pain than suffer long, lingering pain'. The message was clear enough: an imminent liberalization of prices should be expected across the board. What followed is familiar: widespread runs on banks and panic buying during the summer and autumn of 1988. From January to November of that year, the urban consumer price index accelerated for every single month year-on-year, from 10 per cent to the high of 30 per cent (Naughton, 1990, pp. 112, 137). This inevitably gave rise to popular consumer discontent, especially among urban residents, which should certainly be considered as an important ingredient in the political upheavals of the spring of 1989.

The question remains why Deng was prepared to indulge himself in this boldest initiative. Was he really ill-informed about the harsh economic reality, or simply inspired by the liberalist idea of a Big Bang? At any rate, the massive attempt made in early summer 1988 to free the entire Chinese price system was probably perceived to be a most critical, integral part of a programme of action to be launched for the Resolution adopted at the 13th National Party Congress held scarcely six months earlier, in October 1987. Note again that the new Resolution, another landmark in Chinese economic reforms, also provides for quasi or full privatization of small SOEs, as well as enhanced 'management rights' for the larger ones.

As a matter of fact, the new October 1987 Resolution, under the catch-phrase 'the state (should) regulate the market, and the market guide the enterprises', clearly purported to be a 'phased', hopefully smooth, transition from 'guidance planning' and 'mandatory planning', as was indeed envisaged in the October 1984 Resolution, although no indication whatsoever was given that the transition should be completed in such a short spell as three or four years. It appeared therefore that Deng deliberately defied his own famous epigram of 'groping the stone to cross the river' and untypically attempted simply to jump over or swim across the rapid currents of 1988.

The 1988–89 crisis ended, in familiar mode, abruptly, not only with a most severe 'double-squeeze', both monetary and fiscal contractions, but also in a drastic return to centralized physical–bureaucratic control that threatened to pre-empt any further industrial deregulation. There is no doubt that, no sooner had the dust of the Tiananmen upheaval settled, than the new planners in charge were inspired by the grossly ineffective 'fight-inflation' experience in the interregnum between Hu and Zhao, the two Party Secretary-Generals deposed hardly three years apart. Several points of interest emerge.

First is that the earlier 'double-squeeze' as applied subsequent to the outburst of inflation in 1985 (at 8.8 per cent) was by any measure far too moderate in the first place. Note that the rates of inflation in 1986 (6.0 per cent) and 1987 (7.3 per cent) were hardly curtailed relative to the 1985 level, and against the background of continuous accumulation of monetary overhang, as indicated in Figure 11.2.[3]

Second is that the 'twin expansion' in investment and wage outlay on the part of the medium and large-scale SOEs (the very core of Chinese industrial system), had indeed persisted through 1988, as prompted by the new-found freedom in investment decision making and wage determination (Tsang and Cheng, 1999). This of course tended to 'crowd out' government-sponsored investment and forcefully resulted in further increases in state budget deficits (Fan, 1999).

Third, it seemed doubtful that the contract-responsibility system (after-tax profit sharing with the Finance Ministry subject to fulfilment of obligatory enterprise targets) as adopted in 1987 on top of the 'tax-for-profits' method would really help to curb the excess liquidity of SOEs to any substantial extent, given the *modus operandi* of the familiar ratchet principle. As a matter of fact, at least for the medium and large-scale SOEs, capital stock expansion in 1984–88 was also found to be hardly constrained by the profit targets, given improved access to bank loans (Kueh, 1999c).

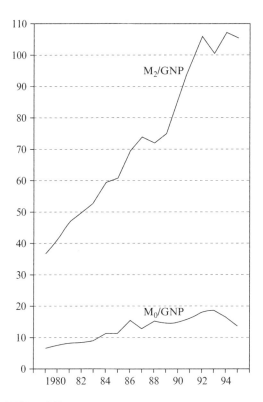

Source: Kueh (1999b), p. 269.

Figure 11.2   Major indicators of monetary overhang in China, 1979–95 (per cent)

Fourth, the 'passive accommodation' of the 1985 bout of inflation by way of ad hoc increases in import supply was clearly not tenable, given the insatiable demand for imports of technology to sustain the country's massive industrialization drive.

Nevertheless, this unsatisfactory background somehow could not help to hold back the promulgation of the October 1987 Resolution for pushing the inflation-prone industrial deregulation to an even higher plane. Even more strangely, it was hardly a month earlier, in September 1987, that, being prompted by widespread *guandao* practices, the central government dispatched a huge ad hoc 'price investigation' delegation (comprising representatives from 28 different state commissions and ministries) to the provinces to help crack down on exorbitant abuses (Kueh, 1989b, p. 389). Hilarious as it was, however, the campaign launched was then hastily made redundant by the draconian injunction from Deng Xiaoping in May 1988.

It is difficult to unravel the mysterious about-face. Perhaps it reflected the inner political dynamics between, say, the so-called 'conservative' and 'reform-minded' factions; nobody knows for sure. But, following the Tiananmen Square crackdown, there came a full-fledged freezing of prices and wages, in the first place, coupled with the resurrection of the Maoist-style ideological campaign. Bank loans and fiscal appropriations were curtailed or suspended altogether for a wide range of investment projects – already embarked on or in the pipeline, productive or 'non-productive'. Mandatory input and output targets returned as well for major industries, together with centralized material allocation. Thus, at a stroke, the entire market-oriented reform was brought to its knees, and the emerging programme of Western-like macroeconomic control swiftly replaced by direct administrative fiats to strictly reduce SOEs autonomy once again (Zhang and Kueh, 1999).

The upshot was, as shown in Figure 11.1, that the inflation rate was drastically reduced, from a high of 18.5 in 1988 and 17.8 per cent in 1989 to a mere 2.1 per cent in 1990 and 2.9 per cent in 1991. Thereby, the ratio of inflation to GNP growth fell substantially, from more than unity (that is, 1.68 and 4.45) to 0.48 and 0.38, respectively.

Severe though it was, no sooner had the situation stabilized than enormous unemployment pressures quickly arose to compel a relaxation in bank loans and credit control, especially to the medium and large-scale SOEs (Kueh, 1991, p. 10.3). The rest is history: Deng Xiaoping's 'South China Tour' in early 1992, the October 1992 NPC Resolution for creating a 'socialist market-economic system', inflation rate accelerating to 5.4 per cent in 1992 and 13 per cent in 1993, and the urgent 16-point programme adopted by Zhu Rongji (the maverick Vice-Premier in charge of economic affairs) in July 1993 for fighting inflation.[4]

Briefly, Zhu's ambitious anti-inflation campaign carried a flavour of Western-style indirect regulation through the use of selective bank loan and interest rate manipulation, a recognition not only of the emerging *modus operandi* of the new market-economic system based on increased deregulation, but also of the need to avoid a repetition of the painful 1989–90 'crash-landing', which had been brought about by a severe and indiscriminate monetary and fiscal squeeze. Even so, over half of Zhu's 16-point directives necessarily took the form of administrative fiats, as, among other factors, relative prices (especially upstream producer goods prices) then probably still remained far from being rationalized (Chai, 1997a, pp. 116–17) to make SOEs sensitive to fiscal and monetary policy leverages.

Interestingly, however, by November 1993, Zhu's programme was somehow overruled by yet another bold set of initiatives – perhaps again with the imprimatur of the Octogenarian leader, formulated at the Third Plenum of the 14th Party Central Committee. Aptly, in pursuit of 'developing the new socialist *market-economic* system by the end of the 20th century' (as the new Resolution puts it), the new initiatives consistently called for wide-ranging economic reforms of fiscal, banking, monetary and foreign exchange systems in China.[5]

The new policy measures include, foremost, the reduction of the 55 per cent profits tax for SOEs to realign with the 33 per cent charged to collective and private enterprises, and the elimination of the supplementary 'regulatory (adjustment) income taxes', although as an offset SOEs would now have to repay bank loans (both principal and interest costs) from after-tax profits rather than gross profits (Chai, 1997a, p. 129). In addition the cumbersome contract-responsibility system was abolished altogether. With this the state as shareholder of SOEs has effectively waived dividend claims. *Postscript*: It was not until lately, in June 2007, that experiments were being carried out for reinstituting the claims, anticipated to be 20 per cent of after-tax profits (*XBCJ*, 1 June 2007; *SCMP*, 20 December 2006).

It is difficult to ascertain how exactly these and similar deregulatory measures in the banking and foreign exchange sectors may have helped to enhance or mitigate inflationary pressures,[6] but, no sooner had Zhu's two-month-old 'fight-inflation' campaign been shelved than, from September to December 1993, loans extended by the state commercial banks soared to the startling amount of some 340 billion *yuan*. The figure accounts specifically for 70 per cent of the yearly total for 1993 (Tsang, 1995, pp. 21.4 and 21.30), and is indeed very much reminiscent of the spectacular mischief of the last quarter of 1984. Perhaps the frenzy was prompted by favourable anticipation of the impending November Third Plenum; we do not know for sure.

At any rate, the rate of inflation accelerated sharply from a mere 5.4 per cent in 1992 to 13.2 per cent in 1993 (vis-à-vis GNP growth of 13.4 per cent) and the all-time high of 21.7 per cent in 1994 (GNP growth, 11.8 per cent), before decelerating down to 14.8 per cent in 1995 (GNP growth, 10.5 per cent) and 6.1 per cent in 1996 (GNP growth 10.2 per cent). Taken as a whole, therefore, the country had (unprecedentedly in its post-1949 history), experienced double-digit inflation for three consecutive years, 1993–95.

Fortunately enough, though, judging by the GNP trends, by 1996 the phased disinflation all pointed to a hoped-for 'soft landing', thereby avoiding a trade-off between economic reform and macroeconomic instability. Perhaps this suggests that the new socialist market-economic system of Chinese characteristics should now finally begin to work properly.

THE INTERPLAY OF THE KEY VARIABLES

The crude quantity theory of exchange has long been used in order to explain the quantitative sources of inflation, according to the familiar equation:

$$PQ = MV,$$

where P denotes the average or general price level; Q, real output or GNP/GDP; M, nominal money supply; and V, the money velocity of income transactions. This shows that, with a given level of output (or a slower rate of increase of output), an increase in money supply (a faster rate of increase) is inherently inflationary, assuming that V remains relatively stable.

Simple as the equation may be, it has nevertheless given rise to many sophisticated econometric estimates made in the West, just to show how inflation in China was caused by 'inordinate' money supply. Hardly any attempt is made, however, to probe beyond the rising monetary veil to discover how the Chinese monetary authority, rather than being the 'culprit *in situ*', represents really none other than the agent designated to accommodate the insatiable demand of SOEs for investment funds. This should apply invariably to the bizarre case of 1984, given that, arguably, any SOEs operating on a 'hard budget constraint' would likely not be conducive to the tantalizing offer from the state banks in the last quarter of the year, as alluded to earlier.

Viewed against these very basics, the other factors influencing the inflationary spells in China, as shown in Figure 11.1, seem to carry relatively marginal weights. A short methodological note is in order, however, before one may proceed further. The time series involved, as shown in the figure, are, in the first place, obviously too short and data points given too scanty to allow any meaningful regression exercise. A 'pooled data' type of regression, for example, with or without 'distributed lag', may yield results that would possibly only help to blur the highly visible causal relations of the variables as exhibited in Figure 11.1.

Note also that the trends of growth for M_0 and M_2 should not be taken as consistently comparable over time. For the early years, when personal saving was practically zero, M_0 should comprise virtually all peasants' cash income plus urban wages. But for the later years, an increased proportion of the potential purchasing powers are subsumed into the M_2 measure, in terms of passbook savings and time deposits. This explains the divergent growth paths of the two measures. Note that, in Figure 11.1, the ordinates of M_0 and M_2 are almost exactly reversed between 1984 and 1995.

Bearing in mind these caveats, a word or two should first be said about the initial inflation spell from 1979 (rate 2 per cent) to 1980 (6 per cent). Undoubtedly this was directly prompted by the first round of decreed increases in both state farm procurement prices and urban wages in 1979–80, which immediately translated into increased state budget deficits. Interestingly, the 'less-harsh' consumption policy as adopted had in fact also immediately triggered the massive 'Economic Readjustment' and the first round of industrial deregulation, though essentially in a passive mood.

There are two aspects to the remarkable changes made in the early 1980s, and both purported indeed to greatly enhance consumer goods supply to help absorb the rapidly rising purchasing power. The first is that the Chinese government felt compelled to cut down production and investment in heavy industry in favour of light industry. The second is to introduce the double-track system (market versus plan) to improve supply efficiency. But, in order not to upset too much the national financial balance, free market prices were nevertheless capped at certain limits until 1985, as alluded to earlier.

It was therefore the 'Economic Readjustment', coupled, fortunately, with three consecutive years of exceptionally good harvests that helped to bring the inflation rate in 1981–84 down basically to the pre-1979–80 standard of near-zero. Note the increased discrepancy between the growth rates of Q (up) and P (down) from 1981 to 1984 as shown in Figure 11.1. And note also that the dramatic increases in both M_0 and M_2 in 1984 are essentially a matter of the mischievous October 1984 banking and wage policies, but that had yet to take their toll in 1985.

Looking at the drastic upsurge in inflation in 1985 (P at a record high of 8.8 per cent, as shown in Figure 11.1), the basic cause should therefore not be seen in any unexpected shortfall in Q (GDP/GNP growth rate only marginally down from the record high of 15.2 per cent in 1984 to 13.5 per cent in 1985), but rather in the dramatic acceleration in M_0 and M_2 towards the end of 1984, in the first place. The underlying key variables given in Table 11.1 are highly revealing. Although agricultural output (in gross value, or GVAO) was somewhat reduced by a relatively bad harvest in 1985, the decline, by 3.4 per cent, was greatly offset by an all-time high in growth of industry output (GVIO), by 21.4 per cent to result in the GDP growth of 13.5 per cent.

Note, in particular, that the robust industrial growth in 1985 was paralleled by spectacular increases in fixed assets investment, by 41.8 per cent, by the state-industrial sector, or by 38.8 per cent in total. Increases in personal consumption and especially wage outlay are equally impressive for 1985 and the following years. And these all took place against the backdrop of an unparalleled growth in 'domestic loans', by 97.4 per cent in 1985 and

Table 11.1   Growth rates of industrial and agricultural output, fixed asset investment and sources of financing, and wage outlay and personal consumption, 1979–96 (per cent)

	Gross output value		Fixed investment		Sources of finance		Wage outlay	Personal consumption
	Industry	Agriculture	Total	State	Loans	Self-raised		
1979	8.81	6.1	—	2.9	—	—	19.4	6.9
1980	9.27	1.4	6.7	2.8	—	—	22.0	9.0
1981	4.29	6.5	5.5	−10.5	—	—	13.1	8.3
1982	7.82	11.3	28.0	26.6	41.9	34.1	12.7	6.8
1983	11.19	7.8	16.2	12.6	−0.3	18.7	12.6	8.1
1984	16.28	12.3	28.2	24.5	47.3	27.6	18.5	12.0
1985	21.39	3.4	38.8	41.8	97.4	41.6	24.8	13.5
1986	11.67	3.4	22.7	23.7	29.0	21.9	35.4	4.7
1987	17.69	5.8	21.5	27.8	32.4	19.9	6.0	21.7
1988	20.79	3.9	25.4	23.3	12.1	32.5	12.1	7.8
1989	8.54	3.1	−7.2	−7.0	−22.0	0.7	3.6	−0.2
1990	7.76	7.6	2.4	6.3	16.1	−1.2	0.2	3.7
1991	14.77	3.7	23.9	24.4	48.5	21.2	6.2	8.6
1992	24.70	6.4	44.4	48.1	68.4	41.0	12.2	7.9
1993	27.30	7.8	30.4	21.3	38.8	69.6	11.0	8.4
1994	24.20	8.6	17.5	13.3	30.1	34.7	11.2	4.6
1995	20.30	10.9	14.8	10.6	5.0	16.3	12.0	7.8
1996	16.60	9.4	8.8	9.0	9.0	15.3	14.6	9.4

Notes: Figures for industrial and agricultural output, as well as those for wage outlay and consumption, are all based on absolute magnitude given at 'comparable prices'. Those for investment and sources of financing are at current prices. Other sources (not given here) include state budget appropriation and foreign capital.

Sources: *TJNJ 1998*, Table 13.4 for industry output; ibid., Table 12.6 for agricultural output, 1980, 1985, 1987–96; *TJNJ 1988*, p. 216 for 1981–84 and 1986; *TJNJ 2004*, Table 6.2 for investment, 1981 and 1985–96; *TJNJ 2001*, Table 6.2 for 1981–84 and *TJNJ 1985*, p. 416 for 1979–80; *TJNJ 2006*, Table 6.4 for sources of finance, 1982–96; and *TJNJ 2006*, Table 3.17 for wage outlay and consumption.

47.3 per cent in 1984 (Table 11.1). Note also that investments financed by funds accumulated by the enterprises themselves show similarly impressive growth in those years, consequent upon the tax-for-profits reform, among other things. Thus all this clearly points to the background of accelerated industrial deregulation and decontrol in the monetary and fiscal regimes.

A close look at the macroeconomic indicators given in Table 11.1, in conjunction with Figure 11.1, would indeed only help to reveal that the short-lived retrenchment, if any, made in 1986, was in effect a veiled preparation for an even bolder round of inflation to come in 1988–89. As a matter of fact, total fixed asset investment continued to grow in 1986–88 at over

20 per cent per year, associated with equally high, if not higher, rates of growth in 'domestic loans' and 'self-financed' investments, as well as total wage outlay. Thus, taken together, the entire 1985–88 episode resembles very much a 'triple-jump' that is bound to collapse heavily at the last, most rigorous, attempt for any athletes aspiring to break the Olympic record.

There seems therefore a good reason to suggest that the maverick octogenarian Deng was made awfully ignorant of the colossal background of monetary overhang accumulated in 1984–87, when he opted for the fateful 'short pain' in May 1988 that immediately triggered bank run and panic buying, to result in the enormous rise in the velocity of M_0 (Figure 11.1) and hence the record high inflation rate in 1988 (18.5 per cent) and 1989 (17.8 per cent). Put plainly, had it not been for the continual robust GDP growth of 11.3 per cent in 1988, the subsequent economic disasters of 1988–89 could have easily reached a totally unmanageable proportion.

Taken together, the instantaneous outbreak of inflation in 1985 and 1988–89, or for that matter that of 1980 and 1993–94 clearly suggests that, unlike the familiar cyclical fluctuations in the West, the Chinese pattern represents a system *sui generis*, very much conditioned by the attempt made by Deng to engineer a breakthrough in the economics of industrial deregulation.

References are made (in the foregoing section) to the possible microeconomic foundation of inflationary pressures in the 1980s. As a matter of fact, in the same study, entitled *Industrial Reform and Macroeconomic Instability in China*, as quoted (Kueh, Chai and Fan, 1999), the medium and large-scale SOEs (in total 300 under study) are all clearly implicated. There are several aspects worth addressing, if only briefly, in order to further substantiate the perceived linkage between industrial deregulation and inflation.

The first relates to the rapid accumulation of the wage-money overhang in 1984–88. This is clearly bound up with the permanent urge common to all SOEs to maintain or expand labour reserves, the continuous built-in rigidity in dismissing workers or in mitigating 'deadweight' wage subsidies and, above all, the powerful workers' aspiration emerging from the economic transition for improving their lot. There appears really no reason why the managers of SOEs, being basically in the same boat, should attempt to strongly subdue workers' rising wage expectation (ibid., p. 279).

Thus, while the 1984–85 wage reform may have brought about some (at times dubious) productivity improvements, the ensuing profitability gains appeared nevertheless to be grossly subjected to wage and bonus claims. The balance sheet analysis conducted by Yang and Han (1999) for the quoted study reveals that, between 1984–85 (wage reforms) and 1987–88, SOEs which displayed a 'negative elasticity' of wage outlay (positive growth) with respect to the combined total (reduced) of profits and taxes remitted to the state, increased from 30 to 58 per cent of the total surveyed. And those which exhibited an 'elasticity greater than unity' (wage outlay growing faster than contributions to state budget) increased from 20 to 45 per cent, respectively.[7]

The second aspect deals with the familiar phenomenon of 'investment hunger'. That is, against the backdrop of a pervasive sellers' market, the prospect for any SOEs should virtually remain 'permanently buoyant' for any investments to be undertaken; hence the insatiable demand for finances. However, with the internally available funds (comprising profit retentions and increased capital amortization as allowed in the 1984–85 fiscal reform package) being increasingly encroached upon by the remarkable 'wage drift', the SOEs were left with no alternative but to turn to the state banks ('commercialized' in 1984–85); notwithstanding that the borrowings practically involved hardly any opportunity costs, as alluded to earlier. Thus, as Fan (1999) estimated for the study, the share of internally-funded investments for the 300 SOEs surveyed declined remarkably, from 41 per cent in 1985 to 26 per cent in 1988 – almost exactly the same level as in 1980. But total investments nevertheless kept on increasing at high speed in 1985–88 (Table 11.1).[8]

The third, and perhaps most important, aspect relates finally to the very issue of whether the monetary and banking authorities could really be made more 'prudent' in lending money. Here again, the harsh fact in the Chinese context is that, subsequent to the 1984–85 banking reform, the local-level branches of the 'commercialized' state banks had actually only become more prone to pressures from the provincial authority for granting the required bank loans to locally based SOEs, be they under the jurisdiction of the central industrial-branch ministries or the provincial counterparts. Note that many centrally-sponsored SOEs were in effect placed under the 'dual-line' control. In either case, expansion in investment and production by the SOEs would all help to boost the local economy and generate employment. Thus, as Fan (1999, p. 181) aptly puts it, the excessive increases in bank loans extended between 1984 and 1988 should be regarded as a 'forced rise in money supply', in that, during the period, the central authority actually did not engage in any expansionary monetary policy.

Taken together, this is clearly also the case of a 'forced rise in consumption', to the extent that the acceleration in inflation in 1984–88 was caused directly by accelerated wage claims and indirectly by added wage expenditure arising from expanded investment as just explained. Undoubtedly, this should also be understood as the background against which continuous realignment between light industry and heavy industry had taken place towards the end of the 1980s for a reintegration in favour of an increasingly consumer-based national industrial structure, as alluded to in Chapter 9. There is also no doubt that the reorientation was, in the first place, arguably built upon, and indeed strongly facilitated by, the material foundation Mao had left behind.

THE 1993–95 EPISODE OF INFLATION

The key to unravelling this extraordinary inflation dynamics should be the historic October 1992 NPC Resolution for the most decisive phase of industrial deregulation, coupled indeed with the imperatives for resurrecting immediately the country from the deepest 1989–90 economic crisis. Thus, as shown in Table 11.1 (see also Figure 11.1), all major aggregates soared instantly in 1991, fixed assets investments up by 24 per cent, and domestic loans extended for financing the investments by a startling 49 per cent. These clearly helped to trigger industrial output growth to accelerate from 15 per cent in 1991 to 25 per cent in 1992, and with this an even more spectacular surge in domestic loans (by 68 per cent) and fixed investments (by 48 per cent for the state sector, or 44 per cent in total) in 1992. Needless to say, wage outlay and personal consumption are bound to rise in tandem, though not as remarkably as in 1984–88.

It is against this background specifically that mandatory planning was dismantled, and the double-track system abolished towards the end of 1992, in favour of a full-fledged system of market regulation and free prices; hence the drastic upsurge in inflation rate in 1993 (13.2 per cent) and 1994 (21.7 per cent). Note that 1993 was an exceptionally good harvest year, in terms of grain output. Barring this, the inflation rate would clearly have turned out to be even higher. Nevertheless, while the case of 1993 may be readily explained by the sudden collapse of the acute monetary overhang, with the freed SOEs immediately exploiting their monopoly privileges, that of 1994 deserves further scrutiny.

To begin with, official estimates show that a massive rise in food prices (by 35 per cent in June 1994) accounted for 12.1 percentage points out of the 21.7 per cent rise in retail prices in 1994 (56 per cent of the total). Together with wage hikes, this was responsible for the 65 percentage-point contribution to total annual inflation in 1994 resulting from 'cost-push' factors. The investment surge accounted for much of the remaining (35 per cent) 'demand-pull' contribution (Kueh, 1999b, p. 271). Several points emerge from the 'decomposition' exercise.

The first relates to the fact that the massive increases in retail food prices – the main culprit of the 1994 inflation – were preceded by decreed

increases in farm procurement prices of a similar magnitude. The earlier
price rises were in turn probably deemed necessary to compensate the peasants for the imposed increases in agricultural input prices resulting from
price decontrol, subsequent to the 1992–93 industrial deregulation (cf.
Chen, 1995). Note, in particular that, paradoxical as it was, the food procurement prices were raised, despite the fact that the 1993 harvest was after
all an all-time record and agricultural conditions in the summer of 1994
highly favourable as well (in the event, 1994 grain output was only 2.5 per
cent below that of 1993) (Kueh, 1999b, pp. 288–9).

The second point relates to the remarkable upsurge of investment expenditure which, together with the food price rise, should account for around 90
per cent of the 1994 inflation component. There seems little doubt that the
upsurge was strongly prompted by the massive increases in bank credits in
the last few months of 1993, in defiance of Zhu Rongji's 16-point 'fight-
inflation' campaign. But, as a factor, it should again not be seen as oblivious
to the broader context of industrial deregulation, especially the extensive,
and most favourable, fiscal reforms of November 1993 for the SOEs. Note
that, towards the end of 1993, even for the large-scale SOEs, around three-
quarters of input materials needed had to be acquired from the market. In
coastal provinces, 90 per cent of producer goods required by the enterprises
were purchased from markets, rather than directly allocated through the plan
(Yi, 1994, p. 199; *Renmin Ribao*, 20 November 1993). And in fact, no sooner
had the October 1992 Resolution been promulgated, than 85 per cent of producer goods sales were transacted at free market prices (Chen, 1995, p. 4).

Note also that, as early as March 1994, the central authorities already felt
compelled to reinstate administrative measures to curb 'unwarranted investment' and 'unscrupulous (price-raising) practices' throughout the country
(Tsang, 1995, p. 21.10). In other words, were it not for the timely renewed
control over investment – selective though it may have been – given the government's determination to keep many strategic industrial SOEs afloat, the
inflation rate in 1994 might even have exceeded the recorded 21.7 per cent.

Perhaps the drive to curb investment in March 1994 was also deliberately
designed to prepare for the subsequent massive increases in farm procurement prices; that is, to help pre-empt the outbreak of inflation on a totally
unmanageable scale; we do not know for sure. However, this clearly appears
to be an absolutely acute case of policy trade-off between avoiding a full-
blown agricultural crisis and pursuing persistently the massive industrialization drive.

At any rate, as a result of the severe investment curbs, markets for producer
goods stabilized during 1994 (the prices of many producer goods actually fell
quite substantially). The timely pervasive crackdown on 'price abuses' in
earlier 1994 also helped basically to enhance consumer confidence – unlike

summer 1988, when Deng's 'short pain' approach immediately prompted bank runs and panic buying.[9] This had no doubt contributed to the impressive rises in urban and rural residents' bank savings deposits in 1994, with the year-end balance recording a 42 per cent increase over the previous year.

The story of the 1993–95 inflation should not be considered as complete without dealing at some length with the emerging external trade balance, as it may bear on the aggregate supply–demand equation. In 1994, burgeoning exports helped generate a record trade surplus. Coupled with accelerated FDI influx, and as a result also of the massive *renminbi* devaluation in January 1994 (part of the comprehensive reform package of November 1993), when the official exchange rate (5.7 *yuan* to US$1.0) was realigned with the market rate (8.7 *yuan* to US$1.0), China's foreign exchange reserves soared to reach US$51.6 billion at the end of 1994 (that is, US$30 billion above the level of December 1993).

On the basis of the new unified rate, additional foreign exchange reserves translated into an injection of some 250 billion *yuan* into the domestic economy. This overwhelmingly constituted most of the base money creation for 1994 (Yao, 1995), and helps explain the impressive growth in money supply, especially in M_2 (see Figure 11.1). The unexpected new factor forced the central bank to institute a policy of restricted loans to domestic enterprises in order to avoid disturbing the already strained monetary balance. The knock-on effect was, however, to delay the expected 'soft landing' (Naughton, 1995, pp. 1102–3).

Consider next the situation in 1995, when the rate of inflation fell to 14.8 per cent. With continued monthly rises in China's trade surplus, foreign exchange reserves grew steadily to reach US$73.6 billion in December 1995, that is, US$22 billion more than in December 1994. This put further pressure on the strained internal aggregate demand–supply balance inherited from the previous year. Meanwhile, in an effort to ease such pressure, in December 1994, the government began to ban exports of rice and maize, while sharply increasing grain imports. The result was to transform net grain exports of 7.94 million tonnes (1993 and 1994 combined) into net imports of almost 20 million tonnes in 1995, as shown in Table 11.2.[10]

In value terms, China's agricultural imports (which are dominated by grain) rose by nearly 80 per cent in 1995 to reach US$11.55 billion. The total agricultural trade surplus was thereby reduced from US$5.9 billion in 1994 to a mere US$0.71 billion in 1995. On the basis of a dollar exchange rate of 8.5 *yuan*, 1995 agricultural imports helped to 'sterilize' almost 100 billion *yuan* – about one-third of base money creation. There is no doubt that increased imports helped slow down the rise in grain prices, which in July 1995 were already 28.5 per cent above the previous year's level (*SCMP*, 17 August 1995; Xin,1995, p. 11).

*Table 11.2   China's agricultural trade, and grain exports and imports,
1993–95*

	1993	1994	1995
Total grain output (million tonnes)	456.49	445.10	466.62
Total agricultural trade (US$100 million):			
Exports (X)	123.00	124.70	122.60
Imports (M)	24.00	65.70	115.50
Balance (X) – (M)	99.00	59.00	7.10
Total grain trade (million tonnes):			
Exports	13.27	11.04	0.64
Imports	7.33	9.04	20.40
Balance (X) – (M)	5.94	2.00	–19.76

Sources: TJNJ 1997, Table 11.2 for grain production. Trade statistics are from Chinese
Customs data, given in *DGB*, 13 Feb. 1996. Estimates for agricultural trade (1993) are from
TJNJ 1994, p. 509.

In addition to the agricultural export ban and increased agricultural
import supply, there were certainly other factors that all contributed to the
slowing of inflation during 1995. These include the introduction in 1994 of
a guaranteed-value (inflation-indexed) bank deposit scheme, two rises in
1995 in bank interest rates, restrictive/selective bank loans for investment,
and continuous bureaucratic curbs on 'unscrupulous' pricing practices.
Coupled with the increasing use of credit cards and the payment of wages
through bank transfers, the impact of such policy measures was then considered by the Governor of the People's Bank of China as quite effective
(*DGB*, 22 January 1966).

At any rate, the growth of money in circulation (M_0) fell sharply, from
24.2 per cent in 1994 to only 8.2 per cent in 1995, while broad money supply
(M_2) declined markedly from 34.4 to 29.5 per cent (see Figure 11.1) in
preparation for the 'soft landing' in 1996.

CONCLUSION

The spectacular 1993–95 inflation episode should perhaps be regarded as
a once-for-all response to the Deng-style 'big push' towards a full-fledged
marketization in 1992–93. If correct, inflation in China may henceforth follow the cyclical pattern as observed in the West, yet the new
Chinese system continues to differ quite significantly from the archetypal

market economy, with implications for the behaviour of the general price level.

Foremost is the quantitative dominance of the large and medium-scale SOEs in national industrial investment, production and employment, and hence the privileges to claim the bulk of state bank loans, and to command consistently the entire national industrial linkages, both forward and backward. No doubt they have survived Deng's colossal 'deregulatory' upheavals, and have indeed become the sole custodian of the new '*socialist* market-economic system', as other lesser SOEs have now all been privatized, de jure, or de facto. In other words, the two basic institutional dimensions, state ownership and monopoly powers, remain intact, and should, *ceteris paribus*, continue to exert synergistic influence on the inflation dynamics in China for some time to come.

In the circumstances, any further acceleration in privatization of the remaining SOEs for purpose of, say, hardening the enterprises' 'budget constraints', or curbing the built-in 'wage drift', would in fact only help to deprive the state of the last lines of political and administrative controls available to it through ownership, for checking monopolistic abuses.[11] Perhaps this would nevertheless help to promote Schumpeterian capital accumulation for R&D and technological progress. We do not know for sure.

There are, however, two emerging factors that may eventually help to break the impasse. The first is the development of the non-state economic sector that has strongly gained momentum since the early 1990s to encroach increasingly upon the reserved economic sphere of the SOEs. The second is that, with increased FDI influx, foreign competition has come in as well. In this respect, the celebrated initiative, also personally taken by Deng himself in 1992, for 'opening up the domestic market in exchange for technology' could indeed prove to be very crucial in the long run.

Meanwhile, the drastic investment and capital stock expansion made during the buoyant years of 1992–95 has also forcefully translated into excess production capacity and supply glut in the second half of the 1990s. Compounded by the impact of the Asian financial crisis, the ensuing protracted disinflation since 1997 has no doubt significantly helped to transform the SOEs, and the Chinese banking and financial system as well, to be in line with what was envisaged in the comprehensive reform agenda of November 1993, for realigning the basic Chinese economic structure with the Western model.[12]

Postscript: As a matter of fact, following the *renminbi* devaluation in 1994 (and especially the country's accession to the World Trade Organization in 2001), mounting accumulation of foreign exchange reserves (to the tune of US$1333 billion by end-June 2007) resulting from continuous increases in trade surplus and the influx of FDI, has already obliged the Chinese authorities to revalue the currency time and again, albeit marginally, in order to keep inflation in check. Undoubtedly the predicament of holding in balance the domestic interest rate against the external value of *renminbi* will continue to haunt the People's Bank of China – the monetary authority of the country. Hopefully the well-tested managed-float exchange rate regime need not be abandoned, to follow the painful experience of Japan consequent upon the signing of the Plaza Accord in 1985.

At any rate, the tumultuous inflation episodes of 1988–89 and 1993–95 have very much become a matter of the past, but China, in joining the rank of major Western countries, still has increasingly to face cyclical fluctuations as elsewhere.

NOTES

*   This chapter draws, by permission of Oxford University Press, substantially on Y.Y. Kueh, 'Prospects for a transition to a market economy without runaway inflation', in Y.Y. Kueh, Joseph C.H. Chai and Fan Gang (eds), *Industrial Reform and Macroeconomic Instability in China*, Oxford: Clarendon Press, 1999, pp. 263–91. New statistics and new materials are added.

1.   The monetary overhang, as may be estimated in terms of repressed inflation, may not appear to be strongly in evidence according to an estimate made by Imai (1997, p. 201).

2.   This is the first ever, albeit relatively marginal, outbreak of inflation in contemporary China history. The inflation rate of 6 per cent in 1980, in terms of the retail price index, represents a mere four percentage-point increase from the low of 2 per cent in 1979, or for that matter, the average of 0.6 per cent for 1955–78, ignoring possible 'repressed inflation'. This first bout of inflation was clearly triggered by the drastic increases in farm procurement prices beginning with the summer harvests of 1979 and concurrent increases in wages for the workers. Both increases were decreed by the government, and in fact occurred before any major programme of industrial deregulation per se was launched. If anything, it should be the massive 'Economic Readjustment' made in 1979–80 (which aimed to curtail production and investment in heavy industry in favour of light industry) that, in combination with consecutive good harvests in 1982–84, helped to deflate the emerging inflationary pressures.

3.   See also Imai (1997, pp. 201–2) for quotes from authoritative Chinese sources about growth in money supply relative to GDP increases in 1984–87.

4.   By June 1993 the monthly inflation rate already stood at 13.3 per cent, compared with 8.6 per cent in January. See Ho (1994) for details of Zhu's programme. The 16-point directive comprised essentially a variety of administrative decrees, which required banks to recall 'unwarranted' loans, stop 'irregular' lending to non-financial institutions, reduce infrastructural investment financing, and fulfil treasury bonds' subscription quotas (by 15 July) in advance of approval of any new schemes to raise capital. Other measures included (*a*) diverting earmarked funds from IOUs (*da baitiao*) for farm procurements in order to prevent earmarked funds from being reallocated to 'undesirable' industrial or real estate projects; (*b*) separating 'policy' loans from commercial loans in order to guarantee adequate supplies of funds to priority sectors, including agriculture; (*c*) curtailing administrative expenses by a uniform 20 per cent to curb the purchasing power of state agencies; (*d*) imposing a moratorium on price reforms in the second half

of 1993; and (perhaps most importantly) (*e*) strengthening the role of the People's Bank as a central bank by adjusting (that is, increasing) interest rates (on savings deposits and loans) in order to address a growing 'disintermediation' crisis (that is, the phenomenon of funds circulating outside the banking sector (*tiwai xunhuan*) to take advantage of higher market interest rates and so avoid 'intermediation' by banks in transferring household savings to the enterprise sector. For a good illustration of the 'financial order' that prevailed in the first half of 1993 and forced Zhu's intervention in June of that year, see Tsang (1995, pp. 20.3–4). Naughton (1995, pp. 1097–9) gives an excellent account of the 'disintermediation' crisis of 1993. Cf. also Hong (1993, p. 4) for consideration of the 'double track' flow of capital.

5. There are different interpretations of this dramatic policy reversal. Many outside observers did indeed suggest that Zhu's programme was compromised by the personal intervention of Deng Xiaoping who, on the analogy of the dramatic 1992–93 recovery from retrenchment of 1990–91, presumably favoured a continuous upsurge in economic activities. But Tsang (1995, p. 10.6) sees the policy reversal as part of a 'stop-go' (*zouzou tingting*) approach, which was deliberately formulated in preparation for the bold and comprehensive programme of reform, launched in November 1993. Nevertheless, there remains little doubt that Zhu's short-lived anti-inflation campaign tended strongly to trigger a deceleration in both investment and current industrial production in the vulnerable state industrial sector (Ho, 1994).

6. Most important is probably the decision to detach entirely the People's Bank of China as a central bank from the Ministry of Finance. This obliges the Ministry henceforth to resort to bond issuance rather than bank borrowing to finance budget deficits. Other new major banking and monetary policy measures include (a) the creation of 'policy banks' (three in total) which should take over from the four specialized state commercial banks the non-profitable 'policy loans', and (b) the 'asset/liability ratio management' method which should help to further 'commercialize' the specialized banks by restricting bank loans relative to the size of deposits taken. In addition, the Third Plenum Resolution also re-emphasizes the need for the People's Bank to readjust the benchmark interest rate more often, and to allow the commercial banks a greater bandwidth to float the loan and deposit interests. It seems doubtful, however, that the new measures could really help to coerce the SOEs (especially the larger ones) to follow a more prudent borrowing practice, given that their interest elasticity of demand for bank loans had proved to be 'practically zero' (Chai, 1997a, p. 129). In the foreign economic sector, the most significant change made is of course the unification of the overvalued *Renminbi* exchange rate with the lower 'swap rate' under a float-management regime.

7. As summarized in Kueh (1999b, p. 280), Yang and Han also consistently show that wage payment (net of bonus awards) as a share of the combined total of profits, taxes and the wage bill itself, increased from the range of 12 to 14 per cent in 1984 to the tune of 18 or 19 per cent in 1988, irrespective of which wage reform package was applied. Zhang and Kueh, and Fan as well, have all come up with similar estimates from different perspectives (ibid.).

8. Basic neoclassical or Keynesian economic principles would dictate that, in the circumstances, interest rates should be raised to help curb investment and inflation. But students familiar with Chinese or Soviet-style economics would readily recognize that, in practice, the lending rates could not be raised to any substantial level for any significant period of time. As with the potential consequences of any effort to raise significantly a depressed wage rate to an 'equilibrium' level, the universal liberalization of interest rates would have been almost certain to reduce the existing fiscal balance and redistributive mechanism to chaos, thereby fundamentally disturbing the order of priorities underlying national economic strategy (Kueh, 1999b, p. 283). This explains why centralized ad hoc administrative fiats were preferred to reign in the tumultuous years, 1989 and 1990, in order to minimize the spill-over effects.

9. Contrary to widespread outside perception (Tsang, 1995, p. 21.9), Chen Jinhua, Chairman of the State Development and Reform Commission at the time, divulged recently (at the 'Oral History' interview programme of Hong Kong-based Phoenix

Television Station in late night 28 July 2007) that there was indeed also panic buying, even in Beijing in summer 1994.

10. Foreign observers have suggested that the sharp rise in grain imports in 1995 reflected renewed problems in grain production during 1994. But Table 11.2 shows that 1994 output fell by only a small margin over the 1993 record and was equal to the previous high, achieved in 1990. Rather, there is little doubt that the surge in grain imports in 1995 reflected 'demand-pull' forces, not crisis management designed to offset any dramatic output decline. Note, too, that grain output in 1995 reached yet another new peak.

11. A highly enlightening note: Wang and Tsang (1999) point out that, in the 1980s, the 300 sampled state enterprises were more constrained by mandatory output and investment targets, government wage policy and enforced profit-*cum*-tax remittances than they were by monetary aggregates, such as bank credits, or cash and demand deposit supplies. By contrast, the 1990s have seen planning and conventional fiscal constraint removed in favour of greater emphasis on monetary policy. Such a change is likely to expand the manoeuvrability and enhance the monopolistic behaviour of state enterprises.

12. Starting in 1998, for example, mandatory bank loan quotas were effectively abolished. The commercial banks are finally free to make their own lending decisions, subject to the central bank's regulation on the basis of asset-to-liability ratios. For these and other banking reform measures, see Kueh (2000, pp. 135–7). For various monetary policy measures adopted to cope with the deflationary pressures, see Kueh (2001).

PART V

From Autarky to the WTO

12. Foreign economic relations readjusted, 1979–84*

THE PRELUDE

Obscure as it may now appear to be, it was in fact Hua Guofeng, the heir-presumptive upon Mao's death for the 1976–78 interregnum, who initiated the most dramatic turnaround towards the West. Falling back on the earlier 1973–74 Mao-Zhou efforts with the urea plants imports from the United States, Hua embarked on a massive technology imports programme for 1978, which was worth double the combined value for similar imports for 1973–77, as is shown in Table 12.1. No doubt Hua was then greatly buoyed by the rapidly improved political relations with the United States and her major allies.

However, this 'open-door' strategy of Hua represented the only major plank of his overall economic programme that had survived through the Deng era. For both Hua and Deng, access to foreign technology was clearly crucial, not only to the continuous pursuit of modernization but also for merely arresting, in the first place, the declining trends in industrial productivity due to years of repetitive investments in capital-intensive but dated industrial technologies. The common orientation towards foreign trade ends here, nevertheless.

For Hua, the key to resolving the economic predicament should be bound up with an overall strategy which favoured economic growth at rates well in excess of those historically achieved, which continued to emphasize heavy industry (symbolized by the ambitious 60 million tonnes target for 1985 steel output), and in which the organization of the economy was recentralized, with no significant concessions for market incentives and 'freedoms'. In short, these all imply continuous physical–bureaucratic control, foreign trade sector included, plus of course 'austerity', as practised in the Maoist past. Note that there also remained an unwillingness to finance imports through credit, other than the customary supplier credit for plants.

The implicit assumptions of the Hua strategy appear to have been that (a) the stimulating effect of imports on growth would operate rapidly, and (b) growth would be biased towards a form that should somehow enable

Table 12.1   Complete plants and technology imports, 1973–81 (US$ million)

	Total value				
	1973–77	1978	1979	1980	1981
(1) Total value of import contracts	3 960	7 700	1 800	2 130	298
(2) Patent trade, industrial					
consultancy, technical services					
and cooperation	166	11	22	329	86
(3) Ratio (2)/(1) × 100	4.19	0.14	1.22	12.61	28.86

Sources: JJNJ 1982, V, p. 284; *1981*, IV, p. 131.

export expansion to generate the foreign exchange needed for the import programme. Perhaps Hua was also thinking of the growing potential of a programme of plant imports to be financed by oil revenues that was resisted by the 'gang of four'. We do not know for sure.

At any rate, the boldest Hua import initiative, which was shortly after his downfall branded as '*yang yuejin*' (Great Leap Outward), immediately turned the large visible trade surplus of 1977 into a deficit in the final quarter of 1978. And, compounded by the huge forward import commitments made, notably 11 major contracts in December 1978 which were signed with extraordinary haste (often to the surprise of Western partners), presumably as ministries foresaw the retrenchment to come (Chen Huiqin, 1981, Lin Senmu, 1981), the trade imbalances persisted through 1979 and 1980. Undoubtedly this had helped to precipitate the need for the Readjustment to come, quite apart from the unreality of the macroeconomics of Hua's programme.

Note that China's policy towards the visible balance has been consistently conservative over the years. Imbalances are explicable by exceptional events and are generally short-lived. This is obviously rooted in what the planners perceive as imperatives for minimizing dependence on foreign supply, in order to maintain a desired degree of stability in the national planning system. Thus, even the import share of capital goods which have consistently been accorded the highest priority had fluctuated with the internal industrialization cycle. Hua's bizarre initiatives have completely upset the balance, however.

Against this background, this chapter attempts to show how China's foreign economic relations were readjusted from 1979, within the broader context of national Economic Readjustment established in 1979–84, and how the initial practical policy measures for the 'open-door' strategy *à la*

Deng were formulated and put into practice. The first section highlights the major readjustments made in trade policy for redressing the excesses committed by Hua Guofeng, and analyses in some detail the quantitative impact on export and import trade structure, and trade balances. The second section provides an overall view on the completely new Chinese strategy for courting foreign capital for both direct and indirect investment, in order to bridge the domestic savings and investment gap.

Section three examines how the entire conventional system of foreign trade planning and organization has been reshuffled to suit the emerging open-door strategy. Section four looks at the operational approaches to attracting foreign direct investment (FDI), including forms of business organization, and tax and other types of incentives provided. A particular reference is made to the fundamental issue of how the FDI strategy which has hitherto been entirely alien to China, should fit in with the country's avowed economic goal of building, at maximum speed, an independent and integrated industrial system of its own.

The last section analyses the difficulty associated with the existing commodity pricing practices, and the absolutely overvalued Chinese currency as inherited from the Maoist past, for further promoting trade, and shows how using the fixed exchange rate regime for *Renminbi* to serve the purpose is inherently destabilizing. The discussion is concluded with a brief note about the prospects of the open-door strategy.

READJUSTMENT IN TRADE POLICY AND QUANTITATIVE IMPACT

The most immediate concern of the Readjustment was obviously to scale down the mounting trade deficits resulting from Hua's unrealistic programme of technology imports, in order not to compound the emerging difficulty with internal balance caused by the decreed increases in farm procurement prices and urban wages in 1979–81. Thus, apart from drastic import curtailments, rigorous efforts were made to promote exports. Light industries were called upon to enhance supply for matching, not only rising domestic consumption demand, but also export requirements as well. More interestingly, heavy industry, hitherto an entirely 'closed system', was also strongly urged to make use of production capacity rendered idle by the Economic Readjustment and the cancellation (in December 1978) of the 60 million tonnes steel output target, to produce machines and equipment for the export markets.

These all seemed to suggest that the massive industrialization drive over the previous three decades had begun to pay dividends, being able to help bail out the country from mounting external indebtedness. Note that, on the eve of opening up in 1978, 'industrial products' as a broad category of exports, as opposed to 'primary commodities', did already account for 46.5 per cent of the country's total exports, although admittedly the exported machines and equipment were at best embodied in 'immediate technology' suitable for other developing countries.

At any rate, the Readjustment has had a dramatic effect on quantitative trends in trade. In 1979, the visible account was in deficit by US$906 million. By 1982, China had achieved a surplus of US$6.868 billion, as shown in Table 12.2. This surplus was achieved in spite of a poor world trade environment and it enabled China to accumulate substantial foreign exchange resources and also to repay, ahead of schedule, loans from the International Monetary Fund (IMF) which had been granted to support the Readjustment programme. No doubt the IMF wishes that it had more clients of this quality.

Note that this feat was accomplished against the backdrop of an unbridled expansion of imports. From Table 12.2 it will be observed that imports increased in real terms in the years 1977, 1978 and 1979, by 32 per cent, 51 per cent and 21 per cent, respectively. Data in Table 12.1 indicate the role of complete plant imports in this expansion. Table 12.3 reveals which of the five different major commodity groups contributed to the turnaround.[1] Several points emerge from Table 12.3.

First, the exports–imports balance for foodstuffs actually deteriorated between 1979 and 1982, thus making a negative contribution to the improvement in overall trade balance. This can be easily explained by accelerated increases in grain imports prompted in part by indirect demand for feed grains to support the growth of meat production for improving the dietary structure.[2] Another factor is the continuous decline since 1976 of exports of rice, which at one time constituted the largest single category of China's agricultural exports (Kueh,1984b).

Second, the mineral sector (mainly petroleum) contributed a startling 35 per cent of the trade balance improvement. This essentially reflects the dramatic increases in exports (since imports are very small) and underlines the crucial role of oil and petroleum in China's balance of payments. (It also explains why China has to allow domestic industry to work below capacity because of fuel shortages.)

Third, the largest contribution (49 per cent) to the improvement is actually by manufactured and semi-manufactured goods (from the textile and clothing industries in particular). Here, the net balance has increased almost tenfold, from US$473 million in 1979 to US$4.662 billion in 1982. Disaggregated, the data for this group reveal that, while imports marginally declined between 1979 and 1982, exports increased by 73 per cent.

Table 12.2   Aggregate trade balances and growth of exports and imports, 1970–83 (US$ million)

	1970	1975	1977	1978	1979	1980	1981	1982	1983
Visible trade									
balance, FOB	112	303	1564	−161	−906	−305	3547	6868	5584
cumulative total (since 1950)	1260	2985	6264	6103	5197	4892	8439	15307	20891
Exports									
total, FOB	2163	7121	8178	10170	13458	18875	21496	23501	23983
real growth (%) (p. annum)		10.1	−1.9	23.9	17.6	21.4	n.a.	n.a.	n.a.
Imports									
total, FOB	2051	6818	6614	10331	14364	19180	17949	16633	18399
real growth (%) of which:		11.6	32.3	51.0	21.0	14.2	n.a.	n.a.	n.a.
Capital goods									
total	411	1996	1165	1994	3705	5131	4343	3068	n.a.
real growth (%)		19.2	−33.0	58.1	76.3	n.a.	n.a.	n.a.	n.a.

Notes: Capital goods cover machinery (SITC 71, 722–4), transport equipment (SITC 73) and precision instruments (SITC 861).

Source: Kueh and Howe (1984), p. 815.

Finally, the trade balance for machinery and transport equipment (the largest import commodity group by value) remained substantially negative in 1982, in spite of a cutback in imports as a result of the Readjustment and an export drive that in percentage terms has been very successful.

The other question of interest is: which trading partners have been involved in these changes? Figure 12.1 shows changes in China's exports and imports with major partners for periods between 1975 and 1982, and the balance can be measured by comparing actual positions to the 45° line, which represents a state of balanced trade. It should, first of all, be noted that a very substantial proportion of China's exports to (and imports from) the United States has been channelled through Hong Kong, but are thus subsumed in the custom statistics of Hong Kong (as shown in the figure), rather than that of the country of origin (Kueh and Voon, 1997). In other words, the balance line drawn for the United States in Figure 12.1 should in reality be positioned much more in the northeast direction.

*Table 12.3   Sectoral contributions to improvement in the visible trade
balance, 1979–82 (US$ million)*

Commodity group	Net balance		Improvement	Contribution to improvement (%)
	1979	1982		
(1) Food, animals, oils and fats	+806	+158	−648	−8
(2) Crude materials and chemicals	−998	+298	+1296	15
(3) Minerals (petroleum)	+2289	+5243	+2954	35
(4) Manufactures	+473	+4662	+4189	49
(5) Machinery	−3417	−2645	+772	9
Total	−847	+7716	+8563	100

Notes: SITC 0, 1 and 4 for (1); 2 and 5 for (2); 3 for (3); 6 and 8 for (4); and 7 for (5).

Source: As in Table 12.2.

There is therefore no doubt that the United States has been most rapidly catching up with the whole of Western Europe, to become an extremely significant trading partner of China. Note, in particular that, following the formal establishment of diplomatic relations in 1978, U.S. exports to China (dominated of course by much-needed capital goods) have continued to increase despite the Economic Readjustment, at the expense of both Western Europe (notably West Germany) and Japan. The politics of trade is indeed very conspicuous.

The importance of Hong Kong as revealed in Figure 12.1 also deserves a particular note. The trade surplus it helped to generate for China during 1978–80 is indeed sufficient to cover around four-fifths of the combined total of trade deficits incurred by the country with the United States, Western Europe and Japan in the same period. Perhaps this constitutes the economics of the political proposal for the 'one-country two-systems' model for the sovereignty of Hong Kong reverting back to China.

THE SEARCH FOR FOREIGN CAPITAL

Accompanying the major changes in conventional trade is a radical new attitude towards the role of foreign capital. In 1979, the Bank of China began open, and substantial, international borrowing. At the same time efforts were made by the government to secure low-interest state loans from foreign lenders, including the World Bank. The pace with which the practice

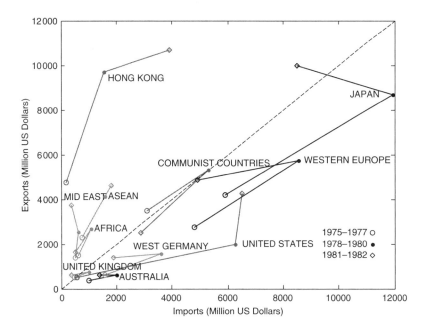

Source: Kueh and Howe (1984), p. 823.

Figure 12.1   *China's exports, imports and trade balances, FOB, by major region and country, 1975–77, 1978–80, 1981–82 (US$ million)*

of capital borrowing spreads out is indeed quite amazing, in terms of both lending sources and beneficiaries.[3]

An even more radical departure from the past has been the concerted effort to attract foreign direct investment (FDI) to China – in simple terms, the purchase of foreign machinery, equipment and advanced technologies with foreign money. In the broadest historical perspective, this programme resembles the 'joint international development' of Chinese resources originally envisaged by Sun Yat-sen at the beginning of the century. Thus, a Sino-Foreign Joint Venture Law was promulgated in 1979, together with various similar provisions including the establishment of the Special Economic Zones (SEZs) for foreign investment. By 1983, foreign direct investment already amounted to the sum of US$910 million, equivalent to 13 per cent of the trade surplus for 1982. Figures 12.2 and 12.3 reveal the trends in capital borrowing and FDI intake.

Note first of all that, over the years, increases in FDI intake have been accompanied by a stable increase in government-to-government loans from

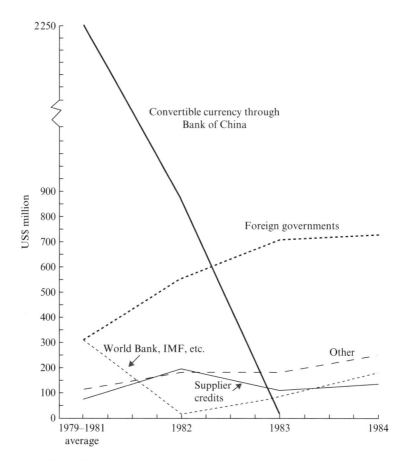

Source: Kueh (1987), p. 469.

Figure 12.2   External loans effectively used in China by sources of the loans, 1979–84 (US$ million)

foreign countries. Total external loans appeared to have decreased most drastically up to 1983, when the assigned obligation of the Bank of China to repay loans for the 22 key equipment sets for the well-known Baoshan Steel Works in Shanghai was replaced by direct payment through hard foreign currency held by the state treasury (*DWJJMYNJ 1984*, p. 1095). The trend since 1979 in the use of loans from foreign governments seems to imply a long-term readiness by the Chinese government to engage in this more stable source of international borrowing, on top of the effort made by the regional and ministerial authorities to attract FDI (Kueh, 1987, p. 470).

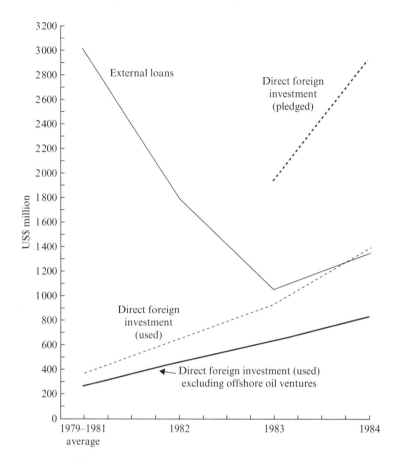

Source: Kueh (1987), p. 467.

Figure 12.3 *Total amount of external loans and FDI effectively used (or pledged) in China, 1979–84 (US$ million)*

The most spectacular foreign investments have been the offshore joint ventures. Most of the oil majors are involved, including the Japanese (Japan National Oil Corporation) and the French (Total and Elf-Aquitaine) who entered in 1981. In March 1983, British Petroleum and associates were awarded five exploration contracts for the South China Sea, to be followed by American, Australian and Spanish contracts in November 1983. Oil apart, the most remarkable event was the long-awaited agreement between China and Occidental Petroleum signed on 29 April 1984, for a 30-year equity joint venture worth US$640 million to develop the Antaibao open-cast coal mine in Pingshuo, Shanxi. No sooner had the interim agreement with Occidental been worked out, in March 1983, than the Ministry of Coal published a list of 23 central and provincial coal mine development projects, with a view to soliciting further foreign capital participation up to a projected total of US$5 billion (*DGB*, 23–4 March 1983).

In addition to these giant, resource-based projects, systematic efforts have been made to attract FDI from Hong Kong and overseas for the manufacturing sectors. As revealed in Table 12.4, both the central industrial ministries and provincial authorities are involved. By 1984, FDI intake had already covered a wide spectrum of industries.

Thus the quest for foreign direct investment has rapidly become an integral part of China's foreign economic relations. As a *Red Flag* editorial put it, 'in the near future courting direct investment should become the most important method (of utilizing foreign capital)' (*Hongqi*, 1982, p. 5). In early 1984, this policy line had been quickly pushed to a new apex, specifically, by the government's decision to 'open up' 14 major coastal cities (Dalian, Qinhuangdao, Tianjin, Yantai, Qingdao, Lianyungang, Nantong, Shanghai, Ningbo, Wenzhou, Fuzhou, Guangzhou, Zhanjiang and Beihai), by conferring on them privileges similar to those enjoyed by the Special Economic Zones (*DGB*, 7 April 1984).

TRADE PLANNING AND ORGANIZATIONAL ADAPTATIONS

The increased volume and the diversification of imports and exports, and the new inflow of foreign capital, all forcefully called for the conventional Chinese trade apparatus to be readjusted accordingly. As a result, a series of organizational changes have been made. These began in 1979.

At the central level, an Import–Export Control Commission and a Foreign Investment and Control Commission were established within the State Council, together with the State Bureau of Foreign Exchange Control and China International Trust and Investment Corporation (CITIC). The Bank of China (the specialized bank for trade and exchange clearing) has also been promoted to ministerial rank. All of these developments indicate the urgent need for greater functional specialization within the overall system of trade, investment and finance. In March 1982, the two Commissions were merged with both the Ministry of Trade and the Ministry of Foreign Economic Relations to become a Ministry of Foreign Economic Relations and Trade (MOFERT). Most, however, of the newly developed institutional specialization has been maintained under the umbrella organization.

Table 12.4   Distribution of FDI value by country of origin, industrial sectors and hosting authorities/regions in China, 1979–84 (per cent)

Country of origin	1979–83	1984	Industrial sectors	1983	Hosting authorities/ regions	1979– 84
Hong Kong	58	34	Offshore oil	53	Central	30
Japan	13	5	Transportation	3	ministries	
USA	12	25	& telecommuni-		Provinces	70
UK	3	16	cations		of which:	
France	3	2	Machinery,	7	Guangdong	(65)
Others	10	18	metallurgy,		Beijing	(12)
			& chemical		Shanghai	(4)
Total	100	100	Electronics &	6	11 coastal	(74)
			light industry		provinces	
			Building/	3	15 open	(12)
			materials		coastal cities	
			Tourism &	7	SEZs	(31)
			commerce		Shenzhen	(21)
			Others	21		
			Total	100	Total	100

Notes: Figures for 1979–83 (country of origin) and 1979–84 (hosting authorities) refer to cumulative total. Bracketed figures add up to more than the provincial total because of overlapped coverage (Shenzhen is also included in Guangdong's figures, for example). The 15 open cities include Weihai in Shandong province, which was subsequently added to the list of 14.

Sources: Kueh (1997), pp. 172–3; Kueh (1987), p. 471.

Within the conventional foreign trade system itself new powers and functional divisions have emerged. It must be recalled, briefly, that, prior to the 1979 reform, nine State Trading Corporations (STC) directly under the Ministry of Foreign Trade monopolized all import and export transactions. The STCs paralleled the industrial ministries in a highly centralized system. Strict vertical control lines stretched from Beijing down to the various branch corporations in the provincial capitals. Compared to domestic economic planning, control in foreign trade was particularly coercive, because of the rule that *all* foreign exchange earnings be remitted to Beijing (where they were used to finance imports ranked according to central priorities).

Thus the import and export plans of the STCs were derived from the material balance system, along with the output targets of major SOEs. The enterprises which consumed imported goods in practice related more closely to their ministerial superiors (and through them to the higher planning and balancing authority, namely, the State Planning Commission) than to the Ministry of Foreign Trade, except in so far as they were allowed relationships to facilitate technical familiarization.

It was here that the first major change occurred. The industrial ministries have now been allowed to establish their own import and export corporations. Within less than three years, 32 such economic entities have emerged at the central level alone. The most significant ones include the following:

> China National Machinery and Equipment Import and Export Corporation
> China National Aero-technology Import and Export Corporation
> China Electronics Import and Export Corporation
> China Precision Machinery Import and Export Corporation
> China Metallurgical Import and Export Corporation
> Petroleum Corporation of the People's Republic of China
> China National Offshore Oil Corporation
> China National Coal Development Corporation
> External Engineering Corporation of the Ministry of Coal Industry
> China National Complete Plant Export Corporation
> China National Light Industry Construction Corporation
> China National Chemical Construction Corporation.

It is clear that many of these new corporations cut across the business competence of the conventional STCs, and some degree of specialization must be agreed, as is explained shortly.

The new opportunities for direct trade were intended to provide not only incentives for industrial ministries to expand trade, but also to improve the efficiency of trade by allowing proper technical contacts between Chinese and foreign enterprises. It is the latter intention that has been hailed as the decisive advantage of the new system: all the more important in view of the increasing technological sophistication of imported goods and also of imports in the form of industrial blueprints, consultancy and technical services.

From the standpoint of the State Planning Commission, this diffusion of import decision-making power may represent a potential source of planning instability, but, given that foreign exchange allocations to enterprises and ministries are still strictly controlled to ensure compliance of imports (essentially capital goods and technologies) with central physical planning, there exists nevertheless a powerful brake on undesirable behaviour. The

problems on the export side have been somewhat less problematic. The Readjustment policy made a substantial proportion of production capacity (especially in the machine-building and metal-making industries) redundant, and exports are thus strongly encouraged as an important outlet for many ministries.

The second major reform relates to regional decentralization. This includes, first, within the ministerial system itself, powers over imports and exports that have been relegated to selected producer enterprises. Secondly, the provincial branch corporations of the STCs have become increasingly free from vertical control by the superior authority in Beijing. Thirdly, an increasing number of provinces (notably Guangdong, Fujian and the three central municipalities) have been allowed to set up their own independent, province-wide, import–export corporations. Finally, selected provincial enterprises have also been granted a degree of autonomy in trade decisions.

An important aspect of this decentralization is that it has not simply been a matter of loosening old ties, because these local-level economic entities (industrial and commercial) have also been encouraged to break both departmental (ministerial) and regional barriers, either to engage in cooperative trade ventures or to form interdepartmental and supraprovincial trade corporations (Ma, 1982, p. 366).

What, then, is left of the central, industrial–ministerial authorities, and especially of the entire Ministry of Foreign Trade system? Within the ministerial category, many producer enterprises have indeed been given full-fledged export autonomy. These include even such large steel complexes as Wuhan, Anshan, Shoudu (Beijing) and Maanshan (Li, 1982). It thus appears that the China Metallurgical Import and Export Corporation may have been reduced to little more than a loosely connected parent company. This is of course not necessarily true of other ministerial corporations. The China National Offshore Oil Corporation, for example, has been heavily involved in direct business negotiations and in preparations for the offshore drilling tenders.

As for the centrally-controlled STCs, specialization along product lines has occurred. Thus the larger ones become mainly responsible for important, bulky and relatively standardized commodities such as grain, coal, crude oil, finished steel and large complete plants (Shao, 1980). As their direct export functions are reduced or terminated, many of the other STCs are converted into general trading agencies for export producers, and also for inland corporations unfamiliar with foreign trade. Making use of their established market and administrative links, the STCs have also had a role in setting up horizontal and vertical export joint ventures. Even more important, they are now responsible for coordinating export prices and for directing foreign buyers to various localities and exporters (Ma, 1982, pp. 365–6).

Significant as these institutional developments are, it should be noted, however, that the scale of export decentralization is much smaller than the drastic nature of some of the organizational reshuffles might suggest. Even during the height of decentralization in 1980–81, when the number of export commodities subject to 'unified control' by the Ministry of Foreign Trade was reduced to 15 or 17 categories, these still accounted for 80 per cent of total export value (Zhong, 1981, p. 15; Chen, 1982, p. 66).

As a matter of fact, the export decentralization drive (especially in terms of producer autonomy) relates most of all to highly heterogeneous products, such as arts and crafts, processed farm products, clothing and other labour-intensive light manufactures. These products enjoy comparative advantage but are evidently not conducive to centralized planning and export control, in the first place. They were formerly monopolized by the STCs simply out of the desire to centralize all earnings of foreign exchange. In other respects, the old system must have been very inefficient.

Clearly the decontrol now is prompted by the strategic thinking that, coupled with the incentives provided for retaining part of the foreign exchange earned, producers/exporters should be greatly stimulated to exert extra effort to exploit local resources and skills for further increasing exports of these lines of products; and that, as a result, total foreign exchange revenue accruable to the central authority net of the proportions retained locally should also increase accordingly.

While reform experiments in the domestic sector seem to be subject to cyclical advance and retrogression, export decentralization has basically remained intact. The reason for this is that, while partial loss of control over capital goods was at times found to be a disintegrating force in central planning, export decentralization, which deals primarily with goods flowing from the peripheral (or secondary) economy, does not challenge the basic operation of the system to the same extent.

Taken together, amidst the decentralization drive, export control by means of volume quotas in physical or value terms has largely been replaced by targets of foreign exchange earnings imposed on provincial and lower-level authorities, and by measures for forestalling excessive price competition among the exporting corporations, enterprises and the various localities (*DGB*, 19, 20 February, 1983, *GJMY*, nos 3 and 4, 1984).

INCENTIVES AND ORGANIZATION FOR FOREIGN INVESTMENT

Several forms of investment opportunities have been made available to foreign investors. These include equity joint venture (EJV), contractual joint venture (CJV), wholly foreign-owned venture (WFOV), compensation trade (CTJV) and offshore oil exploration ventures (OOEJV).[4] The latter type has so far received the greatest attention because of the scale of the operation and the international significance of any major discovery of oil supplies. In this type of contract, however, the Chinese authorities found little scope to manipulate the terms and conditions for agreement with the Western oil giants. China's position is essentially that of an option taker, comparable, as far as the majors are concerned, with other developing countries with oil. Therefore, no further time is spent on this form of foreign investment. Neither will WFOV be looked at, which has so far been of negligible quantitative significance.

Among the other three types of joint venture, EJV appears the least attractive, as it involves long-term capital commitment in an environment almost totally unfamiliar to outside businessmen. For example, the absence of a definitive, tried and comprehensible legal framework creates many difficulties. The Joint Venture Law of 1979 is a characteristically vague formulation, leaving wide room for discriminatory interpretation, although the position has been improved by the publication of the more detailed Implementation Regulations, in September 1983. Another legal issue is the absence of a tried system of patent protection (Sakurai, 1982). This is critical to companies whose technology is being urgently sought by China, and has in fact prompted the promulgation of the China Patent Law in March 1984, to take effect from April 1985.

A second major aspect of the Chinese environment vital to the foreign investor is the problem of industrial supplies. Joint undertakings usually stipulate that materials and equipment should be supplied from Chinese sources, where and whenever feasible. This is clearly related to the government's attempt to maximize foreign exchange earnings, yet, for investors with even limited knowledge of the Chinese economy, the likelihood of secure and timely supplies is known to be low, in spite of the fact that Chinese 'sales cadres' insist that, once a joint venture agreement is reached, the necessary input supplies from domestic sources will be incorporated into the state production and distribution plans (*DGB*, 7 April 1982; Chai, 1983, pp. 116–20).

Another problem which arises for foreign investors is the Chinese government's attempts to combine the earning of hard foreign currency (by selling materials to the joint projects) with an ambitious 'leapfrog to export-oriented foreign investment', whereby foreign investors are also obliged to 'balance their own foreign exchange requirements' (by exporting their output to overseas markets). The effect of this approach is to make the joint venture relationship resemble compensation trade, or even conventional trade. It is an approach in sharp contrast to the practice of most industrializing nations in Asia, where foreign investment is part of a policy of import substitution (Sakurai,1982), and it is certainly an approach unwelcome to many Western investors whose purpose in investing is to get a foothold in the vast Chinese market itself, and not to create a Frankenstein of Chinese competition that will undermine them in third country markets.

The standard corporate income tax rates are also plagued with difficulties built in with the established system of central planning and price control. The nominal percentages are hard to interpret in general terms because of the arbitrary character of official price formation practices and because of pervasive cost–price irrationalities – not to mention the added complication of the artificial exchange rate. Further, the provisions for tax exemptions and reductions are highly differentiated according to the duration of the investment, to the necessity of compensating for illogical intersectoral earnings differentials and also to take into account the role of the foreign partner in providing 'technologies that are up to date by world standards' (Joint Venture Law).

The upshot is to leave potential investors with the impression that the standard tax rates contain a large margin within which the Chinese government can discriminate from case to case. This individualized approach is indeed characteristic of Chinese trade practices, and has long been a source of confusion and complaint.

Nevertheless, given the strong urge to attract FDI, a new series of tax, tariff and other policy measures were introduced between March and May 1983. The measures included (1) reduction of the tax rate from 20 per cent to 10 per cent on interest income for capital brought into China; (2) complete exemption from import duties and industrial–commercial taxes for machinery and equipment imported for joint ventures; and (3) a generous extension of the tax holiday periods for newcomers, especially for investments from Hong Kong, Macao and Overseas Chinese. Taken together, the concessions stipulated will indeed help reduce the effective income tax rate for the joint ventures from the original level of 33 per cent down to 18.91 per cent for the first five years (*DGB*, 22 February 1984). Besides, provisions for accelerated depreciations are also available. Perhaps more importantly, the concessions also come with an enhanced (though still vague) prospect of sales to the Chinese domestic market.

Most of the problems mentioned above relate, not only to EJV, but also to CJV and CTJV. There is, however, an important difference. The two last-mentioned types of contract (especially CTJV) offer the opportunity for agreements which are far more specific and definitive, which can be framed in terms of precise operational programmes, and which are of a short-term nature.[5] In these contracts, therefore, the short-term interests of the partners can be incorporated more easily. If successful, contracts can of course be renewed to constitute a long-term series of cooperative ventures. Against these benefits, of course, there is some loss of the long-term benefits of an equity joint venture.

The changing size and nature of the foreign capital commitment from 1979 to 1984 as revealed in Figure 12.4 bear out the points made above. Thus EJV investment in China, amidst increased difficulties encountered after the initial euphoria, dropped most precipitously, from an annual average of US$39 million in 1979–81 to a mere US$24.19 million for 1982, in favour of continuous increases in CJV and CTJV investment (in terms of the amount pledged by foreign partners). In fact, in terms of the average per project value, the foreign partner share for EJV has also consistently declined and the reverse is true with both CJV and CTJV upto 1982.[6]

It is clearly against this background that the sweeping tax concessions were made in early 1983, as mentioned above. Coupled with the promulgation, also in 1983, of the detailed 'Implementations Regulations' for the Joint Venture Law, the upshot is that foreign investment pledged for EJV in 1983 rapidly rose to a total of US$188 million, compared with US$140.59 million for the entire period 1979–82. And even more spectacularly, in the wake of the opening of the 14 coastal cities and the publication of the Patent Law (both in early 1984), and perhaps also in anticipation of the October 1984 Resolution for gradually phasing out central planning, EJV investment soared to a startling total of US$1100 million in that year. Even if the mammoth Occidental coal-mine project is excluded, the value still represents a 250 per cent increase on 1983.

The SEZs have played an important role. Shenzhen, by far the largest and most important of these, attracted commitments amounting to approximately US$1.5 billion (for some 1400 investment projects) within two years of its opening in 1980. A total of US$240 million has been added since then (*JJTQNJ 1983*, p. 146). These made up the bulk of total CJV and CTJV investments combined, virtually all of which came from Hong Kong, just across the border, for engaging in export-processing (although a sizeable amount was also destined for property development and recreational facilities (Ma, 1982, p. 391; Jao, 1983, pp. 50–53).

Clearly, the successful Shenzhen experience has prompted the Chinese government to open up the 14 coastal cities in 1984. This strongly suggests that China's open-door strategy for expanding foreign trade and investment has entered a practically irreversible stage.

PRICES AND INCENTIVES IN COMMODITY TRADE

In the Soviet-style planned economy, where plans are in physical terms and are determined by central bureaucrats, foreign trade is largely unaffected by incentives offered to enterprises and consumers. Imports are selected either

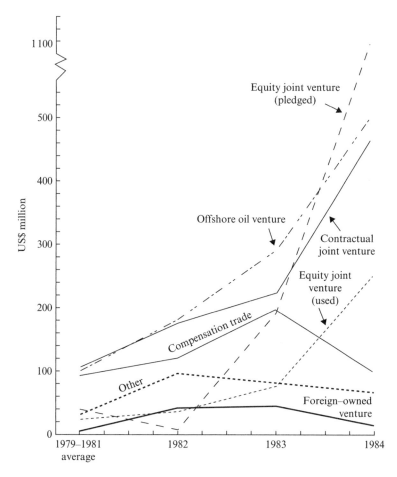

Source: Kueh (1987), p. 468.

*Figure 12.4   FDI used (or pledged) by different types of foreign joint
            ventures in China, 1979–84 (US$ million)*

because they fill unforeseen gaps in the planners' input–output (material
balance) estimates, or because they are commodities not available in the
domestic economy at all, or are only produced and procured with very great
difficulty. The exports required to pay the import bill are generally those
most obviously available (that is, raw materials or traditional exports). In
such a system, the structures of trade (especially of exports) are likely to be
rigid and, as the economy matures to the stage where the range of goods
domestically available is wide, the role of trade diminishes to the point

where, by comparison with market systems, participation in trade is almost certainly suboptimal.

In such a system, although prices play no role either in determining the allocation of resources to exports or in determining the level of imports and efficiency with which they are used, there is a price problem, in the sense that the planners are faced with a trading environment in which the external prices of traded goods are the product of competitive markets, or, in the case of trade with other planned economies, are at least heavily influenced by them. Typically, however, the exchange rate of the planned economy does not serve to relate the internal and external price systems, but is overvalued, so that export procurement requires that domestic producers be subsidized (world prices are lower than domestic prices) while imports allocated at domestic prices earn large 'profits'.[7]

Moreover, particularly on the export side, the irrationality of domestic prices (and hence variations in required subsidies) are often very large, not only because of oddities in the cost structure, but also because of the incidence of the domestic tax system, which uses differential taxes on industrial goods as a means of financing investment (Xu, 1984).

None of this matters too much as long as the system remains centralized, since losses and profits may be used to offset each other, or (as in the Chinese case) may be at average levels that enable the foreign trade monopoly to make 'profits' over the long run. Also, while retaining the overall monopoly, corporations trading in specific classes of goods may be encouraged to maximize the 'profitability' of their own business, although the net effect of this on resource allocation will depend on the nature of the price and tax system.

However, as soon as the planners attempt to infuse dynamism and improve efficiency in the economy by a measure of decentralization (whether decentralization to the individual enterprise, to local industrial systems or to local levels of government), the precise incidence of losses and profits in the system becomes of crucial importance. For, not only will the interests of exporters and importers begin radically to diverge, and not only will the incentives to export of different kinds of producers vary enormously, but the uneven regional distribution of different kinds of trading activity will mean that the geographical allocation of gains and losses will become a major economic and political issue. The unravelling of these problems, which are in practice infinitely more complex than any simple, schematic account of them, is the process which China began tentatively in the export sector in the mid-1970s, and has begun in earnest and on a wide front since 1979.

The first step in the provision of export incentives has been to convert the old administrative trade organs at various levels into accounting entities, or to set up new trade corporations under the trade bureaus (this is a parallel to the establishment of industrial branch corporations in the domestic reform). By introducing an obligation to make profit-and-loss calculations, this step immediately facilitated economic control.

A second stage in the reform has been to allow trade corporations and some producers of exports to retain part of their earnings from profits or foreign exchange. This has proved a powerful incentive, partly, in the case of corporations and enterprises located in the coastal regions, because of familiarity with foreign goods that can be obtained with hard currency.

A third step has been to begin to 'make' industrial export business 'profitable' to both the trade corporations and exporting industrial producers. This was essential because the existing Chinese domestic price structure discriminated very strongly against the export of industrial products. But industrial exports were vital because domestic and market factors made agricultural exports hard to increase.

Two technical terms frequently referred to in the Chinese literature need clarification to facilitate further discussion. The first is the so-called *huanhui chengben* which is the cost in *Renminbi* of earning one unit of foreign exchange (this rate might, for example, be 5 *yuan* per US dollar). The reciprocal of the *huanhui chengben* is the *chuanhui* (or *huanhui*) *lu*, that is, the amount of foreign currency earned per *Renminbi*.[8]

The use of these two criteria to analyse export performance has been widespread. However, in general terms it was clear at the beginning of the reform that, for the foreign exchange earnings of a substantial share of exports measured in *Renminbi* even to cover the *huanhui chengben*, the prevailing official exchange rate of one US dollar to about 1.5–1.7 *Renminbi* had to be raised substantially.

The nature of the situation facing exporters is illustrated by data for Guangdong province (Guan, 1980). Between 1976 and 1979, losses on exports averaged one billion *yuan* per annum. In 1979, at an exchange rate of 1.56 *yuan* per dollar, only 22.8 per cent of the items exported from Guangdong could be exported without incurring losses. And a number of manufactured goods, because of high costs and taxes, would have required an exchange rate of seven to 10 times the official rate to cover costs. Clearly, to encourage exports, drastic action was required, and the course chosen by the government was the introduction of a dual rate system. Under this, the old rate was supplemented by a new rate, which represented a 50 per cent devaluation of the *yuan* for internal purposes. This doubled the *renminbi* value of exports to the exporter and, other things being equal, doubled the *renminbi* price of imports to the domestic purchaser. This reform was introduced on 1 January 1981 and was subject to strong international criticism (notably by the US Department of Commerce) on the grounds that it constituted an export subsidy.

The new system has certainly had effect. In the Guangdong case, an additional 40 per cent of exported items were immediately added to the list of commodities that could be exported without loss. In Shanghai, four major trading corporations were converted to profitability, and throughout China, it was claimed that in only three cities and one province was overall foreign trade not 'profitable' after the introduction of the new internal rate (all specialized in industrial exports) (*GJMYLWX*, 1982, pp. 367–8).

However, on its own, this reform is only a beginning. Many industrial exports still require subsidies and the existing system of trading corporations means that, unless the benefits of the new price structure are passed on to producing industrial enterprises, the incentive effects are likely to be limited. There are still a number of products which enjoy high export prices in international markets, which the trading corporations are eager to acquire and export, but which from the standpoint of domestic producers it is not profitable to produce at all. Silk is a good example of this (Li, 1983, p. 39). This conflict of interest explains why, during the heyday of decentralization in 1980, it was strongly advocated that producer enterprises be allowed to export directly, or to commission local or central trading corporations to export on their account.

Incentives apart, direct trade relations between producers and foreign markets are also thought to be conducive to export efficiency. They enable producers to get direct knowledge of foreign markets and technology (Liu, 1980; Shao, 1980; Wang and Zhang, 1980). Here again there is a parallel with the reform of the domestic system with its emphasis on sales and the market. The danger, of course, is that competition among Chinese exporters becomes excessive and leads to foreign exchange losses. This is why senior officials from the Ministry of Foreign Economic Relations and Trade have rigorously called for 'coordinated export sales'.[9]

This problem created by the new internal exchange rate is particularly severe in the case of exports of agricultural products, since these were profitable at the old rate and their profitability hence was greatly enhanced by the new internal exchange rate. This resulted in severe competition among exporting corporations not only in selling, but also in efforts to procure supplies from domestic producers (Li, 1983, p. 40). The problem was by no means solved, even by 1983. One proposal to solve it is the introduction of a new, third internal exchange rate specifically for agricultural trade. What all this illustrates is how difficult it is to solve problems by reform which is piecemeal, for, without a proper internal price reform, the revaluation of the *yuan* cannot give proper signals to the whole range of domestic export producers.

CONCLUSION

There is no doubt that the entire seaboard of China is poised to be opened up for foreign trade and investment. However, amidst the metamorphoses of the open-door strategy, the very basic trade orientation inherited from the Maoist past has largely remained intact: that is, to facilitate technology transfer from the West to support the massive industrialization campaign.

Thus, while export decentralization is accelerated to help further generate hard currencies needed for technology imports, the import sector itself remains as strictly centralized as in the past, despite added provision for user enterprises to maintain 'technical contacts' with overseas suppliers. Foreign exchange earnings consistently continue to be subject to centralized allocation to ensure compliance with the planners' import priorities, despite new provision for exporting agents to claim 'partial (indeed very marginal) retention' as an incentive.

In the same vein, the new FDI strategy represents nothing more than a double-pronged vehicle for generating foreign exchange earnings through export-oriented FDI, on the one hand, and attracting technology transfer from the West through import-substitution FDI, on the other hand. Investors from Hong Kong (hard pressed by land shortage and high wages) seem poised to take advantage of the offer from the Chinese hinterland to engage in labour-intensive export manufacturing. It seems hard, however, to visualize how the multinationals from advanced countries might readily jump onto the bandwagon with new and high technology, given that the huge domestic market remains highly restrictive, let alone the host of issues concerning legal protection, for patent rights for example.

What of the future? Given the enormous demand for foreign exchange and Western technology, it should be equally clear that readjustments will continue to be made in China in the legal, planning, taxation, pricing and exchange rate systems, in order to further promote exports and attract foreign investment, although the prospects still seem to be remote for the country to be fully assimilated into the global system of free trade and investment.

NOTES

* Reprinted with adaptations (new statistics added) from Y.Y. Kueh and Christopher B. Howe, 'China's international trade: policy and organizational change and their place in Economic Readjustment', *The China Quarterly*, **100** (December 1984), 813–48; copyright School of Oriental and African Studies, published by Cambridge University Press.

1. See Kueh and Howe (1984, pp. 820–21) for detailed breakdown of exports and imports by the five major commodity categories.
2. In 1983, this trend moderated, partly as a result of excellent harvests in 1982 and 1983 (Kueh, 1984b).
3. If commissioned borrowings are included, the Bank of China has extended on its own account total foreign exchange loans amounting to US$19.6 billion for the period 1979–83, of which 45 per cent are for major state construction projects, 35 per cent for energy and transport projects (sponsored by some 40 industrial departments) and the rest for technological renovation in locally controlled medium and small-scale enterprises (Jin, 1983; *DGB*, 14 April 1984).
4. See Kueh and Howe (1984, pp. 834–5) for details about differences among the various types in terms of organization and legal status, right and obligation, contract duration, taxes and profit distribution; and also Ma (1982, pp. 384–8) and Zheng (1983, pp. 27–8) for comparative attractiveness.
5. CJV need not be a legal entity; investment contributions, and risks-and-profit sharing are subject to contract, and taxes to be paid separately by business partners. For CTJV, foreign party sells (exports) equipment or technology on credit or by means of a loan; repayment (compensation) is made by instalment of output in kind (for export).
6. For EJV the per project value (foreign share) is US$8.5 million for 1979–80, US$2.19 million for 1979–81 (and only US$1.2 million for 1982). The comparable figures for CJV are US$1.67 million and US$2.46 million, and for CTJV US$0.53 million and US$0.78 million, respectively (Kueh and Howe, 1984, pp. 837, 842).
7. The subsidy involved in exporting is known in the European context as *Preisausgleich* and is discussed in Wiles (1968, chs 6, 7) and Pryor (1963, ch. 4).
8. Sometimes the two terms are used to mean exactly the reverse relations see Wu Nianlu (1983, p. 39), and Li (1983, p. 38).
9. For a more general policy discussion about how to make use of market regulations without challenging the integrated core of planning in the export sector, see Xu (1983). The partial marketization process in the export sector and the ensuing price competition has met with very strong criticism from responsible cadres of the Ministry of Foreign Trade see, for example, Cheng (1980).

13.   The quest for WTO entry*

WHAT WAS AT STAKE?

There seems no doubt that, by 1984–85, the platform for pursuing or expanding the open-door strategy was seen from the Chinese perspective to be already firmly in place, after the initial experiments with trade reforms and FDI intake were completed (as discussed in the previous chapter). China therefore ventured to apply for admission to the World Trade Organization in 1986. Note that the application had, indeed, taken place in tandem with the promulgation of the October 1984 Resolution for gradually replacing 'mandatory planning' with 'guidance planning' and 'market regulation'. In fact, the application was also synchronized with the first wave of domestic price liberalization, which began in 1985. These all represented bare prerequisites to qualify for WTO member status.

There is also no doubt, however, that with a WTO membership China aspired to take advantage of a stable multilateral global trading system for further enhancing foreign exchange earnings in support of, but hopefully without compromising, the pursuit for an independent industrialization drive.

Nevertheless, the Chinese quest for WTO entry entailed a 14-year ordeal of hard and at times frustrating negotiations with major trading partners, the United States in particular. The latter insisted, interestingly, on China being admitted, rightly or wrongly, as an industrialized member, while the Chinese authority strongly argued for the status of a developing country. This would have of course profound implications for the crux of the issues involved. Should the US course prevail, China's import tariffs would have to be lowered, on average, to as low as 3 to 4 per cent to be at par with that of other advanced nations, while the developing countries generally enjoyed the much higher protective tariffs of 13 to 14 per cent.

For the Chinese authority, this would inherently run against the very value imperatives inherited from the Maoist past for building an independent, integrated industrial system. Perhaps as a matter of the Confucian principle of 'moderation', China finally settled for the industrial import tariffs to be reduced from the high of 24.6 per cent to a mere 9.4 per cent, as against 17 per cent for agricultural goods, down from the prevalent 21.25 per cent.[1]

Added to the predicament is of course the equally, if not even more, crucial problem of WTO requirements for investment liberalization. An influx of import-substitution FDI could evidently threaten to disintegrate the very technological core of the aspired-to independent industrial system, if the country were to yield completely to the WTO dictates for immediately granting 'national treatment', prohibiting 'forced technology transfer' and eliminating the requirements for complying with any 'localization rates' and for 'balancing foreign exchange expenditure' incurred with foreign investors. These all basically implied unrestricted access to the Chinese domestic market for multinational corporations, without their being obliged to divulge details of technological blueprints.

This is not the place for discussing how China has managed to cope with these and other important issues (such as import quotas, import licensing and other non-tariff barriers) since WTO accession. Rather, consistent with the main thrust of the present study, we focus in what follows on how, over the protracted period of negotiations with the WTO, the country has attempted to gradually adapt the Maoist legacy to the global regime of free trade and free investment flows. As a background to the discussion, however, we first show how the Chinese strategy to cope with the predicament has given rise to the coexistence in China between a highly open trading system and a strictly closed, inward-oriented industrial core prior to WTO accession.

THE 'ONE COUNTRY – TWO SYSTEMS' MODEL

In early 1988, shortly before Deng personally made the boldest attempt to free prices across the board, the Chinese government declared, in one single decree, all 11 coastal provinces, from Liaoning down south to Hainan and Guangxi provinces, to be opened for foreign trade and investment.[2] This was the culmination in fact of the opening of the 15 sea ports in early 1984, and the Pearl River (Zhujiang) and Yangze River (Changjiang) deltas, as well as the 'Fujian triangle' (Xia-Zhang-Quan) in February 1985.

The spectacular move was presumably underpinned by a new development strategy called 'the great international circular flow' (*guoji daxunhuan*), which was thought to be favoured by Zhao Ziyang himself, then the Party Secretary-General. Specifically, the entire coastal belt should be converted into an export-processing zone, by taking advantage of abundant labour supply to engage both foreign investors and domestic enterprises in export-oriented manufacturing, whereby input materials needed should be secured from and outputs destined to the overseas markets (hence the Chinese epigram *liantou zaiwai*: to '(place) two heads outside'). The proceeds of hard currencies so earned should nevertheless be used for imports of Western technology and equipment to support the preferential development of heavy industry, which should in turn make use of capital accumulated to help foster both Chinese agriculture and light industry.[3]

Clearly, the 'new theory' amounts to nothing more than a manifestation of the very essence of Deng's original industrialization strategy. As a matter of fact, from the very onset of that strategy the entire Chinese economy had already begun to be bifurcated into two disparate, distinctly different, systems. That is, a widely open, export-oriented system catering to foreign investment and export drives existing alongside a highly protective, strictly import-substituting industrial system. In the latter, since the 1950s, central planning has been used as a means to achieve rapid industrialization and modernization.

This 'one country – two systems' model resembles in a way the one adopted for Hong Kong after its return to Chinese sovereignty in 1997, setting aside, of course, the difference in political system. China's export-oriented, open system is by no means incidental vis-à-vis the well-established, inward-oriented industrial system. On the eve of WTO accession, the open system accounted for over 10 per cent of total capital formation and 50 per cent of the country's foreign exchange earnings. Moreover, it employed well over 10 million workers. This was 10 times the size of Hong Kong's total manufacturing workforce. If taken as a separate economic entity, this export-oriented industrial belt is likely as open as Singapore or Hong Kong, in terms of the estimated transnationality index.[4]

There is no doubt that, from the WTO perspective, the opened coastal region (for which raw materials and machinery and equipment imported for export processing are exempted from custom duties) should in itself be basically qualified for membership, ignoring of course the import-substitution industries which are also concentrated in the areas.

TRADE LIBERALIZATION

As soon as the Readjustment was completed in China's foreign economic relations, a comprehensive foreign trade reform programme was launched, in September 1984. To synchronize with the October 1984 Resolution, the new programme also consistently made a distinction between export and import commodities to be placed separately under guidance planning and mandatory planning. In the words of Zheng Tuobin, then the new MOFERT Minister,

> In the export sector, the mandatory planning of the past for all commodities is to be replaced by aggregate targets, relegated by MOFERT for foreign exchange

earnings and by the Ministry's quantitative plans for a few commodities critical to national livelihood. The former is guidance planning, and the latter an imperative one, but they all fall under the category of the planned economy. At the same time, MOFERT will no longer compile and impose procurement and allocation (of export goods) plans. With respect to the import sector, mandatory planning will continue to prevail over import purchases made by the centralized foreign exchange earnings, and imports of the few bulky commodities and key whole plants, as well as imports made under bilateral national agreements. These are imports based on the state plans, which MOFERT will authorize its own specialized trading corporations to implement. For imports outside of the sphere, there will be no centrally imposed plans with detailed commodity breakdowns. Instead, eligible end users of imported goods, or other imports departments, will just receive certain foreign exchange allocation targets, and they are free to commission any trading enterprises to do the import business. (Zheng, 1984, p. 31)

With this broad sweep the basic parameters of China's new trading system are thus clearly established. However, parallel to domestic reform, it had still taken nearly a full decade for the country to gradually move out of the Maoist shadow of centralized trading control. Specifically, it is not until the landmark Resolution of October 1992 that, along with the dismantling of central planning, export planning was replaced by indirect control through export taxes and export subsidies, coupled with export quotas and licences and that the share of import planning was reduced to the low of 18.5 per cent (in total imports), in favour of control by way of import quotas, licensing and canalization (monopoly or limited imported rights), as well as import duties and the 'import-regulatory taxes' (Chai, 1997a, p. 142).

Note also that it is not until the mid-1990s, when prompted by the 'WTO euphoria', that the Chinese government began to make several rounds of offers for sizeable import-tariff reduction and elimination of non-tariff import barriers, in order to win an early WTO approval (Howe, Kueh and Ash, 2003, p. 351). There is no doubt, therefore, that it was in recognition of the relative merits of preserving the Maoist thrust of pursuing an independent industrialization strategy that the quest for WTO entry had proved to be such an arduous one.

A very important part of the September 1984 trade reform package is the adoption of the 'trade agency system' (*maoyi dailizhi*). This is clearly also built upon the decentralization drive of the Readjustment period, whereby exporting and importing enterprises were all to be increasingly detached from their administrative superior, and become legally independent economic entities, trading indiscriminately on their own account of profits and losses. This is evidently meant to provide the necessary platform for the trading corporations to serve as 'trade agent', by charging commission for linking the exporters and importers to the world markets. Under the system, import users are specifically charged by the trade agent at the *renminbi* equivalent of the foreign price (at the official exchange rate) plus freight, the agreed commission (normally between 1.5 and 3 per cent) and any applicable import tariffs. For the exporters, the *renminbi* equivalent receipts should clearly be understood as net of the commission, freight and export levies, if any.

There is no doubt that this new 'trade agency pricing' (*waimao daili zuojia*) method has (a) greatly helped export producers and import-user enterprises to familiarize themselves with the world market prices, (b) set in motion a competitive system to encourage trading corporations to vie for agency businesses, and vice versa, the exporters and importers to look for the most efficient trade agents, and (c) brought China's trading system closer to the Western practice. However, such improvements conceal the most important, fundamental issue as to whether the new system has effectively or immediately helped to realign domestic relative prices with the prevalent international price relatives.

It was reported, for example, that, scarcely a year after the inception of the agency system, by 1986, the domestic prices of fourth-fifths of all imports were already based on import cost (Lardy, 1997, p. 230). And by the early 1990s, the comparable share had risen to 90 per cent for imports, and 80 per cent for exports (Chai, 1997a, p. 144).

Nonetheless, behind the apparently increased 'link-up' with international prices, user enterprises of a wide range of important imports continued to receive fiscal subsidies for 'balancing the price differentials between domestic sources and import supplies'. A good case in point is imports of pig iron, scrap steel, iron ore and similar materials needed for producing steel products which were subject to 'unified distribution'. The producers had in fact been granted such subsidies ever since 1985 (when such import commodities began to be placed under the 'agency pricing' system) and until as late as 1990. And in fact the subsidies were then terminated not because domestic prices had become at par with those for import supply, but rather, the Ministry of Finance considered the added burden not sustainable and was in favour of encouraging domestic production to substitute for foreign supply (Notice of Ministry of Finance, 7 July 1990).

As a matter of fact, one of the major obstacles to China's bid for WTO membership was the persistent American objection to the country's engaging in 'unfair trading practice' of 'subsidizing exports' and imposing 'the import regulatory taxes' on top of normal custom levies.[5] Rightly or wrongly, this should remain a matter of interpretation, in the absence of reliable 'shadow prices' for gauging the real resource costs of the traded commodities. What seems clear, however, is that despite the abortive attempts made in 1985 and 1988 to float domestic prices, and several rounds of *renminbi* devaluation since 1985, the domestic price system still remained largely distorted and divorced from the world market prices, and the *renminbi* value, far from being an equilibrium one, as inherited from the Maoist past.

It is really not until 1992 that, following the celebrated NPC Resolution, things began to change more significantly. These include not only the abolishment of central planning and accelerated price liberalization,[6] but also consistently import deregulation (partly in response to increased holdings of foreign exchange earnings outside of the state treasury as a result of continuous accumulation of trade surplus), and most of all the realignment of the officially fixed (but overvalued) exchange rate with the basically market-driven rate prevailing at the familiar 'swap centres',[7] to become a unified exchange rate under the new 'managed float' regime, effective January 1994.

Undoubtedly, the new developments had greatly helped to remove the major hurdles for the Chinese economy to be effectively integrated with the global system. Both export and import trade should henceforth begin to relate to explicit scarcity price signals rather than being controversially 'conducted in the dark' – as was characteristic of all former Soviet-type economies. Increased linkage to world market prices should enable Chinese enterprises and consumers to respond to unified market prices and to identify and exploit China's natural comparative advantages in the world system (Howe, Kueh and Ash, 2003, p. 349).

Nonetheless, following these positive changes, it had still taken nearly another decade for the Chinese authority to convince the major stakeholders of WTO, the US and EU in particular, that the country should be a worthy peer.

ADAPTING THE FDI REGIME

Given the basic Chinese government's FDI policy stance (especially on import-substitution FDI), there really was hardly any room available for the negotiators to compromise with the WTO requirements for investment liberalization, as stipulated in the two cornerstone global agreements, TRIMs and TRIPs.[8] Briefly, TRIMs prohibits FDI-hosting countries from imposing 'a foreign exchange balance requirement' and any mandatory 'export ratio' (restricted access to the domestic market). And TRIPs simply pre-empts any 'forced technology transfer' and provides a secure multilateral mechanism within the WTO for protecting intellectual property rights. The choice for the Chinese authorities should thus essentially be a matter of 'take it or leave it'.

Certainly, the negotiations on investment liberalization also covered such complicated issues as geographic and industrial restrictions on FDI and, not the least, access to the banking, financial, commercial and transportation sectors, and as well, a possible timeframe for any transitional arrangements. But these still seem much less complex than problems encountered in trade negotiations, which involved numerous tariff and non-tariff barriers for an enormous nomenclature of commodities carrying diverse weights in total exports and imports. Implications for trade balance aside, any sizeable import-tariff concessions to be hammered out, for example, could certainly all be backed up by alternative deliberations on the relative merits of protecting priority industries concerned, and the latitude for estimating the value of any reciprocal offers should also loom large.[9]

At any rate, before Deng Xiaoping made the emphatic call in 1992 for 'market-for-technology exchange',[10] China's FDI regime remained remarkably rigid, with a strict requirement of 'technology transfer' for import-substitution FDI, and a mandatory 'export ratio' (normally 70 per cent) for export-oriented FDI. Most interestingly, even for Volkswagen, the first to gain a foothold in China as early as 1985–86 to manufacture finished passenger cars exclusively for the domestic market, the 'foreign exchange balance' rule applied as well. VW was, nonetheless, willing and indeed able to commit itself by manufacturing vehicle parts and accessories, and car engines in China for export to Germany.[11]

Prior to Deng's call for changes, readjustments were indeed made to improve the 'investment environment', but the basic tenets of the FDI regime remained intact. These included, for instance, improvements in the procedure for FDI approval (including granting provincial and local authority a higher dollar limit for FDI intake), patent protection, labour and wage regulations, and joint venture corporate governance. Subsequent to the extra tax incentives offered in 1983, generous tax concessions also continued to be made in the second half of the 1980s, including an extended tax holiday, exemption from profit repatriation tax, and full refund of tax for reinvested profits.

Perhaps more importantly, following the 1984–85 central planning reform, problems with uncertainties in domestic input supply to Sino-foreign joint ventures had also been increasingly mitigated. The unfortunate experience of Pilkington Brothers (famous for their float glass technology) which represented, together with the Belgium Bell Telephone, one of the few most treasured equity joint ventures in the 1980s, in terms of capital size and advanced technology, had largely faded away. Note that the company (a joint venture with Shanghai Yaohua Glass, signed in 1983) was privileged to have its supply requirements of reinforced steel for building construction incorporated into the state plans, but an unexpected shortfall in supply forced it to import a more expensive substitute from Japan in 1984. Note especially that the company is precisely located in Shanghai, the single most important source of industrial supplies in China.

For export-oriented FDI (almost all from Hong Kong engaging in labour-intensive export processing), the interface with the domestic industrial core is evidently less pronounced or non-existent, as they rely on the outside supply of raw materials as well as machinery and equipment. Thus the improved 'investment conditions' had prompted many existent or new investors to upgrade to equity joint ventures.[12] By 1989, the share of EJV in total FDI intake (realized, excluding joint oil exploration) already increased to 58 per cent from 28 per cent in 1984, compared to a decline for contractual JV to 21 per cent from 52 per cent respectively (Kueh, 1997, p. 169). And, more interestingly after 1992, virtually all newcomers prefer to invest in the new market-based system without involving any Chinese partners. Or, in the parlance of Dunning, they all attempt to minimize transaction costs and 'internalize' their most valuable, intangible assets, which most notably include global marketing expertise' (UNCTAD, 2000, p. 141).

Nonetheless, import-substitution FDI inflow continued to lag far behind, and was in fact virtually halted following Western sanctions on account of the 1989 Tiananmen affair. The boldest 1992 strategy of Deng Xiaoping did no doubt help to turn the tide around, and discretionary concessions then made to selected multinationals, including such an unlikely candidate as Coca-Coca, in 1993, certainly also helped to add force to the quest for WTO accession in terms of the TRIPs requirements.[13] However, it is a different matter whether the strategy can be considered as successful in courting truly advanced industrial technology. The picture appears to be mixed.

For sure there is no lack of examples for such sought-after import-substitution FDI granted since 1992. A good case in point is the Shanghai Krupp Stainless, a US$1.4 billion project established in 1998 to produce stainless steel for domestic demand which could then only be matched by Chinese suppliers to the tune of some 30 per cent. Another good example of imported high technology is perhaps the German contribution to building the maglev train in Shanghai which has now become a global showcase. It is difficult to ascertain, however, how much overall such cases have contributed to technological upgrading of the home-grown industries in China.

What is clear is that, since the early 1990s, import-substitution FDI has in practice concentrated for the most part on such 'new industries' as sedan manufacturing, and electronics and information technology industries, in particular. Note that, up to the late 1980s, these were almost all alien to the

Chinese setting, and could thus be approved with relative ease for involving foreign capital and technology in line with TRIPs stipulations. Note also that the entire Chinese market for passenger cars is now virtually monopolized by foreign car-makers of German, French, American and Japanese, as well as Korean, origin.

For the electronic and IT industries (TV sets, computers, mobile phones, integrated circuits and so on), FDI would even tend to provide a double benefit for China: not only to help fill the vacuum in domestic supply, but also being able to target output at overseas markets as well (since most investors, especially those from Taiwan and Korea and Japan as well, were then already enjoying extensive global market outlets from their home bases). Their investing in China thus seems analogous to the relocating of export-oriented manufacturing plants from Hong Kong and Taiwan to the country, and was certainly welcome. Note that, on the eve of WTO entry, foreign-invested IT enterprises already accounted for 46, 52 and 60 per cent, respectively, of total sales, gross profits earned and foreign exchange generated for the industry in China.

In short, unlike metallurgy and machine-building industries (the linchpin of the Maoist industrialization drive), FDI intake in the car manufacturing and electronics and IT industries seems relatively free of technical and financial encumbrances inherited from the past.

Nonetheless, the most liberal FDI intrusion is yet to be seen in the consumer goods industries. By way of mergers and acquisitions, in contrast to 'green-field investment', by 1995, foreign-invested enterprises already held sizeable market shares (in percentage terms) in a wide range of such unlikely consumer goods as detergent and laundry powder (35), cosmetics (36), soap (40), beer (20) and beverages (19), with carbonated beverages alone holding 37 per cent (Howe, Kueh and Ash, 2003, p. 388). This was hardly thinkable just a few years before (in the late 1980s or early 1990s, given that the established industrialization drive was then still very much marked by continuous 'austerity', let alone that hardly any high technology is embedded in such consumer products. Perhaps the concessions made should just be seen as a ploy in winning an early WTO approval.

Evidently, prior to the signing of the Sino-American accord on WTO in November 1999, China's qualifications for WTO were already deemed *faits accomplis.*

CONCLUDING REMARKS

China's import-substitution FDI policy has been considered by an authoritative source as a remarkable success, at least in relation to the Shanghai

Volkswagen joint venture – a prototype in such undertakings (*infra*, note 11). From the very beginning the company was also required to manufacture vehicle parts and car engines for export to comply with the 'foreign exchange balance' rule, but this has nevertheless developed into an important integral part of the Chinese automobile industry. As a matter of fact, by 2003, total value of such exports already greatly surpassed that of finished vehicles (*China Daily*, 8–9 May 2004; *DGB*, 4 April 2004). Increased availability of quality parts and accessories is also considered as a factor for increased interest on the part of Japanese automobile conglomerates to invest in China as well. Note also that the purchases of vehicle parts and accessories from Chinese sources now does not necessarily involve foreign exchange outlay, as foreign carmakers may pay with *renminbi* earned from the sales of cars manufactured in China. More importantly, Shanghai Volkswagen has now begun to export sedans to third country markets as well, thus completing the whole FDI cycle from 'import-substitution' to 'export-oriented' (Kueh, 2007).

Meanwhile, however, some radical critics have also started to emerge. As one puts it, the 'great international circular flow theory' that helped to formulate the open-door strategy is 'absolutely nonsensical', in that, in practice, the 'international flow mechanism' not only did not result in Chinese heavy industry supporting agriculture and light industry, but had rather entirely cut off the 'material flows' between the sectors in favour of a linkup of the two latter sectors with the (monopolistic profits of) heavy industries in the United States, the EU and Japan. More seriously, China's equipment manufacturing industry (which by the 1970s had already developed a relatively independent system ensuring a self-sufficiency rate of over 80 per cent), is now seen to be on the brink of a total collapse, as a result of increased import influx. On top of this has come the 'large-scale, unwarranted outflow' of non-renewable resources, as exemplified in the export manufactures. Moreover, workers' wages are also bound to be permanently depressed amidst the '(competitive) race to the bottom' in support of the massive export drives, as the critic sees it (Lao, 2005).

Whatever the interpretation, it seems clear, however, that with WTO the country is poised to be fully integrated in the global system of free trade and investment flows, and the global technological structure as well, hopefully without completely yielding to Western technological supremacy.

NOTES

* A newly completed chapter drawing in parts on Y.Y. Kueh, 'Coping with globalization in China: strategic implications of WTO accession', *Journal of World Investment* (now

Journal of World Investment and Trade), **3**(1) (2002), 37–64; and Y.Y. Kueh, 'Economic decentralization and foreign trade expansion in China', in Joseph C.H. Chai and Chi-Keung Leung (eds), *China's Economic Reforms*, Hong Kong: Centre of Asian Studies, University of Hong Kong, 1987, pp. 444–81.

1. It seems to be a clear case of trade-off, in that China was forced to accept a much lower level of industrial tariffs in exchange for the higher agricultural tariffs; 9.4 per cent is the target for 2005. For US 'priority products' the tariff should be 7.1 per cent, with most in place by 2003. For the European Union, the comparable tariff reduction for the imports of important machinery and appliances is from 35 per cent to between 5 and 10 per cent.

2. Not all but only a total of 288 *xian* (counties) in the 11 provinces were selected for opening up, but they all seem quite representative, nevertheless.

3. The 'circular flow' theory was formulated by Wang Jian, a young economist with the State Planning Commission in 1987. See Zhang Xinjing (1990, pp. 271–2) for highlights.

4. This refers to the standard measurement of UNCTAD (2001, p. 38), defined as an average of four components: FDI inward stocks and value added of foreign affiliates – both as a percentage of GDP; and FDI inflows and employment of foreign affiliates as a percentage of gross fixed capital formation and total employment, respectively. China's index measured some 13 per cent, compared to 2.5, 15 and 8 per cent for India, the UK and the United States, respectively.

5. In contrast to import subsidies granted to enable user enterprises to pay for the (higher) import prices (as discussed), the import-regulatory tax is intended to raise the (lower) import prices (in *renminbi* equivalent) to comparable domestic prices, so as to prevent undue increases in import supply at the expense of domestic producers. For foreign suppliers this clearly constitutes a deliberate import restriction. For the Chinese rationale for 'export subsidies', see the previous chapter.

6. By 1996, prices determined by markets already embraced 80 per cent of producer goods, 85 per cent of agricultural products and 95 per cent of industrial consumer goods (Howe, Kueh and Ash, 2003, p. 118).

7. The swap centre, first established in 1985, enabled approved SOEs and foreign-invested enterprises to exchange, among themselves, excess foreign exchange holdings of *renminbi*. These funds were needed respectively by firms short of *renminbi* to buy inputs from the domestic markets and those requiring hard currencies to import machinery and equipment from overseas. This represents the first step towards foreign exchange decontrol. However, the swap centres were made redundant by the unification of the two exchange rates and the establishment, in April 1994, of the National Foreign Exchange Trading Centre in Shanghai.

8. Short for 'Trade-Related Investment Measures' and 'Trade-Related Aspects of Intellectual Property Rights', as agreed during the Uruguay Round of GATT (precursor of WTO) negotiations concluded in 1993.

9. Let it also be noted that the reduction in the share of imports under the central plan (to 18.5 per cent by 1992, as mentioned above) was compensated by increases in import tariffs from the average (unweighted) of 38.4 per cent in 1986 to 43 per cent in 1992, and in the share to 32.9 per cent of imports placed under such non-tariff types of control as canalization and licensing (Chai, 1997a, p. 142). These evidently helped to provide room for further negotiations with WTO subsequent to the 1992–93 dismantling of mandatory control.

10. The call was made in conjunction with Deng's celebrated 'South China tour' in early 1992, during which he called for China's door to be opened even more widely and the domestic market be opened in principle in exchange for FDI with advanced technology.

11. Personal communication with Mr Wang Rongjun, former Managing Director of Shanghai Volkswagen Automotive Company Ltd, in 2004.

12. In fact, this occurred despite the fact that, even as late as 1995, the '70 per cent export' rule was hardly relaxed, especially for such conventional export industries as clothing and leather (Kueh, 2002b). Truly, by the early 1990s, Hong Kong's export-manufacturing plants were virtually all relocated to the Chinese Mainland to cash in on the much more favourable investment possibilities. Taiwan joined the exodus as soon as politically feasible after 1987, and, within four or five years, the island was already fearful of a 'hollowing out' of the

industrial structure (Ash and Kueh, 1993). Given the enormous economic size of these two 'Little Dragons', it is clear that the Mainland's export-oriented system was by then already firmly established.

13. Coca-Cola was admitted as FDI in 'carbonated beverages' manufacturing as early as December 1978, falling into the category of 'controlled', as opposed to 'encouraged' or 'prohibited'. But in 1993, a singular approval was given for the company to nearly double its production capacity (from 14 to 24 plants across the country) (Peking University et al., 2000, pp. 13, 16).

References

Agricultural Bank of China (Policy Research Office) (1984), 'Developing the rural banking system to boost the rural economy', *NYJJWT*, **3**, 26–9.

Ames, Edward (1965), *Soviet Economic Process*, Homewood, IL: Richard D. Irwin, Inc.

Ash, Robert F. (1988), 'The evolution of agricultural policy', *The China Quarterly*, **116**, 529–55.

Ash, Robert F. (ed.) (1998), *Agricultural Development in China, 1949–1989: The Collected Papers of Kenneth R. Walker (1931–1989)*, Oxford: Oxford University Press.

Ash, Robert and Y.Y. Kueh (1993), 'Economic integration within Greater China: trade and investment flows between Hong Kong, Mainland China and Taiwan', *The China Quarterly*, **136**, 711–45.

Ash, Robert and Y.Y. Kueh (eds) (1997), *The Chinese Economy under Deng Xiaoping*, Oxford: Clarendon Press (first edn 1996).

Atkinson, A.B. (1983), *The Economics of Inequality*, Oxford: Clarendon Press (2nd edn).

Baum, Richard (1975), *Prelude to Revolution: Mao, the Party and the Peasant Question, 1962–1966*, New York and London: Columbia University Press.

Bergson, Abraham (1968), *Planning and Productivity under Soviet Socialism*, New York: Columbia University Press.

Berliner, Joseph (1957), *Factory and Manager in the U.S.S.R.*, Cambridge, MA: Harvard University Press.

Buck, John L. (1937), *Land Utilisation in China*, Nanking: Nanking University.

Campbell, Robert W. (1966), *Soviet Economic Power: Its Organization, Growth and Challenge*, New York: Houghton Mifflin Company.

Campbell, Robert W. (1974), *Soviet-type Economies: Performance and Evolution*, London and Basingstoke: Macmillan Press.

Chai, Joseph C.H. (1983), 'Industrial cooperation between China and Hong Kong', in A.J. Youngson (ed.), *China and Hong Kong: The Economic Nexus*, Hong Kong: Oxford University Press, pp. 104–55.

Chai, Joseph C.H. (1997a), *China: Transition to a Market Economy*, Oxford: Clarendon Press.

Chai, Joseph C.H. (1997b), 'Consumption and living standards in China', in Robert F. Ash and Y.Y. Kueh (eds), *The Chinese Economy under Deng Xiaoping*, Oxford: Clarendon Press, pp. 247–76.

Chao, Kang (1970), *Agricultural Production in Communist China*, Madison, WI: University of Wisconsin Press.

Chen Dezun (1995), 'The causes and prevention of inflation', *ZGWJ*, **10**, 4–5.

Chen Huiqin (1981), 'The trend in technology imports must be changed', *JJYJ*, **4**, 22–5.

Chen, Nai-ruenn (1982), 'China's capital construction: current retrenchment and prospects for foreign participation', in US Congress Joint Economic Committee, *China under the Four Modernizations* (Part 2), Washington, DC: US Government Printing Office, pp. 48–82.

Cheng Jixian (1980), 'Some views on reform of the foreign trade system', *GJMYWT*, **1**, 19–21.

Chiang, Alpha C. and John C.H. Fei (1966), 'Maximum-speed development through austerity', in Irma Adelman and E. Thorbecke (eds), *The Theory and Design of Economic Development*, Baltimore, MD: Johns Hopkins University Press, pp. 67–92.

Chow, Gregory C. (1985), *The Chinese Economy*, New York: Harper and Row Publishers.

Chow, Gregory C. (1989), 'Market socialism and economic development in China', unpublished paper, cited in Dernberger (1989), 'Reforms in China: implications for U.S. policy', *American Economic Review* (papers and proceedings), **79**(2), 21.

CIA (1963), *The Short-lived Liberal Phase in Economic Thinking in Communist China*, Washington, DC: CIA.

Croll, Charles R. and K.C. Yeh (1975), 'Balance in coastal and inland industrial development', in US Congress Joint Economic Committee, *China: A Reassessment of the Economy*, Washington, DC: US Government Printing Office, pp. 81–93.

Da Feng-quan (1983), 'Probe of the system of contractual responsibility in relation to agricultural output', *NYJJWT*, **1**, 47–9.

DGB (*dagongbao – Ta Kung Pao – Impartial Daily*), Hong Kong.

Dernberger, Robert (1989), 'Reforms in China: implications for U.S. policy', *American Economic Review* (papers and proceedings), **79**(2), 21.

Donnithorne, Audrey (1972), 'China's cellular economy: some economic trends since the Cultural Revolution', *The China Quarterly*, **52**, 605–19.

Drewnowski, Jan (1961), 'The economic theory of socialism: a suggestion for reconsideration', *Journal of Political Economy*, reprinted in Wayne A. Leeman (1963), *Capitalism, Market Socialism and Central Planning*, New York: Houghton Mifflin Company, pp. 341–54.

DWJJMYNJ (*Zhongguo duiwajingji maoyi nianjian – Almanac of China's Foreign Economic Relations and Trade*), various years.

Easterly, William and Stanley Fisher (1994), 'What we can learn from the Soviet collapse', *Finance and Development*, **31**(4), 2–5.

Eckaus, R.S. (1955), 'Factor proportions in underdeveloped areas', *American Economic Review*, quoted in Alexander Eckstein (1975), *China's Economic Development: The Interplay of Scarcity and Ideology*, Ann Arbor, MI: The University of Michigan Press, p. 269.

Eckstein, Alexander (ed.) (1980), *Quantitative Measures of China's Economic Growth*, Ann Arbor, MI: University of Michigan Press.

Eckstein, Alexander (1977), *China's Economic Revolution*, Cambridge: Cambridge University Press.

Eckstein, Alexander (1975), *China's Economic Development: The Interplay of Scarcity and Ideology*, Ann Arbor, MI: The University of Michigan Press.

Eckstein, Alexander (1966), *Communist China's Economic Growth and Foreign Trade*, New York: McGraw-Hill.

Eckstein, Alexander, Walter Galenson and Ta-chung Liu (eds) (1968), *Economic Trends in Communist China*, Chicago: Aldine Press.

Elvin, Mark (1982), 'The technology of farming in late-traditional China', in Randolph Barker and Radha Sinha (eds), *The Chinese Agricultural Economy*, Boulder, CO: Westview Press, pp. 13–36.

Fan Gang (1999), 'Industrial reform as a major cause of inflation', in Y.Y. Kueh, Joseph C.H. Chai and Fan Gang (eds), *Industrial Reform and Macroeconomic Instability in China*, Oxford: Clarendon Press, pp. 163–87.

Feiwel, G.R. (1967), *The Soviet Quest for Economic Efficiency: Issues, Controversies and Reforms*, New York: Praeger.

Field, R. Michael (1986), 'China: the changing structure of industry', in US Congress Joint Economic Committee, *China's Economy Looks Towards the Year 2000*, Washington, DC: US Government Printing Office, pp. 505–47.

GJMY (*Guoji Maoyi – Intertrade*) monthly.

GJMYLWX (*Guoji maoyi lunwen xuan – Select Articles on International Trade*).

GJMYWT (*International Trade Problems*) monthly.

Guan Qixue (1980), 'The problem of Guangdong's export structure from the perspective of economic efficacy', *Xueshu Yanjiu* (*Academic Research*), **6**, 25–9.

Gutmann, Gernot (1965), *Theorie und Praxis der monetären Planung in der Zentralverwaltungswirtschaft*, Stuttgart: Gustav Fischer Verlag.

GWYGB (*Guowuyuan Gongbao – State Council Bulletin*), various issues.

GYJJTJZL 1949–1984 (*Zhongguo gongye jingji tongji ziliao – China Industrial Economy Statistical Materials 1949–1984*), Beijing: National Statistical Bureau.

Hensel, K. Paul (1977), 'Der Zwang zum wirtschaftspolitischen Experiment in zentral gelenkten Wirtschaften', *Jahrbücher für Nationalökonomie und Statistik*, **184** (4–5), 349–59.

Hensel, K. Paul (1979), *Einführung in die Theorie der Zentralverwaltungswirtschaft*, 3rd edn, Stuttgart and New York: Gustav Fischer Verlag.

Ho, Lok-sang (1994), 'Financial restructuring in 1993', in Marice Brosseau and Lo Chi-kin (eds), *China Review 1994*, Hong Kong: The Chinese University Press, pp. 10.1–15.

Hong Feng (1993), 'Inflation: outstanding problems in the current economic situation', *ZGWJ*, **6**, 3–6.

Hongqi (Red Flag) editorial (1982), 'Problems concerning China's foreign economic relations', **8**(5).

Howe, Christopher (1978), *China's Economy: A Basic Guide*, London: Paul Elek.

Howe, Christopher and Kenneth Walker (1977), 'The economist', in Dick Wilson (ed.), *Mao Tse-Tung in the Scales of History*, Cambridge: Cambridge University Press, pp. 174–222.

Howe, Christopher, Y.Y. Kueh and Robert Ash (2003), *China's Economic Reform: A Study with Documents*, London and New York: RoutledgeCurzon.

Hsueh, Tien-tung and Tun-oy Woo (1986), 'The political economy of the heavy industry sector in the People's Republic of China', *The Australian Journal of Chinese Affairs*, **15**, 52–82.

Imai, Hiroyuki (1997), 'Is the battle against inflation over?', in Maurice Brosseau, Kuan Hsin-chi and Y.Y. Kueh (eds), *China Review 1997*, Hong Kong: The Chinese University Press, pp. 181–208.

Jao, Y.C. (1983), 'Hong Kong's role in financing China's modernization', in A.J. Youngson (ed.), *China and Hong Kong: The Economic Nexus*, Hong Kong: Oxford University Press, pp. 12–76.

Ji Changzhong (1986), 'An analysis of why Shandong province's Engel coefficient ranks highest in China', *Zhongguo nongcun jingji (China's Rural Economy)*, **4**, 34–8.

Jin Deqin (1983), 'Role played by the Bank of China in technology import', *GJMY*, **12**, 6–8, 64.

JJGL (Economic Management) monthly.

JJNJ (Zhongguo jingji nianjian – China Economic Yearbook), various years, Jingji chubanshe, Beijing.

JJTQNJ 1983 (Zhongguo jingji tequ nianjim 1983 – China's Special Economic Zones Yearbook 1983).

JJYJ (Economic Research) monthly.

Johnson, D. Gale (1982), 'Agriculture in the centrally planned economies', *American Journal of Agricultural Economics*, **64**(5), 845–53.

266 *References*

Kornai, Janos (1980), *Economics of Shortage*, Amsterdam: North-Holland Press.

Kueh, Y.Y. (1966), 'Die weichen Pläne im neuen ökonomischen System Mitteldeutschlands: Eine Untersuchung der Verhaltensweisen in sozialistischen Betrieben', PhD dissertation, University of Marburg.

Kueh, Y.Y. (1983a), 'Economic reform in China at the *xian* level', *The China Quarterly*, **96**, 665–8.

Kueh, Y.Y. (1983b), 'Weather, technology, and peasant organization as factors in China's foodgrain production, 1952–1981', *Economic Bulletin for Asia and the Pacific* (United Nations), **34**(1), 15–26.

Kueh, Y.Y. (1984a), 'A weather index for analysing grain yield instability in China, 1952–1981', *The China Quarterly*, **97**, 68–83.

Kueh, Y.Y. (1984b), 'China's food balance and the world grain trade: projections for 1985, 1990 and 2000', *Asian Survey*, **24**(12), 1247–74.

Kueh, Y.Y. (1984c), 'Fertilizer supplies and foodgrain production in China, 1952–1982', *Food Policy*, **9**(3), 219–31.

Kueh, Y.Y. (1984d), 'China's new agricultural-policy program: major economic consequences, 1979–1983', *Journal of Comparative Economics*, **8**(4), 353–75.

Kueh, Y.Y. (1985a), *Economic Planning and Local Mobilization in Post-Mao China*, Research Notes and Studies Series No. 7, London: School of Oriental and African Studies.

Kueh, Y.Y. (1985b), *Foodgrain Production Instability in China and the World Grain Trade*, Hong Kong: Institute of Social Studies, The Chinese University of Hong Kong.

Kueh, Y.Y. (1985c), 'Economic reforms in Chinese industry', paper presented at the *Workshop on Comparative Studies of Economic Reforms in China and Eastern Europe*, sponsored by the School of Oriental and African Studies, London, 17 June.

Kueh, Y.Y. (1985d), 'The economics of the "second land reform" in China', *The China Quarterly*, **101**, 122–31.

Kueh, Y.Y. (1987), 'Economic decentralization and foreign trade expansion in China', in Joseph C.H. Chai and Chi-Keung Leung (eds), *China's Economic Reforms*, Hong Kong: Centre of Asian Studies, University of Hong Kong, pp. 444–81.

Kueh, Y.Y. (1988), 'Food consumption and peasant incomes in the Post-Mao era', *The China Quarterly*, **116**, 634–70.

Kueh, Y.Y. (1989a), 'The Maoist legacy and China's new industrialization strategy', *The China Quarterly*, **119**, 420–47.

Kueh, Y.Y. (1989b), 'Bureaucratization and economic reform in Chinese industry', in Wolfgang Klenner (ed.), *Trends of Economic Development in East Asia*, Berlin and Heidelberg: Springer Verlag, pp. 381–92.

Kueh, Y.Y. (1989c), 'Where will China go from here?', *The Australian Quarterly*, **61**(3), 358–69.

Kueh, Y.Y. (1990a), 'China's economic reforms: approach, vision and constraints', in Dieter Cassel (ed.), *Wirtschaftssysteme im Umbruch: Sowjetunion, China und industrialisierte Markwirtschaften zwischen internationalem Anpassungszwang und nationalem Reformbedarf*, Munich: Verlag Franz Vahlen, pp. 255–75.

Kueh, Y.Y. (1990b), 'Growth imperatives, economic decentralization, and China's open-door policy', *The Australian Journal of Chinese Affairs* (renamed *China Journal*), **24**, 94–119.

Kueh, Y.Y. (1991), 'The state of the economy and economic reform', in Hsin-chi Kuan and Maurice Brosseau (eds), *China Review*, Hong Kong: The Chinese University Press, pp. 10.1–25.

Kueh, Y.Y. (1997), 'Foreign investment and economic change in China', in Robert F. Ash and Y.Y. Kueh (eds), *The Chinese Economy under Deng Xiaoping*, Oxford: Clarendon Press, pp. 159–216.

Kueh, Y.Y. (1999a), 'Economic reform in Chinese industry: efficiency and instability', in Y.Y. Kueh, Joseph C.H. Chai and Fan Gang (eds), *Industrial Reform and Macroeconomic Instability in China*, Oxford: Clarendon Press, pp. 3–19.

Kueh, Y.Y. (1999b), 'Prospects for a transition to a market economy without runaway inflation', in Y.Y. Kueh, Joseph C.H. Chai and Fan Gang (eds), *Industrial Reform and Macroeconomic Instability in China*, Oxford: Clarendon Press, pp. 263–91.

Kueh, Y.Y. (1999c), 'Investment financing and the profitability criterion', in Y.Y. Kueh, Joseph C.H. Chai and Fan Gang (eds), *Industrial Reform and Macroeconomic Instability in China*, Oxford: Clarendon Press, pp. 121–46.

Kueh, Y.Y. (2000), 'Financial restructuring for economic recovery in China and Hong Kong', in Fu-chen Lo and T. Palanivel (eds), *Financial Restructuring and Economic Perspectives in East Asia*, Tokyo: United Nations University Institute of Advanced Studies, pp. 127–44.

Kueh, Y.Y. (2001), 'The Greater China Growth Triangle in the Asian Financial Crisis', in Shahid Jusuf, Simon Evenett and Weiping Wu (eds), *Facets of Globalization: International and Local Dimensions of Development*, Washington, DC: The World Bank, pp. 57–77.

Kueh, Y.Y. (2002a), *Agricultural Instability in China, 1931–1991: Weather, Technology, and Institutions*, 1st edn 1995, Oxford: Clarendon Press.

Kueh, Y.Y. (2002b), 'Coping with globalization in China: strategic implications of WTO accession', *Journal of World Investment* (renamed *Journal of World Investment and Trade*), **3**(1), 37–63.

Kueh, Y.Y. (2006), 'Mao and agriculture in China's industrialization: three antitheses in a 50-year perspective', *The China Quarterly*, **187**, 700–723.

Kueh, Y.Y. (2007), 'China's new industries and the East Asian production networks', in P. Intal, M. Garcia and M.A. Cortez (eds), *Production Networks, Trade and Investment Policies, and Regional Cooperation in East Asia: Country Cases and Regional Papers*, Manila: De La Salle University Angelo King Institute and International Development Research Center, pp. 95–142.

Kueh, Y.Y. and Robert F. Ash (eds) (1993), *Economic Trends in Chinese Agriculture: The Impact of Post-Mao Reforms*, Oxford: Clarendon Press.

Kueh, Y.Y. and Christopher Howe (1984), 'China's international trade: policy and organisational change and their place in "Economic Readjustment"', *The China Quarterly*, **100**, 813–48.

Kueh, Y.Y. and Zhao Renwei (1990), 'Market-oriented transformation of China's economic system as a development strategy', in Dieter Cassel and Günter Heiduk (eds), *China's Contemporary Economic Reforms as a Development Strategy*, Baden-Baden: Nomos Verlagsgesellschaft, pp. 13–36.

Kueh, Y.Y. and Thomas Voon (1997), 'The role of Hong Kong in Sino-American economic relations', in Y.Y. Kueh (ed.), *The Political Economy of Sino-American Relations*, Hong Kong: The University of Hong Kong Press, pp. 61–92.

Kueh, Y.Y., Joseph C.H. Chai and Fan Gang (eds) (1999), *Industrial Reform and Macroeconomic Instability in China*, Oxford: Clarendon Press.

Kuo, Leslie T.C. (1972), *The Technical Transformation of Agriculture in Communist China*, New York: Praeger.

Kuznets, Simon (1964), 'Economic growth and the contribution of agriculture: notes on measurements', in Carl Eicher and Lawrence Witt (eds), *Agriculture in Economic Development*, New York: McGraw-Hill, pp. 109–19.

Kuznets, Simon (1979), 'Growth and structural shifts', in Walter Galenson (ed.), *Economic Growth and Structural Change in Taiwan*, Ithaca, NY: Cornell University Press, pp. 15–131.

Lao Tian (2005), *On the Economic History of New China: A Preliminary Observation on the 'Non-Western Road to Industrialization' (Xin zhongguo jingji shilun: Dui 'feixifang gongyehua daolu' de yige chubu kaocha)*, www.wyzxsx.com/ebook/007.doc.

Lardy, Nicholas (1975), 'Economic planning in the People's Republic of China: central-provincial fiscal relations', in US Congress Joint Economic Committee, *China: A Reassessment of the Economy*, Washington, DC: US Government Printing Office, pp. 94–115.

Lardy, Nicholas (1983), *Agriculture in China's Modern Economic Development*, Cambridge: Cambridge University Press.

Lardy, Nicholas (1995), 'The role of foreign trade and investment in China's economic transformation', *The China Quarterly*, **144**, 1065–82.

Lardy, Nicholas (1997), 'Chinese foreign trade', in Robert F. Ash and Y.Y. Kueh (eds), *The Chinese Economy under Deng Xiaoping*, Oxford: Clarendon Press, pp. 217–46.

Leeman, Wayne A. (1963), *Capitalism, Market Socialism, and Central Planning*, New York: Houghton Mifflin Company.

Li, Choh-ming (1962), *The Statistical System of Communist China*, Berkeley, CA: University of California Press.

Li Geng (1982), 'Vigorously organize the export of mechanical and electrical products', *JJGL*, **3**, 30–33.

Li Gonghao (1983), 'An initial exploration with regard to the pricing problems of imports and exports', *Shejie Jingji Wenhui* (*World Economy Forum*), **1**, 37–42.

Li Peng (1990), 'Government Work Report', delivered (by the Premier) at the Third Session of the Seventh National People's Congress, *DGB*, 21 March.

Liberman, Evsei (1962), 'The plan, profits and bonuses', *Pravda*, 9 September 1962 (translated in *The Current Digest of the Soviet Press*, 3 October 1962, **36**, 13–15).

Liberman, Evsei (1965), 'The plan, direct ties and profitability', *Pravda*, 21 November (translated in *The Current Digest of the Soviet Press*, December, **47**, 6–8).

Liberman, Evsei (1966), 'Confidence is an incentive', in *Komsomolskaya Pravda*, 24 April (translated in *The Current Digest of the Soviet Press*, 11 May 1966, **16**, 29–30).

Lin Senmu (1981), 'The lesson of the 22 whole plant imports', *JJYJ*, **6**, 12–14.

Liu Guanglie (1983), 'Analysis of some problems concerning agricultural-bank loans', *ZGJR*, **7**, 37–8.

Liu Suinian (1982), 'Planned economy: a prerequisite to the realization of the Four Modernizations', *JJYJ*, **9**, 3–6.

Liu, T.C. (1968), 'Quantitative trends in the economy', in Alexander Eckstein, Walter Galenson and Ta-chung Liu (eds), *Economic Trends in Communist China*, Chicago: Aldine Press, pp. 87–182.

Liu Zhaojin (1980), 'Preliminary discussion on reform of foreign trade system', *GJMYWT*, **1**, 14–30.

Luo Shuhua (1983), 'The development of the agricultural-responsibility system and issues raised in the course of its application', *NYJJWT*, **3**, 3–9.

Lyons, Thomas P. (1987), *Economic Integration and Planning in Maoist China*, New York: Columbia University Press.

Ma Hong (1982), *The Contemporary Chinese Economy. A Compendium*, Beijing: Zhongguo Shehui Kexue Chubanshe.

Ma Hong (1983), *Study on Problems of China's Industrial Structure (Zhongguo Gongye Jingji Jieguo Wenti Yanjiu)*, Beijing: Zhongguo Kexue Chubanshe.

Maoxuan (1977) (*Mao Zedong Xuanji – Selected Works of Mao Zedong*), Volume V, Beijing: Renmin Chubanshe.

Naughton, Barry (1990), 'Monetary implications of balanced economic growth and the current macroeconomic disturbances in China', in Dieter Cassel and Günter Heiduk (eds), *China's Contemporary Economic Reforms as a Development Strategy*, Baden-Baden: Nomos Verlagsgesellschaft, pp. 109–40.

Naughton, Barry (1995), 'China's macroeconomy in transition', *The China Quarterly*, **144**, 1083–1104.

NCGZTX (*Nongcun gongzuo tongxun – Rural Work Bulletin*), various issues.

NCYJ (*Zhongguo Nongcun Yanjiu – China Rural Studies*).

NYJJWT (*Nongye Jingji Wenti – Agricultural Economic Problems*), various issues.

NYNJ (*Zhongguo Nongye Nianjian – China Agriculture Yearbook*), various years, Beijing: Nongye Chubanshe.

Nove, Alec (1964), *Was Stalin Really Necessary?*, London: George Allen and Unwin.

Nove, Alec (1965), *The Soviet Economy*, London: George Allen and Unwin.

Peking University, Tsinghua University and University of South Carolina (2000), *Economic Impact of the Coca-Cola System on China*, Moore School of Business: http://moorecms.graysail.com.

Perkins, Dwight H. (1966), *Market Control and Planning in Communist China*, Cambridge, MA: Harvard University Press.

Perkins, Dwight (1968), 'Industrial planning and management', in Alexander Eckstein, Walter Galenson and Ta-chung Liu (eds), *Economic Trends in Communist China*, Chicago: Aldine Press, pp. 597–636.

Pryor, Frederic L. (1963), *The Communist Foreign Trade System*, London: George Allen and Unwin.

Renmin Ribao (People's Daily).

Riskin, Carl (1987), *China's Political Economy: The Quest for Development since 1949*, New York: Oxford University Press.

Sakurai, Masao (1982), 'Investing in China: the legal framework', *Jetro China Newsletter*, **37**, 7–9.

SCMP (*South China Morning Post*), Hong Kong.

Shanxi College of Agriculture (1975), *Turang Xue (Edaphology)*, Beijing: Remin Jiaoyu Chubanshe.

Shao Gang (1980), 'Problems of foreign trade system reform', *GJMYWT*, **2**, 22–5.

Sicular, Terry (1993), 'Ten years of reform: progress and setbacks in agricultural planning and pricing', in Y.Y. Kueh and Robert F. Ash (eds), *Economic Trends in Chinese Agriculture: The Impact of Post-Mao Reforms*, Oxford: Clarendon Press, pp. 47–96.

Sik, Ota (1967), 'Socialist market relations and planning', in C.H. Feinstein (ed.), *Socialism, Capitalism, and Economic Growth: Essays in Honour of Maurice Dobb*, Cambridge: Cambridge University Press, pp. 133–57.

Sinha, Radha (2003), *Sino-American Relations: Mutual Paranoia*, Basingstoke: Palgrave Macmillan.

Stone, Bruce (1993), 'Basic agricultural technology under reform', in Y.Y. Kueh and Robert F. Ash (eds), *Economic Trends in Chinese Agriculture: The Impact of Post-Mao Reforms*, Oxford: Clarendon Press, pp. 311–60.

Sun Yefang (1984), *Selected Works of Sun Yefang (Sun Yefang Xuanji)*, Taiyuan: Shanxi Renmin Chubanshe.

Tang, Anthony M. (1968), 'Policy and performance in agriculture', in Alexander Eckstein, Walter Galenson and Ta-chung Liu (eds), *Economic Trends in Communist China*, Chicago: Aldine Press, pp. 459–508.

Tang, Anthony M. (1984), *An Analytical and Empirical Investigation of Agriculture in Mainland China, 1952–1980*, Taipei: Chung Hua Institution for Economic Research.

Tang Minfang (2002), 'In solving the *sannong* problem, where should be the point for a breakthrough', *NYJJWT*, **12**, 25–9.

Tang Zongkun (1987), 'Supply and marketing', in Gene Tidrick and Chen Jiyuan (eds), *China's Industrial Reform*, Oxford and New York: Oxford University Press, pp. 210–36.

Tidrick, G. (1987), 'Planning and supply', in Gene Tidrick and Chen Jiyuan (eds), *China's Industrial Reform*, Oxford and New York: Oxford University Press, pp. 175–209.

TJGB (Zhongguo Tongji Gongbao – Communiqué on Fulfilment of the National Economic and Social Development Plan).

TJNJ (Zhongguo Tongji Nianjian – China Statistical Yearbook), various years.

TJZY (Zhongguo Tongji Zhaiyao – China Statistical Abstracts), various years.

Tsang, Shu-ki (1995), 'Financial restructuring', in Chi-kin Lo, Suzanne Pepper and Kai-yuen Tsui (eds), *China Review 1995*, Hong Kong: The Chinese University Press, pp. 20.1–35.

Tsang, Shu-Ki and Yuk-Shing Cheng (1999), 'Empirical evidence of the twin expansion of investment and wage outlay', in Y.Y Kueh, Joseph

C.H. Chai and Fan Gang (eds), *Industrial Reform and Economic Instability in China*, Oxford: Clarendon Press, pp. 215–31.

UNCTAD (United Nations Conference on Trade and Development) (2000), *World Investment Report 2000: Cross-border Mergers and Acquisitions and Development*, New York and Geneva: United Nations.

UNCTAD (United Nations Conference on Trade and Development) (2001), *World Investment Report 2001: Promoting Linkages*, New York and Geneva: United Nations.

US Congress Joint Economic Committee (1975), *China: A Reassessment of the Economy*, Washington, DC: US Government Printing Office.

US Congress Joint Economic Committee (1982), *China under the Four Modernizations* (Part 2), Washington, DC: US Government Printing Office.

US Congress Joint Economic Committee (1986), *China's Economy Looks Towards the Year 2000*, Washington, DC: US Government Printing Office.

Walder, Andrew (1995), 'China's transitional economy: interpreting its significance', *The China Quarterly*, **144**, 963–79.

Walker, Kenneth R. (1963), 'Ideology and economic discussion in China: Ma Yin-chu on development strategy and his critics', *Economic Development and Cultural Change*, **11**(2), 113–33.

Walker, Kenneth R. (1965), *Planning in Chinese Agriculture: Socialism and the Private Sector, 1956–1962*, London: Frank Cass.

Walker, Kenneth R. (1966), 'Collectivization in retrospect: the socialist high tide of autumn 1955–spring 1956', *The China Quarterly*, **26**, 1–43.

Wang Cheng and Tsang Shu-ki (1999), 'Macroeconomic policies, financial conditions and enterprise behavior', in Y.Y. Kueh, Joseph C.H. Chai and Fan Gang (eds), *Industrial Reform and Economic Instability in China*, Oxford: Clarendon Press, pp. 247–62.

Wang Yuxuan and Zhang Yifang (1980), 'Problems concerning the reform of economic management system as viewed from the export of mechanical and electrical products', *GJMYWT*, **1**, 34–49.

Wansui (1967) (*Mao Zedong Sixiang Wansui – Long Live Mao Zedong Thoughts*) (Chinese Red Guard publications 1967; first reprinted in Japan, 5 October 1974).

Wansui (1969) (*Mao Zedong Sixiang Wansui – Long Live Mao Zedong Thoughts*) (Chinese Red Guard publications 1969; first reprinted in Japan, 15 November 1974).

Watson, Andrew (1989), 'Investment issues in the Chinese countryside', *The Australian Journal of Chinese Affairs*, **22**, 85–126.

Wheelwright, Edward L. and Bruce McFarlane (1970), *The Chinese Road to Socialism: Economics of the Cultural Revolution*, New York: Monthly Review Press.

Wiens, Thomas B. (1980), 'Agricultural statistics in the People's Republic of China', in Alexander Eckstein (ed.), *Quantitative Measures of China's Economic Growth*, Ann Arbor, MI: University of Michigan Press, pp. 44–107.

Wiles, Peter J.D. (1962), *The Political Economy of Communism*, Cambridge, MA: Harvard University Press.

Wiles, Peter J.D. (1968), *Communist International Economics*, Oxford: Basil Blackwell.

Wong, Christine P.W. (1982), 'Rural industrialization in the People's Republic of China: lessons from the Cultural Revolution decade', in US Congress Joint Economic Committee, *China under the Four Modernizations* (Part 2), Washington, DC: US Government Printing Office, pp. 394–418.

Writing Group (1974), *Basic Knowledge on Political Economy (Zhengzhi Jingjixue Jichu Zhishi)* (Second Part on Socialism), Shanghai: Renmin Chubanshe.

Wu Nianlu (1983), 'Relations between exchange rate and export transactions', *GJMY*, **1**, 39–41.

Wu Xiang (1983), 'Combine contract-responsibility system with agricultural planning', *NYJJWT*, **3**, 3–10.

Wu Wen and Liu Nianyan (2004), 'Thoughts and policy for co-ordinating the overall development of the urban and rural economies', *NCYJ*, **13**, 1–18.

XBCJ Ribao (Hong Kong Economic Journal Daily), Hong Kong.

XHYB (Xinhua Yuebao – New China Monthly).

Xin Yang (1995), 'Analysis of the inflationary trends in the second quarter of 1995 and forecast for the second half of the year', *ZGWJ*, **7**, 11–13.

Xu Shiwei (1983), 'On the foreign trade system of our country', *GJMYWT*, **2**, 8–13.

Xu Xuehan (1984), 'A discussion of the problem of the fake losses in exports', *Caimao Jingji (Finance and Trade Economics)*, **2**, 5–9.

Yan Fan (1981), 'The important task of present economic work is to clear up left-deviationist thinking', *JJGL*, **1**, 20–23.

Yang Shengmin (1986), *Research on China's Consumption Structure (Zhongguo Xiaofei Jieguo Yanjiu)*, Taiyuan: Shanxi Renmin Chubanshe.

Yang Zhongwei and Han Zhineng (1999), 'Wage reforms and the effectiveness of aggregate wage target control', in Y.Y. Kueh, Joseph C.H. Chai and Fan Gang (eds), *Industrial Reform and Macroeconomic Instability in China*, Oxford: Clarendon Press, pp. 188–214.

Yao Keping (1995), 'An analysis of the 1994 balance of payments and a projection for 1995', *ZGJR*, **4**, 39–40.

Yeh, K.C. (1984), 'Macroeconomic changes in the Chinese economy during the Readjustment', *The China Quarterly*, **100**, 691–716.

Yi Gang (1994), *Money, Banking and Financial Markets in China*, Boulder, CO: Westview Press.

Yi Gang (1995), 'Money supply and demand, and inflation in China', *JJYJ*, **5**, 51–9.

ZGJR (*Zhongguo Jinrong – China Finance*).

ZGWJ (*Zhongguo Wujia – China Prices*) monthly.

Zhang Shuguang and Y.Y. Kueh (1999), 'Measuring the changing degree of enterprise decision-making autonomy and constraints', in Y.Y. Kueh, Joseph C.H. Chai and Fan Gang (eds), *Industrial Reform and Macroeconomic Instability in China*, Oxford: Clarendon Press, pp. 46–86.

Zhang Wei De (1983), '*Baogan Daohu* as the road to a new rural economy', *JJGL*, **1**, 49–53.

Zhang Xinjing (1990), *Theories of Importance in the Ten Years of Reform: A Comprehensive Review* (*Gaige shinian zhongyao lilun guandian zongshu*), Beijing: Xueyuan chubanshe.

Zhang Yanning (1990), 'Intensify enterprise reform and strengthen enterprise management during the process of rectification', *Renmin Ribao*, 7 January.

Zhao Renwei (1986), 'The dual-system problem in China's economic reform', *JJYJ*, **9**, 12–24.

Zhao Renwei (1989), 'Some problems encountered in the market-oriented reform in China', paper presented at the International Symposium on Development Strategies of the Third World Countries, Beijing, 18–21 April.

Zhao Ziyang (1987), *Forward on the Road to Socialism with Chinese Characteristics* (Party Secretary-General's Report delivered at the 13th National Party Congress of the Chinese Communist Party on 25th October).

Zheng Tuobin (1984), 'Problems of the reform in foreign trade' (*Woguo duiwai maoyi tizhi gaige wenti*), *JJYJ*, **11**, 27–33.

Zheng Yinyong (1983), 'Make use of foreign funds to serve the technical transformation of our existing enterprises', *GJMY*, **3**, 27–8.

Zhong Zhi Zhang (1981), 'Problems of adopting the internal exchange settlement rate for foreign trade', *Economic Reporter* (*Jingji Daobao Weekly*, Hong Kong), 2l January, p. 15.

Index

agricultural investment 65–7, 71, 116, 121
agricultural savings 67–71, 108
agricultural surplus, siphoning 6, 20–21, 52, 57, 121, 136, 146, 160, 177, 197
agriculture
  direct taxation 21, 121
  evaluation of 117–18, 120
  factor contribution 121–2
  market contribution 118
  mechanization 132, 135
  product contribution 118, 121
  see also farm procurement prices
agriculture–industry dichotomy 120, 139, 141–3, 150, 158, 161, 174
Ames, Edward 125
Angang Constitution 15–19
'anti-revisionism' treatises 33
Ash, Robert F. 6, 26, 161, 165, 168, 253, 255, 258, 260, 261
Atkinson, A.B. 106
Atkinson index 106
austerity
  absolute 8
  continuous 258
  with degree of 4, 21, 119, 175, 179, 227
  emphasis on 180
  less 11
  maximum 4, 87, 153, 163
  maximum-speed development through 3, 50, 163, 173, 175
  ultimate 9
  see also Angang Constitution

backyard furnaces 5, 48, 126, 136, 146, 203
balance of payments 230
balanced development strategy 119
Bank of China 233–4, 236, 249
baochan daohu 5–7, 21, 24, 69, 81, 88; *see also* responsibility farm system

baochan zhi 80–81
baogan daohu 64–5, 80–81
  direct contracting with households 78
  impact on incomes 91
  impact on irrigation 71, 74
  impact on savings 69–71
  and investment priorities 71–2
  peasant labour released 142
  and procurement ratio 75–6
baogan zhi 80–81
baogong zhi 80–81
base money creation 219
Baum, Richard 9
Bergson, Abraham 135, 136
Berliner, Joseph 22, 190
Big Bang strategy 195, 207
big push paradigm 198, 220
Bolshevichka–Mayak experiment 11, 164
bonus awards 4, 10, 11, 25, 38, 176
Brus, Werner 203
Buck, John L. 136
budget appropriations 9, 13, 65–6, 188, 192, 205
budget constraints
  hard 207, 212, 221
  soft 16–17, 190
Bukharin, Nikolai 7, 8
bureaucracy
  constraints imposed by 194–8
  and economic reforms 190–94
  extent 183–4
  and Mao Zedong 184–6
  problems 189–90
  and property rights 198–200
  structure 186–9
bureaucratic–physical control 59, 77, 153, 171, 192, 198, 208, 227

calorie intake 101, 103, 105, 113
Campbell, Robert W. 7, 147

capital intensity 14, 150, 163
capital movement 82–3
capitalist restoration 3, 10, 17
Cassel, Dieter 181, 202
central planning
    bureaucratic requirements 184–6
    tolerance of market forces 180
centralism, as stabilizing 49–51, 59
Chai, Joseph C.H. 123, 156, 169, 192, 195, 197, 203, 210, 211, 222, 223, 241, 253, 254, 260
Chao, Kang 136
chemical fertilizers 5, 41, 65, 70–72, 77, 117, 118, 126, 130, 132, 140, 170
Chen Dezun 218
Chen Huiqin 228
Chen Jinhua 223
Chen Jiyuan 26
Chen, Nai-ruenn 240
Cheng Jixian 249
Cheng, Yuk-Shing 208
Chiang, Alpha C. 3, 24, 27, 174
Chiang–Fei model 3–4, 20–21, 76–7, 79, 87, 174–5, 177
Chicago school 194, 198
Chinese Communist Party 189
Chow, Gregory C. 136, 172, 179
chuanhui lu 246–7
CIA, predictions following Tiananmen Square incident 58
CJV (contractual joint venture) 240–43, 249
class struggle 9, 10, 24, 116
coarse grain 134
Coase theorem 198–9
Coca-Cola, as foreign investor 257, 261
collectivization
    as agricultural growth strategy 123–9
    to control consumption 33
    evaluation of 116–23
    see also Socialist High Tide
compensation trade joint ventures (CTJV) 241–3
compulsory purchase quotas 86–7; *see also* farm output quotas
consumption
    aggregate trends 89–91
    changes in patterns of 96–100
    elasticity with regard to income 21–2, 68, 178

interprovincial inequality 104–13
    and savings 94–6, 108
    short-run fluctuations 92–4
consumption policy, less harsh 12, 18, 19, 35–6, 41, 63, 65, 175, 213
consumption standard 17
contract-responsibility system 200, 208, 211, 273
contractual joint venture (CJV) 240–43, 249
contractual procurement 64
cooperativization 24, 82, 118–19, 135
Croll, Charles R. 143
CTJV (compensation trade joint ventures) 241–3
Cultural Revolution
    agricultural planning targets 124
    as confined to urban centres 4–5
    growth disruption 35, 201
    lessons learned 48
    as Mao's legacy 31
    political upheaval 3, 9
    strategy built on Great Leap blueprint 126
    trade volumes 55
    see also self-reliance

Da Feng-quan 72
Dazhai model 8–10, 25
decentralization 19, 24
    agricultural 38, 65
    constraints 170–72
    future 179–81
    as growth policy 172–5
    growth versus efficiency 175–9
    industrial 38
    measures of intensity 166–70
    optimum 8, 17, 22, 39–40, 50, 76, 79, 162–6
decollectivization
    and farm procurement prices 38, 63, 65, 130–31
    sanzi yibao as 7, 21
    as transition to intensive growth 130–32
Deng Xiaoping
    agricultural economic reforms 63–78
    economic strategy vii
    'marketization' drive 26

May 1988 liberalization
announcement 207, 209–10,
215, 218–19
policy reliant on foundation left by
Mao 32, 39–46
succession 48–9
transition from Mao as evolution 32,
34–9
departmentalism 190, 193
depreciation 13
Dernberger, Robert 172, 180
direct contractual ties 10, 12, 26, 164
Document No. 1 158–9; *see also* Party
Central Committee, Document
No. 1, 1984
Donnithorne, Audrey 136, 161
double-squeeze 208
double-track system, *see* two-track/
double-track system
Drewnowski, Jan 19
droughts, *see* floods and droughts
Dulles, John Foster 122

Easterly, William 35
Eckaus, Richard S. 21, 124, 146
Eckstein, Alexander 24, 88, 120, 139,
146, 150
economic accountability
(*Khozraschyot*) 8, 12, 38, 164, 191
economic growth strategy
extensive 39, 123–4
intensive 39, 123, 133
Economic Readjustment 4, 65, 89, 151,
181, 191, 213, 222, 228; *see also*
foreign economic relations,
Readjustment after Hua
economics of shortage 185, 189, 198, 204
effort function, labour 4, 20, 76–7
egalitarianism 9, 15, 20, 25, 136
EJV (equity joint venture) 240–43, 249,
257
Elvin, Mark 136
Engel's law/ratio 96–8, 103–4, 108–10,
112–13
enlarged reproduction (new
investment) 13, 17–18, 26
equity joint venture (EJV) 240–43, 249,
257
export control 236, 240
export joint ventures 41, 55

export-oriented FDI 146, 157, 248,
256–7
export processing 172, 243, 251–2, 257
export subsidies 46, 253
externality 198
extractive strategy 119

Fan Gang 208, 215, 216, 222, 223
farm mechanization statistics 132
farm output quotas 5, 86–7
farm procurement prices
applied to voluntary sales 65
and decollectivization 38, 63, 65,
130–31
impact compared to weather 92–4
increases in 63–4, 114, 213, 218
and interprovincial consumption
inequality 107–8
rise enabled by Mao's debt-free
heritage 41
farm procurement scheme 121
farm production, instability 72–4
FDI, *see* foreign direct investment
Fei, John C.H. 3, 20, 174
Feiwel, G.R. 18
Fel'dman model 23
Field, R. Michael 144
Finance Ministry 187–9, 196–7, 223
fine grain 100, 133–4
Fisher, Stanley 35
five small industries (new) 65, 72–3, 77,
134, 146
five small industries (old) 25, 41, 65,
72, 126, 146
floods and droughts 73–4, 77, 126–7,
130, 136
food
adequacy of peasant diet 100–104,
105, 110
interprovincial inequality 105
staples versus non-staples 97,
100–101
see also Engel's law/ratio
forced-draft industrialization 33, 35,
57–8, 114, 157, 163
foreign direct investment (FDI)
attracting 38, 157, 232–5
in coastal areas 144, 146, 150–51
export-oriented 146, 157, 248, 256–7
import substitution 157, 258–9

incentives 241–4
joint investments 171–2, 235–6
    see also Joint Venture Law
regime adaptation for WTO
    membership 255–8
foreign economic relations
attracting FDI 38, 157, 232–5
internal/external price problems 244–8
investment incentives 241–4
organizational adaptations 236–40
overview vii, 227–9, 248
Readjustment after Hua 229–32
foreign exchange
available to central government 181
control 45–6, 165
earnings remittance to Beijing 237
fixed-rate regime 194, 229
huanghui chengben vs *chuanhui lu*
    246–7
tourists 55
    see also swap centres; swap rate
foreign exchange/currency reserves
and open-door policy 157
retention incentives 179
following Tiananmen Square
    incident 58
foreign-invested enterprises
compensation trade joint ventures
    (CTJV) 241–3
contractual joint venture (CJV)
    240–43, 249
equity joint venture (EJV) 240–43,
    249, 257
offshore oil exploration joint
    ventures (OOEJV) 235, 241
offshore oil joint ventures 235, 241
wholly foreign-owned venture
    (WFOV) 241
foreign trade policy 38–9
four modernizations 33–4, 48
free markets 6, 11, 52–3
French *Planification* 181
Friedman, Milton 198

gigantomania 147
Go West campaign 145, 160
Gorbachev, Mikhail 39, 40, 45, 48, 49,
    50–51, 53, 58, 179
gradualist/incrementalist method vii,
    39–40, 204

grain first/pro-grain strategy 89, 124–5
grain self-sufficiency 40–41, 116, 126
Great Leap Forward
agricultural policy reorientation
    following 5
amalgamating collectives into
    communes 126
aspirations for another 4–5
collapse of 4, 8–9, 184
economic strategy 146
food supply downturn 112, 133
growth disruption 35, 116
intentions 185
as Mao's legacy 31
    see also self-reliance
Guan Qixue 246
guandao practice 26, 53, 166, 171, 192,
    209
guidance planning 166, 168, 192–3,
    197–8, 208, 250, 252–3
Gutmann, Gernot 8

harvest stabilizers 74, 78; *see also*
    institutional hedge; subsistence
    urge; technological hedge
Hayek, Friederich 198
He Jiangzhang 11, 13, 17, 26
heavy industry, vs light industry 33,
    151–4, 174
Hensel, K. Paul 8, 17, 24, 184
high and stable yield fields 127
Ho, Lok-sang 222, 223
Hong Feng 223
Hong Kong 44, 46, 56–7, 122, 171, 194,
    231–2, 236, 242, 248, 256
horizontal cooperation 193
housing demand 98–9
Howe, Christopher 26, 122, 135, 136,
    161, 168, 185, 186, 231, 233, 248,
    249, 253, 255, 258, 260
Hsueh, Tien-tung 144
Hu Jintao 120, 134, 135
Hu Yaobang 193, 207
Hua Guofeng 31, 49, 227–9
huanghui chengben 246–7

idealtypus 8
Imai, Hiroyuki 222
IMF (International Monetary Fund)
    230

imports
  canalization 253, 260
  complete plants 228, 230, 238–9
  licensing 253, 260
  minimization of 33
  quotas 253
  technology 157, 227–9, 238, 248
  see also foreign direct investment;
    taxes, import-regulatory
incomes
  consumption elasticity 21–2, 68, 178
  and food consumption 108–9
    see also Engel's law/ratio
  interprovincial inequality 105–8,
    113
  peasant vs urban residents 52–3,
    89–91
industrial deregulation 195, 201,
    208–9, 213–15, 217–18, 222; *see*
    also inflation, and industrial
    deregulation
industrial *gigantomania* 147
industrial imbalances
  coastal vs interior 143–6
  industry vs agriculture 120, 139,
    141–3, 150, 158, 161, 174
  prospects for 158–61
  technological dualism 146–50, 160
industrialization
  forced-draft 33, 35, 57–8, 114, 157,
    163
  regional 146
  socialist 118, 139, 146
  supremacy of viii
industry, vs agriculture 34–5
industry–agriculture dichotomy 120,
    139, 141–3, 150, 158, 161, 174
inflation
  1985 peak 205–7
  1988–89 episode 207–10
  1993–95 episode 210–11, 217–20
  causes 45, 51, 54
  and industrial deregulation 204–5
  overview 220–22
  pressures 22, 24, 41
  sources 212–17
  following Tiananmen Square
    incident 58
inflationary pressures 204
institutional hedge 126–7, 129, 131

intellectual property rights, *see* patent
    protection
interest rates 14, 83, 172, 220, 223
internal prices 65
International Monetary Fund (IMF)
    230
international standing 139–40
intersectoral investment 4
investment
  enlarged reproduction 13, 17–18, 26
  simple reproduction 12, 13, 17–18, 25
  see also agricultural investment;
    foreign direct investment;
    intersectoral investment
investment hunger 198, 216
irrigation
  advances under Mao 117
  area covered 132
  curtailed investment 71, 77
  impacts 41
  projects 5, 25, 84, 88, 126
  see also water conservation works

Jao, Y.C. 243
Ji Changzhong 103, 112
Jiang Zemin 47, 49, 57, 165, 180
Jin Deqin 249
Johnson, D. Gale 86
joint stock corporations 193, 200
Joint Venture Law 233, 241–3

Kapp, William K. 24
Khozraschyot (economic
    accountability) 8, 12, 38, 164, 191
Khrushchev, Nikita 7, 49, 50, 55, 169,
    180, 181, 201
Kissinger, Henry 33
Klenner, Wolfgang 202, 266
Kornai, Janos 185, 189, 190, 198, 204
Kosygin Reform 10, 17, 51, 164
Krupp Stainless 257
Kuo, Leslie T.C. 127
Kuznets, Simon 118, 140

labour accumulation 71; *see also*
    Nurksian accumulation
Lange, Oscar 15
Lao Tian 259
Lardy, Nicholas 44, 117, 119, 122, 124,
    125, 127, 129, 135, 136, 146, 161, 254

lateral cooperation 193
leasehold extension 79, 107, 176
leasehold markets 85–6
Leibenstein, Harvey 8
Li Bening 88
Li Chengrui 201
Li, Choh-ming 9
Li Geng 239
Li Gonghao 247, 249
Li Peng 48, 56, 162
Li Ruihuang 47
Li Yining 203
lianchan zhi 81–2
Liberman, Evsei 10–18, 25, 26, 51, 164,
    196, 200
life expectancy 122–3
Lin Senmu 228
Liu Guanglie 78
Liu Nianyan 135
Liu Shaoqi 3, 16–17, 33, 135; *see also*
    Mao–Liu controversy
Liu Suinian 78
Liu, T.C. 141
Liu Zhaojin 247
living standards 97; *see also* Engel's
    law/ratio
local adaptations 139
Luo Shuhua 72
Lushan Plenum 186
Lyons, Thomas P. 161

Ma Hong 161, 239, 243, 249
Ma Yinchu 6, 23, 79
macroeconomic control 193, 197, 210
mandatory planning 166–9, 172, 192–3,
    197, 205, 208, 217, 250, 252–3
Mao Zedong
    50-year perspective 133–5
    and bureaucratism 184–6
    On Co-operativization speech 116–19
    *On the Correct Handling of
        Contradictions among the People*
        202
    criticism of Stalin 203
    necessity of viii, 31–4
    remarks from October 1955 speech
        and *sanzi yibao* 24
    On the Ten Great Relations treatise
        119–20, 143, 146, 184
    view of collectivization 126

Mao–Liu controversy
    agricultural implications 5–10
    cooperativization and mechanization
        135
    differences in economic thinking 3–5
    economic impacts 19–22
    industrial implications 10–19
    political perspective 22–3
market economy transition 200–202
market-for-technology exchange 256
market regulation 164, 166–8, 172,
    192–3, 195, 217, 249, 250
Marx, Karl 11, 13, 23, 171, 192, 197,
    203
Marxist–Leninist ideology/doctrine
    viii, 11, 13, 23, 192, 197, 203
mass mobilization 5, 15–16, 74, 88,
    126, 143, 154–6
material balances 24, 166–7, 184, 189,
    200
material incentives 11, 15, 18, 25, 26,
    50, 176, 178
McFarlane, Bruce 136, 161
Ministry of Finance 187–9, 196–7,
    223
monetary overhang 204, 208–9, 215,
    217, 222
monetary policy 204, 210, 216, 223,
    224
money supply 58, 206, 212, 216,
    219–20, 222
monopoly overhang 198, 202–4

Naughton, Barry 207, 219, 223
Nove, Alec viii, 26
NPC Resolution
    October 1984 84, 165–6, 168, 172–3,
        181, 192, 193, 199, 202, 205,
        208, 213, 243, 250, 252
    October 1987 193, 199, 207–9
    October 1992 210, 217, 253, 255
Nurksian accumulation 10, 41, 63, 84,
    142

offshore oil exploration joint ventures
    (OOEJV) 235, 241
'one-country two-systems' model 232,
    251–2
OOEJV (offshore oil exploration joint
    ventures) 235, 241

open-door policy
   contributing to three imbalances
      156–8
   future of 172, 181
   as growth policy 174
   reliance on foundations laid by Mao
      vii
   speed of implementation 40
   survival from Hua to Deng 227
   and Tiananmen Square incident
      47–51, 54–5, 165, 181, 257
'optimum austerity' consumption
   strategy 4, 79, 87, 175
optimum decentralization 8, 17, 22,
   39–40, 50, 76, 79, 162–6
output maximizing model 125
ownership reforms 44–5

Party Central Committee, Document
   No. 1, 1984
   background 79–80
   implications 86–8
   rationale 80–86
   see also Document No. 1
patent protection 35, 241, 243, 248,
   256; *see also* TRIPs
People's Bank of China 188–9, 192,
   197, 223
people's commune/production
   brigade/team 6, 10, 22, 69–72, 82,
   126, 146
   accounting units 6–7, 9. 20, 82
   communization drive 9, 79, 116
   depoliticization of communes 84
   dismantling of commune system 63,
      117
   for expanding compulsory deliveries
      86
   see also mass mobilization; Nurksian
      accumulation
Perkins, Dwight H. 4, 8, 13, 24, 86,
   124, 135, 136, 147
physical input/output targets 167, 183,
   186
physical–bureaucratic control 59, 77,
   153, 171, 192, 198, 208, 227
Pilkington Glass 256
'ping-pong' diplomacy 33, 156
'Politics in Command' 15, 123
Preisausgleich 249

price fixing 14, 18–19, 83–4, 171, 189
price liberalization vii, 45, 83
pro-grain/grain first strategy 89, 124–5
procurement ratio 75–6
Produktionpreis 11, 13–14, 26
Produktionsfondsabgabe 14
profit-contracting methods 173
profit-in-command principle 10
profit retention system 25, 38
profit target 25
property law 202
property rights 165, 183, 198–200; *see*
   also leasehold markets; TRIPs
protein:fat:carbohydrates ratio 103–4,
   113
protestant ethic 180
Pryor, Frederic L. 249

quantity theory of exchange 212

Raubwirtschaft 84
realtypus 8
Regan, Ronald 58
regional decentralization 180, 239
regional industrialization 146
regionalism 190, 193
relative product per worker 141
Renminbi
   convertibility 45–6
   devaluation pressures 44
reserve price, *see* support price
responsibility farm system 4, 6–7,
   80–81; *see also baochan daohu*;
     baogan doahu
revisionism 8–9, 11, 17, 33
Riskin, Carl 120

Sachs, Jeffrey 135
Sakurai, Masao 241, 242
sannong problems 120, 135, 143, 158–9,
   271
sanzi yibao 5–8, 9–10, 24
Schumpeter, Joseph A. 221
scissors prices 21–2, 63–4, 77, 83, 91–2,
   121, 124–5, 136, 158, 176
SEC (State Economic Commission)
   188
second land reform, *see* Party Central
   Committee, Document No. 1,
   1984

self-reliance vii, 8, 48, 55, 120, 156–8
service sector, growth 35, 39
SEZ (Special Economic Zones) 165,
    233–4, 243
Shanghai 57
Shao Gang 239, 247
shock therapy 39, 45, 194
Sicular, Terry 170
Sik, Ota 15, 203
simple reproduction (replacement
    investment) 12, 13, 17–18, 25
Sinha, Radha 122
social costs 199
Socialist High Tide 8–9, 116
socialist industrialization 118, 139, 146
socialist market economy 38
SOE, *see* state-owned enterprises
Soviet Gosbank 188
Sovnarchoz 181, 185
Special Economic Zones (SEZ) 165,
    233–4, 243
Stalin, Joseph 3–5, 23, 32, 35, 48–52,
    56–8, 89, 117, 119–20, 135, 142,
    147, 158, 162, 164–5, 174, 180,
    183–4, 203
State Bureau of Materials Supply 11,
    167, 186–8, 196
State Bureau of Prices 197
State Economic Commission (SEC) 188
State Labour Bureau 188
state-owned enterprises (SOE)
    and decentralization 153, 156, 167,
        184–6, 193
    finance 192, 211–12, 218
    fiscal transfer from 160
    large scale 193, 200, 208, 210, 215,
        221, 223
    medium scale 193, 200, 208, 210,
        215, 221
    seeking rice to fill one's own cooking
        pot 202
    share of GVIO 154–5
    smale scale 200
    wages 206–7
    see also guandao practice
State Planning Commission 189
State Trading Corporations (STC)
    237–40
STC (State Trading Corporations)
    237–40

stock-share system 165
Stone, Bruce 136, 182
subsistence urge 73, 78, 126
success indicators 178
Sun Yat-sen 233
Sun Yefang 10–13, 15, 17, 19, 21, 23,
    25, 26, 27
support price 130–31
swap centres 255, 260
swap rate 223
Systemzwang zum Experiment 184, 195

Tang, Anthony M. 4, 5, 23, 120, 121,
    135, 136
Tang Minfang 135
Tang Zongkun 181
tax-for-profit substitution 196, 205
taxes
    agricultural 21, 27, 64, 78, 121, 135,
        178
    corporate 64, 78, 160, 211, 242
    import-regulatory 253
technological dualism 146–50, 160
technological hedge 126–7, 129, 131
technological innovation 15–16, 84,
    123, 126, 157, 188, 205
technology acquisition 48
technology transfer 38, 48, 147, 156–8,
    248, 251, 255–6
third-line construction 143
Third Plenum
    1978 Eleventh NPC 63
    1984 Twelfth NPC 84, 192, 205
    1993 Fourteenth NPC 211, 223
    see also NPC Resolution, October
        1984
Tiananmen Square incident
    aftermath vii, 26, 40, 44–6, 147, 208,
        210
    causes 51–3
    future government direction 56–8,
        162
    implications for the West 58–9
    and open-door policy 47–51, 54–5,
        165, 181, 257
    removal of causes 53–8
Tidrick, G. 203
total factor productivity 129
total inequality amongst sectors 141–2
tourism 54–5

trade agency pricing 254
trade agency system 165, 170, 253–4
trade balance 219, 229–31, 233
trade liberalization 252–5
trade surplus 219, 222, 228, 232–3, 255
transaction costs 183, 190, 198–9, 201, 257
transnationality index 252
TRIMs 255, 260
TRIPs 255, 257–8, 260
Truman, Harry 122
Tsang Shu-ki 208, 211, 218, 223, 224
two-track/double-track system 26, 53, 57, 167, 171, 177, 191–2, 197, 205, 213, 217

unified distribution 167–8, 181, 264
US containment 32, 122
uxorilocal marriage 85

Volkswagen 256, 259
Voon, Thomas 231

wage drift 216, 221
wage fund 11, 197, 206
wage policy, optimum 4
wage rate, relation to labour supply 20
Walder, Andrew 41
Walker, Kenneth R. 4, 79, 116, 135
Walrasian system 24, 184
Wan Li 85, 88
Wang Cheng 224
Wang Gang-wu 54
Wang Rongjun 260
Wang Yuxuan 247
Ward, Benjamin 24
water conservation works 82, 84, 88; *see also* irrigation
Watson, Andrew 182
wave-like strategy 185, 202
weather
    and farm output 92–4, 129, 130–31
    and interprovincial inequality 105, 107, 113
weather index/variability 74, 92–3, 131
Weber, Max 8
Wen Jiabao 120, 134, 135

Wheelwright, Edward L. 136, 161
wholly foreign-owned venture (WFOV) 241
Wiens, Thomas B. 136
Wiles, Peter J.D. 58–9, 135, 249
Wong, Christine P.W. 182
Woo, Tun-oy 144
World Bank 232
World Trade Organization (WTO)
    accession to 157, 221
    application for admission 46, 250–51, 258–9
    FDI regime adaptation 255–8
Wu Jinglian 26
Wu Nianlu 249
Wu Wen 135

X-efficiency 8, 150
xida ziyou 7, 24
Xin Yang 219
Xu Xuehan 245, 249

Yan Fan 72
Yang Jianbai 11, 13, 17, 26
Yang Shengmin 110
Yao Keping 219
Yao Yilin 162
Yeh, K.C. 140, 143
Yeltsin, Boris 39, 40, 194
Yi Gang 218

Zhang Shuguang 210
Zhang Wei De 74
Zhang Xinjing 260
Zhang Yanning 162
Zhang Yifang 247
Zhao Renwei 169, 181
Zhao Ziyang 45, 48, 56, 165, 170, 173–4, 179–80, 193, 194, 200, 206, 251
Zheng Tuobin 252–3
Zheng Yinyong 249
Zhong Zhi Zhang 240
Zhou Enlai 33–4
Zhou Shulian 26
Zhu Rongji 210–11, 218, 222–3
zifu yingkui 5
ziliudi 5
Zinoviev, Alexander 58
ziyou shichang 5